YOU SAY YOU WANT A REVOLUTION

A COMPELLING & CAUTIONARY TALE OF WHAT LIES AHEAD

JAMES F. PASTOR

You Say You Want a Revolution

First Edition: 2022

Printed in the United States of America

10 9 8 7 6 5 4 3 2 1

ISBN-13: 978-1-955937-29-0 (Paperback)
ISBN-13: 978-1-955937-28-3 (eBook)

Published by Defiance Press and Publishing, LLC

Bulk orders of this book may be obtained by contacting Defiance Press and Publishing, LLC.
www.defiancepress.com.

Public Relations Dept. – Defiance Press & Publishing, LLC
281-581-9300
pr@defiancepress.com

Defiance Press & Publishing, LLC
281-581-9300
info@defiancepress.com

Dynamics of Ideologies 139
Ideologies & the Capitalist System 144

CHAPTER IV: Re-imagining Policing: From Defunding to Lawlessness 153
How & Why Did Defunding & Re-Imagining Happen? 154
Defunding Policing 163
Legislation & Prosecution Decisions 175
Police Policies 184
Disbanded Proactive Anti-Crime Units 188
"Broken-Windows" & Quality-of-Life Policing 191
Traffic Enforcement Restrictions or Prohibitions 194
Stand-Down Orders 196
Use-of-Force Restrictions 197
Police Officers-Thin Blue Line 203
Police Killings/Ambushes/Attacks 204
Resignations/Terminations & Morale 206
Lawlessness 210

CHAPTER V: Public Safety Policing 217
Order + Surveillance + Protective Methods = Control 217
Order Maintenance 221
Research Perspective 222
Contemporary Applications 224
Economic & Operational Issues *(Money)* 228
Crime & Extremism *(Fear)* 230
Surveillance (Intelligence + Technologies) 231
Intelligence-Led Policing 234
Technologies 236
Protective Methods 243
Protective Policing Strategies & Supplemental Means 244
Police Tactics & Weaponry 246

CHAPTER VI: Things That Matter 259
Rights & Freedom → Security & Authoritarianism 265
Surveillance 269
Covid 274
Protests/ Riots 282
Freedom of Speech 285
Fear + Control = Power 293

Order + Surveillance + Protection = Control 294
Truth & Love 295
Rational Thinking....296
Media....301
Race Relations....305

CHAPTER VII: Closing the Loop 315
Back to the Beginning 319
GOD 325
COUNTRY 333
FAMILY....342
As We Go Forward....348

ENDNOTES 357

ACKNOWLEDGMENTS

There are numerous individuals who have contributed to this book, sometimes in ways that they may not even be aware. While I cannot name and thank each person individually, please know that you have made a difference in my life.

My regards to those at Defiance Press, especially Cassandra Spencer, Deborah Stocco, Maxwell, the editor, and to other editors and support personnel. Your help and work are most appreciated. Working with Defiance was a great experience. My regards to David Thomas Roberts, who took the initiative to start Defiance to provide a voice to libertarian and conservative thoughts and authors. Your courage and commitment to liberty, truth, and freedom drew me in—and encouraged me to work with Defiance. I respect your values and thank you for providing this avenue to forward these values.

Special recognition to Cyndy Brucato, who conducted certain interviews to help make the "story" of the pending revolution more personal and more human. As a veteran journalist, Cyndy was an excellent resource to help bring this work into the lives of those affected. Her interviews included Stan Penkin, chair of the Pearl District Neighborhood Association and the former Minnesota Governor Arne Carlson. Both men merit our gratitude. Of course, Governor Carlson added another level of significance and depth to the story. Many thanks for your time and consideration!

To my friends and colleagues in security, policing, and public safety; I hope you stay safe and always seek professionalism. The *job* is getting harder and harder. Your work and service are more important than ever. God speed as you work to protect your clients, communities, and ultimately, this country. While I do not "know" most of you, I know your work. For those I do know as individuals, there are simply too many people to name. Either way my respect and regard go out to you. Indeed, your work often goes unnoticed and unappreciated. In some measure, this book is dedicated to your work.

Of course, my special regard goes out to those men and women on the Chicago Police Department, who I have deep respect and admiration. *Serving on the job* was crucial throughout my career. I will always value the work and dedication of my friends in CPD. This is particularly relevant to those in *Gang Crimes South*, where I had the privilege of working with some of the most skilled, courageous, and dedicated officers one can ever hope to know and work with.

As one looks back on life, I realize how important the lessons and the values learned growing up on the East Side of Chicago. These become larger and more important as one grows older. I will always treasure the friendships founded on the East Side, particularly those on 112th Street. I have many wonderful memories and will always love and respect those who helped shape and prepare me for life. The adage holds true: *You can take the boy out of the city, but you cannot take the city out of the boy!*

To my sister, Marge Tarvid, I thank you for your interest in this book. I sought your vantage point to allow me to get a sense of what the audience may be thinking. Your thoughts have been very helpful. You get it—and I thank you and love you.

Finally, and most importantly, to my wife, Rose Ann. We have gone through a lot over the decades. We have grown together and worked together in so many ways that they are impossible to count. Thanks for all your effort, support, and love over the years. And thanks again for helping me through yet another book. It seems that they don't get any easier. Indeed, this is the biggest and most important of all. Your help, encouragement, and support made this book both possible and more worthwhile. My love and gratitude are with you always—and into the kingdom! With God's help we carry on, always seeking to do the right thing!

CHAPTER I

BE CAREFUL WHAT YOU ASK FOR . . .

You probably know the title of this book comes from the 1968 Beatles song "Revolution." The song starts by asking a rhetorical question: *You say you want a revolution?* The answer is what most people want: *Well, you know, we all want to change the world!* This is the quest of humanity. History seems an endless tale of a struggle to find a better way to live. The operative questions are basic. How do we achieve a better world? Who can we trust to provide solutions to our problems? What do these "solutions" look like and how do we get them?

The Beatles' song tapped into these questions—and raised many poignant assertions at a time of great societal change. At its core, the song was a cautionary tale. It denounced supporting those "with minds that hate." This distinction was—and is—crucial. We all seek to change the world. But it is the mindset—the motivation—that will determine the result of this quest. One can view this through the lens of history. Comparing the American revolution to the French revolution is common but enlightening.

Both commenced with idealistic goals, but one devolved into a bloody reign of terror. The horror show in France was described by Jean-Guillaume de Tocqueville, a descendant of nineteenth-century liberal philosopher Alexis de Tocqueville, as such: "the French Revolution was an event that led to a bloody civil war *because the people who were not in agreement with the new ideas, the really revolutionary ideas, were just killed and beheaded. It was not a good way to debate* (emphasis added)."[1] The debate in France can be likened to the blade of a guillotine. Conversely, America's revolution was successful, leading to the strongest, most enlightened country in the history of the world.

At least this was the way historians used to think. Recently, this viewpoint has been turned on its head. Now the American revolution has been reassessed by those who have declared it to have commenced in 1619 and resulted in a "systemically racist" society. Meanwhile, voices on the far left publish their worldview in the magazine by the name that devolved France into a reign of terror. As this book was being drafted, Jacobin magazine, which bills itself as a voice of socialism, published its November 2021 edition entitled: "Lower the Crime Rate." [2]

The setup to this edition provides insight into their mindset. They introduce their "solution to" crime with a quote from Friedrich Engels as follows:

> "Distress due to poverty gives the worker only the choice of starving slowly, killing himself quickly, or taking what he needs where he finds it—in plain English, stealing. And it is not surprising that the majority prefer to steal rather than starve to death or commit suicide."

This quote from one of the founders of Communistic thinking is illustrative of the schism in contemporary America. Some seek socialism, some want to maintain capitalism, and most don't know what is happening—or why!

Using the Beatles' song "Revolution" as a title and intro to this book was purposeful on a couple of levels. Initially, consider that the song was written during the most violent year of the era. In 1968, the assassinations of Dr. Martin Luther King and Bobby Kennedy rocked the nation. Rioting followed in every major city. Later, the Democratic Convention held in Chicago erupted in brutal violence and resulted in widespread condemnation against the Chicago Police Department. The violence was described by some as a "police riot" and drove the need to study the causes of "civil unrest."

That period exhibited revolutionary elements—and these still shape current societal conditions. The revolutionary climate then was the result of many factors, including the introduction of counterculture, the widespread rejection of the Vietnam War, the often violent—but extraordinarily impactive civil rights movement, and the growing notion that the government could not be trusted. With these dynamics in play, this song threw caution into a growing revolutionary climate. This book seeks to do the same.

For now, though, let's continue to set the tone with the seeds that developed in the 1960s "Revolution" contrasted with another genre from that era that promoted a different type of struggle. Songs such as "Ohio" and "Chicago" clearly advocated confrontation—or at least resistance.

"Ohio"—written by Neil Young and performed by Crosby, Stills, Nash & Young—had an ominous message. Written to depict the killing of four Kent State students by National Guard troops in 1970, it denounced these killings with these repeated lyrics: "Soldiers are cutting us down." As the song builds, it continues this ominous tone, with this ending: "Tin soldiers and Nixon's coming: We're finally on our own, This summer, I hear the drumming: Four dead in Ohio . . . four dead in Ohio." These last four words are repeated twelve times as the song ends.

"Chicago"—written in 1971 by Graham Nash, and performed by Crosby, Stills, Nash & Young—followed up with provocative prose criticizing police tactics. It commenced with: "Though your brother's bound and gagged, And they've chained him to a chair . . ." The song continues this theme, contrasting police tactics with notions of freedom: "In a land that's known as freedom, How can such a thing be fair, Won't you please come to Chicago, For the help that we can bring?" Then, using the quest to make the world a better place: "We can change the world, Re-arrange the world, It's dying . . . to get better."

The song ends with these poignant words: "We can change the world; Re-arrange the world (it's dying). If you believe in justice (it's dying), and if you believe in freedom, (it's dying), let a man live his own life, (it's dying). Rules and regulations, who needs them? Throw them out the door!"

These lyrics have lasting meaning. I believe that mindset is more prevalent today than when it was when written. While times change, this worldview has become more permanent. Idealists from the 1960s are now leading many institutions in this country. Academia, media, Hollywood, political leaders, and even military and police leaders were either shaped by those who lived in those times or have lived it themselves. This is not to say that everyone thinks this way. It is to say that the predominant thinking emanating from our institutions thinks this way.

Viewing just these examples in the backdrop of the lyrics advocated in "Chicago," one can see defunding the police, social justice prosecutors, climate change activism, and a host of other initiatives in a different light. Read the words again: "We can change the world; rearrange the world (it's dying). If you believe in justice (it's dying), and if you believe in freedom (it's dying), let a man live his own life (it's dying). Rules and regulations—who needs them? Throw them out the door!" Consider these lyrics related to just one example—defunding the police. This sounds a lot like [throwing] rules and regulations . . . out the door!

Surely many will advocate that these initiatives are appropriate societal—and global—goals. This book will delve deeply into this thinking—and its implications. In any case, asking the question "You say you want a revolution?" is a rhetorical device used to address what we may encounter ahead.

To illustrate the opposing worldviews, consider these summary statements:

- The Left desires to change the fabric of this country to one that rejects its traditional constitutional, capitalistic, and Judeo-Christian framework with a desire to establish a socialist system.
- The Right sees the current system as corrupt, with "the swamp" overriding their rights and liberties. They want to maintain traditional structures but believe that they must replace or destroy those who are running "the system," or they will lose their rights, liberties, or traditional structures.

Both worldviews are deeply rooted. And they are inherently conflictive. Speaking to both audiences is difficult and may even be impossible. Is there a reasonable, rational way that we can speak to, appeal to, or at least . . . warn everyone? In the end, the overriding emphasis and theme of this book is to speak of the coming revolution. A turning point is coming. A crossroad is before us. Articulating what is ahead—and why—is the challenge. Can this be accomplished in a manner that doesn't alienate large segments of the population? This is the challenge. Yet, it is the goal of this book.

Think about the forces driving this revolution. A significant percentage of baby boomers pushed for revolution in the 1960s and early '70s. Years later, many have become hugely successful, holding leadership positions or having substantial influence over societal institutions. Yet—for the first time in American history—their children will not be happier and more successful than they were. As a result, millennials and Gen Zers often feel unfairly treated. Many within these cohorts cannot afford to buy a house, cannot afford to have children, and cannot see themselves living the American dream. Many have no hope. If this is what *you* faced . . . why would *you* have a stake in "the system"? One challenge going forward is to show why believing in the American dream is still achievable—and worth contemplating. This may get more difficult as we go forward.

These constraints are obvious *before* the dramatic impact of inflation along with the "transformation" of society through a *green revolution*. While many believe *this revolution* is necessary for the survival of the planet, the transition from "current" to "desired" is filled with economic implications. Add the "Great Reset" and the "Great Resignation" to this mix. Millions of people resigning from the labor market is bound to reshape how people think about work—and how goods and services are provided. Other elements of society—and the world—are changing post-pandemic. The scope and depth of these are so "great" that they are bound to have an impact in ways that are now impossible to predict. While these are beyond the scope of this book, suffice to say that large-scale societal transformations will inevitably affect our social fabric. Human interactions will be disrupted, and discord will assuredly follow.

We are already on the cusp of myriad divisions and conflicts. As this book is being drafted, the following events are occurring or were significant media events.

Parents and teachers are disputing face masks, Critical Race Theory, and transgender policies. School boards and teacher associations are aligned against parents, with allegations of domestic terrorism being leveled. Truckers are staging protests against Covid mandates and being accused of hatred and Nazism. Street crime and chaos are widespread, with murders rates reaching record levels in numerous cities. Smash-and-grab shoplifting has been detailed and videotaped across the country. Armed carjackings have substantially increased in several cities. Homelessness and open-air drug usage are reaching epidemic proportions in various cities. Subways in urban areas are becoming "no-go" zones, with random acts of violence occurring daily. Restaurants, movie theaters, bars, gyms, and other businesses are requiring vaccination cards to enter while politicians are alleging voter suppression due to enforcement of ID card voting requirements along with the reduction of some election rules enacted during the pandemic. Meanwhile, "cancel culture" shuts down speech and sanctions people for saying things that violate certain political or social standards.

Geo-politically, on the heels of the Afghanistan debacle, the slow-motion disaster at our porous southern border, and the dramatic war in Europe are turning the world order on its head.

These factors will worsen in the months and years ahead. Altogether, these dynamics *will* result in a revolutionary climate. While this may sound provocative, there is a strong case as to why these, along with new post-pandemic realities, will contribute to the *shaking* of the country. In short, hazardous times lie ahead. Chaotic events are already happening—and more serious implications are percolating.

The result will be the proverbial "tug of war" with people—or, in this "woke" society—groups of collective identities, vying for economic resources in a society transitioning from a post-capitalist system to a "democratic socialistic" world order. This is embedded with emotions, resources, and ideologies. This struggle will lead to violence, which will lead to counter-violence . . . and then to more violence.

Cycles of violence can have their own momentum, causing a spiraling deterioration of the values that hold the country together. Much more will be said about this *shaking* of the capitalistic system. But for now, consider the famous "house divided" quote of Abraham Lincoln—who, referencing the gospel, stated that "every kingdom divided against itself is brought to desolation; and a house divided against a house falleth.[3]

A SNAPSHOT IN TIME

This book will demonstrate that vast ideological divisions are upon us. We will articulate why such divisions will result in conflict and violence. Despite the widespread riots of 2020 and the *shallow* rhetoric that resulted, this "revolution" was always larger than police tactics and police use of force. Indeed, examples of police misconduct were commonly misrepresented to demonize the police and drum up resistance and anger. I make this statement knowing that some will object. The facts, in *most* controversial cases, belie the dominant narrative.

For example, "Hands up—don't shoot," was based on a lie. Anyone who wants to know what really happened to Michael Brown can find out. Yet, we are not going to focus on correcting the false narratives that have now become "urban legend." That would be a fool's errand. Those who want to know the truth already know what happened. Those who want to believe "the lie" will believe the lie. Those who *can't handle the truth* will hide from it.

Nonetheless, just as the 60s-era songs illustrate, revolutionary thinkers often use tactics by the police or military to gin up anger and galvanize resistance. I saw this throughout my police career. After a police shooting, pamphlets distributed by Communist groups often found themselves in the hands of protesters. Back in the day, police shootings galvanized anger against "the man." Now, the man has become "the system." After years of controversial police incidents, this dynamic has changed.

When police use force—particularly, deadly force—there is always an undercurrent that questions its legitimacy. This is a proper and instructive part of our system. This sometimes results in police officers being appropriately charged with misconduct or with criminal charges. This has been part of the system for generations. I have participated in these proceedings and have great respect for the checks and balances developed over years of jurisprudence.

Yet, after the summer of 2020, how the police do their job will change. While no one can justify the malicious conduct of Minneapolis Police Officer Chauvin, his actions amount to a "tipping point" that will change policing for the foreseeable future. The new *policing model* will be pragmatic, yet insufficient. It will not be the "solution" to counter the revolutionary climate that we find ourselves in. In short, despite the empty mantras, the police did not start the revolution that many desire. And they will not—indeed *cannot*—resolve it. This is much *larger* than the police. While police occupy an increasingly fragile "thin blue line," this book offers only pragmatic responses that police are likely to implement.

The forces driving this revolution are substantial. Those seeking to "counter" these forces are gearing up. In the middle are millions of Americans just trying to make a living, raising their children, and seeking to make sense of this increasingly uncertain and volatile world. These are the people to whom this book is dedicated. True believers preparing for conflict are probably beyond persuasion.

Now is the time for good people to step up and make necessary changes. Are you ready? Do you want to make a difference? Do you realize what has been happening before your eyes? Hopefully, this book will provide vital information and an effective road map with which to navigate forthcoming chaos.

As we journey through the difficult times ahead, it may be helpful to initially let a man who has served this country through both Democratic and Republican administrations weigh in on where we are. Jim Webb has quite a resume. He is a former Democratic United States Senator from Virginia, former Secretary of the Navy during the Reagan Administration, and decorated Marine Corps officer. He ran for president as a Democrat in 2016. Having seen any number of challenging circumstances in his career, he made this stunning statement regarding our exit from Afghanistan in 2021:[4]

> "In a perverse way, perhaps we should look at the calamitous blunderings in Afghanistan as an opportunity to *demand a*

> *true turning point.* Americans know that a great deal of our governmental process is now *either institutionally corrupt or calcified* . . . (emphasis added)"

Webb continued by criticizing the "distracting debates over the *very premise* of why the American system of government was created and whether the icons of our past were truly motivated by the words incorporated in our most revered documents (emphasis added)." Webb asserted that the military is becoming a "social laboratory" of "leftist activists" to "advance extreme political agendas." His conclusion is rather chilling. He views congressional oversight of the military as leaning heavily toward social issues, consistent with the "woke" agenda, while "good people at the bottom have to implement poorly conceived plans that might kill them."

This is a powerful sentiment to describe a snapshot in time. Yet, it is a snapshot that had already started developing more than fifty years ago. Others would say they were sown in 1619. Loyalists will point to 1776 as the happiest, noblest day in history. James Freeman writing in the *Wall Street Journal* noted this sentiment was not that a new nation was established, but it was the *new principles* of this new nation that made it significant. Three very definite propositions were set out in its preamble regarding the nature of mankind and therefore of government:[5]

- All men are created equal
- We are endowed with certain inalienable rights
- The source of the just powers of government must be derived from the consent of the governed.

These principles tell you what this book is based on—and where it is going. These also tell us what is at stake. This is not to say this nation perfectly applied such enlightened principles. Today, many remind us of our national flaws. Such criticism is sometimes correct. However, no country, no person, and no document are without flaws. Significantly, those who criticize cannot point to any country, anywhere, at any time that is faultless. This part is easy to discern. History has no perfect example. Indeed, the modern world has no perfect example. Neither does the nature of mankind. What remains is a flawed and dying world. Yet, as the song says, we *still* seek a better world. So, we should. The quest is to find one—or rather, the challenge is to construct one. If history is our guide, we will fail. Thus, once again the operative but rhetorical question—*You say you want a revolution . . .?*

The tragic killing of George Floyd and the resultant riots become one focal point of our journey. The brutal, even masochist actions of Officer Chauvin, led to a chain reaction of dramatic events, sometimes euphemistically and sarcastically referred to as the "summer of love." To add context, in just over two months, from May 25 to July 31, there were 574 officially declared riots, with 2000 police officers injured. More than 624 acts of arsons were reported, and ninety-seven police vehicles were burned. Looting was also common, with 2,385 incidents reported in the ten-week period.[6] Approximately $2 billion in damages resulted.[7] In this two-month period, more than 16,200 people were arrested for protest-related crimes. Yet, over half of these cases were not prosecuted. The report cited prosecutors declining prosecution, even in some instances when "those arrested for felony crimes committed during the protests despite the availability of video evidence and suspect confessions."[8]

Comparing this data to the January 2021 capital "riot," approximately 140 officers were injured[9] and $1.5M in damages resulted.[10] As of late November 2021, there were approximately 702 people charged with crimes relating to the Capitol riot.[11] While it is difficult to obtain accurate data, many were held in jail for months. A *Washington Post* article written on September 17, 2021, related that "dozens" were still in jail.[12]

The one-day three-hour riot at the Capitol necessitates a blue-ribbon committee, while the violent summer does *not* need to be studied. Consider another era when America was subject to such violent, damaging, and sustained riots; the Kerner Commission was instituted to study civil disorders and riots of the late 1960s.

Here is my well-founded but provocative-sounding conclusion: We don't need to study the riots of 2020 because those were ideologically connected to similar rioting during the 1960s. As a preview of where we are going, can we conclude that we already know why the riots of 2020 occurred?

All of this discussion, however, is to make one crucial point. No matter the cause of a crime or a "riot" (which in effect represents multiple crimes committed by multiple people), the reporting and the investigations ought to be fairly and consistently applied. Comparing the Capitol riot to the violence and chaos of that volatile summer is *beyond* disproportionate—as east is from the west. Words cannot accurately convey the chasm between the two.

The point that one must glean from these comparative examples is that if the justice system places its resources and enforcement on one type of extremist yet downplays or ignores those of a different political sphere; we will get *more of both*. Let me restate this for emphasis. Focusing resources, wrath, and enforcement of extremists on one political ideology will communicate two very disturbing messages:

1. Those who are aggressively pursued and demonized may conclude that they are being treated as "political prisoners" or worse, as "terrorists." If they see themselves this way, some percentage of them will conclude that the only option they have is to fight back. To wage a war against a war being waged on them.
2. Those who are given the freedom to riot, or to "peacefully protest," will see this as a license to loot and commit other crimes. If left (no pun intended) unchecked, those so inclined will take advantage of weak government policies. They see this as an opportunity. This is *rational* thinking. If one can get away with certain disorderly behavior, why not keep pushing the envelope? Those who do so will increasingly see themselves as "above the law," even untouchable. At some point, government will have to push back. It is then that the true believers will go "underground" and maintain the fight in a more clandestine, terroristic manner.

The seeds of these extremes have been deeply rooted. Following the protests and riots in the 1960s, the Students for Democratic Society (SDS) saw factions break away. One such faction was the Weather Underground. This group was described as a domestic terrorist group by the FBI. Its founding document called for a "White fighting force" to be allied with the "Black

Liberation Movement" (*ironically* "BLM") and other radical movements to achieve "the destruction of US imperialism and form a classless Communist world (emphasis added)."[13]

To get a sense of how ideologies can drive destruction and violence, consider *CNN* reported that the Minneapolis riots following the death of George Floyd were upended by the *far-left* as well as the *far-right*. Note the substance of the below quote, as it is crucial to understand the dynamic nature of extremist groups and how they ally and oppose:[14]

> "Those domestic extremist groups include anarchists, anti-government groups often associated with far-right extremists and white supremacy causes and far-left extremists who identify with anti-fascist ideology.... Federal officials say they believe there is an amalgam of groups showing up in protests from the extremist left and right that normally oppose each other but see common cause in attacking the police and the government."

Based on the turbulent rioting of 2020 and the disorder and chaos that subsequently occurred, one could conclude that the "seeds of destruction" germinated since the 1960s are now deeply planted in our time. Yet, it is tempting to dismiss the potential for history to repeat itself as speculative or even groundless. We can *hope* this is true, but this denies the overwhelming evidence of revolutionary thinking evidenced in this book. One important decision between then and now: America in the 1960s was much more stable, patriotic, and strong than now. Back then, we overcame revolutionary forces. Can we do it again…?

RACE, REVOLUTION & REDEMPTION

I am a product of the 1960s. Though I was too young to be involved in the "happenings" of that era, I was old enough to take in and experience some of the dynamics and the thinking. The song "Revolution" had an impact on my life—as did many of the songs from that era. This was partly because I grew up in a city that was filled with turmoil and was often "ground zero" for the revolutionary climate. As the song "Chicago" states, come to Chicago or "join the other side." Choosing sides is what every revolutionary struggle inevitably requires. Think about Dr. King. He was pulled by the revolutionaries of his time. Yet, he resisted the violent radicals and sought non-violence, advocating character instead of color. Seeing these distinctions deeply impacted me. Let me briefly summarize my story.

I grew up on the far southeast side of Chicago in a neighborhood called the East Side. It was surrounded by steel mills, the Calumet River, Lake Michigan, and the Indiana border. It was known in some circles as the "white island." It was a classic melting pot of ethnicity . . . Irish, Italian, Polish, Slavic, with a smaller proportion of German, Hispanic, and Baltic. They were tough working-class people. Generations of inhabitants populated the neighborhood, which was a stable but modest environment.

One early memory especially impacted me—and stays with me to this day. As a nine-year-old standing on a street corner at 112th and Ewing Avenue, I watched Dr. Martin L. King march through the neighborhood. This occurred in the summer of 1966.[15] Anger, emotion, and turmoil filled the streets. It was an extremely volatile event . . . yet I did not understand *why* it was so.

Less than two years later, on my Confirmation Day at Annunciata Church on April 4, 1968, Dr. King was assassinated. As we sat in church after the confirmation ceremony, a surreal-sounding announcement was made by the presiding cardinal of the Chicago archdiocese. This was the famous Cardinal Cody. As an aside, his name was the origin of the nickname given to the former FBI Director James Comey. Deriding his pompous and overbearing attitude—James Comey was called "Cardinal Comey" by many. In any case, no one knew what was going to be said. Cardinal Cody stood up and said something to the effect that a great man had just been assassinated. He then stated that Dr. King was dead. The reaction was shock and stunned silence.

Yet, once the church emptied, the reaction was different. It was disdain for the dead man and joy that he was dead. I thought back to the march less than two years prior. Dr. King was seen then as an outsider who had the audacity to come into the neighborhood and cause turmoil. The people who lived there did not invite him nor were they looking for trouble. Yet, trouble did come, both during the turmoil on the day of his march—and following his assassination. Rioting and fires lit up large parts of the west and south sides of Chicago. As rioting got closer to the "white island," the bridges over the Calumet River were raised to prevent entrance into the neighborhood. As an aside, years later, one of these bridges (95th Street) was used to film the famous bridge jump in the movie: *The Blues Brothers*. This brings an ironic twist, doesn't it . . .?

More seriously, I mention these turbulent times for a couple of reasons. Firstly, because they had such a lasting imprint on my life. It caused me to examine race and hate. I was taught about race—and that hate was a predictable response to race. Along with this, we were taught to "protect" the neighborhood. Before your thoughts condemn—which you are correct in doing—also consider the context. The 1960s and '70s exhibited rapid and often violent transformations of entire neighborhoods. As neighborhoods turned from white to black, a host of problems came with these transformations. Property values significantly declined. Crime significantly increased. These twin yet dire effects played a huge role in race relations and the dynamics in the city.

As I matured, I rejected hate. But I learned never to underestimate the human reactions associated with fear and uncertainty. Looking back dispassionately, blacks moving into a neighborhood seeking a better life were obviously justified. Yet so too were whites who sought only the stability of their neighborhood and the value of their homes (consider this was before 401(k) s and the family home was the only real asset working-class people had). This also includes the obvious desire to avoid being a crime victim—which despite politically correct rhetoric was, in fact, inevitable during transformations of neighborhoods from white to black.

Second, and more importantly, is the morally corrupt implications of teaching hate. I know from experience that teaching hate is wrong. I have long since "excised" myself from its ill effects. As I write these words, I can honestly say I do not hate anyone, nor have I *allowed* myself to hate since those volatile teenage years. Note that I use the word "allowed" because it is a mindset that you either allow into your life or you refuse. I stand redeemed by the grace and blood of Christ. Yet, this is not a sermon. This goes to public policy. This goes to a safe and secure society. Teaching and focusing on the color of one's skin, as the progressives and their elite mouthpieces desire, is both unacceptable and frightening. Those who are advocating this know the inevitable consequences.

I learned my lessons from childhood and from the tragic death of Dr. King. His legacy still lives in my life. His courage, his conviction, and his message resonated—and still do. Adopting his focus on "character," not color, is the *only* viable answer to race and hate.

Ironically, both individually and collectively, as America grew away from its "original sin," we are now back to a focus on color. Most people know that racism is learned, it is not innate. But it is still a part of human nature. Otherwise known as "tribalism," we all have the tendency to gravitate to those who are most "like us." Despite the mantras, racism is not "one-sided." All of us have the capacity to hate. While racism is "defined" as residing in *only* those who have institutional power, the kids on the East Side had no institutional power.

Despite being hailed as "post-racial" for many years, our "thought leaders" have recently determined that "structural" or systematic racism exists. In keeping with said conclusion, this illogical solution is offered: advocate and teach Critical Race Theory and deride the system as being racist to its core.

While more will be said on this in the next chapter, over thirty-five years ago, I wrote a master's thesis that analyzed the *Critical Theory of Criminology*—which was the formative theory underlying Critical Race Theory (CRT). My research postulated that this Marxist theory would be used as a precursor for terrorism against "the system." Now, the tenets of CRT have adopted Marxist principles and added a racial component. The similarities are obvious.

Back then, the Critical Theory of Criminology was a little-known yet radical theory. It is instructive—and disheartening—to see that Critical Race Theory has been widely accepted by leaders and institutions. This book makes the case that CRT and its attendant racial animus may act as a catalyst for the revolutionary climate we live in. At the risk of sounding provocative, one can reasonably conclude we are *watching societal suicide*. We are entering precarious times, and we need to be careful what we ask for!

Understanding the impact and intersection of culture, race, politics, and the law is crucial to the theme of this book. What most do not know—or will not admit, is that race was always "present" on the street. Usually, it was unspoken but always there. In some areas, it is almost combustible. Both the police and the public must be cognizant of the racial dynamic—which sometimes goes off like dynamite.

Bringing different perspectives into this combustible mix, I *balanced* two very different worlds during a formative time in my life. Engaging "gang bangers" and law professors in the same day while working as a tactical police officer and going to law school gave me an insight into two very diverse ways of life. Both the gangsters and professors I observed used logic, yet they live very differently. Each acted rationally under the circumstances and the constraints within their respective lives. This reality is often missed by those who make policy decisions.

This experience provides insight that few people have. It helps in effectively communicating the extraordinary revolutionary climate that exists today. This is a complicated task, requiring an almost precise balance. Achieving a balanced yet substantive analysis will inevitably create some level of friction. As will be discussed below, the nature of this analysis is inherently political—or it appears to be political. This is because most everything is now imbued with race, religion, and politics. These basic, fundamental distinctions are at the heart of the current divide. This is something that was evident for years . . .

In 2009, I published a groundbreaking book entitled *Terrorism & Public Safety Policing: Implications for the Obama Presidency*. This book predicted a storm was coming . . . indeed the perfect storm of *race, religion, and politics*. In doing so, I provided specific examples and developed the logic and "triggers" that would foster a spiraling climate of violence. For posterity, the reader is urged to review that book. Spoiler alert: it was written to an academic and professional audience. It is backed with citations and packed with facts that are now just manifesting themselves.

One crucial and ironic element of that book is that it was written just before and just after the Obama election in 2008. Most of the book was written in the run-up to the election. As the election neared, my publisher suggested a "pause" to allow the election to determine the outcome—and the direction of the book. With the election, we decided to adopt the subtitle, thereby locking in time the nature of the book and the direction of the country.

With President Obama's election, the media and the establishment trumpeted what they termed the "post-racial" America. Let this sink in. Do you remember the last time you heard this term? For fun—or at least curiosity, do a *Google* search. Even more telling is the notion that the country could devolve from "post-racial" to being "systemically racist" in a little over ten years. How is this possible? Indeed, it is *impossible* to be post-racial and then revert to being systemically racist. The latter essentially means *structurally* or *inherently* racist. With this thinking, *racism is in our DNA*. Despite this obvious disconnect, leaders from the White House to Congress to state legislators, mayors, councils, police chiefs, and corporate leaders—along with media, academic, sports, and entertainment institutions—all have adopted the systemically racist mantra. Many of these same people are black. Examples are vast and widespread. How could such a tapestry of examples and success stories occur in a country that was *systemically* racist? There is a lot to say on this point later.

But in 2009, I predicted a discerning trend going in the opposite direction. It wasn't a "post-racial" society but a society exhibiting a very delicate and dangerous dynamic. I will explain how this was obvious to me later. But for now, consider what transpired in just the last few years. Almost out of the blue, Americans are asked to accept—and believe that certain "revelations" just *discovered* by the "thought leaders," including:

- 1619 project
- Black Lives Matter (BLM)
- Critical Race Theory
- White Privilege
- Systemic racism, and others . . .

Each of these came to the fore—and with a great degree of acclaim—*after* America *was declared post-racial*. Any rational argument to support these "conclusions" in the span of a decade defies explanation. Yet, it now seems that everything is about race . . .? To add a little levity to a serious subject, consider the following. You can determine whether these are funny or just plain ludicrous.

Consider the depth and scope of race in this woke society. In a *New York Post* article, the author derides the National Football League's decision to play the "black national anthem" before games, effectively rebranding "The Star-Spangled Banner" as a white national anthem. Is this sustainable? Can this help heal racial divisions, or will it lead to further racial discord?

Then there is yoga. Even yoga now represents *white supremacy*, according to the new book *Yoke*. The *Post* author mocks this with these words: "Do we really need to bring race issues into yoga? Isn't the whole point of yoga to turn off your mind so your body can stretch and relax? . . . breathe deep, reconnect with your inner goddess and release all tensions, you racist . . .!"[16] *Ludicrous* is too soft to describe such banality.

Using sarcastic and biting humor is another way to cut through woke thinking. For example, a headline in the *Babylon Bee*: "Scientists Warn That Within 6 Months Humanity Will Run Out of Things to Call Racist." Coming from this site, the satire is obvious—yet instructive. " 'At this current rate of coming up with new things that are racist, warned racism scientist Frank Greene, we'll run out of new things to call racist by the end of this year.' " Continuing the joke, the piece describes that "anti-racism activists met this news with both fear and denial. 'Running out of new things to call racist would be devastating,' said activist Brooke Snyder. 'I mean, you'll only get attention if you come up with something no one knows is racist. You can't just say things like 'Ethnic slurs are racist. Everyone knows that.' "[17]

Yet, there are indicators in real life that people are fighting back from the "skin-color Nazis." After Winsome Sears was elected lieutenant governor of Virginia, as the first black to be elected to this position in the state's history, she focused on unity, not race. After being attacked as a "white supremacist," she rose above the racial fray, saying, "there are some who want to divide us, and we must not let that happen." Then, describing her election as "the American dream," reminiscing that she joined the US Marine Corps while she was still a Jamaican. "I was willing, willing, to die for this country." This sentiment belies the divisive rhetoric of many of the *thought leaders*. "We have a saying in church, 'I may not be what I'm supposed to be, but I ain't what I used to be.' And that's America." She went on to put in perspective what so many have either forgotten—or ignored. "Are there changes that need to be made? Most assuredly, there is no country in this world that does not suffer from racism . . . But you have seen people who are dying to cross the border into America because they know that if they can get their foot on American soil, the trajectory of their lives will change—as it did for my father."[18]

These quotes and examples should give you a flavor of where this book is going. And where the divisions lie and why. There are three takeaways.

Firstly, when racial allegories are extended to the national anthem and to yoga, it is hard to deny that something big is happening. The depth and scope have wide-ranging implications.

Secondly, the use of biting humor to make fun of the absurd is a time-honored means to bring people back to reality. The notion that there is "truth in humor" is illustrative and instructive. If a joke doesn't have at least a grain of truth, then it's not funny. The idea that we could "run out of things to call racist," should give us pause.

Thirdly, the election of Winsome Sears should demonstrate—once again how far this country has progressed. We're talking about a black woman who grew up in Jamaica and loved the *ideals* of this country so much that she joined the military even before she became a citizen. This should proverbially be "trumpeted down Main Street." Yet, ironically, her election was used as evidence this country is *systemically racist* and *white supremacist*. One cannot make this up. Illogical allegations such as these are so absurd that no one ought to have the audacity to mouth them. Yet, people think—and say—these things. And most significantly, they were *not* roundly condemned by everyone who heard such nonsense.

The consequence: One should not be surprised to learn that racial relations are worsening. A Gallup poll published in July 2021 found that for the second consecutive year, race relations in the US are at their lowest point in more than two decades, with a 20-point gap in how white and black Americans view the future.

The poll found that 57 percent say race relations are *somewhat* or *very* bad. The percentage of black people with a positive rating of race relations slumped to 33 percent, with white people weighing in at 43 percent. This is not the only bad trend. Only 40 percent of black adults are optimistic about racial harmony, as opposed to 60 percent of white adults. "This is the largest gap recorded in Gallup's three-decades," according to the report. Black-white relations in the United States have eroded since 2013. Then, 70 percent of adults said "they believed the two racial groups had a positive relationship. By 2015, that number fell off a cliff to 53 percent and has continued to decline."[19]

As this trend toward deteriorating race relations commenced during the Obama presidency, one asks why? Why did *post-racial* America result in worsening race relations? Charles Murray argues that "in retrospect, President Obama's eight years in office look like a prolonged inflection point for race relations." [20] He noted that Americans' "perceptions of race relationships had gone from solidly optimistic to solidly pessimistic."[21]

Could these worsening race relation statistics be the result of being told you are racist and live in a racist society? How about consistently telling people that other people hate them? Do this often, by those in authority, and by those who "ought to know." Sooner or later, more and more people will believe it. Why this is happening is an indictment on the "leaders" who help create and foster such divisive rhetoric.

But it is worse than words. Though some equate words *as* violence, racially charged words inevitably result in *actual* violence. Violence then results in counter-violence. The people fostering racial animus know this. One of the themes of this book is to counter such divisive rhetoric with facts, logic, and rationality. I am not optimistic that this will change anything. But my love for this country and for its people drives my thinking.

In this way, racism could be analyzed like any other "commodity." Consider simple supply-and-demand principles. As these examples reveal and as those who are paying attention already know, there is a great "demand" for racism by those who benefit from it. Yet, the supply of actual racist behavior is rather low. Consider the race hoaxes . . . from Jesse Smollet to the Covington Kentucky high school student—and numerous others. These were trumpeted to prove that racism exists! This is *not* to say racism doesn't exist. As I pointed out in 2009 (on the heels of a "post-racial" America), there was (and is) ample evidence of racial strife.

The problem now is that many *want* racism . . . they want to use race as a wedge to divide society. This is *neo-racism* facilitated by those who use race as a shield and a sword. It protects (and shields) those who are black or who are allied with progressives. They are "immune" to criticism and racial attacks. Consider Vice President Harris' poll numbers being explained as the result of *racism and sexism*. It also is used to attack (as a sword) those who say and do things that are not in keeping with the political views or interests of the neo-racists. The inevitable result is that the term racist will be rendered meaningless.

Back in 2009, I expected to be called a racist. Presenting facts, logic, and analysis demonstrating black men commit a substantially higher percentage of murders is often considered "off-limits" or just plain racist. Using this same approach relative to police officers, black men also disproportionately murder police officers. These statistics act to counter the fiction that violence is only one way—police against black victims. Instead, the data revealed a disproportionate number of blacks killing police. When compared to the percentage of the black population, this *could* explain why police use of force against blacks is higher than their proportion of the population.

Making the connection to "both sides" of this violence is unusual. A higher percentage of violence by blacks may help to explain why police may be more inclined to use force against blacks. I presented this data to demonstrate the dynamics, both statistical and psychological, as to why these encounters may result in a greater propensity of police use of force—or what some would call "violence."[22] While this analysis is beyond the scope of this book, what is relevant is this data has been consistent over many years—and it could help to explain "controversial" police shootings.

Nonetheless, I knew presenting these facts would not sit well with "race hustlers." Being called a racist was not hard to predict. Seeing police officers killed or broadly painted as "racists" to further the progressive agenda, though, is hard to take. Even worse, one could readily predict that these volatile allegations would "trigger" rioting and unrest—and would lead to more killings of police officers.

Now, *everything* is racist. Back then, the proverbial racist sword was not nearly as sharp as it is now. Yet, one must take a stand to do what is right. Wading into this racial cauldron is not without risk, yet it's necessary to tell the story of a pending revolution.

APPROACH & FRAMEWORK

From this vantage point, it may be helpful to provide an outline of where we are going. Our approach is to operate from the policy level yet remain cognizant of the realities of "the street."

Policy is driving the dynamics described above. By policy, I mean the initiatives implemented by decision-makers. These range from "defunding" and "reimagining" policing to "reforming" the criminal justice system to implementing changes to police policies, such as "quality of life" and "broken-windows" policing. We will analyze how and why these were done—and the consequences that naturally follow. This may not be direct "cause and effect," but my experience tells me that the connection is there, and a wealth of evidence stands to support as much.

Indeed, I will argue that these measures were not only shortsighted but that in many cases, the *result* (the effect) *was intended.*

We will flesh this out later, but suffice to say, the ideological thinking of progressives, as can be seen in the cited *Jacobin* article on how to "Lower the Crime Rate," centers upon the intent to apply socialist "solutions" to crime. As implied by the *Jacobin* article, society can deal with "crime" in many ways, including what we are seeing now. Prosecutors deciding not to punish certain "minor" crimes. Legislators deciding to defund and "reimagine" policing. Police policymakers deciding to abandon proven police tactics and strategies (such as anti-crime/anti-gang units, "quality of life," and "broken-windows" policing). Mark Levin wrote in *American Marxism* that "if your goal is to 'fundamentally transform' America, that is, abolish our history, traditions, and ultimately our republic—then you must subvert support for the police. After all, without law enforcement, the civil society collapses."[23]

There is the point: Either decision-makers do not know how people *on the street* would react to such thinking—or they know that by creating chaos, the capitalistic system would collapse under the stresses posed by chaos. Either of these is possible, but I conclude the latter.

Making the connection from policy to street, street to policy is often missing. I have found that most policymakers either disregard or do not understand the "logic" of the street. Most people are rational, making decisions based on their understanding of the risks and benefits of their actions. Without this level of analysis, legislative or policy changes, such as increasing the value of stolen items subject to felony shoplifting have real-world consequences. Rational thinkers see this as an *incentive to steal.* Allowing riots to fester during the summer of 2020 is another classic example. As hard as this is to accept, it is deeply disturbing to see these decisions have gravely impacted millions of people—and the viability of this country.

This goes to the summer of love—which at its core was not about the killing of George Floyd or any other "victim" of police action. These events, as tragic as they are from a human and emotional level, are just *triggers* to a much larger agenda. Of course, adding the pandemic into the "equation" has accelerated this agenda. Adding fear derived from the terrible illness, coupled with the government policies seen by some as draconian, has added fuel to the already growing spirit of rebellion. This rebellion and this agenda are intended to take down the capitalist system.

Showing the widespread and complicated unraveling of the fabric of society is a crucial part of telling this story. These slowly but surely unwind the interrelationships of people and institutions that are crucial to sustaining a diverse and sophisticated country. These must be balanced without getting bogged down in dense technical, academic, or political ditches. Painting the picture of what is transpiring may not be pleasant to read. Indeed, it can be so disconcerting that some will not want to see the dots being connected. I certainly appreciate this may be hard for some to digest.

But it is real. What was (and will be) described is coming—and is already upon us. My hope is this book serves to diminish its consequences. It is the reader—and all those in this tapestry called America, who will either be part of the solution or part of the problem. How we think, how we engage, and how we live will either help or hurt.

Most will not admit that they *want* a revolution. The reality is that many live their lives subtly, or even purposely, supporting the climate that will lead to a revolution. Others live as if it does not matter, or that "it can't happen here."

Over 150 years ago, most did not *want* a civil war . . . though some saw it coming. Even those with larger perspectives did not envision how the war would play out. The thinking was a few battles would resolve the conflict . . . as even the most astute observer believed. Yet, the result was a devastating four-year war that almost tore the country apart.

As history has a way of repeating itself, we find ourselves with a divided populous, yet most fail to see (or want) to connect the dots about what this really means. Read on. Let's enter a journey through the "logic" of extremism and ideological movements. Let's see what they are about and *why* they are about to collide. Though it may not be pretty, it is purposeful. So here we are with two trains on the same track going in opposite directions. Is there a *switch* that can be applied in the nick of time?

VIEWING THE MACRO FROM THE MICRO

Before we delve into the substance of this book, one can get a snapshot of the horizon by looking at specific incidents that may be reflective of larger issues and trends. In doing so, consider these incidents as precursors of the future. While we cannot know the "how many" question, one can surmise that these are not isolated incidents. Others that you may know are not listed.

Think of these as examples, not an exhaustive or comprehensive list. Question whether the *reasons* for these crimes (or in criminal justice terms, the *motives*) will be tempered or tapped down by the larger society? This will be fully discussed in context later. But for now, please review these and connect the dots in your own mind.

Daytona Police Murder: In the summer of 2021, Officer Jayson Raynor was shot and killed in a cold-blooded manner. The alleged shooter, Othal

Wallace, known as "O-Zone," was later arrested with multiple weapons as well as body armor. His arrest occurred on property allegedly owned by a militant group called "NFAC" (Not F---ing Around Coalition). According to news accounts, Mr. Wallace's *Facebook* page suggested he was linked to these groups: NFAC, Black Militia, the New Black Panther Party, and the Atlanta chapter of the Huey P. Newton Gun Club, which is named after a founder of the 1960s-era Black Panthers.[24] According to *officer.com*, a past *Instagram* post on Wallace's account contained an ominous message:[25]

> "1 Day I will Take Great Pride And Honor In Getting Me Some [Pejorative term for police] Blood On My Hands and Boots......If U Cant Feel This Energy Following Me Is Not Goin To Be Healthy For U.....I Pray Against My Enemy And Wish Death To All Who Are Oppressive To The Black Culture.......Black Power!!"

Colorado Police Murder: In the summer of 2021, Officer Gordon Beesley was shot and killed by Ronald Troyke. During the investigation, Colorado authorities released chilling excerpts from the twisted writings of the killer. The remarks were contained in a four-page letter seething with hatred for police officers, including this statement: "My goal today is to kill Arvada PD officers." After Officer Beesley was fatally shot, a citizen later described as a "good Samaritan" shot and killed Troyke with a handgun. Yet, to add to this tragic incident, that gun owner, identified as Johnny Hurley, was fatally shot by a responding police officer who had spotted him holding the dead suspect's AR-15 rifle. This double tragedy illustrates the fluid and volatile nature of policing in contemporary America. This hazardous climate was further described in the letter written by the cop-killer:[26]

> "Hundreds of you pigs should be killed daily," he wrote, "I just hope I don't die without killing any of you pigs." . . . "This is what you get, you are the people who are expendable," and "We the people were never your enemy, but we are now."

Denver All-State Game: Fearing a Las Vegas-style attack, Denver law enforcement officers were concerned they had encountered a mass shooting plot at a hotel near the venue of the Major League Baseball All-Star Game in July 2021. Police arrested four suspects on gun and drug charges. One suspect had requested a room with a balcony. Police were called to the Maven Hotel in downtown Denver after a hotel housekeeper entered this room to clean it and noticed multiple firearms. The investigation later revealed a rifle, bullet-proof vest, and high-capacity ammunition magazine, which were recovered from a vehicle of one of the suspects. Police obtained warrants to search two hotel rooms and found twelve guns and a large quantity of drugs.

When one suspect was arrested, his backpack allegedly contained a loaded 9mm semiautomatic handgun with an obliterated serial number, an ammunition magazine, a large quantity of suspected methamphetamine, and black-tar heroin.

Denver Police Chief Paul Pazen said, "we need to identify exactly, to the extent possible, why individuals were here in the first place, why in proximity to downtown. We don't have those answers." Meanwhile, the FBI released a statement saying, "We have no reason to believe this incident was connected to terrorism or a threat directed at the All-Star Game."[27]

Los Angeles – Federal Building-Body Armor/Weapons: A vehicle attempting to enter the employee parking garage of the LA Federal Building was stopped after security guards noticed a firearm in the vehicle. A subsequent search revealed a cache of weapons inside the vehicle. Officials arrested Erik Christopher Younge, who was wearing body armor and was in possession of a 45-caliber semi-automatic firearm, a loaded .556 caliber rifle, and a .762 caliber rifle. According to the criminal complaint, Younge later told Federal Protective Services officials that he went to the building because he needed protection, claiming he was a confidential informant assigned to a confidential federal task force.[28]

Sacramento – Democratic Party Building: Two men were indicted over an alleged plan to firebomb the Democratic Party headquarters in Sacramento, California. Ian Rogers and Jarrod Copeland were charged with conspiracy to destroy a building by fire or explosives. Rogers has also been charged with firearms and explosives offenses. Copeland is also charged with obstruction of justice charge. Prosecutors say the two men were upset about the outcome of the 2020 presidential election. The attack was allegedly designed to jump-start a "movement" to overthrow the government. They hoped to recruit others to their cause and allegedly reached out to the Proud Boys to try to rally support.

Later, Napa County Sheriff's deputies seized between 45 and 50 guns, including assault rifles and three machine guns. They also confiscated five pipe bombs and around 15,000 rounds of ammunition. According to prosecutors, Copeland joined the US military in 2013 but was twice arrested for desertion and was discharged in November 2016. After being discharged, he joined an affiliate of the Three Percenters, an anti-government militia group.

Prosecutors stated, "Copeland's membership in an anti-government militia, and his motivations for planning these attacks are relevant because they are not fleeting or the product of a single, but past, perceived affront . . . His sentiments are deeply felt and long-standing and reflect a belief that the government is illegitimate." According to this media account, the men had settled on a plan to attack the Democrats and were "elated" about the attack on the Capitol. The two men allegedly exchanged texts, including: "REVOLUTION" and "Sad it's come to this but I'm not going down without a fight. These commies need to be told what's up."[29]

Oklahoma – Nazi Flag & Antifa: An Oklahoma man was charged with shooting an unarmed woman in the back as she ran from his home after tearing down one of his Nazi flags—which were illuminated by floodlights. Alexander Feaster claims that he was fearful of an "imminent Antifa attack on his home" when he shot Kyndal McVey with his AR-15 rifle.

According to a court document reviewed in a media account, Feaster was alerted by a neighbor of a "plot" by "Antifa activists and said there was a threat to his life." Wary of partiers in a house on his block, Feaster kept his AR-15 rifle ready in case he was attacked. Feaster's lawyer contends that the Air Force veteran had a "sincere and reasonable fear of imminent peril of death or great bodily harm" when he used "defensive force" against the fleeing victim. These fears "were not unreasonable in the summer of 2020, with the media and left-wing activists drumming up riots and praising violence against their political adversaries," wrote Stephen Jones, Feaster's lawyer.

Jones added that Feaster's flags were a "first amendment display" that was "not dissimilar from the flying of the 'Make America Great Again' flag, or the Gay Pride flag, or the 'Don't Tread on Me' Gadsden Snake flag."[30]

US Capital – Bomb-Threat Suspect: Floyd Ray Roseberry was charged with threatening to detonate an explosive near the Library of Congress, prompting multiple evacuations of nearby buildings and lockdowns. Roseberry drove his pick-up truck onto the sidewalk near the library and allegedly told officers he had a bomb. An officer noticed what appeared to be a detonator in his hand. Roseberry also livestreamed video from the scene and was seen throwing dollar bills out of the truck. The Department of Justice also alleged that during a *Facebook* broadcast, Roseberry stated:[31]

> "The (expletive) revolution starts today, Joe Biden," and "If you want to shoot me and take the chance of blowing up two-and-a-half city blocks, cause that toolbox is full, ammunition nitrate is full."

Massachusetts – Black Militia: Massachusetts police took eleven "armed and dangerous" men into custody after they fled from police during a traffic stop in July 2021. A state trooper spotted the group on the side of an interstate highway. The men, who were dressed in tactical-style gear and armed with both pistols and rifles, refused to comply with orders to drop their weapons. Instead, they ran into woods by the side of the road.

The men claim to be from a group named "Rise of The Moors," but it is unclear how closely they are related to Moorish Sovereign Citizens—an extremist group who do not recognize the authority of the United States government or its laws. MSC's founder Noble Drew Ali taught that black "Moors" were America's original inhabitants and were therefore entitled to self-governing status. He believed that all African Americans were descendants of the Moabites and are therefore Moorish.[32]

Virginia – "The Base" Plot: In a far-reaching plot, Patrik Mathews, a former Canadian Army reservist illegally in the US, and Brian Lemley, a Maryland resident and self-described white nationalist, both said to be members of the group "the Base," were arrested. They allegedly sought to murder police and blacks, with the goal of bringing about the "Boogaloo," or the collapse of the US government by starting a racial civil war. FBI agents intercepted their communications as they planned to use a pro-gun rights rally in Richmond, Virginia to engage in mass murder and attacks on critical infrastructure.

After the two men were arrested in January 2020, just days before the Richmond rally, police found tactical gear, 1,500 rounds of ammunition, and cases of food and supplies in their residence. Subsequent investigation revealed that Lemley and Mathews had both attended military-style training camps with other members of The Base and used an assault rifle at a gun range in Maryland. The two men were sentenced in October 2021 to nine years in prison. Recordings allegedly revealed these statements:[33]

> "We need to go back to the days of . . . decimating blacks and getting rid of them where they stand," Mathews said in one recording. "If you see a bunch of blacks sitting on some corner you f***ing shoot them." Lemley said in another recording, "I need to claim my first victim . . . It's just that we can't live with ourselves if we don't get somebody's blood on our hands."
>
> "You wanna create f***ing some instability while the Virginia situation is happening, make other things happen," Mathews said. "Derail some rail lines . . . shut down the highways . . . shut down the rest of the roads . . . kick off the economic collapse of the US within a week after the [Boogaloo] starts." Lemley added, "I mean, even if we don't win, I would still be satisfied with a defeat of the system . . . and whatever was to come in its place would be preferable than what there is now . . . And if it's not us, then you know what, we still did what we had to do."

New York Professor – Shoot White People: A New York City-based psychiatrist told an audience at the Yale School of Medicine's Child Study Center on April 6, 2021, that she had fantasies of "unloading a revolver into the head of any white person that got in my way." Dr. Aruna Khilanani spewed the race-hating remarks, including that she'd walk away from the shooting "with a bounce in my step . . . Like I did the world a f–king favor." She also stated that white people "make my blood boil" and "are out of their minds and have been for a long time."

A flyer promoting her talk was entitled "The Psychopathic Problem of the White Mind," including learning objectives: "Set up white people's absence of empathy towards black rage as a problem" and "understand how white people are psychologically dependent on black rage"[34]

Dr. Khilanani also described the "intense rage and futility" people of color purportedly feel when talking to white people about racism in that "we keep forgetting that directly talking about race is a waste of our breath . . . We are asking a demented, violent predator who thinks that they are a saint or a superhero to accept responsibility. It ain't gonna happen."

That demented, violent predator that she references is the *white race*. She was sponsored by the Yale School of Medicine! Let this sink in while surveying the many "dots" that demand connection. Reflecting on these examples, there are two points you ought to consider.

Firstly, the targets are instructive: police, government, and political facilities along with the "other" race. These are both relevant and symbolic. Symbolic in representing the government. Relevant because ultimately the true "target" is the system itself. As will be developed, this is the goal of extremist groups across the racial, religious, and political spectrum.

Secondly, the racial animus is almost palpable—and extremely alarming.

Alone, these facts are troubling. Taken together with the guns and targets, they are extraordinarily volatile. Combining race hate with hatred of the system is such a combustible mix as to render urgent need . . . like doing triage in a hospital emergency room.

In November 2021, a classic example of where we are as a society came during a press conference held outside in a public setting in St. Louis. As Mayor Tishaura Jones was speaking about *gun violence*, her words were interrupted by gunfire. A local reporter described the scene. "The gunshots sounded in quick succession, like staccato notes in a symphony. Bam, then a pause. Bam. Bam. Bam. [Mayor Jones] didn't duck. She didn't flinch. She calmly looked over her shoulder in the general direction of the noise." Then she said *she is used to hearing gunfire*. It's like falling asleep with a "lullaby of gunshots."[35]

In another instance of delicious irony, the speech was not just about gun violence. She was advocating using what are known as *violence interrupters* to help stop the violence. As will be discussed in Chapter V, these are social workers from affected neighborhoods, often former gang members, who engage gangs to "interrupt" disputes before they lead to violence. Though the viability of these initiatives is questionable, what is not in dispute is that violence did *interrupt* the mayor's speech!

This is America in late 2021–2022! We are in desperate need of help. While the *triage* analogy may sound alarmist, it's time to go deeply into our circumstances and societal dynamics.

CHAPTER II

RACE, RELIGION & POLITICS . . .

WHAT WE CAN'T OR WON'T DISCUSS—AND WHY IT MATTERS!

Let's start with an obvious statement: this is a hard chapter to write. It may also be hard to read. Naturally, I come at this with some trepidation, yet some experience. For a period of about five years from about 2006–2011, I was actively engaged in getting the message out about a coming storm. The underlying reason for this storm had to do with three basic but powerful factors: *Race, Religion & Politics* ("RRP"). Most people avoid these controversial points like the "third rail" on an electric train track; those who touch it often get electrocuted. Though I did not get electrocuted, some people did not like my message.

Though one must be cognizant of this implication, avoiding RRP detracts from or even negates the theme of this book: *that extremist and terrorist violence will substantially increase*. The quote below is how I introduced this subject in 2009. This has even more relevance for today:

> "The historic presidency of Barack Obama has set in motion an unprecedented opportunity for America and for the world... this is an extraordinary time. His presidency could be so memorable that it will impact the future direction of the country for years

> to come. This impact could be both extraordinarily positive and frightening negative. As I have traced certain trends in this book, I tend to believe the latter is more likely than the former. Since I believe the potentially adverse impact of race, religion and politics is significant, please allow me to flush out the basis for this conclusion."[1]

After this set-up, Barack Obama's speech from the 2004 Democratic Convention entitled "The Audacity of Hope" was quoted.[2] Most know this speech. It rocketed Mr. Obama to great success, including the presidency four years later. A pertinent part of his speech has direct relevancy to this chapter: ". . . there is not a liberal America and a conservative America—there is the United States of America. There is not a Black America and a White America and Latino America and Asian America—there's the United States of America."

These words were powerful then—and urgently needed now. They cut to the core of how we should live and think about each other. Indeed, these words seem "old-fashioned" now. They are so far beyond the mainstream that it even feels silly to type them. In a country that has been declared systemically racist by its "thought leaders," reading these words and remembering what that sentiment felt like is poignant. Do you remember? When was the last time you read or heard them? It may help to remind ourselves that the *neo-racism* driving this culture is not in control of our thoughts, our actions, or our dreams. While we have a long way to go to build a society that values character over color, it can still be accomplished.

An insightful editorial back in 2008 by Joseph C. Phillips speaks volumes as to where we are today. His theme was that Obama's presidential run was always based on race. But he did not mean "race-ism." He emphatically asserted Americans were *tired* of race. They were looking to move beyond race in a concrete way. This manifested itself in real excitement about and for Obama. But it had more to do with America living up to her promise. Americans believed that Obama would bring us one step closer to the embodiment of our national motto "E Pluribus Unum"—Out of many, One.

Phillips emphasized it would be impossible to fulfill this promise "so long as we are stratified by color and class consciousness."[3] The tragic irony, argued Phillips, is that Obama *needs* race, as without it, "the emperor has few clothes." Would America under Obama move to an "idea of racial non-discrimination . . . [to] his vision of an America moving beyond the old conversations about race?" Back then, I suggested one way to demonstrate this commitment to a colorless society was to confront racial provocateurs and racial preferences. I correctly predicted that he could not do so because if he did, it would sever his own party. By failing to do so, he will then prove to the "other side" that it is, indeed, *all about race*. Similarly, Phillips concludes that:[4]

> "finally it must come down to race—not the ethnicity of either candidate, but their willingness to transcend old conversations of race in this country. At the same time, his support of preferences based on race belies the nobility of his speech and the vision that made him a star."

Recall the Obama election was "historic," ushering in a "post-racial" America. The media, his supporters, and the "thinkers" all consider Barack Obama "black." Yet, he is half white. In 2011, the president had an important decision. This decision was symbolic and personal. But it also had significant public policy and public safety implications.

What was this decision? The question was simple: What race are you? Every ten years, the US holds a census to count the number and demographics of people in America. What was his answer? Black.

As Phillips predicted, Obama needed race. He had this perfect opportunity to transcend race. But he didn't. This even goes beyond symbolism. It was also a factual question. In fact, he is half black and half white. Though some contend determining and declaring one's race and gender is both subjective and acceptable, this decision was larger than Obama. It was about that great speech he gave (i.e., "there is not a Black America and a White America."). At the stroke of a pen, Obama could have proven this sentiment. He could have said he is both black and white, just like many other Americans . . .

Enter the Trump era of "Make America Great Again." What happened in his presidency is what I had predicted and envisioned would occur during the Obama Administration. What was missing, and what I missed, was the need for the "counter-weight." This came in the name of Donald J. Trump—who ignited the fire on the Right. With the Right fighting back, playing "hardball" because of Trump's street fighting nature, the Left finally saw that its own street fighting approach to politics actually had an opponent who knew their game—and was prepared to go toe-to-toe. This unleashed a dramatic and likely unprecedented shaking of the system, including a vast investigation into the Trump campaign and administration—which we now know, ironically, was funded and forwarded by the Clinton campaign.

Much can be said about the Trump Administration, but for reasons set out below, the "Make America Great Again" mantra was one of those "dog whistles" that progressives like to perceive. Let me say upfront, I do not believe Trump or Obama are racist. Yet, Trump's speech relating to Charlottesville is one example, among many, to demonstrate that Trump *is* a racist. Like most "racial" things, this too became a deceptive cudgel. Hence, Charlottesville goes to the theme of this book. It has all the elements in one *messy* package: extremists on the Right and on the Left. Plus, media, violence, and layers of controversy and deception. Simply stated, it makes for an excellent case study.

CHARLOTTESVILLE & BEYOND

Seeking to get to the truth about Charlottesville requires some indulgence. As you can see below, the next few pages have many direct quotes. To those following the spectacle, and to those who only vaguely paid attention, this discussion is important for both race relations and for public safety. This is not designed to defend former President Trump. It is larger than Trump. Since much of the controversy was centered on what Trump said, there is little option but to use the actual words he used.

Initially for context, on August 12, 2017, hundreds of white supremacists, neo-Nazis, and the Ku Klux Klan gathered in Charlottesville for a rally called

Unite the Right. The stated purpose was to protest the removal of a statue of confederate general Robert E. Lee on the University of Virginia campus. These protestors were met by others on the Left, including Antifa and BLM. As could be expected, the groups clashed, resulting in violence inflicted by both sides. During these clashes, a neo-Nazi drove a vehicle into the crowd, killing one person and injuring thirty others. The driver was subsequently convicted and sentenced to life in prison.[5]

Trump's initial reference to Charlottesville was given on the day of the event. While intending to hold a press conference for the Veteran Administration, Trump stated:[6]

> "But we're closely following the terrible events unfolding in Charlottesville, Virginia. We condemn in the strongest possible terms this egregious display of hatred, bigotry, and violence on many sides, *on many sides* (emphasis added). It's been going on for a long time in our country. Not Donald Trump, not Barack Obama, this has been going on for a long, long time. It has no place in America. What is vital now is a swift restoration of law and order and the protection of innocent lives. No citizen should ever fear for their safety and security in our society . . .
>
> Above all else, we must remember this truth: No matter our color, creed, religion or political party, we are all Americans first. We love our country. We love our god . . . We love our flag. We're proud of our country. We're proud of who we are, so we want to get the situation straightened out in Charlottesville, and we want to study it. And we want to see what we're doing wrong as a country where things like this can happen. My administration is restoring the sacred bonds of loyalty between this nation and its citizens, but our citizens must also restore the bonds of trust and loyalty between one another. We must love each other, respect each other and cherish our history and our future together. So important. We have to respect each other. Ideally, we have to love each other."

What Trump said was completely legitimate and patriotic. It stressed love, trust, and respect—loyalty to the country and each other. Though not quoted above, he also commended the National Guard, the police, and federal authorities. He engaged the governor (Democrat Terry McAuliffe] and talked about the need to stop hate and the division. He did not blame any politician. Though, he did mention the "hatred, bigotry, and violence on many sides, *on many sides.*" This was his *offense*. He blamed each side!

The media had a fit. Even the title of the *Vox* article that was referenced used quotes around the words "on many sides." Three days later, on August 15, at another press conference, a reporter asked: "Why did you wait so long to denounce neo-Nazis?" Trump responded with a series of points that he said three days previously and how the dead woman's mother thanked the president for his words. Then because the press conference was called to discuss infrastructure, Trump stated, "How about, how about, how about a couple of infrastructure questions." The reporter responded, "Was that terrorism?" Later, when asked again if it was terrorism, Trump replied:[7]

> "I think the driver of the car is a disgrace to himself, his family, and this country. And that is—you can call it terrorism, you can call it murder. You can call it whatever you want. I would just call it as the fastest one to come up with a good verdict. That's what I'd call it. And there is a question. Is it murder? Is it terrorism? Then you get into legal semantics. The driver of the car is a murderer, and what he did was a horrible, horrible, inexcusable thing."

The questions and answers continued in this fashion:

> REPORTER: Mr. President, are you putting what you're calling the alt-left and white supremacists on the *same moral plane* (emphasis added)?
>
> TRUMP: I am not putting anybody on a moral plane, what I'm saying is this: you had a group on one side and a group on the other, and they came at each other with clubs and it was vicious and horrible and it was a horrible thing to watch, but there is another

> side. There was a group on this side, you can call them the Left. You've just called them the Left, that came violently attacking the other group. So, you can say what you want, but that's the way it is.
>
> REPORTER: You said there was hatred and violence on both sides?
>
> TRUMP: I do think there is blame—yes, I think there is blame on both sides. You look at, you look at both sides. I think there's blame on both sides, and I have no doubt about it, and you don't have any doubt about it either. And, and, and, and if you reported it accurately, you would say.
>
> REPORTER: The neo-Nazis started this thing. They showed up in Charlottesville [note this question]:
>
> TRUMP: Excuse me, they didn't put themselves down as neo-Nazis, and you had some very bad people in that group. But you also had people that were *very fine people on both sides* (emphasis added). You had people in that group—excuse me, excuse me. I saw the same pictures as you did. You had people in that group that were there to protest the taking down, of to them, a very, very important statue and the renaming of a park from Robert E. Lee to another name.

Later Trump went on saying, as if to clarify the "very fine people on both sides" comment with this statement:

> ". . . I'm not talking about the neo-Nazis and the white nationalists, because they should be condemned totally—but you had many people in that group other than neo-Nazis and white nationalists, okay? And the press has treated them absolutely unfairly. Now, in the other group also, you had some fine people, but you also had troublemakers and you see them come with the black outfits and with the helmets and with the baseball bats—you had a lot of bad people in the other group too . . . it looked like they had some rough, bad people—neo-Nazis, white nationalists, whatever you want to call 'em. But you had a lot of people in that group that were

> there to innocently protest and very legally protest, because you know, I don't know if you know, but they had a permit. The other group didn't have a permit. So, I only tell you this: there are two sides to a story.

There you have it. Trump has never lived down these words. Politicians, media, and progressives condemned Trump. Even years later, these words were used to tar him as racist. What did he do wrong? Two things: he condemned both sides and he stated there were *fine people on both sides*. This goes to the heart of our divide. The *thought elite* does not allow for "equal wrongs," especially for people who hold beliefs that could be defined as "right-wing." The question by the unknown reporter demonstrated this bias.

The question: Are you putting what you're calling the alt-left and white supremacists on the *same moral plane.* The "answer" on the Left is that the *white supremacists* are the most to blame. He might as well refer to them as drudges of society. The "alt-left" (meaning Antifa, BLM, and other affiliated groups) *are not to be equated* with those white supremacists. This biased position, again, by an *alleged* objective reporter was also reflected in another question: "Neo-Nazis started this thing. They showed up in Charlottesville." Showing up to protest is evidence of "starting it?" These people do not have a right to march, to protest—or to show up? This is what the "reporter" inferred. Turn the question on its head: "*Antifa* started this thing. *They* showed up in Charlottesville." Do you ever think you will hear this question . . .?

This bias was smeared all over the press conference. They wanted to catch Trump in a trap. The best they could get was his "fine people on both sides" comment. And this comment then became the takeaway. It was declared repeatedly to tar Trump as a racist. Numerous public figures parroted this deceptive smear. Of course, few acknowledged that Trump directly qualified the "fine people" comment with [I'm] "not talking about the neo-Nazis and the white nationalists, because they should be condemned totally" and "it looked like they had some rough, bad people—neo-Nazis, white nationalists, whatever you want to call 'em . . ."

Both statements directly called out and distinguished *these people* were not the fine people he was talking about. Yet, this distinction was usually ignored by those who knew or ought to have known.

A classic example came *three years later* in the first presidential debate in 2020. According to the *Los Angeles Times*, Moderator Chris Wallace (then with FOX News) "gave Trump *yet another chance* to denounce far-right radicals." Before we delve into the substance of what was said, note a few points.

Firstly, the reporter characterized the question as "*yet another chance* to denounce far-right radicals." This implies that Trump had never done so previously. What you read above is direct evidence that he clearly had condemned *those people*. Did the *Times* reporter, and for that matter, Chris Wallace, not know this? Of course, they knew what you just read. Yet, they ignored it—as did so many others who seek to forward a divisive fiction.

Secondly, as you will see below, Wallace did not ask Biden the parallel question: Do you denounce *far-left* radicals? Do you denounce Antifa? Ironically, note that Wallace's question to Trump about far-right radicals was premised on this set-up: *add to the violence in a number of these cities*. He did not directly say Charlottesville, which by then was three years prior. Wallace must have been speaking of the summer of love riots. Indeed, rioting was still going on in some places. Its impact was very fresh, as most of the rioting had occurred from May through August. Hence, the premise for the question is itself curious. Though I am sure that some right-wing people participated in certain riots, these were largely, even exclusively, driven by the "alt-left," specifically Antifa and BLM.

Consequently, in a major presidential debate, a crucial racial question was raised on two *false premises*: That Trump had not previously denounced radicals on the right, and that the radical right had some meaningful impact on the riots of 2020. I object to both premises. This may be why Trump did not directly denounce the far-right *again*. Some may contend that Trump should do so at every opportunity. Yet, as we will see in the next chapter, for every "extremist" who is willing to directly get into the fray, there are dozens who are in various levels of support for "the cause." Consequently, Trump was put into a box. He either had to *keep denouncing* the extremists on the Right, which he knows would upset some of his supporters, or he had to find a way to divert the blame or the question itself.

Note that Biden has the same problem—except rarely, if ever, was he asked to denounce the alt-left. Did you ever hear this question posed to Biden: *Are you willing to condemn Antifa and other radical groups?* Instead, when the subject *is* broached, it comes in a generalized denouncing "those who commit violent actions." Of course, everyone should denounce violence. Yet tellingly, remember that hundreds of riots occurred just prior to Democratic Convention in mid-August 2020. Indeed, rioting was still "in progress" in certain cities. Yet, rioting and violence were *never even mentioned* during the entire Democratic Convention. This silence speaks volumes.

In any case, these were the relevant questions and answers posed at the presidential debate:[8]

> QUESTION: "Are you willing tonight to condemn white supremacists and militia groups and to say that they need to stand down and not add to the violence in a number of these cities . . .?"
>
> TRUMP: "Sure, I'm willing to do that. I would say, I would say, almost everything I see is from the left-wing, not from the right-wing," Trump said. "I'm willing to do anything. I want to see peace."
>
> "Then do it, sir," Wallace said. "Say it. Do it. Say it," Democratic nominee Joe Biden then said.
>
> TRUMP: "You want to call 'em—what do you want to call 'em? Give me a name, give me a name," Trump said. "Who would you like me to condemn?"
>
> Wallace and Biden, talking over each other, suggested "white supremacists" and the right-wing group the Proud Boys.
>
> TRUMP: "Proud Boys, stand back and stand by—but I'll tell you what, I'll tell you what, somebody's got to do something about Antifa and the Left," Trump said.

This was not good enough for Wallace, Biden, the *Times* reporter, and for most "objective" members of the media. The *Times* reporter noted that "many listeners, including members of the Proud Boys, saw Trump's response as a sign of support, the opposite of a denunciation." Facing widespread criticism afterward, Trump subsequently added, "I don't know who the Proud Boys are, but whoever they are, they have to stand down; let enforcement do their work." But he reiterated, "now, Antifa is a real problem because the problem is on the left."[9]

Before we move on, let me summarize. Most importantly, *neither side* has a license to hate. Neither side can claim the "high ground" in terms of moral relevancy. Neither side has a "right" to violate the law or commit violence. There is no inherent, objective basis for either of these positions. Hate is wrong. Pure and simple. Significantly, no one can ever convince me that the Left does not hate. In many ways, this book is dedicated to condemning hate, as it is the source and driver for many of our problems.

Hate is largely objectified as the problem of the Right. This premise is often used to distinguish Right from Left. There are many flaws in this thinking.

Initially, this conclusion is objectively impossible to prove. If impossible to prove, why is this premise used so often by so many? We all have our own stories and experiences. Though anecdotal, these belie the false premise used to condemn the Right. I faced hate daily as a police officer—always from the Left. Indeed, many of the radical leftists do not deny that they hate.

A classic example is Darrell Brooks, who mowed down forty people in Waukesha, killing six. He was pictured on social media with a hat that read: I "heart" hate (using the common symbol for the heart). Indeed, many indicators of Brooks' mental state and potential for violence were plain to see for anyone who cared to look. For example, on his now-deleted *Facebook* account, he advocated "knokkin white people TF out" and showed support for the controversial group Black Hebrew Israelites, whose extreme elements claim that white people are agents of Satan and who advocate hatred of the Jewish community.[10] This is but one of thousands of examples one can find connecting the Left to hate.

Yet, let's not get bogged down in trying to prove a negative, that is: Whether those on the Left do not hate. The real point is that hate is wrong. No excuse, no reason, no justification, no political persuasion, no consensus matters. It is plain and simple.

Going forward, our focus should be on the societal consensus of moral relevancy. As shown above, this rests on the false notion that "haters" are those on the Right. Knock this premise down, and what it left (no pun intended)? Accept that everyone (both on the right and the left) are subject to the human flaw known as "hate." This should *force us* to reorient society to address *all* those who hate—not just who some want to blame! This is way too big of a step for some people. It goes to character—which is why abandoning Dr. King's legacy and replacing it with a neo-racist "color" orientation, is both wrong and ominous.

Another element of this distinction between far-right and far-left is political ideology. Nazis are considered worse than Communists or socialists. Why? Why are Nazis worse than radicals on the Left? History does not support this contention. Surely, what Hitler did before and during WWII was barbaric and pure evil. Yet, if history is our guide, Communists killed many more people than Hitler's Germany. Stalin, Mao, Pol Pot, Castro, Chavez; the list goes on. There is no point in comparing the "kill rate" of the Left versus the Right. The Left wins—by far. So, why is Nazism worse than Communism? Why is Nazism worse than socialism or even Anarchism? Using comparative levels of violence as a barometer does not support this conclusion.

So again, why do we almost reflectively put Nazism (or Fascism) at the bottom of the political "pecking order"? This is *not* to say Nazism or fascism is good. For the record, they ought to be condemned. This is basic and consistent. Never should this evil ideology gain traction in our minds or in society. But the same ought to be said for Communism and socialism.

Think back again to the questioning of Trump. The premises were all against the Right, with the silent "wink and nod" to the radicals on the Left. Everyone at the Democratic Convention was silent—no condemnation against the radical leftists who were burning and looting—which was occurring almost while the politicians were speaking.

It was reminiscent of the 1968 Democratic Convention. As police and rioters battled in the streets of Chicago, politicians talked. Back then, Democrats were *not* all progressives—which is the politically correct way of describing socialists. Back then, Democratic Mayor Richard Daley did not sit silent. When he gave the "shoot to kill" order, amazingly, the riots and looting stopped. This is both a policy and a public safety lesson for contemporary America.

Yet, we are too politically correct and weak—too woke to see that there are consequences for being weak in the face of the mob. Yes, America, there are consequences for doing "the wink and the nod" to socialists and anarchists!

Consequently, placing socialism *above* fascism is either misplaced or disingenuous. It is also troubling. Both ideologies are authoritarian. Both seek to assert government control over the population. Both focus on the "collective" to the detriment of the "individual." While both initially need the support of the population, fascism tends to support large businesses (think of "crony capitalism") while socialism tends to *nationalize* business. Because of this distinction, fascism tends to be more efficient in providing for the population (consider much of the "success" of Hitler's Germany was due to the efficiencies of this system—he made the trains run on time—and built a massive industrial sector). So, as in Charlottesville, it is appropriate to be concerned about the *Right seeking to unite*. But it is not the only threat to this representative democracy.

Much more can be said regarding these distinctions, but this is the takeaway: Both fascism and socialism cannot tolerate the freedoms that this country was built on. Both cannot allow the individual to focus on life, liberty, and the pursuit of happiness. Indeed, both systems fall far short of these principles. Hence, it is wrong to think that socialism is better than fascism. Both are wrong and inferior in so many ways to this representative democracy. Yet, we are being told by many, some who are elected political leaders, that not only is socialism better than fascism, but it is better than democracy and capitalism.

Remember the principle: attack one ideology and ignore (or support) the other, you will get more of both.

The reason this dynamic is happening has to do with the "end game." Leftists believe that the only *solution* to this dying planet is to create a *global* governing system, with the United Nations as a typology or model. Correctly understanding that *nationalistic* governments have led to conflict and warfare, they opposed nationalism in favor of globalism. Nationalism often results in "self-interested" decision-making. Doing what is appropriate for *my* country, often means hurting *other* countries. The cumulative effect of hundreds and thousands of these self-interested decisions designed to forward the interests of one country over another is a source of friction and competition. These naturally led to conflict—and war.

History has shown that nationalistic conflict can be avoided by dispersing and defusing self-interested decision-making. The United Nations, and before that the League of Nations, sought to create forums to foster decision-making that benefitted the planet, not individual countries. Yet, the United Nations is too structurally weak, with no real ability to *enforce* world order. This is obvious to any thinking observer. Nonetheless, the Left—read progressives—*know* that the world order is in great danger from nationalistic governments. Therefore, fascism is feared. Think of fascism as socialism in a nationalistic form. Remember Hitler's party was known as the "National Socialists." His vision was to implement socialism, as did the Communists in the 1930s. But Hitler's approach was to forward *Germany*, not some nebulous world-ruling Communist party. This thinking lives on. Russian President Putin said the 2022 invasion of Ukraine was to "de-nazify" the country.

Is there something to Putin's desire to de-nazify Ukraine? An interesting connection between the brutal war in Ukraine and Charlottesville brings ideology directly into play. According to an affidavit filed by an FBI agent supporting an indictment of four members of the "Rise Above Movement" ("RAM"), which is a white supremacy extremist group headquartered in Southern California, the indicted members traveled to political rallies throughout 2017, including in Huntington Beach, California on March 25, 2017; Berkeley, California on April 15, 2017; San Bernardino, California on June 10, 2017; and Charlottesville, Virginia on August 11–12, 2017. RAM members allegedly violently attacked and assaulted counter-protesters at each of these events.[11]

Here is where this connection to Ukraine gets interesting. The affidavit noted that in the spring of 2018 members of RAM traveled to Germany, Italy, and Ukraine to celebrate Hitler's birthday. In Ukraine, they met with the leader of the International Department for the National Corps, which is a Ukrainian political party founded in 2016 out of a regiment of the Ukrainian military called the Azov Battalion. The FBI affiant stated that "the Azov Battalion is a paramilitary unit of the Ukrainian National Guard, which is known for its association with neo-Nazi ideology and use of Nazi symbolism, and which is believed to have participated in training and radicalizing United States-based white supremacy organizations."[12]

The connection of RAM to the Azov Battalion was described by the Stanford Center for International Security and Cooperation, which published a detailed report regarding the connections between US extremist groups and ultra-nationalist Ukrainian neo-Nazi groups, such as the Azov Battalion.[13]

Ironically, these connections may have been fostered by the US government funding of Ukrainian paramilitary forces, such as the Azov Battalion. According to a *Global Times* article which cited reporting from 2015 and 2016, stated that "the US Congress removed a ban on funding neo-Nazi groups like Azov Battalion from its year-end spending bill." This bill provided funding for various Ukrainian groups, including the Azov Battalion. An amendment to this bill sought to limit "arms, training, and other assistance to the neo-Nazi Ukrainian militia, the Azov Battalion." But an amendment was removed due to "pressure from the Pentagon."[14] When Russia invaded Ukraine, the US and other countries ramped up military aide to the tune of billions of dollars into this fray. The Azov Battalion, as a key element of Ukraine's military, will surely receive a lot of military equipment and weapons in their fight against Russian troops.

Beyond the paramilitary groups in Ukraine, the influence of the Azon Battalion is significant. Citing other news reports, the *Global Times* noted that individuals associated with Azon Battalion participated in terrorist acts, including those in Christchurch, New Zealand, where fifty-one people were killed at two mosques in a mass shooting by Australian Brenton Tarrant in March 2019. Tarrant, who displayed a symbol used by the Azov Battalion during the attacks, claimed in his manifesto that he had traveled to Ukraine. Another incident occurred in September 2019 when an American soldier tried to bomb a major American news network. When arrested by the FBI, the soldier, Jarrett William Smith, said that he "planned to travel to Ukraine to fight with violent far-right group Azov Battalion."[15] These connections and the funding from the US led a writer at the *Daily Veracity* to conclude that America "indirectly sent taxpayer dollars to neo-Nazi groups and Charlottesville rioters abroad."[16]

This is very reminiscent of Germany in the 1930s where Communists and fascists fought in the streets prior to WWII. It's why the Left was so afraid of—and hated—Trump. The nationalist thinking of Trump advocating God, Country, and Family was in opposition to the progressives, who saw these as contributing to inequality in society. Hence, Trump's "America First," and "Make America Great Again" campaign was a direct threat to progressive and globalist thinking. It's also why Trump was skeptical of the UN, NATO, and other global bodies, along with various agreements, such the climate and trade pacts. Trump correctly saw these as reducing the interests—the power and influence—of the United States, in favor of nebulous "global interests." Trump's worldview was (and is) directly in conflict with the progressives' globalist worldview—and their ultimate goals.

Consequently, one can cut through the entire notion of race, religion, and politics and reduce it to this: *Globalism vs. Nationalism*. An overriding theme in this book is the fact that progressives use RRP as "sticks" or "wedges" to break down the country. They cannot allow America to be "great again." They want America to be diminished so the world can have a chance for global government. A strong America will, on its face, prevent a global government. Hence, the need to reduce America's power. What better way to do so than to declare that America is "systemically racist"? Much more can be said. But for now, consider that if we focus on the things that separate us—with the most obvious being *race, religion, and politics*; then the goal of diminishing, or even taking down America, becomes much more feasible.

Ironically—and precisely because we are taught *not to even talk* about them—race, religion, and politics may take this country down. Not because we cannot get along. Not because the country is inherently defective or systemically racist. Not because we cannot overcome our "original sin." But because those who are leading and driving the dominant culture and *mores* want to change the country. I believe they do this for what they think is the well-being of the planet. Consequently, their mantra is along these paradoxical lines: *We need to destroy, or at least diminish, this country to save the world!*

With these points as our premise, let's dig into the means—the techniques—being used to divide and conquer.

CRITICAL RACE THEORY

As briefly mentioned in the last chapter, long before this phrase and this "theory" became part of the national conversation, I used its formative predecessor as the basis of my master's thesis entitled: *A Critical Analysis of Terrorism*. The title was designed to merge the Critical Theory of Criminology as a justification for terrorism to accomplish its ultimate goal—which is to take down the capitalist system.

As a summary statement: this theory was a Marxist view of the criminal justice system. Its tenets viewed *crime* and the enforcement of criminal laws as a means to repress those of lower socioeconomic classes. While this theory did not focus *exclusively* on race, as does Critical Race Theory (CRT), its orientation directly lends "credence" to the current view that the criminal justice system is (and has) wrongly discriminated against blacks in a disproportionate and racist manner. This discrimination is so ingrained in "the justice system" that it's structurally or inherently too corrupt to fix. The only way to "solve" these structural defects is to destroy the entire system and start anew.

This theory failed to provide a legitimate mechanism to address the "justice" system's perceived problems. My belief then—which has been sadly reinforced now—is that without legitimate means to remedy the system, those who are so inclined will try to take it down by force, and terroristic violence was the most obvious way to do so. Such was my conclusion back in 1988: Terrorism is the *only real* solution to the problem. Specifically:[17]

> "The analysis of this theory reflects the proposition that the problems of American society can only be rectified through revolution. The operative technique to achieve the revolution is through terrorism."

When my research was conducted in the mid-1980s, this theory had little exposure, remaining limited to law and graduate schools and known only by academics, intellectuals, and students. Briefly, these are the major tenets of the *Critical Theory of Criminology*:[18]

- American society is based on an advanced capitalistic economy.
- The state is organized to serve the interest of the dominant economic class, the capitalist elite.
- Criminal law is an instrument of the state and ruling class to maintain and perpetuate the existing social and economic order.
- Crime control in capitalist society is accomplished through a variety of institutions and agencies established and administered by a governmental elite, representing ruling class interests, for the purpose of establishing a domestic order.
- The contradictions of advanced capitalism—the disjunction between essence and existence—require that the subordinate classes remain oppressed by whatever means necessary, especially through the coercion and violence of the legal system.
- Only with the collapse of capitalist society and the creation of a new society, based on socialist principles, will be a solution to the crime problem.

Read these tenets again. Each reflects a socialistic, or Communistic, critique of capitalism. This is not to say that capitalism does not have its problems. Yet, the theory's obvious conclusions shocked me—especially since it did not provide details for a "solution." Other than a *society based on socialist principles*, the theory was essentially saying *destroy capitalism*—and then create a new society based on socialism. This is how I explained it in my thesis: [19]

> "Advocates of Critical Theory illustrated by both the tenets of the theory, as well as its stated ideologies, fall far short of providing a "blueprint" for the new society. They seem to be content with destroying this "capitalistic" society.

> Clearly this does not constitute the type of framework necessary for intellectual analysis, as well as the basis for advocating revolution. Indeed, Marcuse [Herbert Marcuse, who was a communist theorist and often cited as a significant contributor of the theory] argues that *Critical Theory possesses no concepts which could bridge the gap between the present and the future* (emphasis added and citation removed from the original text)."

As the theory only criticized the problems of the existing system and failed to provide a "blueprint" for how to transform a capitalist system into a socialist society, *my conclusion* was that terrorism would be the means to achieve the desired socialist society. The theory itself did not directly advocate terrorism.

Two qualifiers from my research decades ago are equally applicable today. Firstly, what I did not anticipate was this theory would gain traction in the larger society. Indeed, it is now widely accepted by most of our "thought leaders." This irony is delicious. Could one have ever anticipated those who lead the institutions that support this capitalist system advocating a theory that calls for its destruction? This did not occur to me decades ago. But as we will see below, this is exactly what is happening.

Secondly, using terroristic means to accomplish the transition from capitalism to socialism will still be a necessary component. This is because the system will not be destroyed without a fight.

With the "logic" of the criminological theory established, let's demonstrate the main tenets of its *daughter*—the Critical Race Theory.

Critical Race Theory (CRT) is now deeply connected in contemporary America. Seemingly out of nowhere, mostly in response to the George Floyd killing, this theory has been widely acknowledged and advocated. While writing this draft, I googled the phrase "what is critical race theory." I got 321,000,000 results.[20] As one can imagine, views from all over the political spectrum resulted.

Even advocates of the theory describe it as a "constantly evolving field of study."[21] This notion that the theory is constantly evolving makes it hard to pin down its tenets. Yet, using the elements presented above, this theory has adopted Marxist principles and shaped them through a racial lens. The definition from Britannica:[22]

> "Critical race theorists hold that racism is inherent in the law and legal institutions of the United States insofar as they function to create and maintain social, economic, and political inequalities between whites and nonwhites, especially African Americans. Critical race theorists are generally dedicated to applying their understanding of the institutional or structural nature of racism to the concrete (if distant) goal of eliminating all race-based and other unjust hierarchies."

Note that this definition echoes the now widely accepted "inherent racism" claim about this country. The definition notes the structural and institutional inequalities between whites and non-whites. This is a key distinction from Marxist thinking. Marxists tend to focus on "class" distinctions. Resources, not skin color, drive these inequalities. Indeed, inequalities are real. Nowhere on earth can one point to a place where everyone is equally positioned. Indeed, this would require a "flat" socio-economic and political structure where the leaders are on the same plain as the led. This has never happened in human history. Thus, Marxists are correct in pointing out that inequalities exist. But they cannot show or even explain how they can "level the playing field" and create a truly "equitable" society. It cannot happen—and they know it.

Instead of explaining how they will eliminate inequality, advocates of CRT transform the problem from class to race. Obvious inequalities are "racialized" in CRT. This is how advocates of the theory explain it:

> "The idea is to get people to think *systemically.* As opposed to viewing racism as simply a conflict between individuals based on race, CRT posits that racial bias is perpetuated and inflamed by the very *structure* of our society (emphasis added).
>
> As a legal theory, CRT explores and illustrates how the law can promulgate or support racial disparities. As a social theory, CRT recognizes that racism is a social problem. With that dual focus, it's

> interested in focusing on *institutions, structures, systems*, processes, assumptions, discourses, narratives, and large macro processes that have fostered racial inequality (emphasis added).
>
> So critical race theory is a framework, one developed to help us understand how it is that *structural* and racial disparities endure in our society and how that is engendered in some of our laws and policies. The theory rests on the premise that racial bias—intentional or not—is *baked into US laws and institutions.* Black Americans, for example, are incarcerated at much higher rates than any other racial group. CRT invites scrutiny of the criminal legal system's role in that disparity with a dispassionate view that the law falls far short of the ideals under which it was created" (emphasis added).

Again, the emphasis on the systems, structures, and institutions is crucial to Marxist thinking. Countering this claim would require massive discourse. Yet, consider a couple of points.

Firstly, given the history of slavery in the US, it is correct to identify how laws, structures, and institutions have shaped the black experience. Volumes could be written—and have been—about the evils and impact of slavery. There is no way to adequately negate this stain, this "original sin" that America has and must endure. The bloody and violent Civil War was the most obvious attempt to redeem itself from this sin, but a hundred more years of segregation added salt to this wound. Yet, much has been done to address these evils.

Fifty years after the civil rights movement, the success stories of blacks in every facet of society are legion. Blacks abound in leadership positions. Black success stories are too substantial, too varied, too poignant, too obvious to even try to articulate. Indeed, blacks now and for many years have *led and directed* the very institutions that are being derided as racially inequitable. Many of these institutions, indeed the vast majority (and arguably *all*)—from academic, media, entertainment, government, sports, law, and culture, to name a few, are dominated by progressive thought.

With this level of influence and concentration, how is it that these institutions are still deemed racist? Why have they not been fixed? What have the liberals, and now progressives, been doing all these years? What are these leaders doing to remedy inadequacies in the system?

Secondly, these questions lead to the proposed solutions instituted by liberals and progressives. The widespread "solutions" imposed by the "Great Society" in the 1960s are a notable example. Intending to address social problems, including criminal justice reforms, these programs designed to "help" the poor, including blacks, used welfare and food stamps to provide a "safety net." These programs—and others—are often based on "single parent" status, so that the mother (usually young) can obtain welfare, food stamps, and housing. However, these measures have extraordinarily damaged the black family by isolating black men from the children they fathered.

Similar "logic" supported building monstrosity housing projects to "warehouse" people in rat- and bug-infested hellholes designed to segregate blacks from the larger society. I walked through these projects on numerous occasions. Entering apartments, seeing the chaos and the devastation. It defies explanation as to how *anyone* could come out of these environments healthy, law-abiding—and in one piece. To the thousands that did, they have my respect and I hold them in the highest regard. I could not have done it.

The impact of these "solutions" has been devasting. Black illegitimacy now ranges in the 75-percent range, when in the 1920s–30s the black family had one of the highest rates of intact family units in America. The same percentages hold true of crime rates. *Before* liberals decided to "help" the black families, the rate of black criminality was as low, or even lower, than that of whites. Now, blacks commit a disproportionately higher rate of crime, particularly violent crime—way beyond its population percentage. In fact, blacks commit about 40 percent of the homicides, yet represent only 13 percent of the population. One could go on with many other examples.

These "solutions" instituted by liberals to further the government welfare system did not resolve anything. For example, consider just one factor: out-of-wedlock births. In 1963, 72 percent of non-white families were married and together. By 2017, this data was essentially reversed, with only 27 percent of black households being married.[23] This has had a staggering and devastating impact on black children. This was *after* the Great Society programs sought to *help* blacks and the poor in this society.

Many other indicators of success have either fallen or have not had nearly the "return on investment" that the liberals promised—and taxpayers continue to pay for it. Instead, these programs have marginalized black men, isolated them from the larger society—and created a "cradle to grave" culture in many poor (typically urban) areas. So, after decades of "fixing" led by liberals and the institutions that they've run, progressives now say that the institutions and the structural system are rotten—and systemically racist.

How ironic is this? Use government to "fix" those who government previously discriminated against, institute "reforms" that further their decline, then declare that the system needs to be destroyed—to once again, "fix" the problems of those who (apparently) cannot do so without government help. Now the "help" will come from a *new* system built on socialism. Of course, these promises are made without being able to point to any example, in history or contemporary times, that this desired system has been able to achieve their lofty goal of "equity."

So, here is my point. On one hand, blacks have demonstrated substantial achievement and influence in the American system. They have achieved extraordinary successes. They have accomplished these in a *systemically racist* system. For decades, institutions within the system have been led by blacks, influenced by blacks, and employed blacks. Yet here we are still pointing fingers at *the system*. The illogical nature of this thinking can be illustrated by this quote from the *fairfight* website that was cited above:[24]

> "Beyond simply studying these injustices, critical race theorists are generally dedicated to applying their understanding of the institutional or structural nature of racism to the concrete goal of *eliminating all race-based and other unjust hierarchies* (emphasis added)."

Notice here that the "goal" is to "eliminate *all* race-based and other unjust hierarchies." Of course, no one who advocates CRT wants to abolish affirmative action, which for fifty years has given preferences to blacks and other minorities. This is just one example of the duplicitous "game" that CRT plays. If they really want to become effectively "race-neutral" (which, by the way, is not typically used in its lexicon), they will advocate for the *elimination* (their word) of affirmative-action laws. Consider the famous quote of Supreme Court Justice John Roberts, who in referring to affirmative action stated, "the way to end racial discrimination is to stop discriminating by race."[25]

Also consider the treatment of those blacks who have the audacity to succeed and then espouse conservative political views. A classic example is the treatment of Larry Elders, who came from nothing and succeeded in this *systemically racist* system, only to be called "the Black face of white supremacy," accused of "falling victim to white supremacist narratives" and "promoting white grievance politics." Similarly, Winsome Sears, newly elected Lt. Governor of Virginia, was subject to any number of racially divisive attacks. For example, Professor Michael Eric Dyson, a major proponent of CRT suggested that she is a puppet of white supremacy. He explained, "There is a black mouth moving but a white idea running on the runway of the tongue of a figure who justifies and legitimates the white supremacist practices."[26] Meanwhile, Senator Tim Scott, who is also a black conservative, was called an "Uncle Tom" because he argued that "America is not a racist country."[27]

These are a few of countless examples of black success stories that do not agree with the CRT version of reality. Yet, CRT advocates contend that "fundamentally, CRT is an approach to holistically studying US policies and institutions . . . [and that] CRT does not vilify white people and does not cast the non-white population as perpetual victims. To be clear, CRT is not a study in placing blame."[28] Sure. They also assert that "Some politicians and news pundits claim that CRT furthers racial division, but it's the *opposite*." These words ring hollow. Some may believe these hollow words. But having studied its precursor, this theory is inherently designed to restructure society. The difference is that Critical *Race* Theory is using *race*, instead of "class" to forward its socialist goal.

In short, its current and sustained effort is to divide and vilify. An excellent indicator of this is how hard and consistently black conservatives endure attacks—which are invariably laced with racial insults and divisiveness. There is a larger reason to use black conservatives as targets—and to use racially charged allegations against them.

Black conservatives are threatening, as they refute the contention that the American system is systemically racist. Ignoring the obvious success of black liberals and progressives because they mouth the *racist-system* mantra is the implicit expectation. Achieving riches, power, and acclaim *within the system* they detest contradicts what they often say. Yet, we are not supposed to see their success as a contradiction. If blacks who achieve such success "play along" while they enjoy the fruits from the allegedly corrupt and systemically racist system, they are not deemed a threat to the vacant mantra.

But those who don't play along become immediate targets. Blacks who succeed within the system *and* trumpet its values cannot be allowed to go unchallenged. Therein lies the criticism against Elders, Winsome, Scott, and myriad others.

Criticism of black progressives who benefit from the systemically racist system, however, is seldom heard.

Take, for example, civil rights activist Shaun King, who co-founded the Real Justice political action committee in 2017 with former Black Lives Matter leader Patrisse Cullors. Though he built his image as a champion of the poor and disenfranchised, King lives like a "one-percenter" in a sprawling lakefront home. The property, surrounded by lush, tall trees, was purchased by King's wife, Rai-Tonicia King in November 2020 for $842,000.

Meanwhile, Patrisse Cullors resigned from BLM a month after *The Post* revealed she had spent more than $3 million on *four* different real estate properties.[29] The article went on to describe a series of questionable financial dealings. King has been "dogged for years by allegations of shady dealings in his charitable efforts in movements he has founded—including a lack of transparency in money he has raised for several criminal justice initiatives he has backed." One such group with the stated purpose to "elect progressive district attorneys across the country to 'fight to end structural racism,' took in more than $3.2 million from 2019 to 2020." Contracts by this group that raised questions included the following:[30]

> "Of those funds, *Real Justice* doled out $460,000 in "consulting" fees to three companies: Social Practice LLC, Bernal Alto LLC, and Middle Seat Consulting LLC, which are controlled by some members of their political action committee, including treasurer Rebecca Bond, according to a report.
>
> Other PAC payments included $46,330 to Janaya and Patrisse Consulting, a company run by Cullors and her wife Janaya Khan. Those payments were made between 2017 and 2020, according to the Federal Election Commission."

Using the name of his political action committee as a parody, one can say a lot of *real justice* seems to be directed at those who run progressive outfits. Some who were supposed to be helped by these initiatives questioned their financial distributions.

For example, Samaria Rice, whose twelve-year-old son Tamir was killed by police in Cleveland in November 2014, scorched King on social media, accusing him of soliciting funds in her dead son's name without her permission (or any knowledge of whether Tamir identified as black or biracial). She stated in an *Instagram* post addressed to King, "personally I don't understand how you sleep at night; I never gave you permission to raise nothing. Along with the united states [sic], you robbed me for the death of my son. She continued, you are a selfish self-centered person and God will deal with you . . ." King was also criticized by former members who said in an open letter published in *Medium*, citing King's "lack of accountability." "I just wanted to know how he was using the funds that had been auto-donated," tweeted a donor. When she asked King directly on *Twitter*, he blocked her. "And then for the next month, my mentions were filled up with people calling me racist, a b—ch, etc."[31]

In May 2021, Patrisse Cullors resigned as BLM's leader, following her property-buying spree of four homes with a combined $3 million worth. This occurred despite the organization's claim that she only made $120,000 from

2013 to 2019—an average of $20,000 per year—and received no income from the group since 2019. At that time, she handed the reins to two other members, Monifa Bandele and Makani Themba, who later denied that they led the group. Bandele and Themba released a statement saying: "Although a media advisory was released indicating that we were tapped to play the role of senior co-executives at BLM, we were not able to come to an agreement with the acting Leadership Council about our scope of work and authority. As a result, we did not have the opportunity to serve in this capacity."[32]

So as this book is being drafted, we don't know who leads BLM and we don't know who sits on the "leadership council"? Who is running BLM? Even the organization's website does not identify the leadership. Why? One reason is that there is approximately $30 million that allegedly remains accounted for. These questions go to the nature of the organization and to the character of its alleged leaders. The conclusion from the *New York Post* opinion was:[33]

> "The bottom line is that Black Lives Matter is not, and likely never was, an organization focused on improving policing in America. Advocates for the cause must ask themselves some fundamental questions: Why would the leaders of such a powerful force for good want to remain faceless? If police violence is such a huge problem – and the organization's main reason for being—why is there so little mention of it on the Web site or in the financial report?"

These conclusions are not common knowledge because criticism against BLM is confined to mostly conservative reporting.

This goes to another reason black conservatives are deemed threatening. That is, they can say what whites cannot. They can describe how blacks *can* succeed—and their personal success manifests in their words. Their words are like fingernails on a chalkboard to the progressives! Such stories demonstrate that there is a better way. Extraordinarily talented and caring blacks who had great success can be used as "models" and mentors to help change what really matters: *people* and their *circumstances*. Instead of seeking to *change the system*, we can reach people who need help without being made subject to government bureaucracies, policies, and largess. We will hear more about some change agents later, but for now, consider that the *real* solutions involve family and culture.

One of the strongest voices against CRT in contemporary America is Christopher Rufo. He has written extensively on the subject, calling CRT a "dangerous ideology that will take the nation into racial retrograde." We will present some highlights of what he contends are its tenets and how they are being implemented.

Rufo notes that "progressive politicians have sought to implement 'anti-racist' policies to reduce racial disparities, such as minorities-only income programs and racially segregated vaccine distribution."[34] In one attempt to further this thinking, the Biden Administration proposed farm loans for black farmers only. This policy was rejected by courts as being discriminatory. This failed discriminatory policy was consistent with the tenets of CRT.

In any case, Rufo argues that CRT has divided Americans into racial categories of "oppressor" and "oppressed," promoting radical concepts such as "spirit murder" (what public schools supposedly do to black children), and "abolishing whiteness" (a purported precondition for social justice). Noting that classroom instruction forces children to rank themselves according to a "racial hierarchy," subjecting white teachers to "antiracist therapy," and encouraging people to become "white traitors."[35] After making these assertions, Rufo sensed that the media was "losing control of the narrative on race." In response: articles seeking to knock down "false" CRT detractors. Since the media and Rufo have squared off, here is how Rufo explains CRT.[36]

> "First, critical race theory isn't an exercise in promoting racial sensitivity or understanding history. It's a radical ideology that seeks to use race as a means of moral, social, and political revolution. The left-leaning media has sought to portray it as a 'lens' for examining the history of racism in the US, but this soft framing obscures the nature of the theory, which maintains that America is an irredeemably racist nation and that the constitutional principles of freedom and equality are mere 'camouflages,' in the words of scholar William F. Tate IV, for white supremacy. The solution, according to prominent exponents of critical race theory

> such as Ibram X. Kendi, is to abolish capitalism and install a near-omnipotent federal bureaucracy with the power to nullify any law and silence political speech that isn't 'antiracist.'
>
> Second, the grassroots movement against critical race theory is nonpartisan, multiracial and mainstream . . . The most successful campaigns have been led by racial minorities who oppose the manipulative and harmful practices of critical race theory in the classroom. Asian-Americans in particular have argued that critical race theory will undermine merit-based admissions, advanced learning programs and academic standards.
>
> Third, state legislation about critical race theory bans a specific set of pedagogies—not teaching about history. Left-leaning media outlets have claimed that bills in states such as Idaho, Oklahoma, Tennessee and Texas would ban teachers from discussing racism in the classroom. This is patently false. The legislation in these states would simply prohibit teachers from compelling students to believe that one race 'is inherently superior to another,' that one race is 'inherently racist, sexist, or oppressive,' or that an individual 'bears responsibility for actions committed in the past by other members of the same race.' The same bills explicitly say that teachers may and should discuss the role of racism in American history, but they may not shame or treat students differently according to their racial background."

Rufo is not the only high-profile detractor of CRT. Charles Murray, a black with a decades-long record as a civil rights leader—who promotes conservative values, notes how it is unnatural for humans to treat people as individuals instead of treating them as "members of groups." Murray describes that people tend toward "group think" because for eons it helped keep the *tribe* safe. His point is this: "the combination of acquisitiveness and loyalty to the interests of one's own group (be it defined by ethnicity or class) shaped human governments."[37] Yet, the idealism of the American founders ran directly against what was done throughout human history.

Murray powerfully concludes that the "introduction of identity politics into that carefully crafted constitutional system . . . not only permits but insists that the *power of the state* be used to reward favored groups at the expense of everyone else. The truly grave danger of refusing to confront race differences leads inevitably to thinking the *only* legitimate evidence of a non-racist society is equal outcomes (emphasis added)." As bad as this may sound, the inevitable extension of this thinking is even worse. He concludes with these poignant words: [38]

> "If that's what the people in power truly believe, and if those equal outcomes continue to elude them, the logical conclusion is that the state must force equal outcomes by whatever means necessary. Once the state is granted the power to engineer equal outcomes by dispensing opportunities preferentially and freedoms selectively, it will be one group versus another, 'us' against 'them.' "

Please reread this quote. Whether intended or not, the widespread implementation of CRT will result in a society where *groups vie against groups*. If this is possible, doesn't CRT deserve to be critically examined, debated, and vetted? Indeed, the fact that CRT *came out of nowhere*, should make us suspicious of what is happening before our eyes. Remember that forty years ago, this theory had few advocates. After George Floyd, it has multiple millions—along with the crucial support of decision-makers at all levels of government and other institutions.

In keeping with how we have developed this book, Murray notes the ideological battle lines are drawn as follows:

> "People on the left understand the danger to the nation posed by those on the far right who applaud violence and racism. People on the right understand the danger to the nation posed by those on the far left who insist that whites are irredeemably racist. But we need everyone to understand that what keeps us all safe is the state's impartiality. The nation's commitment to impartiality has been eroding for decades. The most threatening development of all is that whites increasingly seem to agree that identity politics is the way to go."

Any pushback against identity politics—which is inherent in CRT—is met with attacks, usually based on dealing the "race card." It is richly ironic that those who warn of the implications of CRT are attacked as being racist. As mentioned previously, I know that racist attacks will be made against me. But think about those who advocate CRT. They *named* the theory based on *race*. This theory could have been named in many other ways, such as Critical *System* Theory, or Critical *Institution* Theory. Yet, it is explicitly using *race*.

Indeed, since this theory derives from Marxist thinking—it should use "class," as this more accurately reflects Marxist principles. But the neo-racists know that "class" has never been a strong enough incentive in America to foster what they desire. *So, in a sinister manner, they use race because they know that racial divisions run deep in America*. They know that race "sells" much better than class. Americans have overcome class distinctions throughout its history. But race is more volatile—and more likely to "succeed" in their quest for socialism. Predictably enough, when countered by those who object to the tenets of CRT, they use the "race card" to ward off criticism.

This approach was used by the *Washington Post* against Tucker Carlson. The paper accuses Carlson of "time and again . . . look[ing] at an issue . . . through a racial lens."[39] This is rich. Race *is* the issue because it was *made* the issue. But not by Carlson. The whole point of Critical *Race* Theory and *Black* Lives Matter is to view issues through a racial lens. So, goes the circular logic. Use race as both a weapon and a shield.

The consequences of this theory are obvious—or will be by the time you finish this book. Let Victor David Hanson's words be our summary statement on CRT:[40]

> "Race relations have regressed 50 years. Under the fad of critical race theory, the color of our skins is now deemed essential to who we are. Most Americans still integrate, assimilate, and intermarry. But the current woke revolution is an elite, top-down effort to smear a self-critical and always improving nation, as some sort of contemporary racist hellhole."

WHITE PRIVILEGE

Considering the recent "developments" in racial thinking, "white privilege" has both merit and yet is deceptively divisive. Let's first discuss merit.

One cannot honestly dismiss that *some* whites have been privileged in American society. Generations of wealth accumulation have resulted in many elites being rewarded with privileges that make life easier and success more certain. Indeed, some never need to work. "Trust-fund babies" are real. They have a huge head start in life. How could anyone deny this? It's real. It would be disingenuous to deny as much.

However, this thinking is only partly correct. It is not true that whites have some special privilege. Millions of whites, both now and through American history, have toiled through lives of struggle. My father was one such example. His parents came from the "old country" in the early 1900s. His father died when he was twelve, and my father had to drop out of high school to get a job, helping support the family. Other than WWII, his entire adult life was spent working in a steel mill as a welder. Can you imagine what it is like to weld steel bars and machines together for decades? Day after day, in both extreme cold and heat, his "privilege" was to weld things together.

Millions of other stories with similar struggles can be told. Think of the coal miners, auto and factory workers, machinists, farmers, truck drivers, and construction workers. The list goes on. Viewing these as evidence of privilege makes a mockery of the term. Yet, when progressives declare that "work ethic" is an element of white supremacy, one can "understand" how such ludicrous thinking is derived. Even worse, other characteristics of white-supremacy culture that need to be eliminated include the following: perfectionism, punctuality, urgency, niceness, worship of the written word, progress, objectivity, rigor, individualism, capitalism, and liberalism.[41] This list should stun every reader. It reflects a much larger agenda—and much larger implications.

Murray makes some poignant observations about this thinking. He notes that during the summer of 2020, many white college students and young adults "agreed that they had sinned" and adopted the white identity and privilege rhetoric. Yet, Murray noted that many middle- and working-class whites have "not been insulted into agreement." Instead, they were just "insulted" and believe this to be unfair, as they "don't think of themselves as racists and have not behaved as racists." Let Murray's words resonate. Put yourself into the minds and lives of such people:[42]

> "They don't understand why they are being accused of racism. Still other tens of millions live in large cities where racial problems have been real, but they see themselves as having treated black and Latino neighbors and coworkers with friendship and respect. They believe that everyone has a God-given right to be treated equally.
>
> Now all of them are being told that they are privileged and racist, and they are asking on what grounds. They are living ordinary lives, with average incomes, working hard to make ends meet. They can't see what 'white privilege' they have ever enjoyed. Some are fed up and ready to push back."

How widespread might the backlash be? The pushback from millions of whites—and blacks, Hispanics, and Asians is coming. A multi-racial coalition of millions who reject pure racial thinking and who desire to be seen as individuals, not as groups, is what will motivate people going forward. More will be said later, but for now, consider this question posed by Murray: "if a minority consisting of 13 percent of the population [blacks] can generate as much political energy and solidarity as America's blacks have, what happens when a large proportion of the 60 percent of the population that is white begins to use the same playbook?"

For those advocating this playbook, there is still time to step back from race-based thinking. To be clear, I am speaking of progressives who have been hoisted by the media and institutions. If they *want* what will come, then they ought to keep doing what they are doing. Will millions who are called privileged and racists sit back and take it? Will they simply accept their "unconscious" racism? Or, as they toil in working-class jobs, struggle with the pressures inherent in an inflationary environment, is possible that they will conclude that the allegations of privilege and racism against them are unfair and over the top? As salt in the wound?

Know this: *when people are pushed against the wall, some will push back.* This is what worries me. I see no indication that progressives will back off. If this does not happen, then pushback from the Right is certain to come. My hope is this book will sound the alarm. Yet will anyone hear it?

In any case, let's look at some examples of *real* privilege—based not on race, but on wealth. Think of the distinction between Larry Elders and Gavin Newsom. As articulated by William McGurn in a 2021 *Wall Street Journal* editorial, consider the dramatically different life circumstances between these men who ran against each for the governor of California:[43]

Newsome

- His father was a well-connected state judge who once managed one of the trusts for the family of oil magnate J. Paul Getty.
- Coterie of San Francisco's wealthiest families backed him in his political life.
- He raised $70 million in the recall election campaign.
- Elder is attacked as the candidate of the rich and greedy by this new elite—while high tech, teachers' unions, the media, and some of the state's wealthiest citizens support Newsom.
- While many of California's public schools were closed due to Covid, Mr. Newsom's own children were at a private school that offered in-person learning.
- While Newsom prohibited all sorts of public gatherings due to Covid, Newsom was caught flouting his own guidelines by dining out with lobbyists at the French Laundry, where, the *New York Times* reports, "dinner for two costs more than many people earn in a week."

Elder

- His father was a former Marine, took two jobs as a janitor to support his family before opening a small cafe.

- He grew up in South Central LA, and his former high school was featured in the 1991 film *Boyz n the Hood.*
- He raised only $13 million, five times less than was raised by Newsom.

Study these distinctions. Many more facts could be presented. But these alone demonstrate that the two men lived very different lives. Now consider their respective media treatment.

As McGurn asserted, "if white privilege is a thing, Mr. Newsom is drenched in it." Yes, Newsom is a "thing" and Newsom is the *personification of white privilege*. Yet, Newsom was not attacked for his privilege.

One is hard-pressed to think of a better opportunity to describe how white privilege played a key role in this campaign. On one side is a rich, generationally "connected" white man who was showered with campaign money as he violated his own draconian Covid rules. On the other side was a black man from south-central Los Angeles, whose father was a marine and who worked two jobs to support his family. Elders collected one-fifth of the campaign money as his opponent, which largely came from small donors.

If these facts were presented to you, would you guess that the candidate who was subject to attacks was *not* the one who lived a life of white privilege? No, the candidate who was attacked—literally by a white woman in a gorilla mask—was Elders. But this is not all. Elders was declared "the Black face of white supremacy" by the *Los Angeles Times.* This is not all either. MSNBC's Joy Reid accused Mr. Elder of falling victim to "white supremacist narratives," as if Elders was held captive as a victim of Stockholm Syndrome. Yet another *Los Angeles Times* columnist attacked Mr. Elder for promoting the "white grievance politics" of David Duke and the Ku Klux Klan.

If this were not real, it would be amusing. Indeed, one may reasonably conclude that this was another *Babylon Bee* parody. But it's true. Not only did Newsom avoid the white privilege charge, but they also flipped the narrative and called his black opponent a white supremacist, being connected to white grievance politics. Here, once again, are the shield and the sword. The media shielded Newsom from *his own* white privilege mantra. Despite obvious examples of the privilege of *this* white man, and the struggles of *that* black man; the media took the side of the white man—and denigrated the black man with racial smears! Reasonable people should see right through this guise. Just this example alone is so damming that the entire notion of white privilege is made a mockery.

Yet, to be clear, white privilege does exist. More accurately this should be considered *generational white privilege* for those with trusts, estates, and "old money." One can guess that most of these are white people. Most whites, easily about 95 percent, are not included in the group of privileged few. Hence, privilege should be called what it really is: *monied privilege*—not white privilege. This monied or class privilege exists in all societies—even in socialist countries.

So, here is our choice: point to real examples of white privilege or abandon the divisive fiction. Failing to make progressive politicians accountable for their own privilege, while calling working- and middle-class whites "privileged" is ludicrous. If this is what progressives and their media allies want the American people to believe, I contend they will lose what little credibility they have left—no pun intended!

This lack of credibility splashes on to the Biden Administration. As asserted by Liz Peek, Biden called the US "systemically racist" while campaigning; then, as President Biden, he backed away, saying, "I don't think the American people are racist." Vice President Kamala Harris said something similar, stating, "I don't think America is a racist country, but we also do have to speak the truth about the history of racism in our country and its existence today."[44]

This raises a logical question: *Can a country be racist if its people are not?*

Peek provides demographic data to shoot another hole in the white-privilege mantra. Consider that whites constitute 60 percent of all Americans, but they are not even close to the most prosperous group, as measured by median household income. White Americans are only the *ninth* most prosperous group, with median incomes just shy of $66,000, with Indian Americans earning by far the highest incomes in the US, at more than $119,000, followed by Taiwanese Americans, Filipino Americans, and Chinese Americans. While black Americans rank last, with a median average income of $41,500, there is data showing black immigrants earning 30 percent more than native-born blacks. This suggests skin color is not the only issue.[45] As mentioned earlier, skin color must also account for family and culture. If black immigrants are more successful than native blacks, then one can reasonably conclude that something else is going on.

Other data sources also question this white privilege mantra. Consider that in the 2020 election cycle, seventeen of the twenty wealthiest ZIP codes gave more money to Democratic candidates than to Republicans. According to Victor Davis Hanson, this donation data reveals that the Democratic Party "has become the party of wealth." He states that "all too often, its stale revolutionary speechifying sounds more like penance arising from guilt than genuine advocacy for middle-class citizens of all races."[46] Hanson adds that "States such as California have bifurcated into medieval-style societies. California's progressive coastal elites boast some of the highest incomes in the nation . . . He adds that the two parties are switching class constituents. Some 65 percent of the Americans making more than $500,000 a year are Democrats, and 74 percent of those who earn less than $100,000 a year are Republicans, according to IRS statistics." [47]

So, Hanson asks, why are we not talking about class? His answer: "Class is fluid; race is immutable. So, by fixating on race, the Left believes that it can divide America into permanent victimizers and victims—at a time when race and class are increasingly disconnecting." Hanson then concludes with this pointed criticism against the white privilege mantra:[48]

> "Americans who struggle to pay soaring gas, food, energy and housing prices are berated for their "white privilege" by an array of well-paid academics, media elite and CEOs. . . . It's multimillionaire CEOs who bark at the nation for their prejudices, not saleswomen or company truck drivers.
>
> In the pre-civil rights past, race was often fused to class, and the two terms were logically used interchangeably to cite oppression and inequality. But such a canard is fossilized. And so are those who desperately cling to it.

> The more the elites scream their woke banalities, the more they seem to fear that they, not most Americans, are really the privileged, coddled and pampered ones—and sometimes the victimizers."

So, with this as background certain questions can be posed:

1. Since both the president and vice president directly admitted that we are not a racist country, why does this mantra persist?
2. If whites rank ninth in income, which must be considered as part of the privilege scale, why are the other eight races also not deemed privileged?
3. Why do some privileged elites appear to be "immune" to the accusation, while some conservative blacks are derided with racist allegations?
4. Is it possible that those who are most likely to admonish others for being privileged are those who are in fact the most privileged?
5. When one considers the notion of privilege, why has race been replaced by class? Is not class a more accurate reflection of privilege than race?
6. If Democrats are now the party of the rich, does this, at least, partly explain why the progressives ignore class in favor of race?

Ponder these questions as we go forward . . .

WOKISM & THE CULTURE WAR

Being WOKE and the existence of the Culture War are facts of life in America. According to *Merriam Webster*, *woke* means "aware of and actively attentive to important facts and issues (especially issues of racial and social justice)."[49] Wokeness seems to be everywhere, affecting everything. Similarly, what has become known as "cultural war" has been a fixture—being fought on many fronts for many years. Indeed, some declare that Afghanistan was America's longest war. But the culture war long precedes the war in Afghanistan.

Culture war is a term meaning different things to different people. It was defined by Wikipedia as a "cultural conflict between social groups and the struggle for dominance of their values, beliefs, and practices. It commonly refers to topics on which there is general societal disagreement and polarization in societal values." Specifically, these include "wedge issues" such as "abortion, homosexuality, transgender rights, pornography, multiculturalism, racism, and other cultural conflicts based on values, morality, and lifestyle which are described as the major political cleavage."[50]

One can conclude these are not going away. Woke thinking goes hand in hand with the progressive side of the Culture War. Before we delve into certain "triggers" and examples of this war, let's first determine who started this seemingly endless war.

Progressives, as their name indicates, seek "progress." The endless quest for progress has been a consistent feature of humanity for eons. Yet, certain people driven by specific ideologies desire progress more than others. Progressives tend to push the envelope. They push for change, usually based on social themes. As per the definition, the culture war is a struggle for dominance. Hoist *your* values, morality, and lifestyle into the larger culture. Make the culture reflect how *you* see life.

Conservatives, on the other hand—again in accordance with their appellation—gravitate toward stability and tradition. They desire and honor the "way things used to be." This is because stability and tradition have value. The passage of time may be the best evidence of value. Not only does time allow the evaluation to be clear and full, but it also provides more stability and certainty in life. Obviously, some hold these things in higher regard than others.

Managing the culture war is loaded with pitfalls. Like all "wars" violence is not only possible but expected. Think about abortion. Violence has occurred on both sides and will likely continue going forward. This example along with many others are potential "triggers" for violence and "direct action," as it is known in terrorism literature. But before we go to specific examples, let's briefly assess how this war started—and how issues become separate "battles" within the larger war.

Solving a problem is typically much easier when we know its cause—or how it started. As inferred above, the *Left started the culture war*. Progressives are now taking it to another level. Even some leftists admit this is the case. Journalist Kevin Drum authored an article bluntly titled: *If you hate culture wars, blame liberals*. "It is not conservatives who have turned American politics into a culture war battle," he writes. He cites data on hot-button social issues from abortion and religion to guns, same-sex marriage, immigration, and taxes. The numbers suggest "the obvious conclusion that over the past two decades Democrats have moved left far more than Republicans have moved right."[51] The article further suggests that "white liberals have become a larger and larger share of the Democratic Party . . . where white liberals are more left-wing than Black and Hispanic Democrats on pretty much every issue: taxes, health care, policing, and even on racial issues or various measures of 'racial resentment.' "[52]

This—once again—reflects that the heavy emphasis and injection of "race" into the national discussion is misplaced. Just as "class" is a better indicator of privilege than race, so too is "political persuasion" a better indicator than race on a host of issues—including policing and "racial resentment." Progressive whites are using race to seek support from blacks, yet data suggests that blacks are not aligned with this thinking. So, as demonstrated previously, race is being used to create division. This is misplaced, as with blacks who bear the brunt of the "defunding" police movement. Most blacks never backed this idea. Indeed, those living in areas most directly affected *by* crime naturally worry more *about* crime than defunding the police.

Further, Black conservatives and Hispanic conservatives "don't actually buy into a lot of these intellectual theories of racism. They often have a very different conception of how to help the Black or Hispanic community than liberals do." Drum asserts that the "leftward march of the party has been pulled far enough left that even lots of non-crazy people find us just plain scary . . . and that "the whole woke movement in general has turned off many moderate voters . . . Ditto for liberal dismissal of crime and safety issues."[53]

This leads to a couple of assertions: The Left is most apt to push the culture war. Data suggests they are also actually pushing beyond what people want. Why then are conservatives often blamed as being culture warmongers? Drum makes this point. Because "for most people, losing something is far more painful than the pleasure of gaining something of equivalent value. And since conservatives are 'losing' the customs and hierarchies that they've long lived with, their reaction is far more intense than the liberal reaction toward winning the changes they desire." He ends with this poignant statement: [54]

> "And for God's sake, please don't insult my intelligence by pretending that wokeness and cancel culture are all just figments of the conservative imagination. Sure, they overreact to this stuff, but it really exists, it really is a liberal invention, and it really does make even moderate conservatives feel like their entire lives are being held up to a spotlight and found wanting."

What does this mean going forward? Provocations that can potentially tear the country apart are being pushed by progressives. Worrying about any resultant backlash does not cause much hesitation. Indeed, when the backlash comes, they simply blame those who complain. It is another form of sword and shield. They push the culture war sword into society, and when the inevitable pushback comes, they use the racist shield to deflect any criticism.

This game is played by progressives of all stripes, including the media. For example, the 2020 Virginia governor's election victory for Republican Glenn Youngkin was predictably explained away by accusing him of waging a "culture war." McGurn captured a few quotes showing how this victory was characterized:[55]

- Politico headline declaring "One Lesson of Virginia? The Culture War Still Works."
- MSNBC Joy Reid claimed that "education" as an issue is "code for white parents don't like the idea of teaching about race."
- Barack Obama accused Republican opponents of campaigning on "phony trumped-up culture wars."
- Democrat Terry McAuliffe's claimed Mr. Youngkin used "racist dog whistles."
- Lincoln Project sent people to campaign for Youngkin posing as white supremacists to smear his candidacy.

- And the most ridiculous of all, an MSNBC commentator attributed the election of Winsome Sears, a black woman, as a victory for white supremacy.

Is there no shame? Will people just mouth anything, regardless of the ramifications? Facts and truth matter little. Valuing truth is a noble thing. But throwing out racial accusations that spur racial division takes this into another realm. This happens all too often. For petty issues and consequential reasons. Even the founding of America is subject to such criticism.

As McGurn points out, the "1619 Project" was an effort by the *New York Times* to recast America's true founding from 1776 to 1619. This progressive thinking has been adopted in classrooms around the country.

But when parents object, the "paper of record" accuses Republicans of stoking a culture war. As columnist Michael Goodwin noted in *New York Post*, the introduction of the "1619 Project" was *itself* a culture war salvo. Underlying such criticism is the intent to degenerate those who object to "enlightened" theories. Either directly or by inference, those who object must be uncouth or motivated by hate.[56] This results in the Left deeming certain issues *beyond discussion.* The list is long and growing, including abortion, public-school curriculums, guns, crime, or seemingly anything else that affects how we live. McGurn relates Critical Race Theory to the larger culture war:[57]

> "How much easier it is to treat those who express doubts as bigots and racists than engage on the merits. So pronounced is this reluctance to debate honestly that Mr. McAuliffe and the press pretended that because CRT isn't taught in its most formal academic version, it's not in the schools. Who's the real culture warrior here, when any mom or dad can search the state's education website and find many mentions of critical race theory—including a 2019 memo from the superintendent of public instruction recommending the book *Foundations of Critical Race Theory in Education* for school and division leaders.
>
> In short, the culture war charge is lazy. Is the mom whose daughter comes home in tears from a track meet because she had to compete

> against boys a culture warrior? What about an African-American dad— and there are plenty of them—who objects to his son being told he is a victim because of his skin color?"

Other motivations are possible by those who question established mantras. Maybe they are worried about their children being pawns in a great societal transformation? Is it wrong that some parents object? When they object; do they do so because they are racist cultural warriors, or could it be because they worry about the future wellbeing of their children and this country? Does anyone allow for the latter, or must we accept that the only possible reason is the former? Consider what options are available going forward. If the media and the dominant culture simply declare that those who don't go along with the progressive worldview as uncouth or racist, what's the alternative?

Joseph Epstein tells a story about a 1996 conversation he had with Irving Kristol, who declared back then "the culture war is over, and we lost." Epstein explains that by "we," Kristol meant those who viewed success as effort and merit, the value of tradition, and the crucial significance of liberty. These are what "we" lost. Conversely, those who won have the ammunition [my words] of such things as "diversity, inclusion, and equity" as dictated by modern universities. He uses the acronym of DIE: "Diversity, inclusion, and equity—put them all together, they spell DIE, and death to much that is best in American life they bode." The winners use their "putative hunger for social justice" and the desire to render "severe judgments of others based on lapses from political correctness." These people are "they," the woke, who have, as Kristol said, won the culture war.[58]

Epstein then names "they"—media including the *New York Times, Washington Post*, *New Yorker* along with TV networks and a host of what were once prestigious institutions and awards. Meanwhile, the "we" are whose sense the once-great country dwindling to its decline and to the defeat of traditional values, replaced with woke values. He attributes this as the cause (the "why") so many people are angry, "for whom no evidence of progress lessens the intensity of their grievances." He ends with these words:[59]

> "Although the culture war would appear to be over, to surrender to the dreariness of woke culture—which tramples on art, is without intellectual authority, allows no humor, and is vindictive toward those who oppose it— is unthinkable.
>
> So, praise the Lord and pass the ammunition [his words]; it's back to the trenches, for there isn't any choice. The culture war must continue."

Two things can be concluded from the discussion above. First, there is no doubt who started this "war." Progressives and liberals ("the Left") started the conflict. Any attempt to say otherwise is simply false—and most people see this. Consider progressives were even blamed by the French President Macron, stating that woke culture was "racializing" *French* society. Macron noted that France "is becoming progressively racialized."[60]

Second, progressives and liberals are winning the war. Third, is the war over? Or can it *ever* be resolved?

Let's take this one step further. We will briefly highlight certain cultural issues that are both controversial and can be expected to increasingly percolate out into American society. There are so many elements and aspects of each. Plus, this is by no means an exhaustive list. But consider these as representative of issues that generate a great deal of emotion—and tend to inflame people on both sides of the political spectrum.

Before we highlight the triggers, let's end this section with the poignant words of Dr. Hanson. These are hard words to read, yet there is still time to awaken from this woke nightmare! Here is his warning:[61]

> "For the first time in their lives, all Americans of all classes and races are starting to fear a self-created apocalypse that threatens their families' safety and the American way of life . . . What started out as elite woke nonsense now warps everyone's daily life. If we don't wake up from wokeness, we will continue on our sure trajectory to self-inflicted, systemic paralysis—followed by civilizational collapse."

National Anthem

As a crucial symbol and song of the United States, disrespect for the anthem during the past few years has "progressed" to using an alternative song, often known as the Black National Anthem. "Lift Every Voice and Sing" is now being played before National Football League games.

Bill Maher, who has been critical of many progressive actions, was also critical of this practice of playing both the National Anthem and the Black National Anthem. His criticism was to say, "symbols of unity matter." He criticized those who are "purposefully fragmenting things by race [which] reinforces a terrible message that we are two nations hopelessly drifting apart from each other."[62]

Maher then played a clip of then-candidate Barack Obama saying, "There is not a Black America or a White America . . . there is the United States of America," adding that "where we should be now is here" [meaning thinking not black or white, but united]. Maher then correctly took the "dual anthem" thinking to a logical extension:

> "If we have two anthems, why not three? Or five? Why not a women's anthem? A Latino anthem? A gay, trans, Indigenous Peoples, an Asian and Pacific Islander anthem? Because I'm not dealing with you, I'm not speaking to you is not a way you can run a country and most people of all backgrounds understand that already and don't even want to try to do it that way."[63]

Taking the logic even further, Maher then cited a survey of 173 colleges that found that 42 percent offered segregated residences and 72 percent offered segregated graduation ceremonies. In a blistering condemnation of Wokism, he stated, "we're a nation that professes diversity as our strength. But now half the kids' dorm rooms are determined by racial purity? . . . You see what I mean about becoming so woke, you come back out the racist side? Because what's next? What follows separate dorms, anthems, ceremonies, cafes, gyms, separate neighborhoods? That was red-lining!"

He then comes full circle with the logical conclusion of this "thinking" by saying:[64]

> "The *Black silent majority* [emphasis added] seems to be behind the idea that you can't have a melting pot with two pots! Yes, America was born from the original sin of slavery and redress for that is still in order but not at the cost of destroying a country that most Black people now have found a decent life in with a relatively higher standard of living and don't want to lose. And balkanizing our nation will certainly cause us to lose it.
>
> We need to stop regarding this new woke segregation as if it's some sort of cultural advancement. It's not. . . . Countries do disintegrate into madness when they indulge their separatist tendencies; Hutus slaughtering Tutsis in Rwanda, Catholics and Protestants in Ireland, Sunnis and Shiites in Iraq, Hindus and Muslims in Kashmir, everyone in Afghanistan and that one Jew. We need to unite as one nation who come together and sing one anthem always out of key."

American Flag

As with statues that were removed, destroyed, or defaced, coming from this same line of thinking, the flag is way beyond a mere piece of cloth. It is a symbol millions have fought and died for. Yet, it's *subject to hate* and is regarded as a *symbol of hate*. The explosive nature of these polar opposite positions goes without saying. Nonetheless, this is where we are in 2022. Here is but one example of the combustible mixture.

A Utah chapter of Black Lives Matter has called the American flag "a symbol of hatred." According to the chapter's July Fourth post, "When we Black Americans see this flag, we know the person flying it is not *safe* to be around . . . When we see this flag, we know the person flying it is a racist. When we see this flag, we know that the person flying it lives in a different America than we do . . . When we see this flag, we question your intelligence. We know to avoid you. It is a symbol of hatred [emphasis added)," wrote the chapter founder Lex Scott.

His post continued, stating, "We will not pledge allegiance to *that* flag. We will not stand for the National anthem. We will not respect a piece of cloth that you respect more than Black lives . . . We will proactively destroy the systems that continue to give you the power to marginalize people of color. Period." The post continued, "we taste your fear and it tastes delicious."[65]

Mob Action & Justice

Following the summer of 2020, with many cities experiencing nightly demonstrations that often led to violence, people "got the message." It is okay for mobs to run amuck. As we go forward in 2022, my sense is that mob actions—including what used to be called "looting," will increase, possibly dramatically. This will continue until counterforces of police and security stop it. As a tactical police officer who encountered hundreds of gang fights and shootings, I can testify that charging offenders with mob action, or some similar charge, has the effect of regaining control of the environment by getting disorderly offenders off the street. While more will be said about this later, suffice to say that all legal measures ought to be considered.

What is missing from the current equation and what is needed to effectively resolve it are *leaders who can stand up and restore order*. Instituting policies designed to address disorder is the key.

This leads to another question: Are "mobs" driving public policy? Is the weak and often non-responsive government fueling mob violence and chaos? The evidence over the past couple of years appears so. Yet, we know how to regain control. But the failure to do what is needed necessitates the "why" question. If we don't do what we know has (and will) work, then is it possible that mobs are driving public policy? Are decision-makers afraid of the mob? Consider the most important function of government is to keep people safe. When government fails to do so, this creates a vacuum. Nature abhors a vacuum. Something always moves into the void caused by the vacuum.

One can analogize that Kyle Rittenhouse in Kenosha was a classic example of filling the void caused by the vacuum. Without getting into the details and the facts of that case, the shootings by Rittenhouse were legally declared as "self-defense." From a societal perspective, it amounted to a violent "pushback." The leftist media had a fit. Calling him all the words in their arsenal: racist, white supremacist, vigilante, murderer, along with misstating the facts (i.e., crossed the state border with a gun, killed two black men, and other "misstatements"). These were just for starters. What really set off the media is the reality that the mob *can* be countered. Even if the government fails, the mob may be met by a counterforce. Citizens standing up and countering violence with force is not just legal (as per the Rittenhouse decision), but it is a basic element of human nature.

Self-preservation and self-defense are deeply rooted in our DNA. What Rittenhouse did was like what happened early in the summer of love. Remember, Mark and Patricia McCloskey? They too pointed weapons at "protestors." The difference is they did not shoot anyone. They too, were subjected to widespread criticism—and criminal prosecution. But the McCloskey's were protecting their home—and potentially their lives.

In both cases, police and other government guardians failed to keep order. Now, let me be very clear. I am not advocating vigilante actions. In modern-day America, this is so far beyond what anyone ought to expect. The Wild West ended well over a century ago. Yet, there is always a tendency to repeat history. Streets do not create their own order. Order is the result of measures designed to maintain it or regain it. If we fail to implement what are long-standing principles in modern policing—and in civilized society—then the result is easy to predict: *If the government does not do its primary job of maintaining safety and order, then people will do so themselves*. This is not a good development. It is not something we should hope for. But it will occur because people *will* protect themselves.

So, instead of seeing this as a perilous example of pushback against the mob, we should do better. We should demand that our leaders and policymakers give the police and other guardians the *means* and the *backing* to do their jobs. If the leaders and policymakers fail in their job, then people will do what they have to do.

Other related examples occurred against two sitting US senators. Activists confronted Senator Sinema as she used a public bathroom and Senator Manchin in a parking lot as he entered his vehicle. Both are classic examples of the mob pushing the envelope. Two very high-profile people being confronted in vulnerable situations. Same with protestors at the homes of

Supreme Court Justices. These are serious—and a sign of things to come.

Even "ordinary" crime committed against normal people has been politicized. Consider Yeonmi Park, a North Korean defector, who was robbed on the Magnificent Mile in Chicago in the summer of 2021 during a wave of looting across the city. Ms. Park claims she was mugged by three black women—but when we sought to call the police, white bystanders accused her of being racist. Essentially, they accused *her* of being a racist because she accused the black people who robbed her. That's when she stated, "*this country has lost it.*" She has since criticized the "woke" culture in the United States, saying it reminds her of the "censorship" of North Korea.[66]

RELIGION & THE "TRINITY"

One may think that in a chapter entitled "Race, Religion & Politics," the "religious" element has been given short thrift. In some ways, you would be correct. Yet, consider that the entire chapter could be considered "religion." True "believers" of CRT, White Privilege, and Wokism are *living their religion*. This "Trinity" is their religion.

Believers have created doctrines that embrace a worldview built around race and victimization. As with fundamentalist religions, these believers created particular ways to see the world. They envision a "better world," shaped by socialist principles where everyone can live in "equity," where the earth is protected from polluting fossil fuels and evil corporations. Their "Trinity Gospel" is communicated by like-minded elites who understand the fragilities of this world and the urgency needed to bring about the *green revolution*. All know that this must happen soon. It must be soon—before the threat of climate change destroys the planet. They must succeed in their quest to bring about the kingdom in the form of a *One World Government* ruled by elites, from what were once sovereign countries in this failed world. Their mission cannot fail. If it does, so does the planet.

This vision requires conformance. Though they realize many do not understand; they practice and *perfect* CRT, White Privilege, and Wokism. The tenets of these theories, otherwise known as *doctrines*, are communicated far and wide by their media, technology platforms, the academy, and its political allies. Since their mission is so important, lies and misrepresentations are understood to be part of the communication strategy. Elites know that some things are "hard to hear," so they "protect" those who are too simple, or simply uninformed of the hard truth. Hence, they know that lies and half-truths are embedded in their doctrine. These are required, as they help convert the masses in preparation for the utopian world supposedly ahead.

No matter what it takes, they require adherence and enforce all to harken. The failure to do so is *sin*—and brings serious consequences. Indeed, some who are "white-skinned" must repent from the benefits derived from privilege. Repentance also requires a public declaration of past "sins" stemming from being white. Hence, more than repentance is required, believers must confess their sins in a public and contrite manner. Those who speak out of turn, or against the doctrine, will be punished either by canceling their ability to earn money or by imposing pressure on them physically by activist "saints." If these measures don't result in compliance, it is both righteous and appropriate to seek compliance from those who contract with the descender.

Those predisposed to rebel against "righteous" authority, such as those unenlightened nationalists and racists, are deemed enemies of the glorious state—and are considered pure evil. Surely those who hate, deserve to be hated. Hating those who oppose the glorious kingdom is not only acceptable but also required. These are the worst sinners, allowing for no sympathy. Just like the devil, these evil adversaries must be banished and destroyed. Anyone who speaks against the doctrine will be similarly treated and quickly and appropriately punished. In the end, those who conform will be rewarded with a better world. Those who rebel will be destroyed.

The story can go on, but you get the analogy. Yet, this is not just an analogy. To the true believers, this is Armageddon, and we could scarcely be in a more precarious position. The "Trinity" is the answer. Adhering to these doctrines is required. If there is just one takeaway from this chapter, it is this. Obedience and allegiance to the "Trinity" is not optional. It is required.

I trust the reader can see that there is a larger point being made here. Seeing this from a "spiritual" perspective may demonstrate that the belief systems of the true believers will not be easily swayed. Compromise is also less likely—if they believe that the planet hinges on their success. I truly hope that my "analogy" is overstated. Though I have been watching this play out for years, so I think the analogy reflects reality. The depth of conversion, the depth and scope of the "Trinity" embedded into the societal institutions, and the nature and probability of push-back from these make this different—and perilous. Take a step back and think this through.

Let's now transition into more "traditional" religion. Below is a summary of two race-based religions that I analyzed in my 2009 book. Consider that these religions are just as "authentic" as any other religion—but they combine race, religion, and politics into a package called "religion." In some ways, these parallel the "trinity," in that they also combine race, religion, and politics. My belief is that these dynamics are an extraordinarily delicate mix.

Let me explain the significance of my concern. Religions containing racially polarizing orientations will serve to balkanize society around deeply held "spiritual" justifications. Asking this question may coalesce my point: What makes racial churches problematic? Consider two books: *Black Theology and Black Power* and *The White Man's Bible.* Ask yourself, which one is acceptable? Why?

Consider some additional factors: *Black Theology and Black Power* is based on a black nationalistic message—otherwise known as Black Liberation Theology. Like CRT, this theory has Marxist roots and tenets.

Black Liberation Theology was adopted as the fundamental doctrine of the Trinity United Church of God. To get a sense of the larger worldview of this church, in 2009 I quoted its beliefs then posted on its website. "The vision statement of Trinity United Church of Christ is based upon the systematized liberation theology that started in 1969 with the publication of Dr. James Cone's book, *Black Theology and Black Power*."[67]

This is what I saw in 2008. Coming from Chicago, I knew this church was then-Senator Barack Obama's church. I viewed this as an alarming precursor to a predicted increase in extremism. That is, the fact that President Obama's former church, Trinity United Church of Christ, had an overt and underlying racial orientation. The former president was a member for twenty years. He quit the church and renounced Reverend Wright in the spring of 2008. This occurred when the Obama campaign was being criticized for the provocative words of the good reverend.

To my mind, the words of Reverend Wright were a sideshow. Like any other tenured minister, he had made thousands of sermons over the course of a long career on the pulpit. His provocative words did not trouble me nearly as much as the nature of the church itself. Indeed, those who argue that Reverend Wright's inflammatory sermons were taken "out of context," are hard-pressed to explain away the underlying premises of the church. To look at their website, it is hard not to conclude that race is an underlying premise of the organization, which advocated a "black value system."

Consider the overt racial nature of black values. Why does the church focus on black, instead of simply focusing on people? Does God focus on the color of your skin? Indeed, if one believes in God, then God created the races. He did so because He loves *all* people. Would God want blacks to have one value system? Would He want one for whites, one for browns, one for yellows, one for reds? Of course, this is ludicrous.

When a religious institution uses race as an underlying basis of its creed, this can become a source of division and divisiveness. Some points on this latter assertion. First, if a church used the term "white" each time Trinity United Church of Christ used the term "black," how would the white church be viewed? I am quite certain it would be viewed as "racist." If this standard applies to a white church, why does it not apply to the black church? Second, if this "black value system" is not problematic, why did they remove it from their website shortly after their ideology was revealed during the presidential campaign? The black value system was re-installed after Obama's election—and it remains on the website as this book was being drafted.

This leads to the question posed earlier: Is it acceptable to advocate a separatist and balkanized religion? Some would argue it is acceptable for blacks, but not for whites—because of slavery, and the effects of historical and contemporary discrimination.

This assertion, however, must also deal with the implications of opposing views, such as those advocated by the readers of the *White Man's Bible*, which was published by the founder of the "Church of the Creator." This white supremacist "church" openly advocates racial separation. The Church of the Creator (WCOTC- also known as "Creativity") advocates:[68]

> "the proposition that the white race is 'nature's highest creation' and that 'white people are the creators of all worthwhile culture and civilization.' Followers of the WCOTC do not believe in God, heaven, hell or eternal life. They consider Jews and nonwhites, whom they refer to as 'mud races,' to be the 'natural enemies' of the white race. They follow the 'Golden Rule' which means what is good for the white race is the highest virtue. What is bad for the white race is the ultimate sin." The Creativity Movement, whose motto is "RaHoWa" (Racial Holy War), proclaims that its belief system, Creativity, "is a racial religion" whose primary goal is the "survival, expansion, and advancement of [the] White Race exclusively." Their view of religion is simple: "Our race is our religion."[69] To these people, race is everything: the white race is "nature's highest creation."

Their ideology contains obvious extremist rhetoric: "every issue, whether religious, political or racial . . . [should be] viewed through the eyes of the White Man and exclusively from the point of view of the White race as a whole." Ultimately, WCOTC hopes to organize white people to achieve world domination, "free from alien control and free from pollution of alien races . . . Only on the basis of recognizing our enemies, destroying and/or excluding them, and practicing racial teamwork can a stable lasting government be built."[70] The extremist ideology of this group may be best illustrated by this quote from the *White Man's Bible,* which provides:[71]

> "We of the CHURCH OF THE CREATOR are not hypocrites. We openly state that some people need killing, that killing has always been with us and will always be with us . . . Killing our enemies, too, is under certain circumstances a necessary measure for the survival of our own race. Therefore, we condone it, and it, too, is no sin in our religion."

This "racial religion" includes the notion that loyalty to the race is the greatest of honors. Conversely, they view racial treason as the worst of crimes. This movement was gaining steam back in 2009. The scope of these white-supremacist movements gained traction following the election of President Obama. In an attempt to gain membership, the group speaks to these implications: "White people awake! Save the white race!"[72] This blatant attempt to use race to both induce fear and tribal identity is disconcerting.

Given these juxtapositions, I ask the question again: Which one of these books is acceptable? In my mind, the only consistent answer is: *Neither is acceptable.* Consider the words of Dr. Martin Luther King, who so powerfully stated: "I have a dream that my four little children will one day live in a nation where they will not be judged by the color of their skin but by the *content of their character.*"

This principle holds true: If "groupthink" is justified based on *color of the skin,* the likelihood of racial groups opposing each other will also increase. Now add politics into the mix. The emotion, power, and implications of politics *will add violence to the implications of groupthink.* Now, add religion into the mix. The connection to spiritual—even everlasting beliefs adds implications that are extraordinarily risky. More than likely, the same people offended by these statements are those who will justify one of the above books—while condemning the other!

We cannot have it both ways. People naturally find ways to criticize the views of others, while ignoring the implications of our own thinking? We "justify" our views and find the error of others "inflammatory rhetoric." Regardless of how my words are viewed, my intent was to articulate what is deemed controversial because few are willing to do so. Taking this chance is what I choose to do. I did so to try to calm the waters of the coming storm. This chapter showed that the storm is largely based on race, religion, and politics (RRP).

Here is the hard conclusion: *If we cannot address these factors honestly, we have no chance to survive as a country.* If we cannot see our own biases and see how our biases contribute to the combustible mix, then this book has no value.

Let me answer likely criticisms with four provocative questions. Let's view these as rhetorical in nature, as the "answers" are likely to have little consensus—and provoke some consternation . . . and controversy! These same questions were posed in my 2009 book, but please think about your "answers" to these questions, as they have never been more relevant than they are today:

- Question #1: Do you think racial religions are "harmless"?
- Question #2: Do you think they can incite violence?
- Question #3: Can we be "unified" and racially nationalistic at the same time?
- Question #4: Can we have one standard for white nationalistic religions and another for black nationalistic religions? If so, what implications does this portend?

Hopefully, you see these provocative questions as a way of making a point. My main point is that the failure to move away from racial identities will inevitably result in conflict. Clearly, these will not promote a unified society nor a "post-racial" society. Indeed, when group consciousness is promoted by legal and cultural standards, the more logical result is a balkanized society. When group consciousness is promoted by the power of law and by the "thought leaders" within the society, is it unreasonable to believe that this may contribute to the separation of groups around racial, cultural, and political interests?

Let me answer my own question: Group consciousness or group identity will inevitably promote a balkanized society. I made these points in 2009. That was before the "Trinity" became widely accepted in society. Is not the adoption of the "Trinity" (CRT, White Privilege, and Wokism) itself ample evidence that the balkanized society predicted well over a decade ago is occurring? While the media trumpeted a "post-racial" society, my conclusion was the opposite. Now, of course, the system is deemed systemically racist—and the "thought leaders" deem the "trinity" the way forward.

The mere fact that most people shy away from these issues demonstrates we must confront them. For example, when the "Reverend Wright" controversy broke in the spring of 2008, Barack Obama gave a highly regarded speech on race. His speech was proclaimed by numerous pundits. It was hailed as the *definitive speech on race.* Within a week or so after the speech, it seemed to disappear into the campaign. When is the last time you heard a reference to this speech? The larger point is that the mixture of race, religion, and politics is so divisive that people seem to naturally gravitate away from it. When it rears its ugly head, we deal with it—on some level—and then let it go as quickly as we can.

This is what happened to the *definitive speech on race* delivered by then-candidate Obama. I am not optimistic that we will ever effectively deal with this combustible mixture. Regardless of *your race, your religion, or your party*; we all need to be cognizant of these implications. Consider now another important yet less known message that Dr. King delivered in Atlanta a year before his death. As you read these words, think about the two books cited earlier, *Black Theology and Black Power* and *The White Man's Bible.* Here is what Dr. King said:[73]

> "Let us be dissatisfied until that day when nobody will shout, White Power, when nobody will shout Black Power, but everybody will talk about God's power and human power."

CHAPTER III

EXTREMIST IDEOLOGIES & THE CAPITALIST SYSTEM

Coming off RRP, which demonstrates the basic human *dividers*, this chapter presents what drives people toward violence. The most crucial element is ideology. According to *Dictionary.com*, ideology is "the body of doctrine, myth, belief, etc., that guides an individual, social movement, institution, class, or large group."[1] An ideology "guides" the individual into a particular group, which sometimes is embodied by a movement.

Ideologies provides a "window" into the minds of extremist thinking. It is the framework from which one makes sense of this complicated world. This then becomes the individual's "worldview" or mindset. As people tend to seek out people who think like them, forming groups of like-minded people. Groups can grow into something larger, often called a "movement." Movements tend to be more lasting than groups. But ideologies are the most sustaining. They form the necessary support for mindsets, groups, and ultimately movements. Hence, it is crucial to understand the tenets or elements of ideologies.

This presentation will be straightforward. We will highlight relevant ideologies and discuss some important tenets. This can be tedious reading. Ideologies are by their nature rather conceptual, so they may not be "exciting" to read about. They contain tenets that will prove foreign or unusual to many. This is to be expected. People generally do not think in an ideological manner. Further, the "thinking" embedded in certain ideologies can be considered wacky, weird, or even crazy. Conversely, you may find some that make sense or have merit. Arguably, each contain a certain amount of truth. Yet context, balance, and purpose must also be applied. Without these, its adherents could become "extremist." If you are stunned or frightened by what you read, that too would be typical.

Each ideology will be presented in an organized, straightforward, objective fashion—without editorializing on the merits. Implications are offered to demonstrate why a revolutionary pathway is possible—or is *in process*. Illustrating how extremist ideologies add energy to a revolutionary climate is the key to why these are important to understand.

Certain extremist groups within each ideology will be identified, along with examples of violence attributable to them. With this said, specific ideological frameworks can be classified as:

- Single-Interest Groups
- Left-Wing – Communists/Socialists
- Anarchists
- Right-Wing – Fascists
- Nationalist/Racial Groups

As you compare these categories, consider the following points. Firstly, some groups may fit into more than one classification and do not easily lend themselves to a specific, uncompressing category.

Secondly, this presentation is limited to groups who are considered "domestic" terrorist groups with established reach, infrastructure, or support within this country.

Thirdly, there is a fluidity in extremist thinking, with groups rising and falling. This is based on numerous factors, including the amount of support from the population and institutions, the extent and success of engagement by law enforcement, and the overall dedication of its members.

These factors, and others, can cause certain groups to "stand up" or "go quiet," or even become extinct. A good example is Al Qaeda. During the early 2000s, they were the dominant extremist group in the world. Under sustained and considerable pressure, they withered and almost went out of existence. In the void, ISIS was birthed and became so powerful that it controlled an area larger than many countries.

Finally, because of the fluidity of extremism, we will not attempt to "name" all extremist groups. Instead, our task is to present the ideology, not all groups attached to the political mindset.

Though many ideologies have "natural" allies and obvious enemies, all extremist ideologies have one common denominator—to destroy (or attack) the capitalist system. This is what makes the current revolutionary climate so threatening. They all possess a common theme: their existence places great stress on *the system*. In effect, the system is "surrounded" by ideological groups that want to destroy it. See it this way. Take that in. Even now, pressures in many different forms and means are being applied.

With this approach established, it may help to initially provide a definition of domestic terrorism. The FBI defines "domestic terrorism" as:[2]

> "Violent, criminal acts committed by individuals and/or groups to further ideological goals stemming from domestic influences, such as those of a political, religious, social, racial, or environmental nature."

A brief story may help explain the transition to terrorism—and it speaks volumes about being able to connect dots. It has direct implications for our times involving the transition from crime to terrorism.

As analyzed in the discussion around the *Critical Theory of Criminology*, this story involves how this mindset plays out on the street. We will see how a street gang became political and conspired with a foreign leader to commit a terroristic act on US soil. Working in the police district where the notorious El Rukn fort was located, as a young police officer, I had the ideal vantage point to watch this play out.

Here is the backstory. The El Rukn's were a Sunni Muslim organization formed from a street gang known as the *Black P-Stone Nation*. Its leader, Jeff

Fort, changed the gang's name to the El Rukns in 1982.

By any account, this semantic change was far from transformational. Few, if any, individuals within the gang abandoned their life of crime. Though with this newfound status, the "religion" was able to manipulate laws, gaining 1st Amendment freedom of religion, association, and related protections. Further, it gained legitimacy, or at least attempted to do so, as a "religion." No longer was this a criminal organization. They found Allah!

As a young police officer, I saw the El Rukns differently than other officers. This wasn't due to being wiser or more astute, but while working as a cop, I also was a student in the master's program in criminal justice at the University of Illinois at Chicago (UIC). Studying terrorism and listening to terrorism experts at annual terrorism conferences at the school made it clear to me that the *Rukns* were indeed transformed—but not in the way they projected. The transformation was more political and strategic than religious. Groups like the El Rukns were ripe for radicalized thinking. They were rebels. They were political. They advocated a radical brand of Sunni Islam that could lead naturally to terrorism.

I worked with seasoned, tough Viet Nam-era veterans, and they saw the *Rukns* as a deadly and formidable gang. They were killers and drug dealers—but they were "ordinary" criminals. Few fathomed that the gang would conspire to perform terroristic acts. My belief that they had graduated from gang status of full-blown "terrorists" fell on deaf ears.

In early 1985, while researching my thesis, I was transferred to the *Gang Crime Enforcement Unit*—which was the most prestigious and active enforcement group in the city—and one of the best in the country. My role involved tactical enforcement in the most crime-ridden areas of the south side—assigned to *Gang Crimes South.* Those in this unit were tough, smart, and experienced. I was the youngest and least-experienced person in the unit.

I approached the unit's administrative sergeant to inquire about obtaining information regarding the El Rukn ideology. After introducing myself and explaining some of the details of the research along with the overall approach, I mentioned that the *Rukns* could transition into a terrorist group. He paused. The conversation became instantly disjointed. After about ten long seconds, he tilted his head, looked at me, and stated: "*Are you living in the '60s, kid?*" It was obvious this conversation was not going to be fruitful. After a few pleasantries, I walked out of the office having hit a dead end. Later, reframing my research, the *Rukns* were not addressed in the thesis.

Sometime later, while attending the annual St. Jude Parade (which honored fallen police officers), the gang unit hosted a breakfast after the parade and was seated at the same table as the administrative sergeant mentioned earlier. During the breakfast, he looked at me and asked "Jim, did you ever finish that thesis?"

About a year or so after the initial conversation, members of the *Rukns* were accused of obtaining monies from Libyan dictator, Moammar Gadhafi. These individuals conspired to take down an airliner with a surface-to-air missile from O'Hare Airport. The FBI along with Gang Intelligence officers arrested members of the El Rukns with a rocket launcher. I participated in two subsequent raids on the "fort," which were joint federal, state, and gang unit operations. The "fort" was ultimately torn down. Many members of the *Rukns* were imprisoned and the "gang" was dismantled.

Let me summarize this story to give more context and present the conclusion. The P-Stones were a legacy gang dating back to the late 1950s. As previously stated, during the turbulent 1960s, many radicals sought to combine a *white fighting force allied with the Black Liberation Movement*. The P-Stones were precisely the type of gang that would be attracted to this revolutionary mindset. Here is how this was described on *Wikipedia*,

> "Under Fort's command, the BPSN (Black Stone Nation) assumed an increasingly revolutionary outlook as it became associated with the black nationalism movement, eventually attracting the attention of the Nation of Islam leader Louis Farrakhan, who introduced them to Libyan leader Muammar al-Gaddafi and Nicaragua's Sandinistas.
>
> In 1986 four of its members were indicted for conspiring to commit terrorist acts in the United States for the Libyan Government. *The verdict marked the first time American citizens had been found*

> *guilty of planning terrorist acts for a foreign government in return for money* (emphasis added)."[3]

I had a "front-row seat" to see this notorious *first*. This was the first time American citizens conspired with foreign actors to commit terrorist acts. Yet, I conceived—and predicted what no one around me saw. That is: the group had visions and intentions larger than what one would envision within a "gang."

The moral of this story is as follows: *We need to change our paradigm*. This includes having an open mind—even when it comes to what we think we know. Police officers who dealt with the *Rukns* knew them personally, engaging them in street encounters and following them in investigations. They saw them as criminals—not as potential terrorists. Conversely, I did not know them and had no preconceived notions. Instead, seeing the "big picture," I saw the logic of terrorism and applied it to the group. Not knowing the details—the individuals, their notorious crimes, their organizational structure—but knowing the reasons *why* they would "graduate" to a terrorist group was the difference. This is the takeaway for the reader. We must know the reasons "why" a revolutionary climate is coming.

So, as this book is drafted in late 2021 and early 2022, we are witness to Antifa and BLM protests during the summer of 2020. What I saw during my days with the *Rukns* is even more pronounced today. Riots and disorders have *not* been resolved. Most who participated in these have not been made accountable. Those who "got away" have not been transformed away from crime—or from political violence.

So, here is my larger point. Just like the transformation of P-Stones to the *Rukns*, we shall see Antifa, BLM, urban street gangs, and certain right-wing groups transition into more deadly, terroristic groups. This happened in the 1960s when the Weather Underground broke from the larger group, Students for a Democratic Society (SDS). Terrorist acts were the primary means utilized by the "underground" group. But back then, there was no opposing right-wing group. Today, several groups on the Right are likely to also join the fray. This makes finding a peaceful resolution particularly difficult. Simply stated, violent groups will attack each other as they attack the larger society. This transition from criminal groups to terrorist acts, ironically, is even more likely because the media and the government will treat these ideologies differently. With this established, the ideological categories are as follows:

SINGLE-INTEREST GROUPS

- Extremists who seek to force the government or population to alter a specific grievance within the country.
- Usually do not seek to overthrow or greatly alter the government.
- Often represent a popular point of view.
- Often deemed most active in the country, though now less active than in the past. Animal and environmental groups now tend to combine with the larger leftist causes. Abortion groups can quickly grow active depending on court decisions and legislative initiatives.

Anti-Abortion

The proponents and activists are generally Christian, with a small percentage advocating violence against abortion facilities and medical personnel. These groups generally point to four different approaches for their complaints: scriptural, legal, moral/philosophical, and medical.

The *scriptural* basis is often cited in the Old Testament legal code, such as Exodus 21:22–25, which states that:[4]

> "If men who are fighting hit a pregnant woman and she gives birth prematurely but there is no serious injury, the offender must be fined whatever the woman's husband demands and the court allows. But if there is serious injury, you are to take life for life, eye for eye, tooth for tooth, hand for hand, foot for foot, burn for burn, wound for wound, bruise for bruise."

Also, from Psalms 139: 13–16[5]

> "For you formed my inward parts; you knitted me together in my mother's womb. I praise you, for I am fearfully and wonderfully

> made. Wonderful are your works; my soul knows it very well. My frame was not hidden from you, when I was being made in secret, intricately woven in the depths of the earth. Your eyes saw my unformed substance; in your book were written, every one of them, the days that were formed for me, when as yet there was none of them."

The *legal* basis is to criticize the US Supreme Court decision in *Roe v. Wade*. This has taken on additional significance with the current challenge against *Roe* in the US Supreme case: *Dobbs v. Jackson Women's Health Organization.* This legal basis of *Roe* is being seriously questioned by *Dobbs*. The argument against Roe has been summarized as follows:[6]

> "Most of the Supreme Court's verdict rested upon two sentences:
>
> We need not resolve the difficult question of when life begins. When those trained in the respective disciplines of medicine, philosophy, and theology are unable to arrive at any consensus, the judiciary, at this point in the development of man's knowledge, is not in a position to speculate as to an answer."

The *medical* basis can be summarized by asserting that "at conception, the embryo is genetically distinct from the mother." This assertion was developed by Anderson, who stated:[7]

> "To say that the developing baby is no different from the mother's appendix is scientifically inaccurate. A developing embryo is genetically different from the mother. A developing embryo is also genetically different from the sperm and egg that created it. A human being has forty-six chromosomes (sometimes forty-seven chromosomes). Sperm and egg have twenty-three chromosomes. A trained geneticist can distinguish between the DNA of an embryo and that of a sperm and egg. But that same geneticist could not distinguish between the DNA of a developing embryo and a full-grown human being."

The *moral/philosophical* basis can be summarized by asking this philosophical question: Where do you draw the line? When does a [fetus] being become a person? Anderson makes a pointed assertion that has relevance to animal rights advocates, stating:[8]

> "The Supreme Court's decision of *Roe v. Wade* separated personhood from humanity. In other words, the judges argued that a developing fetus was a human (i.e., a member of the species *Homo sapiens*) but not a person. Since only persons are given 14th-Amendment protection under the Constitution, the Court argued that abortion could be legal at certain times. This left to doctors, parents, or even other judges the responsibility of arbitrarily deciding when personhood should be awarded to human beings."

These points are presented for a couple of reasons. Firstly, Anderson's arguments are well-founded and reflect widespread beliefs. Reading his words, he is extraordinarily articulate and well-meaning. This is not the language of an extremist.

Secondly, the logic and passion of his arguments have resonance for many different extremist ideologies, which are needed to develop the intellectual and philosophical framework to further their cause. Anti-abortion advocates examine the question of when life begins. They do this in their desire to prevent the death of a fetus. One can also extend this assertion to its logical conclusion: If it is okay to kill a fetus, what precludes the killing an infidel (or a pig, or a Jew, or a monkey, or a cracker, or whatever)? This is presented to be provocative as some extremist groups *will* make this connection.

The "Army of God" is a significant anti-abortion group, which considers itself "Yahweh's Warriors." Its website considers Paul J. Hill and Scott Roeder American heroes. One was convicted for numerous bombings and the other for killing an abortion doctor. According to Hill, he did these deeds as "self-defense." In his words:[9]

> "You have a responsibility to protect your neighbor's life and to use force if necessary to do so. In an effort to suppress this truth,

> you may mix my blood with the blood of the unborn, and those who have fought to defend the oppressed. However, truth and righteousness will prevail. May God help you to protect the unborn as you would want to be protected."

The Army of God website also trumpets the "accomplishments" of Eric Rudolph, who was convicted of numerous bombings, including the Centennial Park bombing during the 1996 Olympics. Rudolph makes the following statement on his website, which pointedly illustrates the "logic" of extremists. It de-legitimizes the government and the *law* because of the murder of children:[10]

> "I am not an anarchist. I have nothing against government or law enforcement in general. It is solely for the reason that this government has legalized the murder of children that I have no allegiance to it nor do I recognize the legitimacy of this particular government in Washington."

With the current composition of the US Supreme Court, the most volatile aspects of the "abortion debate" may now come from the Left. Abortion proponents see this as a "woman's right to choose" and often characterize abortion procedures as "family planning." No matter how you see it, abortion clearly is a flashpoint of controversy.

A pointed example came as this book was being drafted. Sen. Jeanne Shaheen, (D - NH), issued a warning to the Supreme Court: "reaffirm *Roe v. Wade* 'or else.' " The phrase "or else" stated by Shaheen was this: a promise of "revolution." The writer who quoted her is a highly respected attorney and law professor. His response stated the *very basis—and title*—for this book saying:[11]

> " 'So, you say you want a revolution.' However, these threats are an attack on the very concept of impartial judicial review. 'When you talk about destruction' of our traditions of judicial review, as the Beatles declared in 1968, 'you can count me out.' "

For whatever it is worth, the *title and basis* of this book was adopted months before this assertion appeared in the news. Whether the reader believes that or not, we can all agree that some dramatic events are occurring before our eyes.

Consider this contrast. Quotes from convicted murders were presented above. As alarming as they are, are they worse than a sitting US senator throwing out the "R-word"? This is truly stunning. She did not "qualify" as did Turley—and as we have done in this book. Yet, regardless of what the supreme court does in *Dobbs,* one can reasonably predict that abortion related violence will increase—likely substantially. This is such an emotional subject that it inflames passions on both sides. Plus, there is little room for compromise. Not to make light of a very serious subject, but many are familiar with the well-known wisdom of Solomon in his decision to "split the baby in half." Here, there is no splitting of the baby.

There is no compromise, short of reducing the number of weeks for an abortion to occur. But even this "compromise" will ignite anger. Consequently, violence related to abortion is expected to be more frequent. Understanding the passion and commitment generated by this, which can be said to strike at the core of our political divide, expecting violence is as predictable as it is unfortunate. As this book is being prepped for publication, many are preparing for violence when the *Dobbs* decision is announced.

Animal Rights – Animal Liberation Front *(ALF)*

The most prominent extremist group in this category is the Animal Liberation Front (ALF), which migrated to the United States from England in 1979. Years ago, this group was credited with over 1,000 attacks in the US, causing at least $45 million in damages. Most of the attacks have been relatively minor, consisting of breaking windows, gluing locks, and spray painting. Others have been violent and highly destructive. At least ninety incidents have caused $100,000 or more in damages, and some have resulted in damages that have run into multimillions of dollars. Some enterprises, including fur farms, have been driven out of business by these actions.[12] According to a former FBI Deputy Associate Director for Counterterrorism, groups like ALF and other "violent animal rights extremists . . . pose one of the most serious terrorist threats to the nation."[13]

Their legitimizing goal is to create "rights" for animals, which would put animals on par with humans. Achieving this, the next logical question would be: Do humans have the right to capture, enslave, or kill animals? This thinking raises the provocative question of whether humans can be committing "terrorism" against animals, which is illustrated by this narrative:[14]

> "Is it reasonable to speak of the 'human terrorism' against the animal world?"
>
> "Virtually all definitions of terrorism, even by 'progressive' human rights champions, outright banish from consideration the most excessive violence of all—that which the human species unleashes against all nonhuman species."
>
> *"Speciesism* is so ingrained and entrenched in the human mind that the human pogrom against animals does not even appear on the conceptual radar screen. Any attempt to perceive nonhuman animals as innocent victims of violence and human animals as planetary terrorists is rejected with derision."
>
> "But if terrorism is linked to intentional violence inflicted on innocent persons for ideological, political, or economic motivations, and nonhuman animals also are "persons"—subjects of a life—then the human war against animals is terrorism."
>
> "Every individual who terrifies, injures, tortures, and/or kills an animal is a *terrorist*; fur farms, factory farms, foie gras, vivisection, and other exploitative operations are terrorist industries; and governments that support these industries are terrorist states…"

Radical Environmentalists–Earth Liberation Front (ELF) & *EarthFirst*

Radical environmental or "eco" attacks date back more than forty years, perpetrated by some of the foremost extremist groups functioning in the US. These seek to change the way humans live in the environment. They have leveled numerous direct attacks against businesses and government facilities over the past decades, with more than sixty different attacks causing damages over $100,000 each. One attack in 2003 caused about $50 million in damages to a housing complex under construction.[15] The FBI defines eco-terrorism as such:[16]

> ". . . the use or threatened use of violence of a criminal nature against innocent victims or property by an environmentally oriented, sub-national group for Environmental-Political reasons, or aimed at an audience beyond the target, often of a symbolic nature."

ELF's logic and structure state that "The ELF is an underground movement with no leadership, membership, or official spokesperson. The intention of this website is to inform and chronicle issues related to E.L.F."[17] The website asserted that:[18]

- There is no ELF structure; "it" is non-hierarchical and there is no centralized organization or leadership.
- There is no "membership" in the Earth Liberation Front.
- Any individuals who committed arson or any other illegal acts under the ELF name are individuals who choose to do so under the banner of ELF and do so only driven by their personal conscience.
- These choices are not endorsed, encouraged, or approved of by this website's management, webmasters, affiliates, or other participants.
- The intention of this website is journalistic in intent: to inform and chronicle issues related to ELF.

Earth Liberation Front is an aggressive spin-off movement established by *EarthFirst*. It is a significant political organization, with its main target being capitalism. This is both ironic and problematic. While capitalism certainly has contributed to pollution and other environmental degradation, it is simplistic to only blame capitalism. Yet, the *green revolution* is fueled by this thinking. The pollution emanating from China's industrialization is largely ignored by this movement.

Despite this "inconvenient truth," please consider that none other than bin Laden once asserted that capitalism is the source of the world's problems.

Was it possible he was seeking allies with certain groups in this country? Obviously, he was talking to anarchists and e*nvironmentalists*. The ranting of bin Laden's thinking is reflected as follows:[19]

> "A revolution will occur. It may not be a bloody one, taking place on the streets, but it will be one with equal or even greater force. One which will dry out the feedlots for greedy capitalists and their deadly ways. One which will end corporate rule and environmental destruction by man's thirst for wealth."

LEFT-WING (MARXISM)

- Revolution of the workers, directed by revolutionary elite
- Seek to overthrow capitalism and create a socialist state
- No private property
- Means of production controlled by the workers

Left-wing terrorists/extremists are often referred to as "Marxists" or Communists." They seek to eliminate capitalism, which would require a substantial overthrow—or overhauling—of the US government. Ultimately, its goal is a socialist system where all people would be equal. In this system, people receive their basic needs and give according to their talents and skills, leading to a *classless* nation where cooperation would be stressed over competition. The means of production would be owned in common. In the final stage of development, there would be little or no government. Any government that did exist would be weak and administrative in nature.

Leftist ideologies vary as to the exact form that the new society would take. Traditional leftists believe that a transitional period would be required. During this transition, economic conversion and "re-educating" people would occur. Those with the insight necessary to accomplish the revolution often rule in a dictatorial manner, often referred to as the "dictatorship of the proletariat." Eventually, this would end, and the strong government would cease to exist.

However, many anarchists disagree with the need for a transitional period.

They believe that if a capitalist state were overthrown, people could immediately live harmoniously with little or no government.[20] With this thinking, anarchists are more inclined to destroy without regard for the consequences. Think of the riots of 2020. Destroying symbols of the system and burning sections of cities were the means used by the mob. Who cares now about what they left behind?

One of the best examples of a "successful" terrorist campaign was with Narodnaya Volya in Russia from about 1869–1881. This group published the *Catechism of the Revolutionist*, which taught the revolutionist has "only one science, the science of destruction . . . His sole and constant object is the immediate destruction of this vile order . . . For him, everything is moral, which assists the triumph of the revolution. Immoral and criminal is everything which stands in its way."[21] This movement eventually led to the Bolshevik Revolution in 1917. When the Communists took over Russia, millions of people died. The Soviet Union maintained a brutal, state-run government until its demise in 1990.

Communist-inspired groups were in "vogue" during the 1960s. After the Cuban revolution in the late 1950s, Castro and Che Guevara inspired groups that sought to create a "peoples revolution." They attracted many followers. Groups dedicated to this cause appeared in Peru (Shining Path), in Italy (Red Brigades), in Germany (Red Army Faction), in Northern Ireland (Irish Republican Army), and in other countries. Many of the groups were inspired by the *Manual of the Urban Guerrilla* (Carlos Marighella), which advocated a "scorched earth strategy, the sabotage of transport and oil pipelines, and the destruction of food supplies."

There are numerous left-wing groups that were active during the turbulent days of the civil rights and Vietnam War era. These include the Black Panthers, the FALN, and the Weather Underground. As cited earlier, the Weathermen Underground was a Marxist group credited with at least thirty-five bombings, including the US Capitol, the Pentagon, police stations, and other government facilities.[22] Another group, FALN, which sought independence for Puerto Rico, was "credited" with more than 130 bombings and acts of arsons between the years of 1974–1982. Members of this group attempted to assassinate President Truman in 1950 and shot up Congress in 1954.[23]

For various reasons, I believe that the ideologies like those represented by the Weather Underground, which can influence Antifa and the New Black Panthers, may pick up where the old group left off. This group will be highlighted in the "nationalist section" of this chapter. Suffice to say, the thinking of these groups has not died and will stand up as we go forward.

MS-13

In the 1980s, El Salvador experienced a bloody civil war, killing an estimated 100,000 people. Millions fled this unstable environment, immigrating to the United States. Once in America, Salvadorian youth were victimized by local gangs. To protect themselves, they created a gang called Mara Salvatrucha, also known as MS-13.

Their name came from combining "La Mara," a violent street gang in El Salvador with Salvatruchas, a term used to denote members of the Farabundo Marti National Liberation Front, who were peasants trained as guerilla fighters during the civil war. The "13" was added to pay homage to the California prison gang, the Mexican Mafia, to "13th Street" in Los Angeles, and the letter 'M' is the 13th in the alphabet.[24]

MS-13 members sport numerous tattoos on their bodies and faces and wear blue and white colors taken from the El Salvadoran flag. Membership is at least 10,000 in the US and over 100,000 worldwide.[25] Members typically range in age from eleven to forty years old.[26]

The criminal activities attributed to the group include the smuggling of guns, drugs, and people. Killing for hire, theft, arson, and other violent activities and blatant disregard for the law (threats and attacks on law enforcement officials are common). These made them one of the most feared gangs in the United States. Indeed, they have been known for their "signatures," which are more characteristic of terrorist groups. *Signatures* include "booby-trapping" their drug houses, "announcing" their arrival into a new community with acts of violence, and "planting" females to surveil law enforcement personnel to note where they eat, exercise, drink, live, and conduct business and their daily routines. These activities coupled with killing police and federal agents, and threatening police with "green light" (target) notices are characteristic of this group.

Its violent and political nature makes it poised to "graduate" to terroristic violence. Those associated with the group have committed many politically orientated violent acts, such as:[27]

- In 1997, the son of Honduran President Ricardo Maduro was kidnapped and murdered by MS-13 members. MS-13 members have continued to taunt Central American government officials. Members also left a dismembered corpse with a note for the Honduran president that "more people will die . . . the next victims will be police and journalists."
- In 2004, Guatemalan President Oscar Berger received a similar message attached to the body of a dismembered man from MS-13 members.
- After an increase in crime, Mexico began a campaign in 2004 to eradicate MS-13 when they arrested 300 members calling them a "threat to National security."

Urban Street Gangs

Without naming specific gangs, urban street gangs will become increasingly political. As per my example of the El Rukns, street gangs will see value tied to violent political action. One can be certain that many gang members participated in looting and rioting during the summer of 2020. It defies any explanation that they didn't. Going forward, gang members will commit more brazen crimes, such as ambushes against police, bold and premeditated looting, and other crimes tilting toward urban chaos and societal instability. If one sees gang members as "foot soldiers," it makes perfect sense to think they could be used by those who seek a revolution.

Anarchist

ANARCHISTS

Purist and idealistic anarchists do not believe in government. They believe each person should function free of restraint, though most who claim to be anarchists are more opposed to the capitalist system than they are to the basic concept of government itself, believing that the workers must unite to bring down capitalism, then they will control the means of production and enable them to live in harmony with one another.

Historically, anarchist philosophy significantly impacted terrorist campaigns and groups. An early anarchist, Karl Heinzen, wrote *Der Mord* (translated from German as "Murder"), which justified terrorism on a grand scale. His thinking was quite blunt. "If you have to blow up half a continent and pour out a sea of blood in order to destroy the barbarians, have no scruples or conscience."[28] The desire to kill was strong.

Anarchists were blamed for numerous notorious actions, including the assassination of President William McKinley in 1901, killing eight police officers in a bombing that resulted in the Hay Market Riots in Chicago on May 4, 1886, and for the September 16, 1920, bombing on Wall Street in New York City. The latter attack killed 33 people, wounded 400 others, and caused approximately $2 million in damages.[29]

During the 1990s, anarchists engaged in violent protest demonstrations, dressing in all-black outfits and gathering in "Black Blocs" to prepare for and function in protests. The "Battle for Seattle" was a classic example of this violence at the World Trade Organization (WTO) meeting. The violence generated was far-reaching. This movement sought to attack what was then known as the "New World Order." Consider the following quote from Louis Beam, a right-wing extremist relating to the Battle for Seattle:[30]

> "The new American patriot will be neither left nor right, just a freeman fighting for liberty. New alliances will form between those who have in the past thought of themselves as "right-wingers," conservatives, and patriots with many people who have thought of themselves as "left-wingers," progressive, or just 'liberal.' "

As this statement makes clear, the New World Order is an attractive target to a surprising array of groups. This mindset asserts that international corporations are controlling—and ruining—the planet. One consequence of this internationalization of business is that national identity and sovereignty will be greatly diminished or even abandoned. Because of their strong attachment to sovereignty, white supremacist and Christian Identity groups have applauded leftist groups in their attacks on the New World Order. Each group desires to "purify" the world through murder.[31] With the world undergoing a dramatic geo-political transformation, this thinking is sure to increase.

The attraction of attacking the New World Order is strong to those who see themselves as oppressed. This message particularly resonates with racial and ethnic minorities who see the capitalist system as the cause of their troubles. At that time, these "Black Blocs" were not intended to be long-lasting organizations. As the riots of 2020 reveal, this *did* last.

Antifa

The riots of 2020 made it obvious that anarchists dressed in black "uniforms" have not gone away. Indeed, Antifa has been extraordinarily active in its attacks on "the system." According to *Wikipedia*, Antifa is:[32]

> "far-left, anti-fascist, and anti-racist political movement in the United States. As a highly decentralized array of autonomous

> groups, Antifa uses both nonviolent and violent direct action to achieve its aims rather than policy reform.
>
> Much of antifa political activism is nonviolent, involving poster and flyer campaigns, mutual aid, speeches, protest marches, and community organizing. They also engage in protest tactics, seeking to combat fascists and racists such as neo-Nazis, white supremacists, and other far-right extremists . . .
>
> Individuals involved in the movement tend to hold anti-authoritarian, anti-capitalist, and anti-state views, subscribing to a range of left-wing ideologies. A majority of individuals involved are anarchists, communists, and socialists who describe themselves as revolutionaries and criticize liberal democracy . . ."

Many US political leaders have ignored, diminished, or misrepresented Antifa—largely but not exclusively from the Left. Typically, the perception of Antifa is dependent on one's political persuasion. Famously, NY Congressman Jerrold Nadler stated that Antifa was a "myth."[33] But others who do not have a stake in the US believe otherwise. For example, Slovenian Prime Minister Janša labeled Antifa an "international terrorist organization."[34] As we saw earlier, President Macron of France echoed this sentiment. Similarly, former US Attorney General William Barr stated that "violence instigated and carried out by Antifa and other similar groups in connection with the rioting is domestic terrorism and will be treated accordingly."[35]

Boogaloo Boys (Boies)

The boogaloo movement is a loosely organized far-right, white supremist extremist movement. It has also been described in wide ranging terms: as a militia, pro-gun, neo-Nazi, anti-government, and even as an anarchist group. Adherents say they are preparing for, or seek to incite, a second American Civil War or a second American Revolution, which they call "the boogaloo."

One common thread is that impending unrest will result in a race war. Though some condemn racism and white supremacy, these have been met with skepticism by some.

The movement primarily organizes online, boogaloo emerged on 4chan and subsequently spread to other platforms. Although usage of the term dates to 2012, it did not gain mainstream attention until late 2019. In 2020, members appeared at events including anti-lockdown and George Floyd protests. Heavily armed, boogaloo members are often identified by their attire of Hawaiian shirts and military fatigues.

Individuals affiliated with the boogaloo movement have been charged with crimes, including the killings of a security contractor and a police officer, a plot to kidnap Michigan Governor Gretchen Whitmer, and incidents related to participation in the George Floyd protests. In mid-2020, several social media companies acted to limit the movement's activities and visibility on their media and chat platforms.

According to Alex Newhouse, a digital researcher, the 'boogaloo' movement is considered far-right "because they draw a line directly from Waco and Ruby Ridge." They consider the Oklahoma City federal building bombing and the armed response to Ruby Ridge as "heroic moments in American history." Viewing these incidents as citizens standing up to government oppression, their anti-government posture is obvious. Newhouse also identified adherents of the movement to provide armed protection to private businesses during anti-lockdown and George Floyd protests as evidence of a right-wing orientation. Newhouse emphasized that the importance of private property is part of what makes the boogaloo movement "very much an extreme right libertarian ideology."[36]

In May 2021, a thirty-two-year-old Air Force staff sergeant named Steven Carrillo allegedly fired on a federal courthouse in Oakland, California, killing one security officer and wounding another. A week later, Carrillo allegedly shot and killed a sheriff's deputy. Wounded and on the run, he hijacked a car and, before his arrest, wrote "boog" in blood on the hood.

According to an FBI affidavit, Carrillo was in communication with another person from Texas who had driven to Minneapolis apparently to incite violence during the protests there. Wearing a skull mask and tactical gear, that person allegedly fired an AK-47-style rifle thirteen times at the Minneapolis Police Third Precinct while the building was set ablaze.[37]

RIGHT WING (FASCISM)

Neo-Nazi groups seek to establish a strong central government that would control the means of production, either directly or through corporate monopolies controlled by selected individuals. Nationalism, strong militaries, and patriotism are also stressed. The white race, Aryan nationality, and a quasi-Christian creed would occupy a favored position. Other groups would face discrimination and would have their rights restricted.

- Stresses nationalism above individual Rights.
- Some seek strong central government; others are strongly anti-government.
- Foreigners and minorities are often targets.
- Opposite of left-wing philosophy but not necessarily along a straight line:
    - Some oppose the US government
    - Some believe government has been taken over
    - Some believe they are the government

While these tenets illustrate typical Neo-Nazi thinking, there are other political philosophies (i.e., sovereign citizens, Freemen, Posse Comitatus) that are different from the neo-Nazi cause—yet they are still characterized as right-wing philosophies. For this reason, it is difficult to categorize or classify right-wing extremist groups. No matter how they are categorized, there will be some overlap, as there are many common themes in their thinking. Most of these groups are anti-government in philosophy. Almost all espouse an element of hate towards some other group of people.

Anti-Government Groups

Posse Comitatus is a conspiracy-oriented group that focuses on a "hidden history" and misinterpretation of laws to justify its beliefs. This group derives its name from the legal prohibition on using the military to enforce the law.[38] They view federal and state governments as illegitimate bodies. Instead, they believe the *county* is the highest level of government, with the sheriff as the highest elected official. Given this level of authority, sheriffs ought to never enforce unpopular laws. What entails *unpopular* laws are those that the *Posse* do not like or those that allegedly violate biblical precepts or principles. Sheriffs should not enforce orders from judges, laws from legislatures need not be obeyed, and taxes imposed by federal/state bodies should be avoided—and ignored.

Posse members claim that at one point in American history, there were essentially no laws, and every man was a king (or at least a sovereign citizen). From that point forward, a long-standing conspiracy slowly replaced the true, legitimate (de jure) government with a tyrannical, illegitimate (de facto) government.[39]

Posse also asserts that the Fourteenth Amendment is illegal. This amendment, among other things, extended citizenship to ex-slaves following the Civil War. *Posse* tenets assert that this amendment created an entirely new class of citizens. These citizens were subject to federal and state laws and regulations, which are different from *sovereign* citizens. Though sovereign citizens may adhere to federal and state laws, they believe that people could voluntarily (and unknowingly) become US citizens by "contracting" with federal or state governments (e.g., by using social security cards, driver's licenses, or zip codes). Hence, two types of citizenship exist:

- *Sovereign citizens* who are immune to almost all laws
- *US citizens* who are subject to government laws

Posse Comitatus

Sovereign Citizens are direct ideological descendants of *Posse* beliefs, asserting that an illegitimate government has replaced the lawful government. Because of this, sovereign citizens contend they are subject only to the old common law, forming their own common-law courts. These courts, often called *Our One Supreme Court*, were formed to hear sovereign citizen matters. They believe this is the *only* court that has jurisdiction over them. Through the jurisdiction of these courts, sovereign citizens refuse to "contract" with the de facto government—and believe they are exempt from paying taxes. Common-law courts have *jurisdiction* ranging from settling disputes among sovereign citizens, placing bogus liens on property of public officials and other targets, and issuing arrest warrants for both serious and sundry crimes, up to and including treason. Sovereign citizens generally believe that the only enforceable laws pertain to crimes where someone was harmed. They oppose any statutory law where there was no victim.[40]

Militias believe that citizen militias are authorized under the US Constitution and/or early federal statutes, particularly the 2nd Amendment. This thinking goes back to the Revolutionary War. At that time, all adult males were considered part of the *ready militia*, subject to call, should the nation require defense. Male citizens were expected to attend training sessions at their own expense, providing their own uniforms and weapons. After the War of 1812, the need for a defense force diminished and became unpopular. To circumvent the federal law requiring all males to be in the militia, the concept of having an "unorganized militia" was established. But this was applicable only if the nation was under attack. Over time, states created paid and professional militia bodies, which became known as *the National Guard*.

Militia groups tend to be conspiracy-oriented, being essential to protecting the people from tyrannical governments, which are allegedly increasingly under the domain of the "New World Order" and/or the United Nations. Many believe that the US government has become a puppet to these world-ruling organizations.

Beyond this thinking, most militia groups engage in paramilitary training. Some were involved in criminal activities, particularly with respect to the acquisition of weapons and explosives. Some also engage in violent activity. By the end of the twentieth century, the number of militias functioning had shrunk, and some became quite secretive. This was in stark contrast to the open and notorious way they once functioned in the early 1990s. The Oklahoma City bombing changed how law enforcement viewed these groups, with heavy pressure brought against them. Militias continue into the twenty-first century but are usually small and clandestine. Nonetheless, they present a threat that can suddenly emerge without warning.[41]

An example in 2021 comes from the southern border. As tens of thousands of people move through the border, a militia group has formed to secure the border and protect citizens from the migrants. As this manuscript is being drafted, the group, Veterans on Patrol (VOP), are patrolling the border. While they were formed in 2015, their presence on the border is a new phenomenon.[42]

Ku Klux Klan

Racist/Hate Groups

Some right-wing terrorist groups are animated by the hatred of people of different races or ethnic origins. These hate-based groups include racial hatred as the main plank of their agendas. The obvious example is the KKK.

Ku Klux Klan (KKK) has existed in three distinct waves. Initially, the group started in the ex-Confederate states shortly after the Civil War in response to Reconstruction. At that time, state governments threatened structural white supremacy. In response, whites covered their faces to shield their identities, attacking blacks to make it impossible for them to enjoy the freedom granted by the Fourteenth Amendment. Blacks were menaced, beaten, and killed. Many black-owned businesses, residences, and churches were destroyed. The first wave faded away as conservative white Southerners regained their citizenship and control of local and state governments.

The second KKK period began around 1915 in response to several social issues of the era. Blacks moving north to work in factories, the prohibition movement, labor struggles, the suffragist movement, immigrants—many of whom were Catholics from Ireland and Italy—entering the country in large numbers, and the unrest in Europe that led to World War I. All these factors contributed to its resurgence.

The movie *The Birth of a Nation*, which depicted the KKK in a highly favorable light, also helped fuel its rebirth. By the end of the decade, it was politically expedient to seek KKK support. Over a few years, it spread to every state in the Union and had millions of members. Although the KKK grew, it gradually lost its popularity in the late 1920s, and by the time World War II began, it had dwindled significantly in size. Soon, it ceased to be a legitimate force.

The third period of the KKK commenced in the 1950s, largely in reaction to school integration and the civil rights movement. Although various KKK-related violent attacks against blacks and civil rights workers occurred during the 1950s and 1960s, the KKK never became a national, monolithic organization.

Currently, the KKK is divided into separate groups with little association with each other. Many of these entities have very small memberships. Only a few are known to be involved in terrorist/extremist violence. Some modern KKK groups spread their message through protest marches staged in areas where they know that they will be met by counter-protesters. This, in turn, generates publicity and a variety of security problems for local law enforcement agencies.[43] The basic beliefs of the KKK are as follows:[44]

- *White Race* is the irreplaceable hub of our nation, our Christian faith, and the high levels of Western culture and technology.
- *America First* before any foreign or alien influence, and a foreign policy of military non-intervention (note this similarity to Trump's *America First* mantra).
- *Constitution* as originally written and intended. The finest system of government ever conceived by man, which is based on the Holy Bible and Christian common law.
- *Free Enterprise* of private property and business, but an end to high-finance exploitation (and opposes Federal Reserve Bank & "free trade").
- *Positive Christianity* illustrated by the right of the American people to practice their Christian faith, including prayer in the schools.

Neo-Nazi groups arose in the United States after World War II. Some neo-Nazi groups want to establish a national socialistic regime. Generally, however, most neo-Nazi groups have diverged considerably from the German Nazi ideology of the 1930s and 1940s. Other groups simply focus on the symbolism and white supremacy aspects of Nazism.[45]

The National Socialist Movement, founded in 1974 was the most explicitly "Nazi-like" of neo-Nazi groups, emulating uniforms and paraphernalia of the Third Reich. Typically, they adhere to a paramilitary structure, with former military personnel as members. Its ideology calls for a "greater America" that would deny citizenship to Jews, nonwhites, and homosexuals. Some neo-Nazi groups have ties to various Klan, racist, and other white supremacy groups.[46]

National Alliance is a white-supremacist, anti-Semitic, and anti-Capitalist movement. It was initially founded by Dr. William Pierce and was created to protest the new-Left movement on college campuses during the late 1960s. In 1978, under the pseudonym Andrew MacDonald, Pierce wrote a novel called *The Turner Diaries,* which sold hundreds of thousands of copies. It is regarded as a kind of "bible" for Right-wing extremists. Both Robert Mathews of *The Order* and Timothy McVeigh of Oklahoma City bombing infamy were heavily involved in the promotion of this book. Indeed, the name of Mathews' group came from the novel. Many believe that the attack on the Murrah Federal Building was modeled after an attack described in the publication.

The National Alliance has had a significant influence on Right-wing philosophy in the United States. Those holding extremist, hate, and anti-government views continue to exist, but often lack large groups to join. Instead, they tend to form smaller, clandestine cells around these extremist ideological premises. Some follow the leaderless resistance philosophy and may formant violence on their own.[47]

NATIONALIST/RACIAL GROUPS

- Individuals of Common Ethnic Origin Seeking to Establish or Regain a Homeland.
- Usually Exists in Conjunction with a Broader Racial, Religious or Political Ideology.

These groups represent a major source of potential extremist violence. Groups formed along a nationalist bend, coupled with a broader racial, religious, or political ideology will foster violence in "defense" of their race. Two groups (and their offshoots), the New Black Panther Party and the Aryan Brotherhood, will be key drivers in the years ahead.

New Black Panther Party for Self-Defense

New Black Panther Party for Self-Defense (NBPP) is the proper name of this group. It was founded by Aaron Michaels in 1990. Its ideology combines black nationalism, Pan-Africanism, racism, and anti-Semitic bigotry. Its influences are the original Black Panthers, Black Panther Militia, and the Nation of Islam.

On its website, the group provides a very clear picture of its ideology. Its "ten-point" ideology includes some curious premises and some hostile language. As with white racial ideologies, their thinking is formed around extremist perceptions of race, with little, if any, room for compromise. Its ten-point ideology is as presented in pertinent part, with the emphasis in the original: [48]

1. We want freedom. We want the power to practice self-determination, and to determine the destiny of our community and THE BLACK NATION. We believe in the spiritual high moral code of our Ancestors. We believe in the truths of the Bible, Quran, and other sacred texts and writings . . . that Black People will not be free until we are able to determine our Divine Destiny.
2. We want full employment for our people and we demand the dignity to do for ourselves what we have begged the white man to do for us. We believe that since the white man has kept us deaf, dumb and blind, and used every "dirty trick" in the book to stand in the way of our freedom and independence, that we should be gainfully employed until such time we can employ and provide for ourselves. We believe further in: POWER IN THE HANDS OF THE PEOPLE! WEALTH IN THE HANDS OF THE PEOPLE! ARMS IN THE HANDS OF THE PEOPLE!
3. We want tax exemption and an end to robbery of THE BLACK NATION by the CAPITALIST. We want an end to the capitalistic domination of Africa in all of its forms . . .
4. We want decent housing, fit for shelter of human beings, free health-care (preventive and maintenance) . . . We believe since the white landlords will not give decent housing and quality health care to our Black Community, the housing, the land, the social, political and economic institutions should be made into independent UUAMAA "New African Communal/Cooperatives" . . .
5. We want education for our people that exposes the true nature of this devilish and decadent American society. We want education that teaches us our true history… and our role in the present day society . . . .
6. We want all Black Men and Black Women to be exempt from military service . . . We will not fight and kill other people of color in the world who, like Black People, are being victimized by the white racist

government of America. We will protect ourselves from the force and violence of the racist police and the racist military, "by any means necessary."

7. We want an immediate end to POLICE HARRASSMENT, BRUTALITY and MURDER of Black People. We want an end to Black-on-Black violence, "snitching," cooperation and collaboration with the oppressor. We believe we can end police brutality in our community by organizing Black self-defense groups (Black People's Militias/Black Liberation Armies) that are dedicated to defending our Black Community from racist, fascist, police/military oppression and brutality. The Second Amendment of white America's Constitution gives a right to bear arms. We therefore believe that all Black People should unite and form and "African United Front" and arm ourselves for self-defense.
8. We want freedom for all Black Men and Black Women held in international, military, federal, state, county, city jails and prisons. We believe that all Black People and people of color should be released from the many jails and prisons because they have not received a fair and impartial trial. "Released" means 'released' to the lawful authorities of the Black Nation.
9. We want all Black People when brought to trial to be tried in a court by a jury of their peer group or people from their Black Communities, as defined by white law of the Constitution of the United States. We believe that the courts should follow their own law, if their nature will allow (as stated in their Constitution of the United States) so that Black People will receive fair trials . . . To do this, the court will be forced to select a jury from the Black Community from which the Black defendant came…
10. WE DEMAND AN END TO THE RACIST DEATH PENALTY AS IT IS APPLIED TO BLACK AND OPPRESSED PEOPLE IN AMERICA. WE DEMAND FREEDOM FOR ALL POLITICAL PRISONERS OF THE BLACK RED AND BROWN NATION!

Their political objective is stated as such: "NATIONAL LIBERATION in a separate state or territory of our own, here or elsewhere, 'a liberated zone' ('New Africa' or Africa) . . . for the purposes of determining our will and DIVINE destiny as a people. FREE THE LAND! 'UP YOU MIGHTY NATION! YOU CAN ACCOMPLISH WHAT YOU WILL!' BLACK POWER!"

New Black Panther Party

Comparing CRT and BLM to New Black Panthers' ideology demonstrates that this is not a fringe and limited segment of the population. These vary only by a matter of degree. Further, when one compares the "ten-point platform" of the New Black Panther Party" with the twelve-point "black value system" of Trinity United Church of Christ, one is struck by the overwhelmingly racial orientation. While the New Black Panther Party has a much more hostile and confrontational edge, it is obvious that Trinity United Church of Christ's value system is also demonstrably based on race. Though there is obvious value of racial pride as a positive force within the black community, other factors identified in this book have more divisive and harmful implications.

The potential connection between black nationalist groups, such as the New Black Panther Party, and black nationalist churches is not limited to "Christian" churches. Many recognize that Islam is suited for people of African descent due to racial prejudice, the doctrine of brotherhood, and the value placed on learning Islam.[49] For example, the Nation of Islam doctrine believes that Arabs are seen as a "sign" of future people, a people chosen by God to receive the Koran (Quran). However, since Arabs strayed, God selected American blacks as his people to spread Islam to the West.[50]

Another group, known as the "Five Percenters" (or 5 percent Nation), has adopted a particularly hostile ideology. Founded by Clarence Smith (also known as Father Allah), who was a former Nation of Islam (NOI) member formed this group in New York City in 1964 after he was expelled from the NOI for disagreeing with the group's teachings. While the Five Percenters do not consider their beliefs a religion, they do follow non-traditional variants of Islam.

They believe that blacks are the original people of Earth and founded all civilizations. Because blacks founded all people, the "Blackman" is god. They also believe that whites have deceived the whole world, causing the world to honor and worship false gods and idols.

Some Five Percenters profess their beliefs through rap and hip-hop music, with some striking similarities between Islam and hip-hop culture, which express anger at structures of domination, government indifference, and US foreign policy. This connection—and the implications of such were summarized by Aidi, who stated:

> "the cultural forces of Islam, black nationalism and hip-hop have converged to create a brazenly political and oppositional counterculture that has powerful allure."[51]

The potential for direct action by an inter-relationship with gangs and radicalized black groups can be seen in numerous examples, recall the killing of the Floridan police officer Jayson Raynor in 2021 by Othal Resheen Wallace (also known as O-Zone Wallace).

While the manhunt for Wallace was still underway, the New Black Panther Party (NBPP) posted a *YouTube* video podcast titled "NBPP LIVE! HANDS OFF OZONE, TRUTH OF A COURAGEOUS BLACK NATION WARRIOR." In the video, NBPP National Chair Krystal Muhammad said, "Wallace officially announced that not only was he the founder of Black Nation . . . but that he was becoming a member of the New Black Panther Party." Using similar language, a woman claiming to be Wallace's wife, posted images on *Instagram* of what appears to be Wallace and wrote, "I told you I will fight to the end of the revolution with you . . . together we will fulfill the purpose of THE MOST HIGH GOD YAHWEH!!!!!."[52]

Wallace's actions and words are not isolated. Consider that NFAC's leader, John F. Johnson was indicted for pointing an assault-style weapon at several federal officers at a protest in Louisville, Kentucky, on Sept. 4, 2020. According to a criminal complaint, he also urged NFAC members to attack and kill law enforcement and their families and urged members to dismantle the body cameras of police they assault. Officer Raynor's body camera was indeed dismantled.

In an interview with *NBC's* Morgan Radford, Mr. Johnson said the NFAC was growing "by leaps and bounds." He said its goals are self-defense and creating a Black *ethnostate*. "NFAC was born out of the last four years under the Trump administration, the deterioration of racial relations in this country," Johnson stated. Calling violence, the "last option," he noted the US "was built on violence as an option."[53]

J.J. MacNab, a fellow in the Center on Extremism at George Washington University, said in written testimony to the US House Subcommittee on Intelligence and Counterterrorism in July 2020 that left-wing militias are "the newest entrant to the militant world," including NFAC, as a black militia. MacNab added, "to date, armed left-wing militias and gun clubs have generally arisen in response to the perceived threat from armed right-wing militias, Three Percenters, and Oath Keepers, but some express strong anti-police and anti-government beliefs."[54]

Volusia County Florida Sheriff Mike Chitwood added there is "no difference in the threat posed by militia groups, left or right . . . is a grave crisis that's facing America right now because any extremist militia group, I don't care whether they're white, Black or Hispanic, whatever they are, they are a danger to society and they are a danger to democracy." He noted that all such groups share a hatred for law enforcement and the rule of law. "That's the commonality between these extremist groups."[55]

Chitwood argued that these groups "formed in response to Charlottesville and some of the other things that have occurred but clearly the police shootings also played a role in that group being formed." Adding that extremist violence is "nothing new" while referring to several police officer killings in the 1960s, he noted the obvious advantage that social media now gives extremist groups in their ability to recruit."[56]

While publicity around black militia groups is often limited to photos of armed groups, a long and thoughtful analysis of the Not F****** Around Coalition (NFAC) was done by Graeme Wood. His talk with the leader of NFAC, John Fitzgerald Johnson, was revealing. Known as *Grandmaster Jay*, Mr. Johnson, who was formerly in the US military, has a recruiting strategy consisting of these criteria:

- "You must be Black."
- "If you're biracial, your father must be Black."
- Recruits' must arm themselves without attracting attention of law enforcement.
- "Military experience is preferred," and members must have an AR-style rifle.

The recruits are "sworn in" and must be ready to "put your life on the line" by standing armed in an NFAC formation. Weaponry includes "AR-15s galore," sniper rifles with scopes and bipods, high-capacity magazines, and "enough 'tactical' clothing to resupply an Army-surplus store.[57]

"We don't come to sing, [w]e don't come to chant." Instead, they stand in formation. Wood compares this to "a praetorian guard for some unseen emperor." They wait for any situation where other armed groups might start trouble. Wood summarizes the group as having a "military like structure, an army of hundreds of heavily armed men and women, subscribing to esoteric racist doctrines."

The "Grandmaster" believes we live in a period of "apocalyptic tribulation, and . . . speaks prophetically, and sometimes apocalyptically." In a concise summary that has widespread implications, Wood said this "sectarian racist is raising an army, stockpiling weapons, demanding total loyalty, and suggesting that he is a 'messiah.' "[58] One way to understand this dynamic is to imagine what a paramilitary wing of the Black Hebrew Israelites would be like, providing the spiritual, ideological framework for groups like NFAC.

The stunning implications belie the relative silence from the media and political leaders. Though Jay Johnson boasts "we have a zero-incident record, "[w]e've never destroyed a piece of property, or had our people arrested for anything." Yet, as alleged in a criminal complaint against Johnson, in a video he advises members to burn government officials' homes, murder their children, and destroy police body cameras if they assault cops, to remove evidence.

Following an incident during a protest, the police raided his apartment. Among the small armory of assault rifles, they also found a "prodigious amount" of marijuana. After jay's arrest, he ordered his followers into a "stand-down position."[59]

Despite the "stand down" order, Johnson's goal is to "establish a racially pure country called the *United Black Kemetic Nation* (UBKN- Kemet is the original name of Egypt, which means 'land of the Blacks'). Calling for Black self-reliance and segregation from white people, Johnson said the time "for the Black race to come into its own—then arm and train themselves to act as an immediate bulwark against the continued human-rights abuses."

Seeking a segregated, armed, and racialized quest to create a separate country is quite a dramatic goal. This fits right into the "logic" that race-based thinking will take us. Such race-based "solutions" inevitably lead to violence. Wood offers this pointed conclusion that "Jay's answer—[to] create a parallel, quasi-fascist race army with its own flag and homeland—strikes me as a particularly bad case of becoming that which you hate."[60]

Wood aptly warned that "public order is the hostage of the most radical gunman present." By this he suggests that one radical gunman who decides to start shooting could "trigger" grave consequences.

Think about two opposing militia groups who start shooting at each other during a public protest. This is not just some far-fetched fatalistic delusion. For example, the *Grandmaster* posted a video from Louisville showing white militia members expressing concern that the NFAC would annihilate them. "There's no cover there," one militia member laments to a police officer. "NFAC shows up and decide they want to wipe us all out—we're gone in seconds." Amy Iandiorio, an investigative researcher for the Anti-Defamation League's Center on Extremism, noted the obvious: "These are volatile situations . . . [NFAC] are a lightning rod that attracts opposing groups, and that's a recipe for conflict."[61]

In July 2020, in Louisville, Kentucky, NFAC descended on the city dressed in black, marching through downtown streets. Some wore body armor, and others had gas masks. They wore pistols on their belts and carried shotguns and AR-15-style rifles. This was described as "the biggest public display by an armed militia I have ever seen," by J.J. MacNab, who has studied the militia movement for twenty-five years. "Nobody was expecting that."[62]

While this took some by surprise, going forward we have no excuse. The time for being "surprised" is over, and so is the notion that these racially based groups and movements will not lead to racial violence.

This includes the widely accepted, and widely acclaimed Black Lives Matter (BLM) movement. Notwithstanding some redeeming elements of this movement, including raising attention about police brutality, the troubling reality is the movement is *not about police brutality*—and it's *not about black lives*! They only focus on "black lives" when a black is injured or killed by the police. Not only are police incidents "microscopic" as compared to black-on-black crime, but the incidents that BLM calls attention to are most often reflective of "legal" use of force by the police (this will be addressed in Chapter IV).

So, what is BLM? The fact that two of its founders, Alicia Garza and Patrisse Cullors, are both admittedly "trained Marxists," should raise some caution to an objective observer. Seeing the Marxist foundations of Critical Race Theory, it does not take an expert on political ideology to connect the same dots around BLM. Its website speaks to this connection:[63]

> "Black Lives Matter is an *ideological and political intervention* in a world where Black lives are *systematically and intentionally targeted* for demise. It is an affirmation of Black folks' humanity, our contributions to this society, and our resilience in the face of deadly oppression" (emphasis added).

The larger agenda of BLM is obvious—and they go far beyond what most people naively think. Let me be clear: *BLM is a destructive movement*. Yet, it has gained so much acclaim that American corporations have endorsed and urged its employees, shareowners, and customers to do the same. Of course, the media have been useful cheerleaders. The "mostly peaceful" protests of 2020 spurred by BLM is a classic example.

While it is appropriate to protest, it's simply an excuse to create discord against both the police—and against the capitalist system. How ironic that major media and institutions in this *system* help to bankroll such a radical organization, that was founded by "Marxists." Authors of a Heritage piece assert its goals are to "transform America completely." The BLM leaders themselves revealed their thinking. For example, Cullors said, "myself and Alicia in particular are trained organizers. *We are trained Marxists*." In 2015, Tometi visited Venezuela's Marxist dictator Nicolás Maduro, saying this about the regime: "we have witnessed the Bolivarian Revolution champion participatory democracy and construct a fair, transparent election system recognized as among the best in the world."[64]

This is not the only "clue" about BLM's ultimate goals. According to the Heritage Foundation, the BLM once proclaimed:[65]

> "We disrupt the Western-prescribed nuclear-family-structure requirement by supporting each other as extended families and 'villages' that collectively care for one another."

A partner organization, the Movement for Black Lives, or M4BL, seeks to abolish all police and all prisons, and calls for "the retroactive decriminalization, immediate release and record expungement of all drug-related offenses and prostitution, and reparations for the devastating impact of the 'war on drugs' and criminalization of prostitution."[66]

Since defunding police was advocated by BLM and its supporters, one can conclude this is not about police misconduct against black victims. If black lives are the focus of BLM, why are black victims ignored when they are victimized by black criminals? According to the FBI crime reports in 2020, there were nearly 3,000 more black victims killed from criminal violence than were white victims. Because blacks represent about 13 percent of the US population (which is only one-fifth the size of the white population), this data reveals that blacks are six to seven times more likely to be murdered than whites.[67] The vast majority of blacks will have been killed by black criminals. Why does BLM say little or nothing about 10,000 black homicide victims who died in 2021 that were *not* killed by police?

Indeed, as the Heritage piece declared—the goals of BLM "are hiding in plain sight, there for the world to see, if only we read beyond the slogans and the innocuous-sounding media accounts of the movement." It concluded that BLM's "radical Marxist agenda would supplant the basic building block of society—the family—with the state and destroy the economic system that has lifted more people from poverty than any other. Black lives, and all lives, would be harmed." This, they rightly declare, "is a blueprint for misery, not justice."[68]

Beyond the underlying concepts, we have seen that ideologies are the key, providing the framework for any group. BLM's ideology is Marxist. We have seen the implications of RRP as divisive—and destructive. The riots of 2020 were a direct by-product of the movement. While many naively "joined" the movement to support blacks who were killed or injured by unlawful police conduct, the riots that resulted were a natural consequence of something larger: the hatred for *the system*—and the desire to take it down. Police misconduct was simply the means to generate support—and to create chaos.

Just one more example of this thinking can be seen from a BLM "Jail Killer Cops" rally in Washington, DC in April 2021. An activist speaking at Black Lives Matter Plaza asked how long before "people are really *ready to get blood on their hands*" to make change happen (emphasis added)? Rahim B., a twenty-one-year-old activist speaker, made these statements and asked these questions:[69]

> "Bringing about that change is not going to always be pretty, and it's not going to be peaceful.
>
> I don't condemn who loot, I support them for looting. I support people who take matters in their own hands. If you want to set something on fire, go do that.

> The system is killing people every single day . . . In the courtroom, you got people locked up doing twenty years, facing life sentences, for crimes they didn't commit.
>
> How far are you willing to go for this justice?"

While this is one person in one rally in one city, this thinking is much larger than an individual. It is ingrained in human nature. It is a natural consequence of divisive thinking. This is how Joseph Epstein described how BLM thinking can be contrasted with Dr. King's thinking:[70]

> "Integration called for fairness across all American institutions. Black Power for endless struggle and conflict.
>
> Integration was a call to conscience. Black Power a call to guilt, which is radically different.
>
> Integration implies a vision, the vision set out, specifically, in King's famous "I Have A Dream" speech. Black Power implies, generally, resentment, rancor and the need for retribution.

Aryan Brotherhood

Aryan Brotherhood (AB) is the other side of the racist coin. The Aryan Brotherhood originated in 1967 at San Quentin Prison. Originally, this gang was established to provide protection for white inmates from black and Hispanic groups. Although the Brotherhood is a white supremacist organization, for most AB members, crime is their priority and racial hatred is a secondary goal. Since 1972, the Aryan Brotherhood has had an alliance with the Mexican Mafia.

AB uses the Odinist religion to conduct gang meetings and disguise illicit business practices.[71] This "religion" views Christianity as defective since it allows blacks, Hispanics, and other non-whites in the congregation. Derived from the pagan god Odin (Odinism), a key symbol of this religion is three intersecting triangles (known as volknut or valknut). In white supremacist groups, wearing these triangles signifies the person is willing to give his life to Odin in battle. It symbolizes that the person is a chosen warrior, who is prepared to sacrifice himself at any time necessary.[72]

This group is affiliated with numerous like-minded groups, such as neo-Nazis, the National Alliance, and various racist organizations. There are some specific requirements to be affiliated with the group. These include lifelong allegiance, a "blood in, blood out" oath, and often a "hit" or significant act of violence is required before full membership is earned. Candidates for membership must serve a year or more in some probationary status. As would be expected, membership in the AB has traditionally come from white male inmates.[73]

The group also uses certain symbols and methods, such as the Shamrock cloverleaf, the initials "AB," swastikas, double lightning bolts, and the numbers "666." The number "666" has biblical significance as symbolic of the "Anti-Christ" in prophecy. The group is also known to use Gaelic (old Irish) symbols as a method of coding communications. Another numerical symbol and slogan are known as "the 14 words." These are: "We must secure the existence of our people and a future for white children."

The overall creed of the Aryan Brotherhood illustrates the racial attachment of the group. Their creed is:

> "I will stand by my brother
> My brother will come before all others
> My life is forfeit should I fail my brother
> I will honor my brother in peace as in war"

While the precise number of Aryan Brotherhood members and associates is not known, the gang has chapters in virtually every major state and federal prison in the country. Estimates of AB's total strength vary widely, but nearly all exceed 15,000 members and associates nationwide. Roughly half are in prison and half are on the outside.[74] They have traditionally nurtured a deep hatred toward black individuals and members of black groups/gangs, such as the Black Guerrilla Family (BGF), Crips, Bloods, and the El Rukns:[75]

Unlike the New Black Panther Party, the Aryan Brotherhood does not maintain a website that announces its beliefs and ideologies. However, like radical black groups, radical white extremists also have certain "religious" components to their ideology. Aryan Brotherhood members throughout the country have typically joined Aryan Nations under its alter-ego name, Church of Jesus Christ Christian. This racial nationalist thinking was based on the larger movement known as Christian Identity, which is a "religion" founded by the late Richard Butler. His "prison ministry" promoted the doctrine that non-whites are "mud people" and Jews are the literal descendants of Satan.[76]

Christian Identity evolved from an eclectic set of beliefs known as British-Israelism (or Anglo-Israelism) that began in the eighteenth century in England. This theory held that the people of the British Isles were direct descendants of the "chosen people" of the Bible. These people were carried off from the Promised Land by the Assyrians around 730 BC. This belief reasoned that the people of England (and later the white Christian people of Europe) were, in fact, the chosen people for whom the Bible was written. This philosophy spread to the United States, where it evolved and changed during the early twentieth century.

Christian Identity differed from British-Israelism in that it taught that God had created the white man in His image and given him a soul. He also created manlike creatures of various colors that were not human. Instead, these "creatures" were animals. They did not possess a soul. It also teaches that the Devil came to Eve in the Garden of Eden and impregnated her. The result of this pregnancy was the birth of Cain, who committed the first murder when he killed his "half-brother" Abel. Christian Identity teaches that the bloodline of Cain continues to exist today in the form of people who now call themselves "Jews." Christian Identity churches exist in many parts of the country and are usually small. Nationally, though the data may be dated, there are probably fewer than 50,000 people who adhere to Christian Identity beliefs. However, this is still a significant and alarming movement.[77]

Christian Identity

This mindset has ironic similarities to radical Islamists. For example, some Islamists await the twelfth imam, which can be analogized as an "Islamic Messiah." Both worldviews have a strong adherence to the prophetic event of Armageddon. For these people, Armageddon will take place when the second coming of Christ ushers in a cosmic war between the white race and the "forces of evil." This apocalyptic belief corresponds with those radical Islamists who desire to provoke worldwide chaos designed to usher in the Islamic messiah. Indeed, this also reflects the thinking of NFAC who are influenced by Black Hebrews. Each of these groups has within their worldview the desire to facilitate this cosmic battle.

According to Yungher, the true believers of Christian Identity should be viewed as a potent terrorist threat, as they bide their time, awaiting some "political, economic or security calamity to impact the American political landscape to unleash their holy war."[78] Inherent in this statement is the desire for chaos. Think again about current circumstances. If economic circumstances get worse, and if direct action results, the possibility for chaos becomes increasingly possible.

Proud Boys

According to Wikipedia,[79] the Proud Boys are an "American far-right, neo-fascist, and exclusively male organization that promotes and engages in political violence." The group "originated in 2016 under the leadership of Vice Media co-founder and former commentator Gavin McInnes." Taking its name from the song "Proud of Your Boy" from the 2011 Disney musical *Aladdin*, the Proud Boys initially emerged as part of the alt-right. A "rebranding effort" intensified following the white supremacist *Unite the Right* rally in Charlottesville.

According to Samantha Kutner of the International Centre for Counterterrorism, the group believes "men and Western culture are under siege". Though the group officially rejects white supremacy, Kutner believes that "western chauvinism" is a code for the white genocide conspiracy theory. The Buffalo supermarket shooter, Payton S. Gendron, appears to adhere to this thinking. Furthermore, members have in the past participated in overtly racist events and events centered around fascist, anti-left, and anti-socialist violence.

The Southern Poverty Law Center (SPLC) has called the Proud Boys a "hate group" and an "alt-right fight club," that uses rhetorical devices to obscure its actual motives. The Anti-Defamation League (ADL) also described them as "extremist conservative" and "alt-lite," "overtly Islamophobic and misogynistic," "transphobic and anti-immigration," "all too willing to embrace racists, antisemites, and bigots of all kinds," and notes the group's promotion and use of violence as a core tactic.

The group has been banned from numerous social networks, including *Facebook*, *Instagram*, *Twitter*, and *YouTube*. On February 3, 2021, the United States Justice Department announced the indictment of members for conspiracy related to the 2021 United States Capitol attack. Since then, at least two dozen Proud Boys members and affiliates have been indicted for their alleged roles in the riot. The organization was also subpoenaed by the House Select Committee on the January 6 Attack in November 2021.

DYNAMICS OF IDEOLOGIES

My premise is that all extremist groups are detrimental, acting as a type of cancer in the social fabric. Yet, we have seen that not all cancer is treated the same way. Groups on the Left tend to be seen as less problematic, or even as a natural response to groups on the Right. Leftist groups are often deemed to act in a "defensive" posture in response to hate groups. As with the cultural war, I am not so sure that the Right is the "cause."

Regardless of "which side is to blame," two wrongs do not make a "right." Of course, the presence of hate groups on the Right may inspire those on the Left to counter what they think must be countered. This dynamic could also go the other direction, with the Right reacting by pushing back against the Left. Either way, as Wood noted of NFAC, the hatred exhibited by that group does not justify the hatred that they seek to counter. In short, fighting hate by adopting hate is wrong—and is counterproductive and heartless.

On another level, criticism against those on the Left who advocate hatred, racial divisiveness, and even a segregated black nation is not widely heard or condemned. Indeed, it's largely ignored. Similarly, advocates of CRT and BLM are widely accepted and adopted. Yet, those who advocate conservative thinking, for nationalism and patriotism are almost reflectively deemed outcasts and even threatening. Consider just one example.

As hearings for the January 6 committee commenced, *New York Times* reporter Katie Benner suggested that Trump supporters should be considered "enemies of the state," which she indicated was the ongoing threat within the US. Specifically, in a now-deleted tweet, she spoke to America's current, essential national security dilemma: "Work to combat legitimate national security threats now entails calling a politician's supporters enemies of the state."[80]

Let's state this directly: A *reporter* of the *paper of record* essentially declares that American citizens who supported the previous president are "enemies of the state." This is so far beyond the pale that it leaves one breathless. While some who attacked Congress were disorderly, even volatile; focusing on a generalized notion of "Trump supporters" while ignoring others who have declared their desire to destroy this country is outrageous and disingenuous. After reading the ideologies that you just read, *this is intellectually impossible to justify*.

Adding to this thinking, the Biden administration unveiled its national strategy for countering domestic terrorism. This National Security Council (NSC) report found that among the "wide range" of ideologies, "racially or ethnically motivated violent extremists (principally those who promote the superiority of the white race) and militia-based violent extremists are assessed as presenting the most persistent and lethal threats." Calls for violence can be explicit or not. For example, the NSC wrote that "lurking in ideologies rooted in a perception of the superiority of the white race that call for violence in furtherance of perverse and abhorrent notions of racial 'purity' or 'cleansing.' "

The report makes larger statements encompassing the spectrum of ideological threats, being reflective of what you just read in this chapter. "Another key component of the threat comes from anti-government or anti-authority violent extremists . . . the significant component of today's threat includes self-proclaimed 'militias' and militia violent extremists who take steps to violently resist government authority or facilitate the overthrow of the US . . . including "racial or ethnic bigotry and hatred, as well as anti-government or anti-authority sentiment."[81]

"We must be clear-eyed about this challenge: the unlawful violence that constitutes domestic terrorism is the result of a complex, multi-layered set of society dynamics," the NSC wrote. "We cannot—and will not—ignore those dynamics, such as racism and bigotry that perpetuate the domestic terrorism threat."[82]

President Biden advocated efforts to "unite all Americans" and work together to "root out the hatreds that can too often drive violence." He added that it's "critical to condemn and confront" domestic terrorism, "regardless of the particular ideology that motivates individuals to violence." Yet, the president then said that white supremacy "is the most lethal threat to the homeland today."

Are these statements mutually consistent? Can we condemn and confront extremists regardless of the ideology, yet declare one ideology as the most lethal threat?

While the NSC assessment is fair and objective in many respects, I question the emphasis on white supremacy. Consider that threat assessments are based on several factors, including those that are most probable and most critical. Probabilities and criticalities are key. This would include the nature—and the consequences of relative threats.

Watching from afar over the past several years, I do not see the white supremacist threat in the same way. Granted, trying to "quantify" a threat can be difficult. Even if the data and the analysis are available, the assessment is still somewhat subjective.

One obvious indicator we all can see is when the "threat" becomes real—and a criminal act occurs. Short of the chaos of Charlottesville and January 6 plus the plots highlighted in chapter I, the threat from white supremacist groups has not been apparent. Even the well-publicized plot to "kidnap" the governor of Michigan has been exposed in court proceedings as mostly facilitated by the FBI. Though, the Buffalo supermarket shooting is obvious and accurate example, this lone and hateful act, as terrible as it was, does not constitute a widespread threat.

In short, white supremacist groups have not acted out in a manner consistent with being the *most significant domestic terrorist threat.* Yet, being tagged as the greatest threat will result in greater law enforcement suspicion and pressure. Maybe they deserve this attention. My concern, however, is that this is more political than real. Either way, if the government declares an enemy, it will come after them.

In the meantime, what happens to those who seek to foster socialism and attack the capitalistic system? What about those who rioted and looted in cities across the country? What about the mobs who enter and pillage stores and business districts? What about those who commit "normal" crimes such as murder, robbery, carjacking, and the like?

My point is this: recall the principle. *Attack one ideology while supporting or ignoring the opposite, and the result will be more of both.* As we have seen, the overwhelming bias from institutions and from the elites is toward blacks, progressives, and socialism—and against whites, conservatives, and traditional democratic principles. How much of this bias is reflective of the threat assessment by the National Security Council? It is impossible to know, particularly since threat assessments by their nature are subjective, considering that when one focuses on something, they will see what they want to see. This is not to say that white supremacists are not toxic. They are—and they ought to be appropriately dealt with.

Yet, one cannot also dismiss the obvious political influences inherent to these assessments. Consider also that this assessment comes after four years of investigations into the Trump Administration—that proved *exactly nothing*. Indeed, we now know that the ill-fated "Russian Collusion" myth was ginned up by the Clinton campaign as opposition research. The media and societal institutions reflectively and enthusiastically supported this fiction.

So, is it far-fetched to wonder if this threat assessment is also premised on false or faulty thinking? Again, this matters because the dynamic of extremism is very volatile. What is not a threat can *become a threat* if you back it against the wall. Everyone knows this principle when dealing with wild animals. As noted in chapter I—*we ought to be careful what we ask for*.

To conclude this section, when thinking about the potential for racial, religious, and political conflict, I realize this may have been hard to read. My intent is not to create distress, yet it's critical that we see things as they are. The rationale is twofold.

On one level, it is easier to ignore what we don't want to address. The image is the ostrich sticking its head in the sand. Most people live this way. The fact that you are reading this book makes you different. You are ahead of the crowd. You may be able to both help diminish the impact of extremist thinking and proactively do things to protect yourself and your family.

In this sense, we all contribute to this dynamic. Some are part of the solution. Some are part of the problem. I suspect all of us are partly the former, partly the latter. In any case, please look at the figure below. Where do we place ourselves in this continuum? If we are not as close as possible to the middle, then we may be more part of the problem than the solution.

Where do you come in?

Copyright, James F. Pastor, 2009–2022

IDEOLOGIES & THE CAPITALIST SYSTEM

Given the ideologies outlined in this chapter, assessing how ideologies may result in violence can be seen on two levels: Individual & Group *and* Ideology & System. Let's discuss this distinction and the dynamics created by extremist thinking and violence.

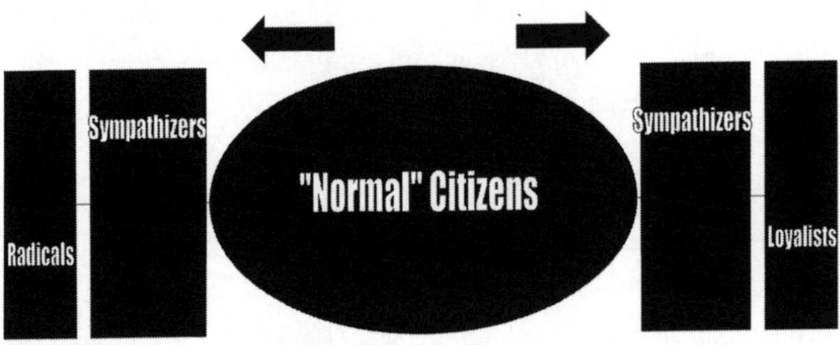

Copyright, James F. Pastor, 2009–2022

The application of individual to group dynamics is highly dependent on the pressures derived from extremism within society. While there are many factors that may inspire people to radicalize, think about this dynamic as illustrated in the figure above.

On your left, is the term "Radicals." This term applies to individuals who seek to make significant changes in society. These individuals are true believers in their "cause"—and seek to forward their beliefs.

Next to this is the larger group called "sympathizers." They care about the issue, but they are not willing to forward it with the passion of a radical. They may be too old, too frail, too afraid, or simply nonconfrontational by nature. They also may hold positions where they need to avoid controversy. Or they simply care more about other matters to get directly involved. Likely, this latter thinking is the most common. In any case, this group of sympathizers wants certain changes forwarded, but they want to do it through peaceful means. If violence is deemed necessary, they want someone else to do the "heavy lifting." To help, however, they may be willing to donate money, encouragement, contraband, votes, and any number of other "contributions."

On the other side is the term "Loyalists," which applies to individuals seeking to maintain the status quo. They feel passionately about and desire to fight for traditional values and norms, seeking to maintain the representative democracy—with a capitalist economic system. Next to the "loyalists" are their "sympathizers." These people are similar as those sympathizers on the other side of the political spectrum. Though they care about these issues, they are not willing to join loyalists in direct action.

The middle is the large segment of society that just wants to live their lives, raise their children, plan for retirement, and stay out of the political fray. They are not political. They are not moved by strident sentiments. However, they may be sympathetic and want to do the right thing, and as with most Americans, they desire to support the "underdog."

But these people are not educated on the issues. Either because they do not know enough to care, are too busy to care, or are not willing to take the time to learn. They simply do not want to get involved in public policy debates. They *avoid* race, religion, and politics. These people are normal in society—and is how most Americans see their world. Most are disengaged or disconnected from the larger issues facing society. This could change—possibly dramatically.

Getting the attention of the stable middle (which used to be called the "silent majority") is the key. If life for those in the middle is "normal," chances are they will stay disengaged. However, if circumstances begin to deteriorate, either through violence or dramatic changes in the economy, then people will start to pay attention. For example, crime in cities may leave people uncertain or afraid. If inflation spikes, energy costs rise, and the economy is sluggish for a long period of time—people will start to pay more attention to what is happening. When this occurs, people will also make judgments regarding who to blame for their situation.

Think about how this plays out. Both "sides" blame the other. As opposing groups blame each other, their respective positions harden and they begin to personally attack each other. When frustrated and passionate, it is near impossible to stay focused on substance and facts. People will make personal attacks instead of carrying out substantive analysis. Think of all the accusations of "racism" that you have read in this book—and what you hear in media accounts.

Inevitably, the dynamic will turn increasingly hostile. As violence occurs, it serves to harden positions. Particularly when deaths occur, the loss of loved ones "die hard." Their loss serves to spur others to fight harder. It also serves to inspire deeper levels of commitment from the participants. As these commitments deepen, the respective sizes of the groups change. The extremes grow, the sympathizers grow—and the middle decreases. The below figure illustrates this change.

Copyright, James F. Pastor, 2009–2022

Now take this a step further. Consider the impact of sustained violence. Particularly, if violence is used as a strategy, then the dynamic changes considerably. In this scenario, the Radicals and Loyalists grow larger and bolder, though these extremes never become too large. Killing and dying are limited to certain individuals who are willing to kill and die. This is generally limited to certain personalities, age groups, genders, and those most directly impacted by the violence. Nonetheless, the sympathizers on both sides grow proportionately larger, as these limitations are not as applicable for those who sympathize but do not directly engage.

The group most affected by this dynamic is the middle—the normal citizens. As the most vital to a stable society, it is also the most difficult to maintain. If violence gets too disruptive, the tension between the competing sides becomes too intense to maintain a "middle ground." This tension can force people to "pick sides." The dynamic is this: *if you are not with us, then you are against us*. Recall the lyrics, "come to Chicago, or join the other side."

Circumstances can become so tenuous that even people who do not want to be involved are *forced* to get involved. The status quo can become impossible to maintain. Since this "process" is inherent to human nature, it is also illustrated in counterinsurgency. Speaking about tribal groups in Afghanistan, insight into fear and violence in a terroristic environment found that village elders wouldn't commit to opposing the Taliban "if they and their families are vulnerable to Taliban torture and murder."[83]The lesson is that forced compliance and forced resistance are dependent on the level of violence and vulnerability imposed on the group.

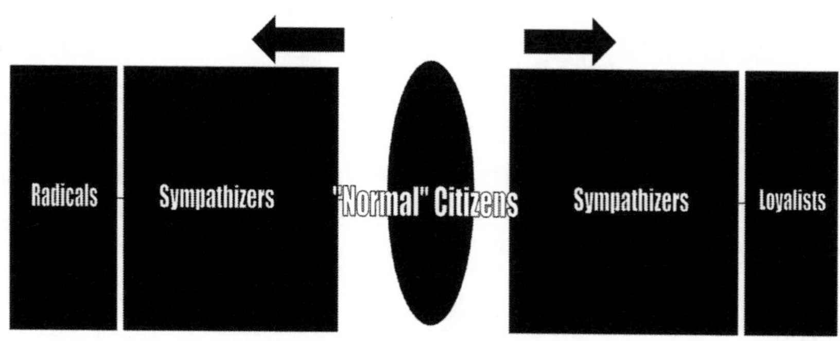

Copyright, James F. Pastor, 2009–2022

Consequently, this dynamic separates individuals into groups—or tribes. The social fabric in society can become increasingly reflective of group identities. Whether that group is racial, religious, or political; it is a powerful cohesive factor. This is especially true if people are effectively forced to identify with the group or risk being branded as traitors, sympathizers, or worse.

The reader can extrapolate ongoing events in society and consider how these can become so emotional as to turn violent. As violence occurs, the "other side" is motivated to respond in kind. Violent response, in turn, inspire more violence. Each time this occurs, it gets more difficult to stop. Each time this occurs, it gets more difficult to maintain "neutrality." Each time this occurs, the stability in society becomes more tenuous. Each time this occurs, the police are placed in the middle—and often are targeted by the violence. Each time this occurs, the government is placed in an increasingly difficult position. The government seeks to balance the need to stop the violence while at the same time avoiding draconian police tactics. The result of this dynamic is a spiraling cycle of violence and its resultant implications on society.

To summarize my premise: *the incidence of inter-group conflict will be the result of, and response to, increased extremist ideologies*. As demonstrated, extremist ideologies are percolating just underneath the social and political framework of the country. As such, a crucial question is this: what will trigger a rise in extremist ideologies?

The ideologies outlined in this chapter, coupled with the impact of RRP and this country's history, play a significant role in fostering extremism. Simply stated, some people cannot or will not let go. While it is true, that we cannot "change the past," it is also true that the past can create ample "ammunition" for extremist ideologies. As we explore the potential for this eventuality, certain groups are poised to impose their radical agendas through direct action. When groups violently act, what they do, how opposing groups respond, how the media and larger society reacts, and whether public safety forces can control the violence are the resulting challenges. Consequently, it is not whether extremist violence will increase but how and when it manifests itself—and how it is managed.

The below graphic may help to conceptualize the pending threats. Note that some of these groups may directly oppose each other while some groups may ally with each other. To illustrate these potentialities, I show arrows from one circle to another. Sometimes, this can represent a potential ally. Sometimes it may represent a potential adversary. Other times, the line is contained within the circle. For example, racial and nationalist groups exclusively oppose each other. This is because their respective interests leave little room for even tactical cooperation. To illustrate this, the line is contained within the circle.

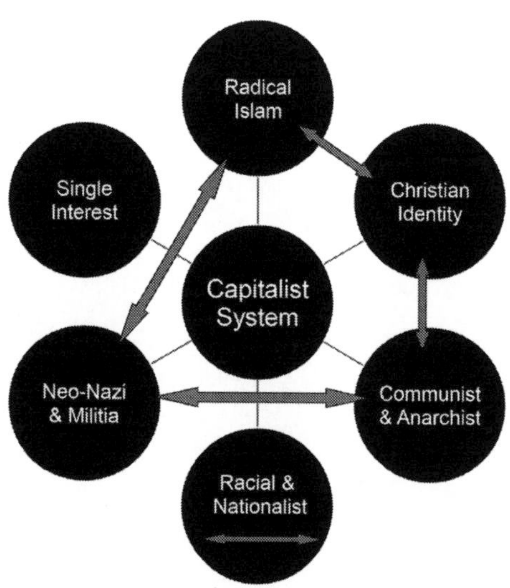

Copyright, James F. Pastor, 2009–2022

Consider the graphic that shows each extremist category with a "bubble." While we did not discuss, radical Islam (often referred to as "Islamists") as currently this threat is mostly connected to international influences, it is still clearly a factor. Consider the Boston Marathon bombings, the Pulse Night Club killings, the San Bernadino attacks, and of course, 9-11.

Groups, such as Neo-Nazis and Leftist/anarchist groups are likely to be natural enemies. Others, such as radical Islamic and Christian Identity groups possess numerous inherent conflicts, not the least of which stems from their interpretations of the Koran and the Bible. However, some assert that their common, mutual foe—the Jews—may inspire some tactical cooperation against their mutual enemy. When thinking about these potential inter-group conflicts, it is crucial that you deeply internalize the notion that the *enemy of my enemy is my friend.* If you get this notion, you could imagine groups cooperating at one time and then opposing each other at another time. Yet, they could still be true to their ideological beliefs.

In the end, however, all of these groups—from the religious to the political to the racial/nationalist, have one common theme: the destruction of the government, or more broadly, the capitalistic system.[84] The impact of this fact is wide-ranging—and extraordinarily problematic—for policing agencies and public safety providers. This is because they are the most visible representatives and symbolize government.

This makes the police and public safety providers as "canaries of the coal mine." They act of early warning indicators of the viability of the government. While targeting police and other "guardians," the *real target* is what they represent—the government and the capitalist system. The viability of the system is what prevents each ideology from achieving its ultimate goals. Since the system is the ultimate target—consider:

- Islamists cannot create a religious state ruled by Sharia law in a representative democracy.
- Christian Identity groups cannot facilitate the coming kingdom of God while the capitalist system and the American government prevail.
- Communist/Anarchist groups cannot institute socialist principles and economic conditions if the capitalist system and the American government prevails.
- Racial and nationalist groups cannot institute their idea of a "pure" segregated society serving its racial brothers and sisters if the capitalist system and the American government prevails.
- Neo-Nazis and militias also cannot exist and thrive in an environment where the capitalist system and the American government prevail.
- Nor can single-interest groups highly focused on very important yet more narrow goals relating to abortion, the environment, and animal rights exist. These cannot thrive in an environment where the capitalist system and the American government prevail, at least without dramatic changes in the way we live.

In effect, the system is "surrounded" by ideological groups that want to destroy it. In all cases, it is *the system* that is the impediment. Each ideology focuses its criticism on systems, institutions, and their structural components. They are saying, sometimes directly but usually indirectly, that *the system is what needs to change*. This was obvious to me decades ago.

What is different today is those who "govern" the system and constitute its chief beneficiaries are *fostering its own demise*. I did not expect this dynamic. Instead, I expected this to be driven by extremists who would pressure and force the system to its knees. Seeing the "leaders" of the system do the "wink and the nod" to those who seek its destruction is stunning. Sometimes, this even includes active participation and acclaim, as per CRT and BLM. The logical result is trouble, danger, and destruction. Those in leadership positions must know as much. Yet, acclaim and the advocacy of these "theories" are supported as if they blind to their inevitable consequences.

There is a concept in public policy known as "unintended consequences." This usually relates to circumstances when leaders seek to "fix" a perceived problem. Sometimes, or even often, when change is instituted, this causes an unrelated problem in another area. This is the "unintended" consequence. Policymakers do not want to break something when fixing something else. Not foreseeing the "domino effect" is common in the complex organism called "society."

Yet, the natural consequences of favoring certain groups, races, and ideologies are obvious. These consequences are not hard to discern or predict. What is hard to understand is "why"? Why allow—and support—policy changes that a reasonable person knows or should know will lead to discord, violence, and the potential destruction of the society that they govern and benefit from? This is the ultimate question. I will let the reader draw their own conclusions.

In the meantime, we are now in the "calm before the storm." How long this calm will last is dependent on the introduction of some dramatic event. Events can trigger great emotion. This is because people are on edge. Yet, know that the storm will worsen when the next direct action occurs. When (not if) this occurs, watch to see what happens. If the country comes together, waving flags, advocating unity, and caring for the victims, then we as a country have an opportunity to weather the storm. Whatever happens, do what you can to bridge the divide without losing your dignity or your values. Truth and love go a long way. So do rights and freedom. Develop and maintain these as we go forward . . .

CHAPTER IV

RE-IMAGINING POLICING: FROM DEFUNDING TO LAWLESSNESS

Continuing the story of how extremist thinking and policies have directly impacted people and property, policy decisions are driving a dramatic rise in crime, particularly violent and chaotic crime, such as looting, organized "smash-and-grab" shoplifting, and other disorderly behaviors. This chapter will discuss *why* and describe the implications if law and order are not restored.

Law and order ultimately stem from the criminal justice system—which consists of police, prosecutors, courts, and prisons. These include related service providers, such as drug rehabilitation programs and treatments, diversion programs, work and training projects, and a host of others. What is important to understand is that each aspect of "the system" is dependent on the others. As a system, one "leg" directly affects each of the others.

Yet, one can trace the interworking of the system back to the voting booth. Voters elect legislators, prosecutors, judges, and of course, mayors and other city officials. All directly impact what happens in the streets, homes, schools, and businesses.

HOW & WHY DID DEFUNDING & RE-IMAGINING HAPPEN?

In the past several years, progressive prosecutors and legislators were elected around the country. Without naming names, simply looking at the urban areas hit hardest by violent crime and chaotic conditions, one will find each jurisdiction's local prosecutor is *progressive*.

In August 2019, *NBC News* published a piece trumpeting a "new wave of progressive district attorneys across the country." The piece explained these progressive prosecutors favor "decriminalization, diversion programs over jail time, and holding law enforcement accountable." Speaking with glowing optimism of reform-minded progressive prosecutors, as they "begin to change the criminal justice system *from the inside out"* [emphasis added], they cited these reforms:[1]

- Reforming the bail system
- Curbing enforcement of lower-level marijuana offenses
- Increasing the use of diversion programs over jail time
- Pledging to end mass incarceration
- Pledging to hold police accountable for alleged wrongdoing

Progressive prosecutors also sought to change prosecutor offices by *adjusting* priorities designed to reduce prison populations. Their intent is "trying to think creatively about changing the status quo." Americans are now living with the consequences of such reforms. Some saw this coming, including former Attorney General William Barr who stated:[2]

> "the emergence in some of our large cities of district attorneys that style themselves as 'social justice' reformers, who spend their time undercutting the police, letting criminals off the hook and refusing to enforce the law . . . is demoralizing to law enforcement and dangerous to public safety."

Let's understand why and how these reforms *seemed* to make sense. First of all, they stem from mantras such as "over-policing," "culture of prosecution," and "mass incarceration." Each of these terms has no real meaning. They are soundbites. They are impossible to define. Because these mantras sound good, the *purpose* and *effect* were hard to detect or predict. Let me explain.

What is *over-policing* to me may be too lax to you. A *culture of prosecution* is the same. What do these mean?

Let's isolate the latter. Ironically, this term was used to describe . . . hold your breath: *the prosecutor's office*! So, the culture of an urban prosecutor's office ought not to be prosecutions? Though prosecutors have discretion, and they should, their job is to *prosecute*. This does not imply that every defendant must be charged and prosecuted. But prosecutors have a *duty to protect* the citizens who elected them. It seems too simplistic to say that their priority should be with the citizens, not the perpetrators. Yet, the opposite seems to be in play.

Next, following the death of George Floyd came the second development. With "peaceful protests" breaking out across the country, the idea of "defunding" the police quickly gained traction. Its widespread acclaim followed. On its face, this was ludicrous.

While this mantra was too subjective to quantify, to some it was literal. Defunding the police means *defunding the police*. Progressive politicians, BLM, and other activists animated the mantra. Indeed, if one takes "defund" seriously, it can be quantified—*zero dollars* for policing budgets! No serious person wanted to get on this side of the "ledger." For example, senate Democrats were attacked by BLM for opposing attempts to defund the police. In response, BLM called the vote a "universal attempt to silence the demands from the streets," and significantly: "No one, we repeat NO ONE, had the back of our *revolutionary* movement in the Senate (emphasis added)."[3]

Yet, the *defund* mantra rolled on in cities around the country. Minneapolis, the place of Floyd's death, was one of the first cities to reform its budget. Other cities jumped on the "defund bandwagon," including Seattle, San Francisco, Los Angeles, New York, Oakland, and Austin, and hundreds of other cities, large and small, did the same.

As this bandwagon gained momentum, so did another mindless mantra: *Re-imagining Policing*. Here again, what you imagine policing should be, may be very different than how I imagine policing. Imagination, by its very nature, is so subjective that it's limited by literally *nothing.* No one has even remotely "bothered" to define what "reimagining policing" means.

Every serious researcher starts by defining the problem—and the proposed solutions. Unlike CRT, seemingly oblivious to the implications of admitting that the theory is fluid, those who advocate reimagining do not even pretend to call it a "theory."

Let's step back and assess what this means. Defunding advocated by the social justice mob was adopted by policymakers throughout the country. The same occurred in reimagining policing. So, police budgets were cut while policymakers *imagined* what future policing would look like. In retrospect, this was utter folly. The speed of change and the intellectually vacant manner in which it was delivered were stunning. So much so that only two explanations are possible: That policymakers cowered to the social justice mob, or it was planned.

I think both drove what can only remotely be called a "policy decision." I say this sarcastically. Having a doctorate degree in public policy, I care about how and why policy decisions are made. Seeing how rapidly decisions were made, during and following the summer of love demonstrates that these were not thought through. Plus, the *results* of these decisions have been disastrous. With violent crime and chaos reigning in cities across the country, any claim that defunding and reimagining were sound policy is almost laughable—if the consequences weren't so serious.

Indeed, not only were the policy decisions laughable, but so was the "excuse" used by the Biden Administration to "explain" the rise of violence and chaos. It is *Covid* that is causing these increases. In December 2021, Covid is *still* being blamed for crime. So, it was Covid that caused roving bands of "smash-and-grab" shoplifters to pillage luxury stores? It was Covid that caused people to use hammers and other tools to smash glass counters as they beat and intimidated store clerks? It was Covid that caused bands of youths to beat a bus driver in downtown Chicago while fighting and taking over the streets of a major business and tourist area? It was Covid that caused a twelve-year-old girl and fifteen-year-old boy to be shot in the same disturbance? It was Covid that has caused a 20-percent increase in murders and a

56-percent increase in shootings in 2021 in this downtown Chicago business district?[4]

These are just a few of hundreds of incidents happening as this book is being drafted. It is impossible to chronicle these incidents, as the fluid nature of crime makes any "list" effectively outdated as soon as it is created. Crime statistics, however, are useful and will be presented later to demonstrate the folly of our "leaders."

More pointedly, dismissing Covid as the cause, which I do, leads to an inevitable question: What is the cause of our current conditions? Are they the product of the policies described above? If so, why were these policies enacted? Did the rioting of 2020 trigger these policies? Or was the "mob" the intended direct beneficiary? Again, based on the rapid—and vacant public policy decision-making, is this unreasonable to consider? Not only is this conclusion reasonable, but one is also hard-pressed to think otherwise.

But let's go even deeper. Is it also possible that these confounding policy initiatives were planned—planned to create chaos? With more than four decades of experience in policing, security, and public safety; I find that no prior example can be even remotely compared. As an attorney with a doctorate in public policy, my conclusion is that "reimagining" policing is not anything *even close* to sound legal analysis or public policy. So too with defunding the police.

When one thinks about how major changes are made to public policy, the "process" typically looks something like this. Public discussions and debates are made, and researchers and policy experts are engaged. Data in support and often against the initiatives are analyzed and debated. Legislators call witnesses to testify in committee hearings. Debating the merits in committee hearings and in open forums typically occur. This is how public policy is "made." Like *sausage*, most people do not want to see it made. However, decisions impacting public safety should be done in a prudent and open manner. Usually this takes time and a good deal of thoughtful discourse, both in public and in legislative sessions.

The *results* are also an indication of how they were enacted. Cities around the country are quickly "undoing" the defunding decisions. As violence and chaos increase, the *defunding* is being questioned—and in several places reversed. Hence, even if one wants to believe these are well developed and meritorious, they are being "undone" as rapidly as they were "done." This speaks volumes as to the how and why they were done in the first place.

With this as the setup, here is my conclusion: *these policy decisions were planned.* Not in the typical way outlined above. They were advocated by progressives in a similar fashion as CRT, Systemic Racism, the 1619 project, BLM, "reforming" criminal justice, and other lesser "thinking." Essentially, when the right "trigger" occurred, they were quickly initiated. The influence of the "mob" may have also played a part.

But the "mob" may have also been *part of the play*. Is it possible the mob was also fostered by those who controlled this agenda? Activists from various parts of the country often showed up at protest sites. How? Why? Who funded those who travelled? To my knowledge, there has not been any serious attempt to explore these questions. Compare the time and resources devoted to the January 6th "insurrection." Why not do a similar deep dive into the summer of 2020? Yet, there has not been any public inquiry.

The silence is deafening. As was the rapid nature of the initiatives—and their withdrawal. Remember the adage: *never let a crisis go to waste*. Its modern attribution is to Rahm Emanuel, the former mayor of Chicago and chief of staff to President Obama. Since these policy changes were enacted mostly, if not exclusively, in 2020, why *can't* we connect the dots? As argued above, the answer is obvious. What was missing in this "crisis plan" was the public reaction.

While the media played its "mostly peaceful protests" song, vehicles and buildings burned. When the burning stopped (at least for a time), murders skyrocketed and chaotic "smash-and-grab" shoplifting took over. Aside from blaming Covid, those who tried to make hay *with* the crisis then had to deal with the fallout *from* the crisis. Streets and business districts were pillaged. While businesses and their employees tried to "manage" through this crisis, the sheer magnitude of the chaos was impossible to ignore—and explain away. If "media silence" continued, any credibility that major news sources had left would be drained.

Though allegedly about seven percent of the 2020 protests were violent, the fact remains that some protestors transitioned into rioters. Those who took part in the rioting were either opportunists or "hardcore" believers with an ideological aim. Regardless of what motivated the rioters, the fact remains they were *allowed* to commit approximately $2 billion dollars of damages in 2020.[5]

As the damage may have been unprecedented, one can ask why Antifa and BLM were not demonized in any comparable manner as those who rioted at the Capitol? The adage holds true: two wrongs don't make a right. But more poignant words come from the former Baltimore Mayor Rawlings-Blake, who stated, following the death of Freddie Gray in 2015, [we wanted to give] "those who wished to destroy space to do that as well." Mayors and governors in the summer of 2020 gave *plenty of space to destroy.*

Let's look underneath the "crisis" of 2020 and see another "reason" for these policy initiatives. When I googled "define reimagine policing," I got 873,000 hits.[6] The top of the search list: *The Obama Foundation.* Quite a coincidence! Why would the Obama Foundation have so much influence on this subject? Is this part of *not letting a crisis go to waste?*

The Obama Foundation website has substantial "resources" devoted to "reimagining policing." Some quotes may help to set the stage:[7]

> "We can take steps and make reforms to combat police violence and *systemic racism* within law enforcement. Together, we can work to *redefine* public safety so that it recognizes the humanity and dignity of every person."

The website did not *define* reimagining. Instead, it points to a "to-do list," which can be described as a blueprint for change. What was missing in the list of suggested changes, however, were the goals. Other than in the most general "feel good" terms, such as "common sense" limits, no objective goals were articulated.

Now let me be clear. There is nothing wrong with seeking reform. The Obama Foundation outlines certain steps for change, including reviewing *use of force* policies, seeking community input, reporting the findings, and then instituting reform. This is exactly what should have been done in 2020 *before* these disastrous policies were enacted! But this did not happen.

So, they did this: *ready, shoot, aim*. They forgot—or intentionally avoided what would be the prudent and reasonable thing to do. This too was not an "accident." It was *planned chaos*—a planned crisis spurred by policy changes allowing the mob to cause even more chaos. In essence, the intent of these policies was to cause chaos. This is my opinion, which is grounded in what you have read so far. But keep reading, as the dots get even more obvious.

Can we "reimagine policing" while keeping people safe? Can we have public safety *and* social justice? Can we balance "systemic racism" *with* law and order? These questions are hard to balance or hard to achieve. Clearly, they are noble goals—if we can define the goals? Which, of course, is part of the problem. How do we define and quantify public safety and social justice?

- Crime levels?
- Arrest rates?
- Conviction rates?
- Prison population?
- Recidivism rates?
- Survey data?
- Education levels?
- Employment rates?
- Out-of-wedlock births?

You get the point. How we define the issue and what measures we use to "prove" the issue *is the issue*! It is circular logic. Using ill-defined terms, such as *reimagining*, guarantees that we will not be sure of our "success" or even the measures used to gauge "success." Understand this is the nature of the criminal justice system—and it is inherent to the social sciences. We are as imperfect in our methodologies as we are in our characters. Flawed and biased thinking comes part and parcel with who we are. This is natural and predictable. Throughout our history, we have "agreed to disagree" on how to improve the criminal justice system and society at large. Most people accept these limitations as being best left to the political process. Those who "win" can impose their policy preferences (at least as far as the law and public opinion allow). Famously, President Obama declared "elections have consequences." He was right then, and this notion is still correct.

But what if the justice system (or this country) is widely accepted as systemically racist? What implications does this portend? How do we fix a systemically racist system? Indeed, how do we prove this conclusion? Can this notion even be proven or disproven?

These rhetorical questions matter. Yet, they are value judgments that are impossible to prove. Even worse, it is a precarious premise to articulate. Having spent so much time developing this in previous chapters, without reasserting what has already been said, I can say this: the premise is an impossible starting point for any public policy initiative. Yet, it's exactly where we are. This is where the progressives put us. This is what they *planned* to do.

As humans, we crave a better life. We want to find solutions to problems. So, back to the unanswerable questions posed above. Though unanswerable, these questions have value. They can inspire reasonable people to find better answers to vexing societal problems. Those who enacted defunding and reimagining policing were *not* thoughtful or prudent. This is clear. This will be hard to read: *the only logical reason was to create chaos.*

Chaotic conditions can cause people to question the system that allowed it to arise. So, follow the logic. If you want to destroy the system, create chaos. Chaos, in turn, will cause people to question or even lose faith in the system that allows this to happen. It breaks down the social fabric. It causes people to separate themselves from others, causes suspicion between people (particularly those in different groups), and it leads people to conclude that the system is corrupt, ineffective, racist—and needs to be destroyed. Consequently, if you want to destroy the system, create chaos . . .

Ironically, the failure of the institutional mechanisms to stop the chaos actually *proves* that the system must be changed. Once again for emphasis, *chaos is the catalyst for revolution.* By creating the chaotic conditions, capitalism, and its attendant systems will be shown to require change. Indeed, if you really believe that the country is systemically racist, why would you support it? Why would you even seek to "fix" it? Remember *systemically* means its foundations. The *foundations* are racist. These along with its institutions are broken and racist. Why would anyone want to maintain an ineffective, corrupt, and systemically racist system?

As current conditions demonstrate, the police and those in the criminal justice system have been unable to resolve the chaos. This could change, but it will take some dramatic action. Significant support from people of all races, communities, and religions is needed. Support is also required from different political stripes. It could still happen.

Yet, those who want to restore law and order are losing to *the chaos activists* and the radicals and criminals who act out in urban settings. Do not misconstrue the message that our criminal justice system is sending. That is, inaction equals weakness. With the police being significantly weakened, who else is going to confront those who commit chaos? Chicago mayor Lori Lightfoot blamed *businesses* for failing to stop "smash-and-grabbers," when she asked this rhetorical, yet ludicrous question:[8]

> "Some of the retailers downtown in Michigan Avenue, I will tell you, I'm disappointed that they are not doing more to take safety and make it a priority. For example, we still have retailers that won't institute plans like having security officers in their stores."

There you have it. Blame businesses for failing to stop chaos—when the city fails to control the streets and prosecutors fail to lock up the "bad guys." Yes, there are criminals with evil intent out there. What does a policymaker do when BLM says "there will be bloodshed" if you go back to pre-Covid policing? This is what the leader of New York's BLM chapter said:[9]

> "If he [new NYC mayor Eric Adams] thinks that they're going to go back to the old ways of policing, then we are going to take to the streets again. There will be riots, there will be fire, and there will be bloodshed because we believe in defending our people."

How do you put a lid on chaos unless you have some enforcement mechanism from your police department? Clearly, Mayor Lightfoot is unable to make this happen. Instead, she shifts the blame. And according to the BLM leader, there is no going back to the "old ways of policing." So, we are dammed if we do and dammed if we don't.

One final and related point in this setup. Think back to May 2020. What does a liberal (or progressive) politician do when riots and mobs rule? Can they "crackdown" on those who are rioting and looting? Progressive politicians got elected because they *criticized the system.* They criticized the police—often as racist, brutal, and corrupt (or white supremacists). Can they later backtrack and say: *We must obey these racist, brutal, and corrupt police*? Could they support the police when they got elected by criticizing the police? Instead, they abided by the mob. At least until it got too "hot" to ignore.

Going further, when (or if) they come out in support of the police, why would the police believe the person who had previously demonized them? Police officers must believe that city officials have their backs. Those who have never done this job or have never known police officers intimately may not understand the significance of this statement. Those who have *been there* or *love those who have* will agree with this statement.

In short, this is the only natural conclusion: either policymakers wanted the riots and lawlessness to occur (remember the Baltimore mayor saying *we must give space for people to destroy*), or they were too cowardly to apply the constitutional and moral duty to protect people. Instead, they blame others (businesses "allow" shoplifting), hide behind false premises (Covid as the cause of crime), and fabricate news (mostly peaceful protests). Remember the first and principal duty of government is to protect its citizens. With respect to this duty, leaders throughout society failed miserably.

DEFUNDING POLICING

A classic example of how many progressive politicians see their priorities can be found in the city on the bay. San Francisco Mayor London Breed announced that the city would spend $120 million removed from law enforcement budgets, and "reinvest" the money into the city's black community. Calling the reinvestment "reparations," Breed said the transfer of funds from law enforcement to the black community was to make up for "decades of disinvestment." The plan calls for the funds to be used for workforce development, health campaigns, youth and cultural programs, and housing support.

Mayor Breed, the city's first African American Mayor, said that her motivation for carrying out the initiative was her own life:[10]

> "I grew up in poverty. I've had to live in poverty over twenty years of my life. And the frustration that came from living like that and then seeing so many of my friends who had been killed or in jail or on drugs—that is my motivation.
>
> Because *just imagine* if we can change the outcome of African Americans in San Francisco. What an incredible, thriving city we truly will be" (emphasis added).

The city's president of the board of supervisors, Shamann Walton, echoed the mayor, saying the funds would help improve the black community. "This initial investment to improve outcomes for the black community and overturn years of disinvestment and inequitable resource distribution is just the *first step* in righting the wrongs of history." Ms. Walton further noted that "we now have to continue to prioritize communities that have never had a chance to build true wealth, and this is a *first step* towards true reparations for the Black community here in San Francisco. We are proud of this work and looking forward to doing more (emphasis added)."[11]

Funding for the initiative will come from the budgets of local law enforcement agencies, with $80 million from the San Francisco Police Department (SFPD), which amounts to 6 percent of their budget, and $40 million from the Sheriff's Department. To account for the budget reduction, the mayor ordered the police department not to respond to non-criminal complaints. Yet, as above, this was the *first step*. When Mayor Breed asked SF Police Chief Bill Scott to enact further budget cuts, he said doing so was not possible, saying:[12]

> "The majority of our budget is personnel staffing, and we've cut pretty much everything we can cut. Which will equate, because we've cut everything we can cut, in a reduction and a loss of 210 full-time employees.

> . . . I am not supportive of these cuts. They will be devastating to the police department."

Even as these initiatives were taking effect, crime was surging in San Francisco. Burglaries have been spiraling out of control, with a rise in property crime of 342.9 percent in the Richmond District alone. Robberies, assaults, and arsons were also rapidly increasing over last year's numbers.

Similar cuts occurred in Los Angeles, where Democratic Mayor Eric Garcetti and the city council voted in July 2020 to cut Los Angeles Police Department (LAPD) budget by $150 million. One council member who voted against the measure offered some prudent thinking. Though the LAPD is not a perfect organization, "there's always room for improvement, but . . . other police departments throughout the nation strive to follow them (LAPD) on their community policing, use of force, de-escalation, and implicit bias training." With these training programs already in place, and with two-thirds of LAPD officers being minority officers, it is hard to contend that the department was rogue or "racist."

Yet, their budget was cut in the haste to chasten the mob—and to execute the plan! Similarly, Oakland Police Chief LeRonne Armstrong said the department chose to cut walking patrols, a team that worked to prevent retaliatory gang shootings, and added this obvious connection: "What's missing in the defunding conversation is our city is facing a huge increase in violent crime."[13]

The Seattle City Council cut the 2021 police budget by nearly $35.6 million, or about 9 percent, compared to 2019. Councilor Kshama Sawant claimed "the role of the police under capitalism" is "to defend the system's deep inequality through ongoing repression of the poor, the marginalized, and communities of color." Other councilors signed a pledge to address "the ongoing assault on Black lives perpetuated by a well-funded police state that acts with near impunity."[14] How do elected leaders walk back such words? Can such sentiments be resolved?

The now infamous summer-of-love idea was conceived in the spring of 2020 by then-Seattle Mayor Jenny Durkan to create a police-free protest zone. This was done not specifically in response to the George Floyd murder but to condone and encourage protest under the banner of freedom of speech.

But as protestors took up the George Floyd mantle, they became violent, overwhelming the police response. Two people died, several were injured, and one woman reported she was raped. Graffiti, garbage, and damaged property dotted the landscape of the sixteen-block protest zone. As the protests and destruction spread over weeks, Mayor Durkan continued to defend the protestors' rights to be heard.

The father of one of the victims, a nineteen-year-old man shot and killed, filed a lawsuit against the city and its administrators, which alleged: "Despite having knowledge of exactly what is happening at CHOP by being there every day and in apparently constant contact with area residents and business owners, the city acted with deliberate indifference toward the safety and care of residents and the public." The lawsuit quotes a Durkan tweet saying that CHOP "is not a lawless wasteland of anarchist insurrection—it is a peaceful expression of our community's collective grief and their desire to build a better world," referring to the outpouring of anger and sorrow over the murder of George Floyd, which sparked anti-police protests nationwide."[15]

Mayor Durkan later canceled the summer of love and ordered police to return to the protest district. But her actions did not occur soon enough to fend off other lawsuits by property owners against the city claiming it unconstitutionally *took their property* by the lack of police presence and response. One lawsuit describes in harsh detail what the plaintiffs claimed they endured. "The complaint stresses the plaintiffs' support of free speech rights and the work of Black Lives Matter but reveals urban dystopia in CHOP much closer to the movie *Escape from New York* than the communal days of Woodstock."

According to the complaint, the CHOP activists used concrete barriers left behind by the police to blockade the neighborhood from police cars, garbage and recycling pickup trucks, and other vehicles. Armed activists effectively decided who could enter CHOP. The police stopped responding to emergency calls except those involving the most serious safety threats, and even then, the responses were slow. Incidents of arson and assault went without a police response.

Over one weekend three people, all black men, were shot in CHOP, and one died. When the Seattle police showed up, they were prevented by CHOP protesters from quickly reaching one of the victims. In the absence of police investigators, private individuals took it on themselves to search for bullet casings. So far, no one has been charged in these shootings.

Meanwhile, garbage piled up, graffiti covered storefronts, music and fireworks prevented residents from sleeping, and the local park became a drug-use haven. People on crutches who needed physical therapy could not get to their therapist in the CHOP zone because of the barricades. A maintenance worker who tried to remove graffiti was threatened. Employees of local businesses stopped coming to work because they did not feel safe, which financially jeopardized the businesses. Residential condominiums had to hire armed guards. One Monday morning, there were two more shootings, leaving one *dead and a fourteen-year-old in critical condition.* "[16]

The city of Seattle's response to the summer of love chaos was to move three million dollars from the police department budget to social programs. Partly as a result, the number of police officers in the department continues to decline. The state of Washington responded in a similar fashion. New laws enacted in July 2021 limit the police use of tear gas to special circumstances and situations, bans law enforcement agencies from acquiring or using military equipment, and substantially limit the way a police officer can use force.

The state of Oregon has passed similar laws restricting police. The consequences were immediate. After a group of self-described anarchists caused a half-million dollars in damages in October 2021, Portland police acknowledged that a new state law prevented them from intervening.

A Portland business owner described the destruction from a March 2021, riot. "There was graffiti and smashed windows [one] night after a march turned into a destructive vandalism spree." Some of the targets: a Starbucks and Umpqua Bank. One business owner said they knew the destruction was coming. "We knew this was going to happen," said Jim Rice. "I spent Tuesday through Thursday communicating with anyone that would listen, begging for help." Rice and his wife own a local restaurant and had a window broken. That prompted them to board up for what they saw coming the following day.

The restaurant employs eighteen people and is trying to make a comeback with a partial reopening after COVID-19 closures. "Only for us to be hit with this group coming in and destroying our neighborhood, forcing us to react by putting up boards and protections for our business that we really don't have the money to invest in," said Rice.

Rice knows frustration is widespread. "I'm frustrated but you should hear some of the community around here," he said. "Yesterday, all day long, we had people coming in and sharing their piece. Their stories of what they experienced. Their shock. Their frustration."[17]

Consider this story from Stan Penkin, the chair of the Pearl District Neighborhood Association. Penkin, a baby-boomer liberal from New York, moved to Portland because it was "culturally and politically aligned with our values . . . and the Pearl [District] specifically because it's a mixed-use urban area with excellent accessibility, with some comparison to New York, although far less dense." The Pearl District was the target of multiple destructive protests.

Now, Penkin is trying to create a coalition of what he calls the "silent moderacy," people left and right of center who value public safety and strong civic institutions. He worked for the election of a moderate candidate for city council. He writes opinion pieces critical of cuts in police funding and the elimination of programs that promote public safety. And he regrets that, as a liberal, "We are seeing the dangers of the left side of this. So much has gone too far to the left. Political correctness rules . . . People are tired of this extreme."

Penkin and others have run out of patience. Consider his explanation. It provides some historical and geographic context as to why Portland and Seattle are the way they are. Here is his quote:[18]

> "My original reaction to BLM was positive, in terms of those who were legitimately protesting on behalf of BLM, but unfortunately, it was seen as an opportunity by those who would want to cause destruction to insert themselves. And it just created chaos as I think you know. And that's unfortunate.

> I think historically it's always been supportive of protests, but I know that long before I arrived here, there were elements of... and I don't know what it would have been called at the time. I heard it when I moved here, heard it referred to as anarchists. There was a group of anarchists who found Portland a comfortable place to express their ideas, or lack of ideas, and then it was always some element of the far-right white supremacists.
>
> We're adjacent to Idaho where we know back in the day, where the skinheads existed. So, I think some of that just became a confluence point for some reason, and I think partly because it's a place that is open and liberal and just creates a friendly environment, I guess, for legitimate protest."

After more than a year of protests, there was a pause and Penkin was hopeful. But more violent events broke out in August and again in October 2021. Hundreds of far-left and far-right protestors gathered in various parts of Portland, hurling paintballs, chemicals, and fireworks, and confronting each other with violence. Again, Portland Police declined to intervene. "Portland's Bizarre Experiment,"[19] "Anarchy in Portland, Political Leaders Yawn,"[20] "Portland Police Give Up, Proud Boys, Antifa Brawl"[21] are just some of the headlines that followed, along with demands and questions from Portland citizens. Citizen response included the exasperated reaction from Mr. Penkin:[22]

> "Things had quieted down for a while, and we were so hoping that we can bring the downtown core back, and every time something like this happens, it's a huge setback. And, when businesses start taking the plywood off their windows, and opening up, and cleaning up the graffiti and all of that, and then we have another protest, and I wouldn't even call it protest. That was not a protest. That -that was pure riot, yeah. And it hurts us tremendously in the eyes of the entire world. Let alone the eyes of those of us who live here."

Clearly, the defunding *idea* has been a disaster. While exact numbers are hard to verify, nearly half of 258 police agencies surveyed by the Police

Executive Research Forum (PERF), a Washington, DC, think tank, said their budgets had been cut or were likely to be cut. The cuts hit purchases of new police equipment hardest, followed by training, hiring new officers, and overtime spending.[23]

As police budgets were being cut, activists encouraged burning down police stations. Showing a photo of the burnt-out police precinct in Minneapolis, the group CrimethInc. (which describes itself as a decentralized anarchist collective of autonomous cells) posted on *Twitter* saying, "when we say abolish the police, we don't mean beg politicians to defund them. We mean take grassroots action to prevent them from continuing to do harm—until flowers grow in the wreckage of their system." The post continued, "abolishing the police means developing ways to resolve conflicts and address crises that do not depend on concentrating all coercive force into unaccountable institutions. It is a project that extends from our interpersonal relationships to mass action against state violence."[24]

The desire to affect change is not limited to politicians and anarchists. It is also supported by some big-money donors. The Open Society Policy Center, an advocacy nonprofit in the George Soros network, provided a $500,000 donation to a Minneapolis ballot initiative to amend the city charter to replace the police department. Though this initiative failed (largely due to the increase in crime and disorder), it was backed by a coalition of at least thirty-three activist organizations and collected more than $1 million in total cash (with Soros' being the most significant contribution). Other contributors included $430,000 in in-kind contributions from the Washington, DC-based MoveOn.org, providing staffing, access to email lists, and other services. The American Civil Liberties Union (ACLU) added $75,000 in cash and $4,000 in staff time.[25]

The impact of the "defunding" movement directly affected police departments and communities served by them. For example, Seattle Police Chief Adrian Diaz describes how "amidst often hostile rhetoric," the department "experienced an unprecedented exodus of officers to other jurisdictions." Since Jan. 1, 2020, to August 29, 2021, some 287 Seattle cops have retired or resigned. The Seattle Police Department said that the "demand for services is occurring during a staggering loss of number of officers in a short period."

This caused an increase in response time. Reduced resources coincided with increases in emergency calls, including higher levels of gun violence and homicide. Ironically, because of budget cuts and staff shortages, "essentially there is no community policing happening in Seattle." So, budget and staff cuts result in increased crime, higher response times, reduced service provision, and little or no community policing. All this in the quest to defund the police. The federal consent decree monitor for Seattle commented that "there's only so much a federal monitor and judge can do if Seattle's political leaders won't help." Judge Robart who supervises the consent decree added:[26]

> "The city and the mayor and other elected officials and the City Council need to be constructive, not destructive to progress. I have seen *too much of knee-jerk reaction and not enough forethought.* We have to be diligent in continuing to reduce bias and disparities. At the same time, we need to recognize public safety is an imperative for all residents and communities (emphasis added)."

Stories with this theme played out across the country as defunding and reimagining became a reality. As crime and disorder rose, so did the clamor to "undo" these ideas. In just a few examples, in New York City, $92 million was reinstated to fund a new police precinct after scrapping the project during the summer of 2020. The mayor of Baltimore, who previously led efforts to cut the police budget by $22 million, subsequently proposed a $27 million increase. In Oakland, following attacks on Asian-Americans and a rise in homicides, policymakers restored $3.3 million of the $29 million in police cuts, with another proposed increase of $24 million. Los Angeles's mayor has proposed an increase of about $50 million after the city cut $150 million from its police department the previous year. In Minneapolis, the city cut $8 million from the department in 2020, only to restore $6.4 million to hire new officers amid mass retirements and rising crime.[27]

To add insult to injury, after the smoke cleared from this debacle, research suggests that people did not want the defunding movement in the first place. For example, Seattle University conducted what it calls the Seattle Public

Safety Survey where it asks residents questions related to policing. People are saying "they want *more*, not fewer police," said Professor Jacqueline Helfgott, the study's principal author. Respondents were asked to rate their perceptions of various public-safety issues on a scale from 0 to 100. The study showed that white respondents rated police legitimacy lower on average than any other racial/ethnic group, at 57.5 (Black respondents rated police legitimacy at 61.3).[28] So, black residents trust the police more than white. Surely this study was proclaimed far and wide . . .?

We could go into more details but suffice to say that the defunding idea has not gone well. The bottom line—no pun intended—is this: Cut police funding, and you get less policing. Austin Police Department is a case in point. Beginning in October 2021, the department asked the public *not to call 911* for the following incidents:[29]

- "Non-emergency situations" if "there is no immediate threat to life or property
- Crimes that are no longer "in progress" (i.e., happening now)
- When the suspect(s) are no longer on the scene or in sight
- Applies to burglaries, thefts, prostitution, vandalism, and several other crimes

Instead, both victims and witnesses were urged to call 311 or file a report online. Austin Chief of Police Joseph Chacon noted this policy is in large part "a result of recent staffing challenges that we have had . . . we are looking to see how we can deploy staff in the most appropriate manner and respond to those calls that need them the most." The service adjustments will be exasperated as three cadet classes were canceled and 150 officers were cut from the budget. The *Wall Street Journal* noted that the department is down about 300 sworn officers since the beginning of 2020, with 200 vacancies and an additional 96 officers on long-term medical, military leave, or restricted duty.

Looking at these numbers, their conclusion is consistent with a key theme of this book: *It's easy to defund and demoralize a police department but harder to rebuild one.*[30]

Meanwhile, some progressives who were instrumental in defunding police are buying their own security. Take for example, "the squad." Most will know the squad refers to four progressive congresswomen who have banded together to fight the socialist fight. Each supported defunding the police, in both vocal and legislative means. Alexandria Ocasio-Cortez (AOC) said a month after George Floyd's death: "Defunding police means defunding police." Massachusetts Congresswoman Ayanna Pressley said in a July 2021 *Facebook* video that she stands "ready to continue the systemic work necessary to radically reimagine a system of public safety in our country that finally censures the dignity and humanity of all." Minnesota Congresswoman Ilhan Omar said on *CNN* that Minneapolis must "rebuild" its police department, describing it as "rotten to the root and impossible to reform."[31]

Their rhetoric also reflects their legislative agenda. Here is a sampling of bills sponsored (or co-sponsored) by Pressley:[32]

> BREATHE Act: Seeks the total elimination of federal law enforcement agencies, particularly those assigned to curtail illegal drug and immigration activities. Initially apply only at the federal level but would ultimately affect state and local policing.
>
> Ending Qualified Immunity Act: Makes it easier for individuals to sue state and local officials, primarily police.

Pressley and Bush are also among the sponsors of this bill:

> People's Response Act: Designed to create a public-safety agency within the Department of Health and Human Services, replacing incarceration in favor of health-based alternatives.

Given their words and the proposed legislation seeking to defund, shut down, or make police more exposed to lawsuits, one could conclude that *the squad* did not need the police—that they abhor any supposed protection they bring. Taking police off the streets via defunding was their quest. If this leads to rising crime and disorderly behavior, well, it is a small price to pay for the larger goal of ridding society of racist and white supremacist cops. People living in the communities would be safe from racist cops, and they ought to be grateful for the valent efforts of *the squad.* This is what *the squad* wants you to believe.

But *the squad* is different. They are not subject to their own legislation. Their soundbite, mantra-based, and meaningless words are for public consumption. But these words are not to be taken too literally—at least as they relate to the lives of squad members.

Between April 15 and June 28, 2021, Bush spent nearly $70,000 of her campaign funds on personal security—the highest expenditure in Congress. Even more astonishing are these security costs compared to her constituent's income levels. Bush spent almost $20,000 *above* the median household income for residents in her district! She did so in a little over two-plus months. Hypocrisy has no limits.

Let me restate this for emphasis: Bush paid more money for her own security than her constituents annually earn, while "the people" pay taxes for police protection that is being systematically taken away. You can't make this up. But it gets worse. Did Bush apologize and say she would change her ways? Of course not. She doubled down, describing herself as a:[33]

> "black woman who puts her life on the line," claiming that white supremacists, including cops, have made threats and "racist attempts" on her life, and that her "*body is worth being on this planet right now* (emphasis added)."

Bush went on to suggest that people would have to "suck it up" because "defunding the police has to happen. We need to defund the police and put that money into social safety nets because we're trying to save lives."[34]

Meanwhile, AOC spent about $50,000 on security during the first half of 2021. Pressley spent almost $8,000 in the first half of 2021, while Omar spent just less than $6,000 in the same timeframe.

Finally, the newest squad member, New York Congressman Jamaal Bowman, who has called cops agents of "white supremacy," has requested the Yonkers Police Department to provide extra protection for his home. Keith Olson, Yonkers Police Benevolent Association president, summarized the hypocrisy when he aptly compared his words and his actions:[35]

"Not long ago, the congressman called for dramatically less policing in the most violent, crime-ridden neighborhoods . . . Asking these same police officers to protect your family while creating policies that make communities of color less safe is simply disgraceful." Here's to *the squad*! The politics of "good for thee, but not for me!"

LEGISLATION & PROSECUTION DECISIONS

This section will highlight the progressive legislation and prosecutorial policies behind the criminal justice *reform* movement. As stated in the setup, this movement commenced several years ago but gained momentum during the summer of 2020. A few examples to illustrate this thinking and the impact of such "reforms" will be highlighted.

Let's recall that progressives believe that since laws are inequitable, devised to maintain the racist system, holding down blacks and other minorities, the natural solution would be to "decriminalize" minor crimes, which are not worthy to be enforced anyway. Indeed, since enforcement of these crimes disproportionately affects blacks and other minorities, one way to diminish or negate such disparate treatment is to change these laws or stop enforcing them. Both approaches were used. Progressive legislators changed laws. Progressive prosecutors changed office policies relating to charging decisions. Essentially, this was dual.

By changing laws and by changing charging policies, the criminal justice system could be "reformed" from the inside. These also took power away from *racist* cops. By making certain behaviors no longer "criminal" (or lowering the repercussion from a felony to a misdemeanor), police have less authority to enforce and less discretion to abuse. Further, by reducing the number of arrests, the court system would reduce its backlog—and the jails would be depopulated. Mass incarceration would end. People would be freed from the draconian criminal justice system, which has been used to support the systemically racist society.

On one level, the desire to divert people away from the criminal justice system was a worthy goal. The system tends to operate like an assembly line.

Police arrest suspects, who are processed and charged, then appear in court, go through bond hearings and arraignment, then through discovery with the intent to "plea bargain" the case away from trial. Very few cases go to trial, usually less than five percent. So, through this process, the individual is subject to a series of discretionary decisions based on prosecutorial policies, court procedures, the relative backlog of the court docket, jail space, and a host of other administrative and bureaucratic limitations. Simply stated, the system is often overloaded and overwhelmed, making it hard to manage all the nuanced—but important—decisions that are made daily.

Participants in the system often cope by seeing people as *just another case*. So many individuals, so many cases. So little time to understand exactly what happened and why. The default position is to just keep them moving. Move defendants through the system. Getting bogged down on any case or trying to get "inside the head" of any individual defendant is too difficult, too time-consuming, too complicated.

To be clear, this explanation is not to impugn those in the system. The vast majority work hard and try to help as much as they are able. Yet, time constraints and the limitations of job descriptions usually prevent a great deal of personal involvement.

The influences and pulls on the individual from *outside* the system are more pronounced. These are typically stronger and more impactful than anything that can be countered from within the system. In short, what matters most is usually not found—or possible coming from a bureaucracy, even when the participants have good intentions.

What the system *can* do is get the attention of those who are going in the wrong direction. Sometimes this is enough to show individuals where they are headed in life. For most people, however, forces and influences outside the system are stronger and more impactive than what the system can counteract. Many of these people are inevitably incarcerated. The aggregate of hundreds of thousands of these cases leads to "mass incarceration." Taking people off the streets, thus, is often the best that the system can do. Because it has a limited capacity to "change lives," progressives seek to divert people away from the system.

Consider what Joe Gonzales, the Bexar County, Texas District Attorney, told *NBC News*: "I believe the jail is for people that we're afraid of, not for people that commit minor offenses that are nonviolent." He elaborated: "one of the reasons that I believe in restorative justice is because punishment, like life, is gray, it's not just black and white. There's a lot of gray, and there's a lot of opportunity for someone like me to give people a second chance."[36]

I agree with his sentiment. Most people would also agree. Yet, it is much more complicated. Most people would be happy "giving people a second chance." The problem comes with multiple chances. When does diversion give way to incarceration? This is also gray. This is where judgment, experience, and time prevail. Again, when dealing with overwhelmed and often understaffed circumstances, one can predict the *gray* will get very difficult to manage.

Without getting too sociological, dealing with youths (typically males) during what is considered the "criminogenic" years, usually from the middle teens to the mid-twenties, used to be the target population of the system. As people age, they tend to *divert themselves* from crime. During the criminogenic years, however, they are both more prone to committing crimes and more visible to those who enforce laws. Hence, police tend to engage this age group because they spend more time on the street, thereby making them more visible *and* more likely to violate criminal laws. The typical legal basis of police engagement is traffic enforcement, disorderly behavior on the streets, and drug use and possession.

In conclusion, *the system cannot change the lives of young people*. The influences they face are too big for the criminal justice system. I believe the answer goes to family, culture, and education. Yet, these take consistent effort and are hard to establish. So, the "vicious circle" continues. If positive influences of life, such as family, culture, and education (and in many cases religion and sports) are not sufficient to draw the person away from crime, then they will be subject to the *depersonalization* inherent in the system. From the perspective of *law abiders* who are trying to make their way through life, getting *law violators* off the streets and preventing them from committing crimes may be the only way to cope as a society.

Progressives see the limitations of the criminal justice system and seek those who were *subject to* the system be *diverted from* the system. This is a two-fold approach. Diverting people *from the system* will inevitably put *pressure on* the system. Pressures will be in the form of increased crime and increased disorder. Progressives must know this end game. By diverting people away from enforcement and prosecution of criminal laws, or allowing them to be released without bond, they understand these were simply "band-aids." These are not "solutions" to anything—unless one desires to change the system from the inside. Which is their stated goal.

Hence the dual strategy: change laws and change charging policies. A perfect example is California's Proposition 47, which amended the California penal code, Section 490.2, to lower penalties for certain thefts. The 2014 law provides that theft of property valued at less than $950 is punishable as a misdemeanor, with a fine of up to $1000 or six months in jail. This law directly affects shoplifting—which then spurred mass and strategic thefts designed to steal items valued below $950, thereby avoiding felony charges.

If arrested, a misdemeanor charge is simply a slap on the wrist. No need to be afraid of this charge, as the system has no real remedy for shoplifting. People know there is no desire to incarcerate them. Restitution is nearly impossible when people have little or no ability to repay. Further, the system will be hard-pressed to cope with the volume of cases from widespread shoplifting. All this *tells* offenders they will not be hurt by the system—no bond, no restitution, no jail time—NO problem.

The result is more shoplifting. The incentive is to steal more. Rationally, this is the message that is being communicated. People on the street read this very well. They are very good at discerning the ways of the system and manipulating it for all it is worth. Consequently, strategic shoplifting has grown to "smash-and-grabs."

Criminals will continue to push the envelope until they are stopped. There is no "governor" to this thinking. It is rational yet sinister. So is the thinking of the progressive legislators and prosecutors. If they cannot think through the logical result of their policy decisions, then they are either too inept or incapable to do the job they are paid to do. Yet, I believe they understand very well what they are doing. Connect the dots from prior chapters. See how these issues weave through as a mindset, as a worldview, as an ideological endeavor for a larger purpose. We have described this conceptually, and here we see the real-world application of such thinking. One retailer made this clear: "this is a real issue that hurts and scares real people, [it] is traumatizing for our associates and is unacceptable."[37]

This goes beyond shoplifting. Changes in laws also affected the enforcement of other crimes. Police discretion was limited regarding vehicle pursuits. Vehicle burglaries must now prove the car was locked. Police use of force restrictions were also enacted. All of these enable people intending to take advantage of the system.

- If police seek to pull your car over, just speed away. Vehicle pursuits are restricted—even prohibited.
- Go ahead, steal from vehicles. It is nearly impossible to "prove beyond a reasonable doubt" that the vehicle was *in fact* locked.

This is a simple cost-benefit analysis for prosecutors. Even those who *want to do the right thing* will avoid taking such cases to trial. It is extraordinarily difficult to prove that the car was locked. Even breaking the vehicle's window does not "prove" that the vehicle was locked. Testimony from the owner that the vehicle was locked can be questioned by a good defense attorney, creating reasonable doubt as to the memory and habits of the vehicle owner.

While this may sound too much like "inside baseball," the reality is when legislators make it more difficult to prove the elements of a crime, overworked prosecutors will hesitate to charge these cases—and almost ensure they do not go to trial. Too uncertain, too difficult to prove, a "waste" of prosecution time and effort. Consequently, what this says is *the flaw lies within the laws themselves*. Get this and understand the implications of such.

The conclusion: The legislative intent . . . and the unintended (or intended) consequences have started the domino into a very hazardous and uncertain future. Cities downplay (or try to ignore) things that used to be crimes, such as shoplifting, thefts from vehicles, and public disorderly behavior such as drug use and urinating/defecating on streets—while fining people for not wearing masks.

People who do not wear masks are easier to manage—and more apt to pay their fines. Those who commit disorderly acts are often too disoriented or too poor to fine. There is a saying in the law: some people are *judgment proof.* They are immune because they have nothing to lose. It is not practical to pursue those who have nothing, so the tendency is to squeeze what you can from those who have something. It is a vicious cycle—and it leads to two inevitable results: It incentivizes those who are inclined to *violate* the law, and it makes the law appear illegitimate to those who are inclined to *abide* the law. This is exactly the opposite of what the law is designed to do. This is where we are in contemporary America.

Let's bring more reality to the text. The following examples are illustrative of the incentives given to rational people when they are given a "license to steal." These are by no means exhaustive. By the time you read this book, circumstances may have gotten worse, or as I hope, reasonable people will have interceded to diminish or negate perverse incentives offered by progressives.

Consider that Walgreens has hired off-duty police officers to guard its San Francisco stores. These stores spend many times more on security than Walgreen's nationwide average. Estimates range from 35–45 percent more for security.[38] Yet, the San Francisco stores endure five times greater cost of theft than their national average. Near the end of 2021, Walgreens closed at least five of its stores in the city, bringing the total number of closings to twenty-two since 2016.[39]

True to form, like the Chicago mayor, San Francisco Mayor London Breed said that San Francisco's drugstore market was "saturated," limiting profitability. A member of the Board of Supervisors, Dean Preston, a self-described democratic socialist, went a step further. He tweeted that Walgreens has "long planned to close hundreds of locations," but "media reports have accepted without analysis Walgreens' assertion that it's closing due to retail theft."[40] Jason Riley notes that this justification does not hold water, as other large retailers had similar problems. For example, a spokesman for CVS, which has closed at least two stores, told CNN that of its 155 locations in the Bay Area, the twelve in San Francisco account for 26 percent of all shoplifting incidents in the region.

One reason why San Francisco is worse than the rest can be attributed to its local prosecutor. San Francisco District Attorney Chesa Boudin's life is a case study in progressive politics. His parents were part of the notorious Weather Underground group from the 1960s–70s. They were convicted of violent crimes and sentenced to decades in prison. Boudin was then raised by two other radicals, the founder of the Weather Underground Bill Ayers and his wife, Bernardine Dohrn. Both of whom were federal fugitives in the 1970s.[41]

You may remember Bill Ayers as Barack Obama's friend from Chicago. Ayers famously hosted Obama's first campaign fundraiser at his home in Chicago. Bill Ayers worked as a professor at the University of Illinois at Chicago, where I obtained a doctorate in public policy and a master's in criminal justice. I did not know him but knew he was a highly regarded man on campus. One can only wonder what lessons he taught young Chesa. With his parents in prison and fellow Weather Underground fugitives as adopted parents, it is predictable that Boudin would have progressive, socialist values.

Regardless of his background, the work product of Boudin as a prosecutor has been riddled with controversy. As of October 2021, at least fifty lawyers from Boudin's office quit or were fired since he became district attorney in January of 2020. This represents roughly a third of the department's attorneys. Boudin is facing his second recall election as this book is written.

Two high-profile prosecutors quit to join the recall efforts. Their narrative is devastating. Prosecutor Brooke Jenkins detailed Boudin's "radical approach that involves not charging crime in the first place and simply releasing individuals with no rehabilitation and putting them in positions where they are simply more likely to re-offend." Ms. Jenkins emphasizes that "being an African American and Latino woman, I would wholeheartedly agree that the criminal justice system needs a lot of work, but when you are a district attorney, your job is to have balance."[42] The other prosecutor who resigned, Don Du Bain, added that he believed Boudin "disregards the laws that he doesn't like, and he disregards the court decisions that he doesn't like to impose his own version of what he believes is just—and that's not the job of the district attorney."[43]

"Police are the bad guys, and the bad guys are the good guys in the mind of a progressive," said San Francisco Police Officers Association President Tony Montoya. With drug markets and homelessness flourishing and with violence increasing, he adds that citizens are "starting to wake up to the reality that's now become their nightmare as far as public safety and crime goes."[44]

Tracy McCray, vice president of the San Francisco Police Officers Association, asserts that district attorney Chesa Boudin's "insistence on dropping or downgrading charges of those caught red-handed" has allowed "those very same crooks to further victimize our communities over and over again."[45]

The result is that businesses are faced with a double-edged sword—and a stark choice. They can tolerate anarchy and theft. Or they can shut down. If they decide to stay open, they face significant security costs to "guard" their store.

However, guarding the store comes with its own consequences—beyond the costs of paying for security. Trying to stop shoplifting often results in allegations of racial profiling and/or the threat of lawsuits. Guards who confront shoplifters have been assaulted and threatened. Adding to this mix, paying for security guards that cannot deter or confront is not cost-effective. Paying security guards to *watch* shoplifters steal is hard to justify. As ridiculous as this sounds, it often is the reality. Getting descriptions of the offenders and their images with security cameras has some value, but this, in turn, is dependent on the police taking the initiative of investigating and making arrests. It also depends on the prosecutor's cooperation. As discussed earlier, this is not to be expected—at least in many jurisdictions.

This same dynamic is occurring elsewhere. Consider that survey from the National Retail Federation, which revealed that the average cost of crime rose five years in a row, amounting to a 60-percent (approx.) increase since 2015.[46] Of course, the cost of "shrinkage" must be accounted for. Inevitably, these are passed on to consumers.

Because shrinkage is not the same in all locations, shoplifting tends to be greater in urban areas. For example, Target has closed stores in predominantly black sections of Chicago, Milwaukee, and Flint, Michigan. These decisions came from increased store thefts but also from rioting, looting, and violent anti-police protests. Closures can have a detrimental impact on the communities and most directly on those who are least able to find suitable alternatives.

Think of the single mother without a car who has lost access to food, medicine, and other essentials. These are seldom spoken, usually overlooked implications of progressive policies. Policies allegedly seeking to help are often very costly. Poor people are also least able to absorb the costs. Jason Riley makes this powerful connection:

> "But indulging criminal behavior in the name of 'social justice' only helps criminals, who are not representative of all blacks. *Public policies that give priority to the interests of lawbreakers only lead to more lawbreaking, and by extension to more economic inequality.* Businesses have every incentive to flee these communities and the jobs follow them [emphasis added above and below].
>
> Tempting though it may be to blame the social dysfunction in poorer communities on heartless business owners or racists cops, the *bigger blame surely lies with public policies that condone counterproductive behavior and make successful businesses much more difficult to operate.*"

Riley also connects back to the riots in the 1960s, which left many communities in ruins. Businesses fled thereafter, usually never to return. The fallout from the summer 2020 and the continuing saga over progressive policies has been all too predictable. We are seeing companies leaving urban areas just like after the riots of the 1960s. Time will tell how long and widespread this may be. But one thing is certain: Until the rule of law is restored and enforced, *cities that tolerate such public disorder will get more of it.*

Yet, progressives will not get this message—or as stated previously, they have a completely different purpose. Ironically, as Boudin faces recall, he participated in a national organizing call for the group "Our Revolution." The group was "celebrating five years of electing progressive champions from coast to coast."[47] Can you see their larger agenda?

If one believes that crime is ultimately the fault of law enforcement (and not criminals), it becomes an "article of faith" to believe that fewer cops and fewer prosecutions are the key to safer communities. As we have seen throughout the text, the ideology of progressives is to forward "reform" policies. Though some say this approach is supported by data, the Sacramento-based Criminal Justice Legal Foundation calls into question whether progressives are in fact "following the science." Their conclusion should give us pause:[48]

> "The US criminal justice system has a lengthy history of rapidly implementing sweeping policy change without comprehensively considering the potential effects, often resulting in damaging consequences that are difficult if not impossible to reverse."

POLICE POLICIES

Using the same approach as above, this section will use examples of the current state of policing. The goal is to paint a picture of how the events of 2020, commencing with George Floyd's murder, have affected policing—and how police departments have reacted. This extends to what the immediate future of policing may look like.

Let's start with the reimagining policing mantra. As analyzed and dissected earlier, this mantra does not mean anything. Mouthing sound bites of something impossible to define and quantify has no real value beyond the purpose that it was devised. *It was a way to change policing—and society, without saying so.* It's a deceptive tool to accomplish what few people would knowingly desire. It sounded good but was not even close to describing the road ahead (the next chapter will outline what policing could look like). Because the progressives failed to do more than mouth the mantra, let's create a picture of what policing looks like now, and what it may look like in the years ahead.

As a summary statement, there are several issues that are directly affected by policing. Each of these is connected to proactive policing, including:

- Ending "broken windows" and quality of life policing
- Disbanding proactive anticrime units

- Instituting traffic enforcement restrictions or prohibitions
- Limiting or preventing pursuits, both vehicle and foot
- Issuing stand-down Orders
- Restricting the use of force options

These changes have one underlying theme. They all limit police powers. This does not mean taking away their legal authority, though that may later occur. More accurately, it entails limiting what they are allowed to do as per internal policies.

Policies are driven by the leadership within each department. Since leaders in local police departments are appointed by the politicians in each city, one can expect that police leaders are politically or ideologically in accord with those who selected them. Even if they are not, they would be expected to adhere to the directives given to them by their political leaders. This is not wrong. Leaders have every right to choose those who will adhere to their vision and directives. No quarrel with this.

You probably know where we are going. If progressive leaders pick police leadership, one can expect police department policies will reflect the values and mindset of the political leadership. Since most political leaders in urban environments are liberal, and more likely progressive, one can expect their policies to be implemented in the cities they lead. The policies cited above are reflective of what I call "reactive policing." The common theme of each is to avoid direct, proactive engagement with citizens.

As a former tactical police officer who spent most of my time being proactive, my conclusion is this simple reality: When police officers decide to engage, either at a traffic stop or on a street encounter, the citizen typically knows that the officer did this on his or her own accord. The officer made the decision. They were not assigned by a supervisor, nor did someone call the police to ask them to do so.

This distinction is crucial. When this occurs, the citizen who was stopped often asks the question: Why are you stopping me? This is a legitimate question, yet it's a loaded question. It's legitimate because everyone who is stopped deserves to know why. The *why*, however, in this racially charged environment is usually attributed to racism.

Let me paint what this typically involves. When a black person is stopped, the allegation is often: "You stopped me because I am black." Working high-crime areas on the south side of Chicago, my response was to say, "look around, everyone around here is black." "Do you see anyone else who is not black?" The answer was usually no or no response. My point is (and was) this is not about being black; this is about the law and my job is to enforce the law. The typical response was, "Well why don't you bother someone who is violating the law?" This interaction would often go back and forth. Cutting through the chaff, the conversation would ultimately lead to this conclusion: *It is not about black or white; it is about right or wrong.*

These stops and encounters are loaded with racial accusations. Accusing the police officer of being a racist is a *strategy* used by some to dissuade police from proactive policing. Gang members even target active cops with "racist tags." These allegations are almost impossible to prove in a street encounter (at least prior to body cameras). Even black police officers are subject to criticism that must be hard to hear. How would you react if you were called a "race traitor," "Uncle Tom," and supporter of white supremacy—and hear this daily? This is said not to complain but to explain.

Because race is so loaded and potentially volatile, the "simpler" answer is to avoid these encounters. Hence, reactive policing policies, like those bulleted above, are designed to diminish the potential of racial incidents. By avoiding proactive stops and encounters, difficult conversations as described are diminished. These situations can go bad quickly, particularly if the officer or the citizen is having a "bad day." Of course, police officers have days when they are not as tolerant and professional as they should be. This is the reality of life. No one in any job can maintain an optimal level of emotional control. When the citizen resists or incites, things can quickly get complicated, even volatile.

This explains why reactive policing has now become the norm. These policies are not effective for crime prevention, but they can *reduce the potential for racial strife* (at least for a time). Yet, these reactive policies are much more damaging than they are useful. Here's why.

First, reactive policing negatively impacts the ability to intercede and prevent crime. The message is this: When those who intend to commit crime believe police will not engage them, they are emboldened. Recall the logic of the street. Those who frequent—and often rule—streets know very well what they can get away with. If they believe the police will not engage, they will be more inclined to carry guns and drugs and seek opportunities to commit crimes.

Second, while reactive policing reduces the number of police encounters with citizens, it does not diminish the racial undertones when police and citizens *do* interact. These policies lessen the *number* of encounters, but the *mindset* of the encounter would not change.

Third, reactive policing will lead to increased crime. Not only will criminals understand that they now "rule" the street, but they will also take this as a license to commit crimes. Understand this. A delicate balance for control of the streets takes place in many areas of this country. Too much police power will be seen as repressive. Too little police power will be seen as weakness. Somewhere in the middle is the optimal balance. The balance, like all other areas of life, requires constant resetting and recalibration. Going too far in either direction will cause a predictable response: Either more crime or more racial strife.

Currently, policies are driving more crime. Racial strife is deemed so risky that the *preference* is more crime. Of course, this presupposes that the policymakers do not *actually want more* crime and chaos (which is more likely than not). Consider this point in light of what Maxine Waters, a sitting US congresswoman said *during* the Derek Chauvin trial for the murder of George Floyd:[49]

> "We've got to stay in the street and we've got to get more active. We've Got to get more confrontational. We've got to make sure that they know that we mean business."

Though the trial judge criticized Water's comments, the congresswoman paid no consequence for making such explosive comments during the trial. Yet, she knows the impact this statement had on those on the streets. She spoke directly to the *logic* of the street. This is how policies interact and intersect with street logic. One must understand how each impacts the other. Unfortunately, what is typical is that policies are enacted without understanding street logic or they are *designed to support it.*

Now let's highlight certain policies and see how they play out in this dynamic. This should not be considered comprehensive, but as an overview as to why crime and chaos is increasing, and what should be done to remedy the current circumstances.

Disbanded Proactive Anti-Crime Units

As a pointed example, New York City disbanded its anti-crime units following controversies of excessive force and racial profiling. Cities around the country followed suit over the past few years. Without going too deep into the data or the issues, the one typical statistical deficiency is comparing the number (or percentage) of stops to demographic data. This is the wrong assessment. Yet, it is almost universally used as a comparative measure.

A typical study was also conducted by the Center for Policing Equity. The study assessed Seattle Police Department's data from 2014–to 2019 on stops and uses of force. It showed that *per capita*, Native Americans were stopped nearly nine times more than white people, and black people were stopped over five times more than white people. Specifically, Native Americans, account for only 0.5 percent of Seattle's population yet amounted to 3 percent of people stopped. Blacks, who make up 7 percent of Seattle's population, accounted for about one-third of SPD's stops. The report also shows that blacks were seven times more likely to be subjected to force by a police officer than whites.[50]

Using demographics instead of crime data queues the findings. I did a comparative analysis of the incidence of violent crime to race in *Terrorism and Public Safety Policing*. The data shows that blacks commit a disproportionate number of violent crimes as compared to their percentage of the population.[51] This data has been consistent for years. For example, Singleton noted that blacks committed 28 percent of the total crimes yet represent only 13 percent of the total population.[52]

Hence, using per capita data is deceiving. Since blacks commit a greater percentage of crimes, one can expect they would have a greater percentage of engagement with the police. Since police, at least until recently, focused on reducing the incidence of crime; we should not only expect but desire that police focus their limited time, attention, and resources where it would statistically have the greatest impact. Yet, this is now deemed wrong and racist. Study after study uses per-capita data to paint a picture of police discrimination. Crime rates are somewhat "lost" in these studies—and in the larger conversation of police proactive engagement.

What often happens is what the Seattle study recommended: that the police should record every pedestrian or vehicle stop and use-of-force incident, including:[53]

- Reason for the stop
- Type of stop
- Nature of the contact
- Type of force was used
- Information about the person including age, race, address

The collection of this information is not inherently wrong. But it creates yet another procedural and bureaucratic burden on already understaffed police officers. There is much that can be said but let me summarize with this conclusion: *The documentation requirement will result in fewer police stops and encounters.* Taking the time to record this information is one reason. Plus, the data can be subsequently used against active police officers, who will be compared to those less motivated. Inevitably, such comparisons will make the active officer's behavior appear *suspicious* while allowing the less-motivated officer to appear more *reasonable.* In short, it diminishes the incentive to do proactive police work. Without proactive policing, crime and disorder will increase. This is vicious cycle that many will resist any attempt to stop.

Another example was found in Portland. During the summer of 2020, Portland disbanded its gun violence unit. As crime predictably increased, the city sought to reinstitute the unit. Also, predictably, they found that police officers were not interested in joining the once elite unit. Since fourteen openings were announced in May of 2021, only four police personnel have applied, and none have been assigned.[54]

Here is the back story. Amid the uptick in gun violence, Portland Mayor Ted Wheeler proposed a new unit renamed the "Focused Initiative Team." The *Fox News* article describes that "uncertainty" related to the unit, including incorporating a citizen advisory board designed to oversee the unit's work. Of course, officers remember that city officials railed against the old unit for alleged racial profiling. To negate this concern going forward, the job qualifications for the new team include this ridiculous requirement: *Applicants must show the "ability to identify and dismantle institutional and systemic racism in the bureau's responses to gun violence."*[55]

So, does Portland want police officers to reduce crime, or do they what them to "dismantle institutional and systemic racism" in its anti-crime bureau? Do they want social workers and criminal justice researchers instead of tactical police officers?

Consistent with progressive thinking, this "analysis" does not admit that blacks commit a much greater percentage of the crimes. When Portland disbanded the old team in 2020, city officials cited data showing that 52 percent of stops conducted in 2019 were for blacks, who represent 5.8 percent of the city's population. But Jami Resch, assistant chief of the Portland Police Bureau's investigations branch, noted that the unit's past work was beneficial in minority communities, as shootings have disproportionately impacted the 23 percent of Portland's population that is non-white.

Other data reveal even more stark evidence. For example, blacks make up 83 percent of all homicide offenders in Chicago whose race is known *and* 83 percent of all homicide victims, though they constitute less than 30 percent of the city's population.[56] One way to limit or reduce homicides is through proactive policing. Catching criminals with guns before they use them would seem like a socially desirous goal . . .?

Once again, if this was not so serious, one can have fun with the illogical nature of progressive thinking. Here is how Daryl Turner, leader of the Portland Police Association described it: "They're demonizing and vilifying you, and then they want to put you in a unit where you're under an even bigger microscope."[57]

"Broken-Windows" & Quality-of-Life Policing

These will be defined and analyzed in the next chapter, but for our present purposes, consider the aim is to focus on relatively minor, disorderly crimes, which send a message that the police—and the public are serious about the rule of law.

A classic example of the importance of these can be seen in deteriorating conditions, homelessness, drug usage, and a host of other behaviors that lead to disorder and chaos. This was shown in graphic detail in Washington Square Park in New York City. This park was described as a *battle of wills* between the NYPD enforcing midnight curfew laws and revelers determined to "reclaim public space." The park was aptly described as "the misery of numerous addicts who call the park and nearby streets home; a world bathed in crack smoke, drenched in urine, murmuring with the fragmentary, delusional self-talk of lost souls."[58] This quote comes from a powerful article written by Sohrab Ahmari that you would be well advised to read in full.

He highlighted a compelling account of the people, the environment, and the attitudes of those who essentially took over the park for months:[59]

> "In the most generous telling, I think, that's the moral fire that animates the militant kids in the park. Something is profoundly wrong with urban America. It's sick. No one cares. This should prick the young conscience, any conscience.
>
> Yet the *defunders'* obsession with police violence, and the warmed-over critical theory that warps their thinking, serve to further obscure the source of the problem, a much deeper crisis of solidarity. Cops deal with the tail- end of the social crisis, and that means more police interactions with people like [names subject from the article] and, therefore, a higher likelihood of police-civilian violence . . ."

Ahmari goes on to describe that the "long-term solution is a recovery of a sane and genuine politics of solidarity, a recognition that some of our fellow citizens need more help, help they may not always accept or appreciate without a degree of humane coercion." Meanwhile, who will be there to pick up the pieces? The police, of course.

Because the chaos in the park grew increasingly controversial, then-Mayor de Blasio was questioned about illegal drinking, pot-smoking, and other behavior that contributed to the mayhem and numerous complaints. The mayor pretended to *rediscover broken windows policing,* which he had previously criticized and rejected. "There's more to do in making sure that we set the right parameters . . . we're starting to be able to focus on the quality-of-life concerns as well."

While this sounds good after the fact, the city council passed a bill that encouraged police to end arrests for quality-of-life offenses such as public drinking or public urination. This was *signed* by de Blasio. On his watch, city district attorneys also decided not to prosecute certain misdemeanor offenses.

As political pressures come from the predictable chaos, he says, "we're starting to be able to focus on the quality-of-life concerns as well." If he didn't shut down quality-of-life policing, maybe he would not be thinking of quality of life "concerns." So it goes. Shut down what maintained law and order, then have "concerns" about what inevitably occurs. This is the worldview of progressives. See the problem as the police, then subsequently ask the police to clean up the mess made by progressive policies.

The results have been predictable. In September 2021, more than 160 CEOs from prominent businesses warned about security and livability in New York. These corporate leaders complained of a "widespread anxiety over public safety, cleanliness, and other quality of life issues that are contributing to deteriorating conditions in commercial districts and neighborhoods across the five boroughs."[60]

Another big city that is struggling with quality-of-life policing is Philadelphia. Coming off a lawsuit over stop-and-frisk encounters, the department issued a new policy prohibiting issuing citations to or arresting individuals engaging in quality-of-life crimes. Instead, the officer is now required to initially engage in a *mere encounter* and request the individual stop engaging in the prohibited behavior. The policy stresses that during the *mere encounter,* the individual will not be detained and will be free to leave.

Officers are required to follow specific procedures, including:

- Activating body cameras.
- Notifying police dispatchers of the "mere encounter."
- Request individuals to stop doing the "quality of life" crime.
- Record the encounter and categorize the video as a "Mere Encounter –Quality of Life" incident.

The policy also stresses that its purpose is "not to abandon quality-of-life enforcement, but rather to provide offenders an opportunity to cease and desist such activities, prior to the issuance of any citations." Describing the policy as a "balanced approach," its goal is to "enable and address community complaints while striving to reduce or eliminate the racial disparity that has been associated with this type of enforcement."[61]

Ironically, the article noted that "at least half the department" doesn't have body cameras required to commence the *mere encounter*. Without these, they cannot even follow the first step of the new initiative. Amazing. The department institutes a new policy that cannot be followed by half its officers. Not surprisingly, Philly police officers do not believe the new program will stop people from committing quality-of-life crimes. This is progressive "window dressing." Pretend to care about quality-of-life policing, while enacting a policy that has little support and lacks the equipment to be fully operational.

Consider that these changes are supposed to be done to protect blacks from "over-policing." Opposition to such progressive policies is given voice in this quote: [62]

> "I cringe when I hear people say black communities are over-policed," Sandra Wortham, the sister of a slain Chicago police officer, My neighborhood is not over-policed. My lived experience has shown me that policing that tackles the small things prevents the big things."

Traffic Enforcement Restrictions or Prohibitions

In yet another attempt to limit the negative impact of racial controversies, police departments are even changing the way traffic laws are enforced. "No one should die over a traffic stop," said New York City Councilman Brad Lander. When lives are reduced to mantras, few disagree. Yet, the impact of traffic enforcement is crucially important to overall public safety.

Removing police from traffic enforcement is another progressive idea. For example, New York State Attorney General Letitia James has proposed that New York City police cease routine traffic stops. Berkeley, Calif., has banned officers from making stops for many traffic offenses, with Lansing, Mich., and the District of Columbia doing the same. They perceive the "solution" is to use unarmed civilian traffic agents, along with cameras to enforce the rules of the road. Though these have some value, high-crime areas *need* traffic enforcement.

The National Highway Traffic Safety Administration has studied the "nexus of crashes and crime" for decades. Its research has found this significant correlation: *Neighborhoods with the highest rates of fatal accidents also have the highest rates of violent crime.* [63] Consider the experience of Oakland where nearly 60 percent of fatalities and serious injuries occur on only 6 percent of the city's streets—which are overwhelmingly in minority neighborhoods. Blacks in Oakland are twice as likely as others to die or be severely injured in traffic incidents. Black pedestrians are three times as likely to die. Yet, Oakland police were ordered to decrease traffic enforcement following a Stanford study accusing them of racial profiling. The predictable result has been growing disorder. A city councilman reported that people sense a "general lawlessness and a lack of accountability for driving however you want." Traffic deaths were up 22 percent in Oakland in 2020. Most of the victims were black.[64]

Similarly, Milwaukee has documented the inverse correlation between car stops and nonfatal shootings, robberies, and car thefts. When traffic enforcement declines, those crimes increase," said a former police chief. He mentioned a "truism of policing," that I can attest to. Criminals "don't follow traffic laws or update their vehicle registration." The thinking goes like this.

If you are *willing and able* to commit murders, robberies, and car thefts, why would you care about violating traffic laws? The answer is they don't.

The human consequences are substantial. Consider this *plaintiff cry* by a high-school principal in Minnesota who publicly begged for more police enforcement after a student was fatally shot. "We are literally in a city that is completely and entirely out of control, I can see outright laws getting broken, traffic laws, people driving outright through red lights, speeding, going 60 to 70 miles per hour. We got kids on skateboards getting hit by cars."[65] Significantly, inadequate attention to traffic violations by police results in people feeling they "may break the law with impunity." This goes to "broken-windows" and "quality-of-life" policing. Minor law violations spur more serious crimes.

Traffic enforcement has a vivid history in this country. Since the first traffic fatality in 1899, approximately 3.9 million have died in traffic accidents. While it is too early to definitively know, something is causing a recent uptick in deaths and disorderly driving. Read this quote broken into sections related to this uptick:[66]

- "In 2020, despite lockdowns across the country, traffic fatalities spiked to their highest levels since 2007, with 38,680 deaths nationwide, according to the National Highway Traffic Safety Administration.
- But today something else is happening. If you've ventured out over the past year, especially in New York, you will see cars running stoplights, speed limits being ignored, motor scooters barreling down sidewalks and dodging pedestrians, and stop signs being treated as a mere suggestion.
- So even with fewer cars on the roads during the 2020 lockdown, 243 people were killed in traffic accidents in New York City, the deadliest year since Mayor Bill de Blasio introduced his grand plan for safer streets in 2014.
- Another baffling oddity: The city has more than 1,300 automated cameras to capture images of speeding cars. But the cameras were

> inexplicably turned off from 10 p.m. to 6 a.m., when one-third of the fatal crashes in 2020 took place."

The author makes this connection between the breakdown of traffic laws and broken windows. He asserted that "when traffic laws can be flagrantly ignored, the door opens to more chaos. This makes not only our streets but our public spaces, homes, and businesses less safe. It reduces the quality of life for everyone."[67]

Stand-Down Orders

When two extremist groups clashed with paintball guns, bats, and chemical spray in Portland, the city decided to let them fight. Mayor Ted Wheeler contended that with "strategic planning and oversight," the policy mitigated the impact of the violence, saying previously "these same groups have clashed with extremely violent and destructive results. This time, violence was contained to the groups of people who chose to engage in violence toward each other. The community at large was not harmed, and the broader public was protected. Property damage was minimal."

Notwithstanding this explanation, the policy received widespread criticism. A tourist reported that "your city terrifies me; these aren't protests; they are planned violence. And your leaders just let them keep doing it; the police tacitly support it. Horrific." A more pointed critique from Amy Herzfled-Copple, who monitors right-wing extremism, said that without the rule of law and law enforcement to intervene and protect public safety, it only "reinforces the lawlessness and fear that anti-democratic groups thrive on."[68] The *Wall Street Journal* came to the same conclusion. Its editorial board stated the message of the policy is clear: "Anarchy is tolerable as long as you're merely shooting at each other. The chaos will continue until the city's political leaders muster the will to stop it."[69]

The underlying assumption of the stand-down policy is instead of maintaining law and order, the city of Portland thinks it is acceptable for extremist groups to fight if they do not hurt anyone else! What can go wrong with thinking like this?

Portland's stand-down policies are further complicated by Oregon House

Bill 2928, which places restrictions on crowd-control devices. The legislation prohibits the of use pepper spray and rubber bullets for crowd control. However, the law allows exceptions when circumstances constitute a riot, and if the officer using the chemical incapacitant reasonably believes its use is necessary to stop and prevent more destructive behavior.[70]

Put yourself in the shoes of that officer who will have to "justify" why it was necessary to use these prohibited crowd-control options. Would you take the chance that your judgment will be deemed appropriate? Indeed, would you not *assume* that policymakers would disagree with *any use* of these options, particularly since the state legislator prohibited them? This in police parlance, is putting the cop into the "trick bag." The "easy" answer is to let the crowd do as it pleases. Don't risk your job or even being arrested for using crowd-control devices that the legislator has deemed inappropriate—even though they say there are "exceptions." Again, progressive thinking makes the police clean up their mess—while simultaneously making the police accountable if something goes wrong. Again, what could go wrong with this "reasoning"?

Use-of-Force Restrictions

This is a very emotional and complicated subject. Having spent hundreds of hours representing police officers and reviewing and critiquing hundreds of other use of force cases, I speak with authority on this subject. While some details are beyond the scope of this book, we will speak to the areas of this controversy. We will see how department policy, the law, and the *Use-of-Force Model*, are used to guide encounters with citizens.

Let me set this up with a perspective of what it is to be a police officer. The very nature of the "job" holds the power of life and death, freedom or prison. Discretion to make split-second, momentous, life-altering decisions are not only predictable, but they are also inevitable.

There is something about carrying a badge, wielding a gun, and having the authority of the government that can be intoxicating—including fostering tendencies to be outright abusive. My understanding of human nature is that *all* people can be swayed by power. The adage "power corrupts, and absolute power corrupts absolutely" is appropriately relevant.

This is not to infer that being a police officer results in being corrupt or abusive, however. Indeed, I think the opposite is true. Having worked with and taught literally thousands of police officers, my conclusion is that they are caring, service-oriented people. Many give their life in the line of duty. Most go to work each day with the possibility of being killed. Think about this for a moment. Very few people go to work with this possibility in their minds. While cops ought not dwell on this, the fact is that the job itself invites danger. Police go toward gunshots and chaos, while others run in the opposite direction.

Understanding the dangers and difficulties of the "job," my bias is toward the police. This is not to say that police are always right. They are not. They can have "bad days," they can lose their temper, they can make bad decisions (often in split-second circumstances), and they can be downright abusive. The gamut of human nature—and of humanity—can be seen in police officer behavior. This should not be surprising. Nor should this even be controversial. Employees of every profession fail in their jobs. As do police officers. Sometimes, this is because they are too emotional or fearful. Based on my experience, this is usually the "why" when "bad shootings" occur.

The George Floyd killing triggered a reflective, emotional, and ideological response. While emotional reactions are understandable, the ideological agenda is not. Indeed, progressives used these to further what they always wanted to do. Mr. Floyd was a "trigger," not a cause. The cause is *the system*—and *the target.*

How *should* these incidents be viewed? Since we are a "nation of laws," how are these viewed from a legal perspective? A brief legal framework ought to help us understand how these often-controversial incidents are assessed.

Police use of force is governed by the *Use-of-Force Model.* This model has been around for decades and is constantly subject to different ways to explain and assess its principles. It is designed to categorize the dynamics of police-citizen encounters into a legally acceptable framework. These encounters are fluid. The subject and the police officer may both be thinking and seeing different things, though they are part of the same encounter. These result in actions and reactions by both the subject and the officer. As this often plays out like a dance—or a wrestling match—it is important to know that police use of force must be commensurate with the subject, and all force must stop when the subject stops resisting.

In application, this can be very dynamic. Let's start with the obvious: *the law does not enforce itself.* Laws written on paper are powerful, yet they are worthless unless people are willing and able to enforce them. Words, when applied in fact patterns, called "elements," are what constitute laws. This is often called the "letter of the law." Outside the words (the letters) is another crucial factor called "discretion."

By the very nature of their job, police have substantial levels of discretion. This ranges from the decision to issue a traffic citation to the decision to pull the trigger. Officers are required to act within the letter of the law, yet they are afforded discretion in how or whether they enforce the law. Discretion can be both wide and deep. It can be applied to routine tasks and to the most consequential acts. Discretion can be construed as the "spirit of the law."

Let's acknowledge yet another basic fact: *the dynamics of a street encounter can be difficult to control.* Relevant factors are fluid and are often based on perceptions. What one is thinking typically reflects how one acts or reacts. Since the *subjective* perception of the officer counts in an *objective* assessment of whether the proper amount and level of force was used, the threat level that the officer believes he/she is encountering is a crucial question. Here the officer must assess the subject. The words, demeanor, physical stature, mental state (drugs or alcohol?), presence of weapons, and a host of other factors ought to be considered.

Yet, as important as these are, the two most relevant factors are the skills of the officer and the willingness of the citizen to cooperate. These factors are magnified—and intensified—when guns or other deadly weapons are involved. Having recovered hundreds of guns in my police career, I can attest that *every* case involved a certain level of stress. Some more than others. Experienced officers may engender less stress simply because they have been "conditioned" to life-threatening situations. This can be analogous to a well-worn combat veteran, who is no longer afraid of battle. This is not to say that policing is like war. But potentially dying by gunfire on the streets of a violent city can feel like war!

Whether or not you accept this analogy, let's agree that more experienced officers also typically develop more skills to manage hazardous encounters. Consequently, stress levels can vary based on experience and skills. The greater the stress level, the more likely fearful and inappropriate actions will result.

However, no matter how experienced and skilled, every encounter has this unknown variable: *How will the suspect respond?* In this sense, the otherwise "routine" street stop can turn ugly—even deadly. Since the law allows police officers to use *slightly more* force than the civilian, the subject typically drives the outcome of the encounter. Subjects can choose to cooperate, resist, or even turn into aggressors.

When "thought leaders" are telling citizens, particularly blacks, that they are consistently subject to police abuse or discrimination, the question becomes: *Why should they cooperate?* Being told repeatedly that the police are out to *get you* has ramifications. Since cooperation is the key aspect of every street encounter, this repeated mantra creates a disincentive to cooperate. One can argue, that these inflammatory allegations even foster and encourage resistance, and the desire to fight back. Is this just a coincidence? Or is this too part of a larger agenda? Think again of what Congresswoman Waters said: "We've got to stay in the street and we've got to get more active. We've got to get more confrontational. We've got to make sure that they know that we mean business." Calling this an agenda seems like an understatement...

Nonetheless, the dynamics of police encounters are reflected as options and alternatives within the *Use-of-Force Model*. It is beyond the scope of this section to delve any deeper, but suffice it to say that the police officer is legally required to adhere to the parameters of the law. Applying the model (and the law) allows the officer to use proportionally more force than the subject. When the subject is under control, all force must immediately cease.

In every controversial case leading up to the Floyd killing, the suspect did not cooperate with the police. In each of these, some level of resistance or even aggression was present. This is not to say that the deaths of these suspects were conclusively and legally proper. Recall that resistance and aggression from the suspect can generate higher levels of force by the police.

Once this dynamic commences, emotion and adrenaline kick in. These can be hard to control—though police officers are legally required to exert controls consistent with the *Use-of-Force Model.*

It is undisputed but largely ignored that Floyd exhibited both resistance and some level of aggression prior to his death. What is crucial is that the application of force is only appropriate while resistance and aggression are occurring. Force tactics or responses that may have been legally justified moments previously must cease when the suspect's resistance or aggression ceases. This is where the nine-minute, knee to neck application of force was well beyond the parameters allowed in the force model.

At some point during this time, the officer's actions transformed from legitimate use of force to excessive force to murder. This is the legal analysis. This is how the letter of the law conforms to the *Use-of-Force Model.* Ironically, the law also provides a remedy—criminal prosecution, which resulted in the conviction of the police officer. While this does not bring back George Floyd's life, it is the best that humans can do in a civilized society. One can say this should never have happened. This is correct.

However, police officers are subject to the same frailties as everyone else. When they use force, they are subject to investigation and possible prosecution. When they cross the line, which is bound to sometimes happen, they are subject to legal consequences, as was Officer Chauvin. Beyond these remedies, there are few ways to completely avoid and mitigate such behavior.

So, to summarize, it is true that police can overreact, they can cross the line, and they can violate the law. There are established mechanisms to investigate and assess these encounters. Legal remedies are available, including arrest, prosecution, and imprisonment.

Other remedies, including changing immunity statutes, have become part of the "reform" movement. Without getting into the details of these, my conclusion is that these will only serve to make police less proactive. As has been the theme in this chapter, so many of the "reforms" being instituted are driving a less assertive, even purely reactive police mindset.

The irony is this less assertive, cooperative mindset is exactly what should be communicated *to the public*. If people are less assertive and more cooperative, then police use of force will be rarely used. Recall, that the citizen cooperation *variable* drives these encounters. With less resistance to lawful police orders, the probability that force will be used is greatly diminished or even negated. Instead of communicating *this message*, the opposite often occurs.

Two things are happening simultaneously: People are being told that police are racist and discriminate against blacks *and* policies are being implemented that make the police less apt to engage. These then lead to increased crime and increased disorder.

Instead, the solution is known—but ignored. It seems simple, but the cleanest, surest, and the most principled approach is to just comply with officers' lawful commands, and don't resist arrest. Is this too hard to say and do? Here is a powerful quote that closes this loop—and this section:[71]

> "In the America of just a few years ago, it would have been sayable, and widely said, that no matter how badly the police sometimes perform their duties, it's exceedingly foolish to resist arrest. No lawyer would advise you to do so. You create a situation for yourself that can't possibly end well.
>
> You commit a chargeable offense when you might have ended up facing no charge at all. You put police, who are public employees, in a terrible position, of having to apply force to vindicate the lawful authority of the state, which all of us rely on for our personal security (that is, unless the left wants to give everyone in America more incentive to arm themselves) . . .
>
> While punishing police misconduct is eminently desirable, making martyrs out of people who resist arrest only encourages others to make the same foolish, self-defeating decision. The results will be predictable unless police stop trying to apprehend lawbreakers altogether: more deaths in custody like that of George Floyd, more accidental shootings like that of Daunte Wright, tens of thousands of injuries to suspects and officers each year, more situations of the sort that produce an estimated 2,000 officer-involved shootings (fatal and nonfatal) annually."

POLICE OFFICERS-THIN BLUE LINE

This section will take the reader inside the police mindset, perhaps providing a new vantage point. Initially, see the police as the *canaries in a coal mine*. They are the most obvious representatives of the government. They are also charged with enforcing laws, statutes, and ordinances that are promulgated by the government. They are the gatekeepers of the criminal justice system, often deciding who and why an individual ought to be made subject to such laws. Their role in a civilized society is crucial.

Yet, as we have seen above, how police and citizens interact is a critical indicator of the health and well-being of society. This dynamic is complicated—and extraordinarily important to the viability of a society. When police are attacked, it signals that the normal constraints are breaking down. Also, consider that since the police are both armed and trained and they represent the government (read "the system"), an attack on the police is equated with an attack on the system. Hence, the notion of *canaries in a coal mine*. These signal that something is wrong inside the society (or in the cave).

Let's make this premise clear: *the problem is not the police*. Though police sometimes do wrong, they are simply the "excuse" to tear down a society that many hate. As a convenient excuse, they are targeted for being symbols of this "repressive" society. As demonstrated throughout this text, the police are being "targeted" in many ways. Of course, direct attacks are part of this. But so are provocative communications from all levels of society. From elected officials to street activists, a common theme is to demonize the police. One can ask *why*, but we have already demonstrated the design of the progressive agenda.

One aspect we have not delved into is that police authority—and the power derived from it—is a crucial impediment to *their* goal: taking down the capitalistic system. Hence, the need is to break through the gatekeepers. As alarming as this sounds, it is what I believe is intended. If I am correct, one hopes this book serves to provide the support that the police need to maintain that "thin blue line." As we explore the viability of this thin blue line, consider this basic principle of human nature. Peace is achieved when good people are stronger than bad people . . . I think the vast majority of police are the good people. I trust you do as well.

Let's first look at this in a symbolic way. Do you think it is wrong for police officers to wear the "thin blue line" flag on their uniforms? The patch consists of a black-and-white US flag with one blue stripe. It honors fallen cops and recognizes the role police play in protecting society from anarchy. Would it surprise you to learn that police chiefs in various parts of the country are banning these flags?

The village of Mount Prospect, Illinois recently prohibited its police officers from wearing a "thin blue line" patch on their uniforms, joining the cities of San Francisco, Middletown, Manchester, and elsewhere that also banned it. Opponents say the patch makes them feel "unsafe."

Despite this "concern," according to the *Washington Post* database, police shot and killed 999 people in 2019, including 424 whites and 252 blacks. Twelve of the black victims were unarmed, versus 26 of the white victims. In a country where annual arrests number more than 10 million, if those black death totals constitute an "epidemic" of police use of lethal force against blacks, then the word has lost all meaning.[72]

The category of "unarmed" is broadly construed to include when a suspect grabs at an officer's gun or is fleeing in a stolen car with a loaded pistol on the car seat. MacDonald uses the number derived from the *Post* and projects the total number of deaths in 2021. She estimated that 10,000 blacks would be murdered in 2021. At this level, deaths of unarmed blacks would make up less than 0.2 percent of all black homicide victims. The vast majority of these 10,000 have been killed by black criminals.[73] She rightly concluded that whether police are allowed to wear the thin-blue-line patch or not, the idea that they are the only thing standing between order and chaos is borne out daily. Ironically, people say they would feel "unsafe" if police wear a patch, say little or nothing about 10,000 black homicide victims who will die this year that were *not* killed by police. What is wrong with this picture?

Police Killings/Ambushes/Attacks

How about the other side of the coin? If deaths caused by police amount to a small fraction of the total murders, what about the total number of times people have killed or attacked police officers? Is it possible that the progressive agenda would contribute to increased violence against officers?

Police union leaders think that the "defund the police" movement and overall hot rhetoric against police have created a culture of disrespect. "I think that the present climate that we see throughout the country right now and the dehumanization of law enforcement is certainly, I think, having some impact on the aggression towards law enforcement," said Patrick Yoes, National FOP president. "All we have to do is simply look at the increase in ambush attacks on law enforcement officers, that shows that there's definitely a lot more aggression towards law enforcement than there was in previous years." He added this statement consistent with the theme of this book, "If you look at the constant and relentless attacks by public officials and by media, it is disheartening for law enforcement and, not only that, in my opinion, we're creating a crisis that is going to take us years to overcome."[74]

These attacks skyrocketed in 2020. There were 60,105 officers assaulted in the line of duty in 2020, with 30.9 percent suffering injuries as a result. This represents over 4,000 more assaults than the prior year. Breaking this data down further, the means to assault officers included:[75]

- Personal Weapons, such as their fists, hands, or feet (44,421)
- Firearms (2,744)
- Knives or other cutting instruments (1,180)
- Other types of dangerous weapons (11,760)

According to preliminary data compiled by the National Law Enforcement Officers Memorial Fund (NLEOMF), as of December 31, 2021; 458 federal, state, tribal, and local law enforcement officers died in the line of duty in 2021. This is an increase of 55 percent from the 295 officers killed during the same period last year (about 301 deaths were Covid-related). This is the highest total line-of-duty officer deaths since 1930 when there were 312 fatalities.[76]

In 2021, eighty-four officers died from felonious assaults including 61 officers who were killed by firearms, which represents a 36 percent increase over the forty-five officers killed feloniously by firearms in 2020. The leading circumstance of firearms fatalities were officers killed in ambush-style attacks. A total of nineteen officers were killed in ambush attacks in 2021, a significant increase over only six such attacks in 2020.[77]

FBI Director Christopher Wray echoed this sentiment saying, "law enforcement officers these days are dealing with a whole range of threats at a time when, in many ways, the job is more dangerous than ever. The dangers are very real and constant."[78]

Another indicator of the dangers inherent in policing that often does not get communicated is the number of times police officers are shot and shot at. For example, as of early August 2021, in Chicago, there have been thirty-eight officers who have been shot at or shot during 2021. Of those, eleven officers were shot by gunfire. In 2020, seventy-nine officers were shot at or shot, which represented a 500-percent increase from the number of officers shot at or shot in 2019.[79]

Resignations/Terminations & Morale

Halfway through 2021, the Seattle Police Department officers are leaving the job at a "record pace," with at least 249 people leaving over the past year alone. This is consistent with departments across the country. From April 2020 through March 2021, Police Executive Research Forum, a think tank based in Washington, D.C., recorded an 18 percent increase in resignations and a 45 percent increase in retirements compared to the same time a year prior.[80]

"Morale is not good, and that's because we don't have the political support from our elected officials," said Seattle Police Officers Guild President Mike Solan. He notes that prior to the death of George Floyd, Seattle officials "publicly applauded" the department as "the model of reform." But after Floyd's death, "these same politicians couldn't run away from us faster." To make this even worse, Solan also said that "hundreds" of officers were injured during the riots, elected officials blamed them "for being the instigators," which further contributed to the decline in police morale.[81]

This sentiment is familiar. For example, an Albuquerque police union leader explained why several officers left the Emergency Response Team following a protest, stressing that "morale is gone." Police Officer Union

President Shaun Willoughby stated that officers don't feel supported and "don't trust their leaders." He stressed that Albuquerque officers are "tired of being managed by politics." Seventeen officers, one lieutenant, and two sergeants resigned from the team that handles protests following a counter-protest. Willoughby made this point of emphasis: "There is a lack of trust with our administration, noting that "they [police] were not supported, and who wants to live under that type of scrutiny?"[82]

"I think that the overall anti-police sentiment has really accelerated the separation aspirations [meaning retirements and resignations] by police officers in this city." Solan said he is struggling to understand activists' and politicians' endgame. "They will decimate numbers to fill the uniforms to protect our citizens, and to what gain, if any? What's the end game? "I don't see how that's a recipe for our communities to feel protected."[83] I think we know the end game . . .?

Chuck Wexler, the head of the Police Executive Research Forum, called the current climate a "combustible mixture." It's creating "a crisis on the horizon for police chiefs when they look at the resources they need, especially during a period when we're seeing an increase in murders and shootings," Wexler said. "It's a wake-up call." Yet, in the same way, the line-level officers expressed such feelings as, "some are angry, some are fearful, some are confused on what we do in this space. Some may feel a bit abandoned."[84]

The operative question may now be: Who would want to be a cop in America? That is the question posed by Miranda Devine. She characterizes the climate as "open season on anyone who wears a badge," with the resultant conclusions: "No wonder recruitment is down, retirements are up, and the streets are growing ever more violent." She continues that by "swallowing the false narrative of systemic racism, we have demonized and criminalized police while turning criminals into civil-rights martyrs. This won't end well."[85]

Writing after the police shooting of a black man, Daunte Wright, during a traffic stop in the Minneapolis suburb of Brooklyn Center, she noted it "was a stupid, horrible accident. But it's not racism." She made this connection about the response from leadership:[86]

> "You would think, at such a time, that our nation's leaders would find a way of lowering the temperature. But no. Former President Barack Obama, who could wield more influence for good than anyone, did the worst possible thing. Instead of using the opportunity to teach young men not to resist arrest, he fanned the flames of fear by falsely asserting that Wright's death was racially motivated.

Quoting the former president, Devine noted he said, it was "yet another shooting of a Black man . . . at the hands of police." It showed "just how badly we need to reimagine policing and public safety in this country." Squad member Rashida Tlaib also fanned the flames. She tweeted that Wright's shooting "wasn't an accident. Policing in this country is inherently and intentionally racist . . . No more policing incarceration and militarization. It can't be reformed."[87]

Yet, much of the media is invested in this false narrative and will not let it go, no matter how much mayhem it unleashes. Here is an interesting point made by Devine that directly connects with my thinking:[88]

> "Police are the thin blue line between violent criminals who take what they want from the weak. Yet now people protected by wealth or the security apparatus of the state are telling those victims that they are on their own. A world without law and order is a very scary place."

One would not be surprised to learn that police officers may not be afforded due process. For example, Atlanta Mayor Keisha Lance Bottoms defended her decision to dismiss a police officer following the death of a suspect, even though the decision to terminate the officer was ultimately overturned. The Atlanta Civil Service Board announced its decision to reinstate Officer Garrett Rolfe, citing several procedural errors made in the quickly decided termination. "Due to the City's failure to comply with several provisions of the Code and the information received during witnesses' testimony, the Board concludes the Appellant was not afforded his right to due process."

The decision to reinstate the officer came after some questioned the swift termination. They correctly connected the desire to quell protests and riots that erupted in the aftermath of the incident that led to the officer's termination. Mayor Bottoms said she "stood by the decision" to terminate the officer, insisting it was "the right thing to do." Significantly, she effectively admitted that her decision was based on mob rule, not the rule of law, when she said, "had immediate action not been taken, I firmly believe the public safety crisis we experienced during that time would have been significantly worse."[89]

In a blistering critique of progressive thinking, Gerard Baker writing for the *Wall Street Journal* noted that actress and comedian Chelsea Handler's advocacy was reflective of progressive thinking. In implying that there is no need for a trial, she tweeted that [it is] "so pathetic that there's a trial to prove that Derek Chauvin killed George Floyd when there is video of him doing so." Baker then sought to enlighten her and other progressives with these mocking words "800 years after the Magna Carta and 230 years after the Bill of Rights, some notions of due process, presumption of innocence, and protection against arbitrary justice might have embedded themselves in the minds of even our densest celebrities." Baker aptly summed up what we were and where we are:[90]

> "The Handler standard, or the Maxine [Waters] maxim—the idea that we don't really need a trial to know whether someone is guilty of a heinous crime—has always had its adherents. There have surely been miscarriages of justice—acquittals of guilty people and convictions of innocent ones—throughout history. The jury system is never perfect.
>
> But what's frighteningly new about our current climate is that the rejection of apparently unwelcome trial outcomes is now part of the dominant progressive critique of our longstanding political and civic order. If US institutions are the product of white-supremacist exploitation—as is essentially the consensus of the people who run the government, most corporations, and leading cultural institutions— then the judicial system itself is inherently and systemically unjust. If the principle of equality before the law is

to be supplanted by the objective of 'equity' in outcome, then only outcomes that serve the higher objective of collective racial justice can be considered legitimate.

So trials that produce the 'wrong' verdict are not just miscarriages of justice. They are an indictment of the entire system.

This rejection of the legitimacy of the judicial process is rooted in the same neo-Marxist ideology—a race- and identity-based interpretation of structuralism—that holds sway over the minds of much of our ruling class.

To the old Marxists, the capitalists were the exploiters. *In The ABC of Communism*, published in 1920, Bolshevik leaders Nikolai Bukharin and Yevgeni Preobrazhensky used language that sounds strikingly familiar today. They denounced the courts as instruments of "bourgeois justice," which was "carried on under the guidance of laws passed in the interests of the exploiting class," and recommended instead the establishment of "proletarian courts."

In one of the more savage ironies of history, some two decades later the authors themselves were tried by such courts under Josef Stalin and sentenced to death.

Yet, even Stalin thought some kind of judicial proceeding was necessary. Our modern revolutionaries would dispense even with show trials."

LAWLESSNESS

As this chapter ends, the section entitled Lawlessness is not intended to be *just* the section. Each element in the chapter builds toward this conclusion: *Lawlessness is the result of defunding, criminal justice reform, and progressive policing policies, which all have an impact on the police as a body.* Underlying these is the ideology that drove reimagining the police and the assorted racially based theories and movements. *It is the cumulative effect of these that will lead to lawlessness.* Hence, it will take more than just one element being restored to "normality."

The obvious negative impact of the defunding movement is manifesting itself in cities across the country. Citizens are making sure "defunding" will turn to "refunding." This is progress, but it is not enough. Put another way, it is necessary though not sufficient.

What happens when cities refund? Let's answer the question with a series of rhetorical questions.

With refunding, will this lead to abandoning the progressive "reforms" of the criminal justice system? With refunding, will police departments reinstitute "broken windows" and "quality of life" policing? With refunding, will police departments restitute anti-crime and anti-gang units? With refunding, will local and national politicians "call off" and disclaim their anti-police mantras? With refunding, will these same politicians advocate and strongly encourage all citizens to cooperate with police officers during encounters? With refunding, will the leaders of our institutions abandon the race-based theories and the notion that this country is systemically racist? With refunding, will "leaders" abandon the attempt to rewrite history and tear down statues and other symbols of this country? With refunding, will we as a country come together to honor the flag, the anthem, and the principles of our democratic republic? With refunding, will we all agree that as a people we should treat everyone equally, and agree to be judged by our character, not the color of our skin?

I trust you get this is *much larger than money*. Indeed, the money mantra was just one small piece of the larger puzzle. As we have made clear in these chapters, the agenda is wide and deep. Neo-Racism and neo-Marxism are deeply entrenched. Though the defunding element of their plan has been seen to be inappropriate, no matter; the momentum has started. Getting police departments back together is a lot like putting "Humpty-Dumpty" back together again.

Putting policing back together will need answers to these questions. Why would young people want to be the police? What kind of "personality type" will police departments look for? And maybe most challenging, why would those police officers who lived and worked through the "reimagining" police movement ever trust political leaders to have their backs? Why would they not believe that they would be thrown under the bus the first time that a suspect wanted to fight instead of going to jail?

Remember this is a critical element of street logic. Bad guys know "the game." They know how to manipulate the system. When they play the game to manipulate the system, how will they be characterized? Will they be called out as criminals or radicals, or will they be deemed "victims" of police brutality? I would be happy to believe the former, but my experience tells me to believe the latter.

So, let's not yet answer the rhetorical questions. Instead, use these questions as your road map. Use them as indicators of the health of our society. After the devasting summer of love and the Covid pandemic, the stage is set for difficult times ahead. As we go forward, it is useful to benchmark to understand *where we were* and *where we are.*

First, where we were. One year after the death of George Floyd, going back to "ground zero" in Minneapolis may be an instructive exercise. As of May 24, 2021, nineteen children were shot since Mr. Floyd was killed. This represented a 171-percent increase over the same period in 2020. Losing these young people was obviously difficult and tragic. Grieving relatives wonder where the protesters are. "Why ain't nobody mad about a ten-year-old, my grandson, fighting for his life?" asked Sharrie Jennings, Ladavionne's grandmother. Answering her own question, she continued "Because a cop didn't shoot him. Is that why?"

Killings of children are just part of the story. Minneapolis homicides between Jan. 1 and mid-May were up 108 percent compared with the same period in 2020. Shootings were up 153 percent, and carjackings increased 222 percent. At least three-quarters of Minneapolis's homicide and shooting victims are black, though the city is less than a fifth black.[91]

Crime rates are not the only problem either. Police officers are routinely punched, kicked, and hit with projectiles. At least 200 officers have resigned or gone on leave since May 2020, leaving the Minneapolis Police Department understaffed by nearly a third.

Just days short of the one-year anniversary of Mr. Floyd's death, there was a near-riot in downtown Minneapolis following a shootout among club patrons. Two people were killed and eight were wounded. Responding officers called other police departments for backup in what they called an "exceptionally chaotic scene." The previous weekend, officers were maced and pelted with rocks and debris while trying to disperse disorderly crowds.[92]

The area around what is now called *George Floyd Square* is still burned-out and desolate. It sits isolated within a *civilian-enforced police-free zone*.

A year later, citizens are still feeling the impact of the riots. "I am afraid. I am frustrated. I am mentally ill right now," says a local shop owner. City Council member Alondra Cano says she hears from senior citizens who sleep in the bathtub to avoid being shot at night. Their bus routes have been disrupted by the autonomous zone—the burned-out and desolate "tribute" to George Floyd, which makes it very difficult to obtain medications and groceries. Yet, as lawless as Minneapolis has become, it is hardly atypical.

The US saw the largest annual percentage increase in homicides in recorded history in 2020. That increase has continued in 2021. The media and Democratic politicians attribute the crime increase to the pandemic and attendant shutdowns. But the violent surge of 2020 began only *after* the George Floyd riots, more than two months after COVID-19 devastated the economy. No industrialized country saw anything comparable; crime dropped in the UK and Canada, where lockdowns were more severe than in the US.[93]

Atlanta is another city hit hard with rioting and chaos—so much so that a wealthy neighborhood is seeking to set up its own town, separate and apart from Atlanta. Bill White, the group's CEO and chairman of Buckhead City Committee, said, "we have three major issues and that's all we have . . . crime, crime, and crime. "People believe truly that this is an emergency— that's the message I'm getting—and that we are living in a war zone." He said it creates issues for the residents, such as that 911 calls placed in Buckhead aren't being answered adequately. "It is life-threatening. It is unfathomable."[94]

When asked about the public perception of Buckhead's quest for more cops and policing at a time when some in the nation are calling for police budgets to be cut, White said the anti-police efforts are falling on "deaf ears."

White said what many are not saying. "The thing with crime is it's colorblind. It's hitting Black people; it's hitting White people . . ." Some of the recent public safety improvement efforts include acquiring the necessary funding for three patrol vehicles to canvass the neighborhood, creating a weekday bike patrol program, hiring officers to monitor the area, and bolstering its network of security cameras.[95] This Buckhead Security Plan was brought into motion after the neighborhood's "unprecedented spike in crime."

As 2021 neared its end, *ABC News* noted at least twelve major US cities have broken annual homicide records in 2021—with three weeks left in the year. Five of these cities topped records that were set or tied just last year. Cities that made the infamous list include Philadelphia, which had more homicides, totaling 562, more than the nation's two largest cities, New York (443 as of Dec. 5) and Los Angeles (352 as of Nov. 27). That's an increase of 13 percent from 2020, a year that nearly broke the 1990 record. The homicide record was also broken in Columbus, Indianapolis, and Louisville.[96] Chicago police recorded 797 murders in 2021, the most since 1996. But more than 800 homicides happened within the city, including expressway shootings, which are investigated by a different agency (Illinois State Police).[97]

Homicides were also up by 12 percent in Los Angeles from 2020 and 4 percent in New York.

Other major cities that have surpassed yearly homicide records are St. Paul, Portland, Tucson, Toledo, Baton Rouge, Austin, Rochester, and Albuquerque, which broke its record back in August. Capt. Frank Umbrino, of the Rochester Police Department, which broke its thirty-year-old record, stated that "We're extremely frustrated. It has to stop. I mean, it's worse than a war zone around here lately." Among the major cities on the brink of setting new homicide records are Milwaukee, which has 178 homicides, twelve short of a record set in 2020; and Minneapolis, which has ninety-one homicides, six shy of a record set in 1995.[98]

According to the FBI's annual Uniform Crime Report released in September, the nation saw a 30-percent increase in murder in *2020*, the largest single-year jump since the bureau began recording crime statistics sixty years ago. Robert Boyce, retired chief of detectives for the New York Police

Department, said that while there is no single reason for the jump in slayings, one national crime statistic stands out to him. "Nobody's getting arrested anymore, people are getting picked up for gun possession and they're just let out over and over again." The FBI crime data shows that the number of arrests nationwide plummeted 24 percent in 2020, from the more than 10 million arrests made in 2019. The number of 2020 arrests, totaling 7.63 million, is the lowest in twenty-five years. FBI crime data is not yet available for 2021.[99]

With these statistics in mind, we will now transition to what policing may look like going forward. Please consider how this data and the dynamics described in this chapter will impact policing as we go forward.

CHAPTER V

PUBLIC SAFETY POLICING

ORDER + SURVEILLANCE + PROTECTIVE METHODS = CONTROL

Coming off the lawlessness chapter, we will switch gears and offer some suggestions to diminish unruly conditions. Delving into straightforward yet complicated suggestions requires some explanation. Explaining this tapestry has not been easy—either organizationally, intellectually, or emotionally. Many dots have been connected. The image depicted may be appalling. Similarly, the policing model devised to encounter lawlessness and extremist violence must be strong enough to control the dynamics described in this text. This requires detail to flesh out.

Lawlessness is not measured by an "on and off switch." Instead, think of it as a rheostat, where it moves from cooler to hotter, then back to cooler. America in 2022 is registering on the "lawlessness rheostat." Exactly where is subjective and varies by jurisdiction, but this chapter will offer ways to move toward the "cooler" level, or even negate any notion of lawlessness.

We will focus on one "leg" of the criminal justice stool. That is policing. Many reasons go to this focus.

First, my expertise is in policing and public safety. Understanding the logic of the street and the dynamics of policing by incorporating the theories, the techniques, the laws, and the people as a former police officer, as a criminal justice theorist, as a police and security expert, as a police union attorney, and as a professor of public safety brings depth and breadth.

Second, the defunding and reimaging policing controversies directly affect the police. Because police are often "easy targets," both literally and figuratively, in this dramatic and divisive dynamic, understanding how police can limit or negate lawlessness is our central goal. Consequently, solutions to lawlessness and chaos must also come from the police.

Third, since the other "legs" of the criminal justice system are largely and directly related to voting decisions, these are "cleaner" in their application. Voting in prosecutors or legislators who advocate a "law-and-order" agenda is closer to an "on-and-off" switch than the rheostat analogy. Laws can be changed, and prosecutorial policy decisions can be made relatively quickly. These would have an almost immediate impact on the system. Demonstrating that laws and policies matter, the reader—and society—can vote for a solution. Hence, voting for law-and-order candidates is easier than policing a racially charged and often volatile environment.

For these reasons, we will focus on what police can do to impact lawlessness and extremism. This approach is not only due to my preference but because it is widely acknowledged as the key to any solution. For example, in a recent *Vox* article, which is liberal, if not progressive in its orientation, German Lopez presented a fair and thoughtful analysis as to what can be done to reduce crime and violence. He concluded it is *the police* that is best suited to accomplish these dual goals. His conclusion was grounded in research and data.

Initially, he cited a 2020 study published by the *National Bureau of Economic Research* (NBER) that concluded, "Each additional police officer abates approximately 0.1 homicides. In per capita terms, effects are twice as large for black versus white victims." This study supported a 2005 study in the *Journal of Law and Economics*, finding that during high-alert periods, when more officers were deployed, less crime occurred. Similarly, a 2016 study looked at what happened when more New York City police officers were deployed in high-crime areas as part of an effort called "Operation Impact." The conclusion: these deployments were associated with less crime across the board.[1] Of course, it is more complicated than the number of police and how they are deployed. What they do is just as crucial.

Most significantly, another NBER study found that the number of police officers led to a reduction in homicides. Reducing homicides was tied to officers making "more arrests for low-level "quality-of-life" offenses, with effects that imply a disproportionate burden for black Americans." Disproportionate enforcement has been criticized by Black Lives Matter and a host of other progressive groups. Contending that police disproportionally focus on blacks in quality-of-life infractions and arguing that these can escalate to police killings—as seen in the deaths of Eric Garner and George Floyd.[2]

At first blush, this looks like a dilemma. Data shows that enforcing quality-of-life offenses can lead to a reduction in homicides. Yet, enforcing quality-of-life offenses can also lead to disproportionate enforcement against blacks. But, like most race-based thinking, this is more rhetoric than reality. There are ways to get past this misleading dilemma.

Initially, just as comparing police stops to per capita data instead of crime statistics, the problem with this dynamic is reality. Let me illustrate with a series of questions that a casual observer of public safety may find controversial: What if blacks spend disproportionately more time on the street or in public areas? Could this contribute to the disproportionate arrest data? While congregating, would you expect offenses, such as drinking, drug use, panhandling, and other disorderly behaviors? Could simple *presence* in public areas correlate with arrests for loitering and trespassing?

Answering these questions reveals the reality of the street. While this is more anecdotal than statistical, my experience is that the black culture encourages time in public settings, such as streets, parks, porches, and around homes. Statistical evidence to support this claim is missing but not because the claim is untrue. Few studies, if any, even attempt to measure this question.

So, how ought we think about this? Use your own experience. When driving through an urban setting, do you see more people on the street than in the typical suburban environment? When driving through an urban setting, look around at those who are moving along. Comparing those to others who are standing around loitering, congregating, and exhibiting disorderly behaviors, it is the latter who the police will likely engage? This should be expected. Extensive research (that will be presented below) reveals that disorderly behaviors and the presence of loiters on the public way is troubling.

Though this is only my conclusion, I say this with experience. This is supported by criminological theories and the realities of policing. As with crime rates in relation to street stops, the relevant data point is not based on *per capita* data but based on levels of *criminality*. Consequently, police ought to focus on those who are most likely to commit crimes and/or quality of life infractions—regardless of the racial component.

The point is this: The enforcement of quality-of-life infractions should focus on those who are engaging in these behaviors. If the offender is black, white, homeless, or not is irrelevant to the enforcement decision. The key is law and order, not race or status. If other means, such as social services remedies are deemed to be a better resolution, then this is a separate and distinct question. My point here is that disorderly conditions must be resolved. Achieving this is crucial as current conditions are exasperating lawlessness and chaos.

While this conclusion may be deemed controversial, the bottom-line question is this: What is more important, fostering and sustaining an orderly environment or seeking to achieve some preconceived notion of social justice or equity? If the latter is valued over the former, then expect more disorderly behaviors—even lawlessness. Yet, this dynamic is very complicated. If order maintenance reduces crime and violence but also causes a community backlash due to a perception of widespread mistreatment, that too is likely unsustainable. Indeed, it could even make crime worse by creating a community backlash where people may stop cooperating with the police. Even deeper, it can cause a breakdown in trust in the law and result in violence against the police.

Yet, this is where we are anyway. Police have largely backed down from proactive enforcement methods, but they are still being targeted, both verbally and violently. And because they have backed away, chaos and violent crimes are increasing. So, what do we do? Here is what Aaron Chalfin, a criminologist at the University of Pennsylvania, stated: "evaluating police work, from stops to more aggressive actions, is nuanced, requiring a comprehensive look at the effects on a community. Stops can be good or bad. People on the left think [all stops] are bad; people on the right think they're good. And it's not that at all."

This supports Lopez's conclusion that there is solid evidence that more police officers and certain policing strategies reduce crime and violence.[3] This conclusion is supported by a series of criminological theories and recent history. The most effective crime-and-disorder-reducing method is order maintenance.

In short, order maintenance is integral to *Public Safety Policing*. This policing model was introduced in my groundbreaking 2009 book. What I saw then was a crime and risk environment that would necessitate pragmatic "solutions" to policing. What you will read here is a condensed, more concise presentation of this policing model. An important takeaway is this equation: *Order + Surveillance + Protective Methods = Control.* We will detail this equation later, but as you read the narrative, consider these components.

Each element will develop this equation. The first is to create order. Particularly in a chaotic and lawless environment, it is crucial to start by establishing some level of order.

ORDER MAINTENANCE

This element is not new. Indeed, it is as old as policing itself—even older, it is as old as *law and* order itself. Yet, there are new and innovative aspects that are applicable in this policing model. Examples include "broken-windows" and "quality-of-life" policing. Order maintenance is a shorthand way of describing both.

Delving into the layers of order maintenance requires a rather detailed explanation. First, research powerfully demonstrates that *order maintenance* is highly effective at reducing crime and fear. Second, due in part to the defunding and reimagining policing movement, we have seen police backing away from enforcing order maintenance (or quality of life) offenses. Third, the reduction of order maintenance enforcement has contributed to increasing crime and chaos, leading to lawlessness. Fourth, due to financial and operational constraints, along with the predicted rise in extremist and terroristic violence, police will not be able to perform order maintenance enforcement as previously performed. Finally, due to the crucial factors of crime and fear, private security and other alternative service providers will perform order maintenance functions to replace or supplement the role previously played by the police. Let's go deeper.

Civilized societies seek to maintain order through the rule of law. As illustrated throughout this text, this is complicated when people disagree on the means to achieve order or even question *whether the goal itself* is appropriate. Because the criminal justice system has been accused as racist or reflective of white supremacist thinking, order maintenance has become more difficult to enforce. Could we even ask if law and order are too controversial to enforce?

Applying order maintenance methods will require *remembering* why it is valuable. This also requires innovative applications to achieve what has been proven successful and is indeed a worthwhile goal. Discerning *why* it is valuable could be seen from a brief review of the research.

Research Perspective

First, we must understand what is at stake and why this is so important. Order maintenance—which was widely utilized in community policing—has proven beneficial in both reducing crime and in reducing the level of incivility or disorder.[4] Conversely, the opposite is also true. An area can transition from relatively few crimes to a high incidence of crime or a heightened fear of crime, caused in part, by lack of order.[5]

Order maintenance is the belief that crime problems initially occur through relatively harmless activities. Drinking on the street, vandalizing buildings, panhandling, and loitering on street corners can be common in certain areas. Some see these as harmless activities. If these activities go unchecked, however, the level of fear and incivility increases. Left to fester, more serious crimes, such as gang fights or drive-by shootings may take place. Disorder can also be seen in "smash-and-grab" violence and chaotic mob actions.

Consequently, disorder reduces the social controls. This results in increased crime. Increased crime, particularly serious crime, in turn, contributes to the further deterioration of the physical environment and of the social and economic wellbeing of the community.[6]

The development of order-maintenance theories can be traced to a line of thinking that initially focused on conditions in cities. Conditions such as "physical deterioration, high-density traffic areas, economic insecurity, poor housing, family disintegration, transience, conflicting social norms, and an absence of constructive positive agencies" were all considered contributors to criminal behavior.[7]

Over time, researchers shifted their focus from socioeconomic factors to the physical characteristics of the community, or in other words—the "environment." Focusing on the physical characteristics contributed to a substantial body of research leading to this formula: "*Committing a crime requires the convergence in time and space of an offender, a suitable target, and the absence of guardians capable of preventing the violation.*"[8]

In keeping with the theme of this book, Gibbs and Erickson argued that the daily population flow in large cities "reduces the effectiveness of surveillance activities by increasing the number of strangers that are routinely present in the city, thereby decreasing the extent to which their activities would be regarded with suspicion."[9] The implication of their conclusion is obvious: the more people in a geographic area, the less likely strangers would be noticed. When natural surveillance from community residents is reduced, crime increases.

Lewis and Maxfield took this logic to the next level. They focused on specific physical conditions within the environment, seeking to assess their impact on crime and the fear of crime. Assessing such things as abandoned buildings, loitering, vandalism, and drug use, they concluded that these factors draw little attention from police, as they have limited resources to effectively deal with said problems.[10] Yet, the researchers noted that they are important indicators of criminality within any community. This conclusion has been echoed by several other researchers.

Citizens regularly report their biggest safety concerns to be things like "panhandling, obstreperous youths taking over parks and street corners, public drinking, prostitution, and other disorderly behavior." These factors were identified as precursors to more serious crime. Moreover, the failure to remedy disorderly behaviors may be perceived as a sign of indifference. This indifference communicates that "no one cares"—which, in turn, leads to more serious crime and urban decay.[11] Consequently, the key to crime control is to address both the physical and social conditions that foster crime.[12].

The implications are clear. When faced with disorderly conditions, individuals tend to feel a greater exposure to risk. People connect the loss of control over their immediate environment with pending criminal attacks.[13] This thinking advanced the concept of "situational crime prevention," which takes into account the "intersection" of potential offenders with the opportunity to commit crime. Consequently, the commission of a particular crime could be avoided through certain preventive measures designed to reduce the offender's ability (or even propensity) to commit crimes at specific locations.[14]

Contemporary Applications

As we have chronicled in this book, the growing levels of disorder, even chaos, have affected many urban areas. Littering, public urination, graffiti, public intoxication, "smash-and-grab" thefts, and other antisocial behaviors signal that disorder is tolerated or even accepted. *Disorder begets disorder.* The prevalence of "quality-of-life" infractions creates conditions conducive to more serious crime.

Addressing these conditions is best done through preventive methods designed to improve conditions within a specific geographic area. This can be accomplished in several ways, including the rehabilitation of physical structures, the removal (or demolition) of seriously decayed buildings, and the improvement of land or existing buildings by cleaning and painting. Other relatively simple environmental improvements are recommended, such as planting flowers, trees, or shrubs. These are designed to enhance the "look and feel" of an area.[15] Physical improvements, coupled with efforts to reduce or eliminate certain anti-social behaviors, such as loitering, drinking and drug usage, fighting, and other disorderly behaviors are critical components of an order-maintenance approach to crime prevention.

Viewed in this broad manner, "security" can encompass a wide array of factors—from trash collection to planting flowers to private security patrols. Each is designed to improve conditions within the area. With the logic derived from this line of thinking, the need to control physical conditions and public activities is paramount. The threat of terrorism and extremist violence will magnify this environmental focus. For example, an unattended package left on a street corner may be a lethal bomb. An unidentified vehicle may become a tragic and lethal explosion. With these demonstrated tactics of terrorists, the importance of an orderly and clean environment cannot be overstated. This focus on the environment has been considered *the* security issue of the twenty-first century.[16]

Discouraging crime by manipulating the environment has many facets. In the security industry, Crime Prevention through Environmental Design (CPTED) has been used successfully for years. Changing certain features of the environment reduces the incidence of crime. Natural surveillance is emphasized, with environmental design structured so that users can see *farther and wider*. In addition, CPTED encourages territorial behaviors and natural access controls. As with the larger notion of order maintenance, proper care and control of the facilities are critical.[17]

Order maintenance techniques were also a core goal of *Community Policing,* which sought to extend beyond the traditional goal of crime-fighting to focus on fear reduction through order-maintenance techniques.[18] Preventing crime was more important than capturing the offender after the crime had been committed.[19]

In the private sector, the focus on prevention, as opposed to enforcement, has dominated the decisions of security industry officials.[20] The similarity of private security and community policing techniques can be narrowed to one core goal: both are intended to utilize proactive crime prevention that is accountable to the client or the citizen, respectfully. Since order maintenance is suited for both police and security, describing this symmetry will explain why security personnel will increase their presence on public streets and areas.

At least partly because of its crime-prevention focus, private security personnel already control and protect business facilities, assets, employees, and customers. Private security personnel did what the police could not accomplish. Security firms serviced specific clients, focusing on the protection of certain assets, both physical and human, as their primary and even exclusive purpose.[21]

Considering the criminological theories outlined above, a substantial body of law has grown around the notion of the environmental aspects of crime. Tort causes of action, known as either *premises liability* or *negligent security*, have provided explosive business for personal-injury attorneys. Legal exposures created a significant consequence. Property and business owners were motivated to institute security measures within and around their businesses. This can be viewed as both a carrot and a stick. The carrot is a safe, secure place to do business, live, and/or work. Of course, a safe and secure environment will not hurt the reputation of the business, or the viability of the property. Conversely, the stick is a substantial potential liability with substantial jury awards. Plus, media exposure coupled with reputational damages associated with criminal incidents are powerful reasons to secure premises from criminals. Consequently, *security can be seen as an asset and crime control as a duty*. Both often supersede merely relying on police for protection.[22]

The result of the carrot and stick was an increased use of security personnel and methodologies. Business and property owners started to think and worry about security, becoming more proactive in fostering a safe and secure environment. This relationship of the security industry to the public also increased the scope of the services provided by private security.[23]

As the liability for security increased, the perimeters of security expanded farther and farther from the "protected facility." Now it is common for security patrols for properties and businesses to extend into the streets and other public areas. Extended perimeters serve to reduce crime by providing a secure environment. By expanding perimeters, security patrols can be seen as an additional security layer in the public domain.

We have seen that public police are facing an increasingly difficult task incorporating crime prevention or public safety. On the heels of defunding and reimagining, what we think about policing is changing—or has changed.

Overburdened police are also faced with economic and operational constraints. Due to these factors, it is not unreasonable to conclude the role of private security will increase and play a larger role in the prevention of crime in areas traditionally and exclusively patrolled by police.[24]

Twenty years ago, I predicted the rise of private policing. In fact, it was the subject of my doctoral dissertation.[25] Ironically, I defended my dissertation on September 10, 2001. At that moment in time, it was only an esoteric subject. The next day, it became relevant. My thinking was that private policing would be driven by terrorism and extremism. But I didn't anticipate that ideologies spurring extremism could become "mainstream." Yet, this is where we are. Hence, here is my summary statement:

Order maintenance techniques will prove to be an increasingly important function of both police and private security, particularly in a chaotic or extremist climate.[26]

Given the already volatile climate, the introduction of security personnel (or what can be considered *private police*) into the public domain will cause concern or even alarm. Yet, to others who are afraid and even desperate for protection, this is precisely what is needed. Either way, many legal and functional challenges must be addressed to appropriately contribute to the order maintenance needs of the community. Suffice it to say that extending the scope of private police into public and semi-public property will necessitate increased professionalism.

As terroristic and extremist violence accelerate the delivery of order maintenance services, private police will fill the void caused by defunding and reimagining policing. While police officers will perform certain order maintenance tasks, the amount or the percentage of this work will likely decrease—possibly significantly. Security will provide more "eyes and ears" on the public way. In the chaotic environment of 2022 and beyond, this will be needed. Though police are chiefly responsible for managing law and order, *alternative service providers* can be viewed as an additional layer of security and as a division of labor.[27] This could be accomplished by focusing sworn police officers on tactical functions and shifting service and order maintenance functions such as loitering, public drinking, rowdy behavior, abandoned vehicles, and vehicle lockouts, building checks, alarm response, and providing "street corner security" in business or mixed commercial/residential districts to private police or other alternative service providers. Others have advocated engaging social workers to treat people under the influence of drugs/alcohol, dealing with mental or emotional problems, or servicing panhandlers or homeless people.

While many alternative service providers are available to fill the void, private firms provide cost savings to municipal budgets. This is achieved through lower salaries, and less costly benefits such as pensions, medical, overhead savings, and other similar factors. Indeed, some privatized arrangements are exclusively funded by voluntary real-estate tax increases or direct payments from business and property owners. These have clear benefits to already overburdened municipal budgets. Many of these arrangements are contained within Business Improvement Districts (BID). There are more than 1000 across the US.[28]

The prospect for alternative service providers—particularly private policing—conducting order-maintenance functions can be derived from two basic factors: *fear* and *money*. Both factors will independently contribute to the market need for these services.

Economic & Operational Issues *(Money)*

From a purely financial perspective, cost saving is a significant driver. Even rather dated police expenditures reveal that it costs at least $100,000 per year per police officer when salary, benefits, and overhead expenses are calculated into the equation.[29] Personnel expenditures are typically the single-largest line item for cities and towns.

Beyond salaries and benefits, certain operational functions increase costs associated with public safety services. For decades, citizens have been urged to call "911." This computerized call-taking system has led to huge increases in workloads in police departments where people call the police for more and more service-orientated requests. Calls for such things as barking dogs, streetlight repairs, noisy neighbors, unruly children, alarm response, and the like have created a difficult "unintended consequence" for police agencies already strapped with resource constraints.[30]

Types of service calls were distinguished in a recent study. Researchers reviewed around 4.3 million calls from nine different police agencies in cities both large (with a population over 1 million) and smaller (with under 80,000 residents) over the years 2016/2017. These are some of the findings:[31]

- Mental health incidents **at 1.3 percent** (only 4 percent of those calls resulted in an officer being dispatched)
- Traffic-related **at 16.8 percent**
- "Disorder" **at 16.2 percent**
- "Suspicion" calls—from individuals worried that a crime might happen or has happened—**at 12.8 percent**
- Violent incidents **at 6.4 percent**

While this study did not set out to assess defunding, it criticized the defunding approach, stating it "generally proceeded *without adequate research* about either the scale or nature of issues that the police handle and the potential consequences of the proposed reform efforts (emphasis added)." It also pointedly stated we "must focus more on what officers are actually doing and where their duties can best be adjusted. 911 data can clearly serve as another potential piece of this puzzle, but also as a reminder that police reform remains a *far more complex and nuanced* issue than many realize (emphasis added)."[32]

Trying to discern what police do and what they *should* do has been debated for years. For example, many years ago, researchers foretold that "citizens [are] bringing problems to the police that the police may not be best suited to address."[33] While the desire to insert social workers into policing is not without merit, the above data shows that only a tiny percentage of 911 calls involve mental health cases. Yet, experts like University of Missouri St. Louis criminologist Richard Rosenfeld says there's no reason if the goal is to fight crime, that communities shouldn't expand both policing and social services—what he calls a "both-and" approach.

This suggested innovation is consistent with reforms instituted over the years. For example, reducing the level of service calls by using "311" (non-emergency police response), and call stacking (prioritizing calls for dispatch based on level of seriousness) had some real success.[34] However, these have not resolved the basic dilemma—servicing the community through the resources allocated to police. Defunding and reimagining have complicated this.

Plus, extremism and terrorism—and lawlessness—have further exasperated this situation (and will only continue to do so). Ironically, these may provide an impetus for police to transfer to or supplement forces with private security personnel. Contracting certain service tasks can be equated to "outsourcing," which is common in business.

My underlying conclusion is that *private police* will be increasingly utilized to respond to service calls that the police ought not do. This assertion is echoed by Stephanie Mann, the author of *Safe Homes, Safe Neighborhoods*, who asserted that "people need to take responsibility for their safety. . . . Citizens are the law and order in a community . . ."[35] In the current extremist and lawless climate, it's particularly appropriate to assert that government cannot implement the necessary remedies to deal with crime and terrorism (including the attendant fears) without the contribution of private security.

Crime & Extremism *(Fear)*

Crime and fear have been systematically demonstrated.[36] Incivility is equated with disorder, in that both purport to represent chaotic conditions that result from more serious criminal activity. Think about this dynamic during the summer of 2020 along with "smash-and-grab" and armed carjackings. These crimes—and the brazen nature of the respective criminals—are very disconcerting.

The levels of fear are greatest where crime *and* incivility co-exist. Now, add terrorism and extremism to this equation. Remember this key distinction: while crime causes fear, terrorism is *designed* to cause fear. Terrorist acts are designed to play to the audience. Think of this distinction. If a mugging occurs on a subway, it is likely that the offender was interested in one thing: *the money*. Publicity is not the desire. Neither is acclaim. Instead, the criminal simply wants money. Certainly, the desire is not to have the "deed" appear on the news. Contrast this with terrorism where victims are often deemed irrelevant. Usually, those injured or killed are simply part of communicating the "deed." The message is: Pay attention to us because you may be next!

This dynamic speaks volumes. It will create a need for more security. It will help explain "why" policing methods need to be changed. Conveying the message that people are vulnerable and that the government may not provide protection. More "guardians" will be desired.

These guardians include *alternative service providers*, such as civilian governmental employees, volunteers, and private police officers. An example comes near the close of 2021 when a Chicago neighborhood hired armed private police. The local alderman noted that "I always say that any extra set of eyes in the neighborhood is important."[37] The reality is they need more than eyes. *Armed* guardians are often what people want—and need.

We will close this section with the acknowledgment that "combining" police and security into a larger "public-safety" policing model will not be easy. There are numerous pitfalls and complications to this transition. The dangers inherent in this work and within this transition are real. Time will tell how the current economic woes and public safety concerns will coalesce.

While identifying or encountering obstacles during the transitional years ahead, recall two words: *fear* and *money*. These will be the drivers. Many have already worked long and hard to develop "partnerships" and other relationships between professionals in security and policing. These will go a long way in facilitating this new model of policing.

SURVEILLANCE (INTELLIGENCE + TECHNOLOGIES)

Combining order maintenance with surveillance is the next element of *Public Safety Policing*. Together these elements provide a fuller, more robust view of what *public safety* will look like. Intelligence and technological advancements in public safety can be traced back decades, but its formal acknowledgment may be best presented in the Department of Homeland Security's "Urban Area Security Initiative" (2007) which offered grants to help local police strengthen their ability to collect and analyze intelligence. These grants were designed to enhance the intelligence capacities of state and urban policing agencies.

A strategy called Intelligence-Led Policing (ILP), which is critical to public safety, came from these homeland security initiatives. Yet, this alone does not adequately explain the dynamics of interfacing and collating information from public camera systems, crime mapping, predictive software, access control systems, and similar technologies. Each is critical to public-safety services and represents a key source of information within the intelligence process.

One way to bring this element into a structural assessment is to consider the acquisition of information. Inherent to policing (and almost anything) is the need to obtain, process, analyze, and disseminate information. In the old days, this was rather straightforward. A crime was committed; it was observed by a citizen, who yelled for help; the police came and arrested the offender based on the statement of a witness. This "information flow" was sometimes enhanced by observations by the officer, or by statements made by the offender. Over time, various technological enhancements made the acquisition of information more readily obtainable.

As police moved in vehicles enabling them to observe much more "data" as they drove from location to location, from beat to beat, from beat to sector, and from sector to the larger community. Telegraphs, "call boxes," and then radios within the vehicle, and later handheld devices, greatly increased the acquisition of additional information. Telephones used to report crimes facilitated this information flow. Other technologies like burglar and hold-up alarms helped transmit information from the protected facility to monitoring centers, to police dispatch centers, and on to responding police vehicles. These and other technologies have fostered the rapid flow of information designed to prevent crime and capture the criminal.

As a society, we are swimming in data. The amount of data and information transmitted within society is overwhelming. Police are processing substantial amounts of information from seemingly ever-increasing sources. Indeed, one of the "innovations" of *Community Policing* was to cultivate the flow and quality of human information by emphasizing relationships within the community. For example, foot patrols enabled police to observe crime indicators that may go unnoticed by rapid-vehicle patrols.[38] Walking also helped facilitate conversations with citizens and business owners, fostering relationships and enhancing data and information flows. Beat meetings also opened dialog to a larger audience, enabling community concerns to be aired. Meetings fostered information flow both ways, from the community to the police and from the police to the community. Other more strategic information flows were fostered by community and political leaders at face-to-face meetings.

Internally, police agencies developed information reports and special-attention notices. Information also came to be transmitted via bulletins, teletypes, emails, and other electronic means. Accountability sessions are used to assess the effectiveness of tactical and strategic remedies designed to impact crime patterns and trends. These are facilitated by increasingly sophisticated data analysis methods, by crime mapping software, by "real-time" information transmitted by such technologies as cameras and alarms, and by an overall increase of technologies designed to transmit and discern information.

These technological enhancements, like those in the larger society, have resulted in "information overload." Seemingly ever-increasing sources of information, more sophisticated layers of data, and the rapid transmission of both have created operational dilemmas within police agencies.

Added to this dilemma is the fact that failing to "connect the dots" from any information source can result in a tragedy. The challenge is not just obtaining intelligence but making sense of it and sharing it with those who can use it.

Traditionally, police have been trained to focus on criminal behavior. The threat of terrorism, however, requires police to focus their attention on data or observations that *do not necessarily indicate criminal intention or conduct.* The difficulties are multiplied when "connecting the dots," involves actions that do not constitute a crime, or are only minor crimes and/or involve multiple jurisdictions. Hence, the key is to recognize indicators, and report them in a timely and thorough manner, thereby enabling the intelligence personnel to "connect the dots."

The "War on Terror" required the military to identify small networks that blended into local populations. To ferret them out, US policy called for vast new databases and powerful intelligence-collection authorities to identify patterns and signatures of terrorists within the general population. "There was a massive expansion in intelligence data and analysis programs after 9/11," said Alan Butler, executive director of the Electronic Privacy Information Center.[39]

Over the years, US intelligence authorities were expanded to obtain access to the communication records of Americans—and the power to wiretap calls without warrants in limited circumstances. One big trend was to shift from targeted surveillance of specific individuals toward bulk surveillance aimed at gleaning information from population-wide data. Meta-data emphasis resulted in the government storing massive amounts of data.

Intelligence-Led Policing

A useful starting point is to provide a definition. According to the *National Strategy for Homeland Security,* Intelligence-Led Policing is:[40]

> "management and resource allocation approach to law enforcement using data collection and intelligence analysis to set specific priorities for all manner of crimes, including those associated with terrorism."

Distinguishing ILP from traditional police investigations is instructive. Information is unprocessed (raw) data gathered or collected in its original form by an officer. Data includes raw print, images, and signals. It can be *classified* (such as technical intelligence signal intercepts) or *unclassified* (such as fliers distributed during a demonstration or posts on Internet message boards). Information is data that has been collated and processed to produce a document that is of generic interest, such as police reports and/or from informants, documents, surveillance, wiretaps, observations, cameras, alarms, and the like. Processing this information, however, does not transform it into intelligence.

Differentiating between intelligence reporting and police investigations is best done by examining respective goals. Investigations are typically based on leads and evidence associated with a specific criminal act. These are designed to identify and/or apprehend offenders for prosecution. Intelligence is designed to capture information based on reasonable suspicion of criminal involvement that can be used in developing criminal cases, identifying crime trends, and protecting the community by means of intervention, apprehension, and/or target hardening.

More specifically, intelligence is much more defined and refined. It is the output of analysis, generated by a trained analyst and assessed for validity and reliability, through inductive and deductive logic. These techniques enhance decision-making, such as an intelligence briefing.[41] In the end, intelligence is designed to assist leadership in making the best possible decisions with respect to crime-control strategies, allocation of resources, and tactical operations.[42] Overall, proper intelligence is built with information that:

- Has an appropriate crime predicate
- Has originated from a verified and evaluated source
- Is enhanced by research and analysis

Intelligence requires the systematic exploitation of information including putting together several, often disjointed and seemingly unrelated bits and pieces of information.[43] An excellent analogy is to picture intelligence much like putting together a puzzle. But a puzzle has a picture of what it should look like when completed. The challenge is not having an advance "picture" of the completed puzzle.

Intelligence, then, is not about merely reacting to issues as they develop. It is about being proactive. It requires discerning and preventing crimes/events before they happen. Understanding threats, criminal organizations, and crime targets within communities is key to managing crime threats and *preventing crime.* Doing so requires an element of surveillance, whether physical or more commonly through electronic means. Instead of relying solely on the federal government for intelligence, many state and local departments are taking the initiatives to create their own systems.

Consequently, ILP is crime-fighting that is guided by effective intelligence-gathering and analysis.[44] In an extremist climate, capturing, analyzing, processing, and distributing intelligence will become increasingly important in the years ahead. As we will see below, the use of artificial intelligence (AI) in technology systems mirrors this intellectual gathering process.

This should serve as a primer on how intelligence methods contribute to the surveillance means of individuals and communities. Connecting this to technologies is part of the "dot-connecting" common in ILP and in overall public safety. The following equation is illustrative: Information/Data + Analysis = Intelligence.

Technologies

Using technologies to enhance security and public safety has been an effective aspect of police work for decades. As these are ubiquitous, they also became "smarter" and more efficient. Smarter devices, often using analytics based on artificial intelligence (AI) software applications, allow the user to set parameters and other "rules" used to alert and hone in on specific behaviors, circumstances, or changes in the environment. Much more can be said, but for now, here is a brief list of these technologies including, but is not limited to:

Networked camera systems	Remote Traffic enforcement
Predictive crime mapping	Access control systems
Identification systems	Facial recognition systems
Perimeter-intrusion detection systems	Infrared/night vision systems
Explosive detecting scanners	Global positioning systems
License-plate readers	Sensor systems
Drones	Fusion centers

Most will know each of these, except possibly fusion centers. These are tech- and intelligence-driven facilities designed to assist with real-time information and actionable intelligence. Fusion centers are a valuable tool—even indispensable—to public safety and combating extremism and terrorism. The information-gathering process described in the previous section is a key to obtaining useful and valuable information. So is information that is obtained from cameras and other technological systems used to "connect the dots" of the *Public Safety Policing* model.

Cameras have made crucial contributions to the public domain. Private firms began using cameras (CCTV) in the early 1960s in banks and commercial buildings. By the 1970s CCTV was deployed in hospitals and all-night convenience stores. In the 1980s video recorders were introduced, and in the 1990s digital technology followed.[45]

The first generation of cameras installed in *public environments* involved wide-angle cameras that were placed in crime hotspots. The second generation brought remote access by using a joystick and zoom capabilities. The third generation used software for facial and license-plate recognition—and for motion detection systems.[46] Predictive and behavioral-based systems constitute the fourth generation of security systems. Yet, even with these, we are still at the front end of the trend toward public camera and surveillance systems.

Surveillance comes in many different forms and types of devices, which can be used for crime deterrence, enforcement, and prosecution.

Surveillance from camera systems transmit video images that can be instantly sent to police dispatch or fusion centers. Video surveillance networks equipped with analytics enable searchable, actionable, and quantifiable intelligence from live or recorded video content. Analytics software is used to detect and extract objects in a video based on certain defined criteria, with users creating criteria to trigger an "event" for such things as unattended bags, unattended vehicles, dwelling vehicles, crowd formation, and even physical distancing compliance. Each of these can be identified by the software with real-time alerts provided.

Depending upon the nature of the event, police or security can be dispatched to respond directly to the area of concern. For example, ShotSpotter cameras detect gunshots in neighborhoods, using audio sensors and remote operational capacity. Once gunshots are detected, the cameras can be remotely tilted or zoomed in to react to the events on the street, turning the camera in the direction of the sounds while alerting police dispatchers and recording images before or as police are dispatched to the scene.

Police also typically have cameras on their chests and in squad cars. Cameras on cell phones are ubiquitous. House doorbell cameras can also be shared or transmitted to the police. In short, cameras are everywhere, proving instrumental to deter, detect, respond to, and record events for investigative, prosecutorial, and even auditing purposes. Cameras and related technologies have significantly changed the way policing agencies operate. Indeed, the nine-minute video that chronicled George Floyd's tragic death was taken from a cell phone.

Artificial Intelligence can expand a system's coverage beyond a camera's field of view, alerting camera operators of an audio alarm or audible request for help. These could be used to pan/tilt/zoom to provide a visual of the area where the audio originated. Audio can also be used by police or security personnel to communicate with visitors or intruders, alerting them that help is on the way or that they have been detected. More advanced technology will even allow audio surveillance systems to detect the tone of voice or certain words that are generally a precursor to violent incidents.[47]

Cameras equipped with speed monitors take photos of passing vehicles that fail to stop at red lights or stop signs or fail to obey the speed limit. Fines against the registered owner result. Cameras also can scan license plates to identify drivers with outstanding parking tickets, warrants, and other infractions.

Widely used Automatic Number-Plate Recognition cameras take pictures of cars, recording the license-plate number, color and make of vehicle, and the time of the photo. This information is then sent to a central computer, where it is stored for a specified time period. The information is also checked against data contained in the law enforcement data systems, a license database, and other intelligence databases. This system can also detect stolen automobiles and vehicles wanted in "Amber Alerts," screen for vehicles driven by terrorists or other criminals, and even locate people who have not paid their tickets, taxes, or whose owners are wanted on warrants.

Now, take this a step further. Interfacing over thirty million cameras used in the private sector with police fusion or dispatch centers would dramatically increase the surveillance capacity of policing agencies. The impact of these "intelligence" sources is substantial. Imagine these cameras interfaced and feeding in "real-time" to police or public-safety personnel as they approach a crime scene. Consider a bank hold-up alarm, which immediately transmits images from cameras in the bank to the police responding unit as they drive to the scene. Technology transmitting images from private cameras to responding police units for any number of crimes or calls for service has obvious value. Officer safety and the safety of those in the affected business location are greatly enhanced by such real-time information.

Other surveillance technologies such as backscatter X-rays, are used at airports to screen passengers. Radiation detection devices are used in seaports. Both provide crucial and timely details. For example, radiation devices scan cargo containers for materials that could be used to construct a nuclear device or "dirty bomb." The scanners provide a graphic visual profile of a container, activating an alarm if radioactive materials are present. This technology is consistent with research in explosive detection and facial recognition software that can pinpoint distress in a crowd to hone in on erratic body movements.[48]

Heat-sensing cameras are used to screen people at train or bus stations without requiring a mandatory wait at a security checkpoint. These cameras can be placed anywhere, to screen people as they walk by, being able to take a thermal image of the body many feet away. Images highlight materials colder than body temperature, signifying objects such as metals, plastics, and ceramics. Objects matching certain pre-set criteria will set off an indicator prompting a screener to do a more thorough search. These can also be used in a variety of settings, including military bases, arenas, malls, stadiums, and landmarks.[49]

Researchers are developing cameras capable of seeing hidden objects under a person's clothes. ThruVision cameras pick up Terahertz rays (also known as T-rays) that are emitted by all objects. T-Rays can pass through fabric and walls, enabling the camera to detect metallic and non-metallic objects such as explosives, liquids, narcotics, weapons, plastics, and ceramics. Since the camera screens people in large, open areas, people may not even be aware they are being screened.

Technology that detects improvised explosive devices (IEDs) is also part of these initiatives. One camera system seeks to identify a person in possession of a bomb by analyzing the way the person moves. Another system uses sensors to identify chemicals used to make bombs. These could help to lock in on suspicious people or activities in airports, border crossings, and other high-risk areas. Live video images are shared with public safety and law enforcement officials.

Other technologies include biometric systems, such as the Automated Biometric Identification System (IDENT) and the Integrated Automated Fingerprint Identification System (IAFIS). Both technologies were instrumental in the interoperability of the *Secure Communities Program* used to identify and remove criminal aliens from local communities.

Smart surveillance software utilizing multiple functions can quickly and efficiently observe and monitor a wide area and improve situational awareness. Focusing on how individuals move and behave, these systems are designed to analyze and model the patterns of people and vehicles moving through particular areas, even distinguishing between a "lost" and a "suspicious" person. "We are trying to automatically learn what typical activity patterns exist in the monitored area and then have the system look for atypical patterns that may signal a person of interest," says one researcher.[50]

Finally, one other surreal-sounding technology is known as Project Hostile Intent (PHI). Its goal is to predict "current or future hostile intentions" through remote behavior analysis systems. PHI technology, if perfected, could identify physical markers (body temperature, heart rate, respiration, blood pressure, facial expressions, etc.) associated with hostility or the desire to deceive. These assessments would then be applied toward the development of "real-time, culturally independent, non-invasive sensors" that can spot such behaviors. These sensors could include infrared light, heart-rate and respiration sensors, eye-tracking, laser, audio, and video. According to the DHS website:[51]

> "Project Hostile Intent (PHI) is a research effort by the Science and Technology Directorate to ascertain whether screening technology can aid DHS screeners in making better decisions by supplementing the current screening process (wherein a human screener evaluates an individual's behavior) with training and computers."

As a precursor to this technology, since 2003, the Transportation Security Administration (TSA) has been using the Screening Passengers through Observation Techniques (SPOT) program to detect suspicious people through the study of micro-expressions, which are involuntary facial telltales that indicate attempts to deceive. This, however, is costly and arduous. It also requires specialized training. The automation of the SPOT program, with computers instead of people screening for micro-expressions and other suspicious bodily indicators, is the impetus behind PHI. The next generation of such a complex system would focus on the ability to identify hostile micro-expressions of an individual *intending* to commit a crime.

The next-generation system called MALINTENT is defined as "the mental state of an individual intending to cause harm to our citizens or infrastructure."[52] This technology searches the body for non-verbal cues designed to predict if the subject intents to harm. But this is not a polygraph test. Subjects do not get hooked up or strapped down. Instead, the sensors do the analysis without any physical contact whatsoever. As an analogy, this technology is like an X-ray for bad intentions. It is the "mind-reading" element of the pre-crime squad illustrated in the movie *Minority Report.*

The system works to recognize, define, and measure seven primary emotions and emotional cues that are reflected in contractions of facial muscles. These emotions and relays are identified and communicated back to a security screener almost in real-time. The analyst then decides whether to flag the individuals for further questioning. The next step involves micro-facial scanning, which involves measuring minute muscle movements in the face for clues to mood and intention.

Similar technology, also known as "Future Attribute Screening Technology" (FAST), is said to be good enough to tell the difference between a harried traveler and a terrorist. Even if someone sweats heavily by nature, FAST technology allegedly can distinguish "normal" sweating from that of a terrorist. Years ago, an undersecretary at DHS declared the experiment a "home run." The results are classified but consider this thinking. As cold and inhuman as this *electric eye* may be, one benefit is that the scanners are unbiased and nonjudgmental. "It does not predict who you are and make a judgment, it only provides an assessment in situations," said the DHS undersecretary. "It analyzes you against baseline stats when you walk in the door, it measures reactions and variations when you approach and go through the portal."[53]

In short, the system reads body movements, called "illustrative and emblem cues." According to DHS, this is achievable because people "move in reaction to what they are thinking, more or less based on the context of the situation." FAST may also incorporate biological, radiological, and explosive detection, but the primary focus is on identifying and isolating potential human threats. Supporters argue that the application of FAST is almost limitless because it is a mobile screening laboratory. It could be set up at entrances to stadiums, malls, airports, and other places with mass gatherings.[54]

Consider also technology designed to be predictive, or at least provide "forecasting" of future crimes before they are committed. Using AI-powered algorithms, the goal is to use data to put cops in the right place at the right time. The software firm Geolitica says they do not make "predictions," but they "identify high-risk locations that officers could patrol." Using core data from incident reports about shootings, burglaries, and other crimes; the firm says it can discern trends used to forecast an objective methodology. "It's not the police who are deciding there's a crime; it's you, the victim, who's saying crime happened here," said Geolitica's chief executive.[55]

This goes both ways. Police departments are also using the software to install global-positioning systems into squad cars or radios to track where individual officers are patrolling. It can track individual officers' locations and compare deployments with crime forecasts. Hence, police agencies can monitor officers' movements and improve accountability, forecasting crime hot spots. As the executive inferred, "digital policing leaves digital trails [and] those trails are susceptible to oversight."[56]

This is the next-generation software of crime-forecasting software and predictive analytics started by CompStat, short for computerized statistics, which was introduced decades ago to analyze data about recent crimes to help cops identify hot spots.

The complexities of such data sets pose questions that many governments aren't currently equipped to answer, says Robert Cheetham, CEO of Azavea.

These technologies pose both promise and frightening implications. Promise in that by analyzing patterns of crime, one gets closer to predicting future crimes. But this can be frightening as we are getting closer to predicting that *specific individuals* are about to commit crimes—or have an intent to commit hostile actions. Consider this in our discussion on liberty and authoritarianism in the next chapter. Though much can be said, the basic questions are still relevant.

These go to the heart of the potential value and the pitfalls of intrusive surveillance technologies. Yet, the threat levels posed by an extremist climate will drive more and more surveillance techniques, both through intelligence methods and technologies. Both go to a policing model using surveillance as a critical element to maintain public safety. While these systems are pragmatic responses to demonstrable threats, there are obvious privacy and public policy concerns raised by a surveillance-based policing model.

To summarize this element, the combination of intelligence-gathering methods coupled with the widespread use of technologies have contributed to *surveillance* being an integral aspect of public safety.

PROTECTIVE METHODS

A descriptive way of describing this element is to focus on *protection* instead of *service.* Its purpose contrasts with the *Community Policing* era which sought to *clean* the environment of physical and social incivilities in order to combat crime. In the *Public Safety* era, the purpose will be to *control* the environment in order to protect the community. Due to the devastating impact of extremism—and of lawlessness—the following formula summarizes this approach:

Order + Surveillance + Protective = Control

Surveillance technologies coupled with an "enhanced" order-maintenance approach—with more eyes and ears on the street—will result in an almost "clinical" focus on the environment.

Considering this environmental focus, the idea of "policing terrorism" was once advocated in much the same way as the "broken-windows" strategy.

Both advocated focusing on minor crimes before they turn into serious crimes. The key difference was shifting police officers away from the idea that they're *only* first responders. Instead, the idea was to train them on prevention techniques.[57] Getting police orientated toward prevention is consistent with the tenets of *community policing.* Though much of the focus of police should be on prevention—this is better characterized as *protection*. Protection is more accurate because the police will need help in securing the environment—and themselves! We saw this with private security and security technologies. Here we will see it with policing tactics and weaponry.

Protective Policing Strategies & Supplemental Means

Exploring the trend toward protective policing methods, highlighting specific methods include:

Hot-Spot Policing focuses on problem areas with disproportionate levels of crime and violence. In this approach, officers are sent to problematic areas with the goal of deterring crime or disorder. Depending upon circumstances, sometimes police don't even need to engage people. Simply watching and conducting surveillance can affect crime. Police presence often deters people—known as the classic scarecrow effect, similar to parking an unoccupied police vehicle to reduce speeding or reduce criminal behavior in the area.

A 2019 review in the *Journal of Experimental Criminology* looked at dozens of studies and found *hot-spot policing* reduced crime without displacing it to other areas. Even better, evidence reveals "diffusion" in which crime reduction *benefits* spread to surrounding areas. The review relied on several strong studies, including randomized controlled trials, suggesting that the findings were solid and accurate.[58]

Problem-Oriented Policing focuses on chronic issues, bringing together local resources and services to address specific problems. This highly regarded approach uses a "scanning, analysis, response, assessment" model. Known as "SARA," the acronym is used to highlight its structured approach. The process is as follows: Scanning to detect the problem. Once a specific problem has been identified, the next step is to analyze how to solve this problem. As solutions are devised and evaluated, the next step is to execute a response.

When implemented, the last step is to evaluate those efforts. Is the problem resolved? Was it resolved in a manner consistent with legal parameters and community standards? Hence, the goal is not just to treat the problem in the short term, but to cure it in the long term. Depending on the specific problem and the ensuing analysis, police might play a major role or as a supplement to other service providers.

Focused Deterrence entails police focusing on specific individuals, particularly gangs, and delivering a clear message: *Stop engaging in violent or criminal activity.* As with wider community-based approaches, the community is to provide resources and support to help this message resonate. Getting community involvement can be accomplished by partnering with other groups in and out of government to provide a carrot—job training, education, government benefits, and so on. These are designed to help people get out of the criminal life. The stick is the threat of punishment. Both the carrot and stick, experts said, are crucial to the idea.[59]

Violence interrupters is a widely publicized approach where trusted community liaisons are inserted into situations that are ripe for violence. This is typically done by people who were formerly gang members. They engage the community, seeking to break up conflicts before they escalate into violence. Research in this approach ranged "from weak to disappointing." A 2020 John Jay report described their findings as to the viability of this approach as "mixed." You may remember from Chapter I that the St. Louis mayor's speech on violence interrupters was interrupted by gunfire. One can wonder if this is symbolic its viability.

Skill-and Life-Development includes summer jobs programs, drug addiction treatments, and skills training and education. Obviously, crime control is larger than the police. But if these do help, they are longer-term solutions, as most "non-police interventions" require longer-term solutions and future perspectives. These cannot quickly reduce crime, especially violent crime. Interventions to help address the root causes of crime and violence, from poverty to drug addiction, are needed but difficult to achieve.

Time is the key. Lifting people and places from poor or dysfunctional circumstances takes time, effort, money—and people who care. This is where "the system" has not been successful. Ultimately, there is little harm in trying to deter and prevent crime through life and career alternatives. Finding socially desirable ways to impact crime and disorder through a "holistic" approach seems best. Yet, we know that policing has been successful in deterring crime or violence—and this can be done quickly and efficiently. Lopez summarized the alternatives as follows:[60]

> "But, at least for now, there's no good evidence that the alternatives can replace the police. Meanwhile, policing has strong evidence suggesting it really can work to cut crime and violence. The idea that we can reduce the violence we've been seeing without any use of the police is not evidence- based; it's an aspiration, and it's a high-risk idea. A balanced portfolio feels like the lowest-risk strategy to me."

Police Tactics & Weaponry

With police and non-police approaches highlighted, the more controversial and poignant aspect of this protective element goes to the tactics and weaponry of police officers. When I initially raised this in 2009, this element was entitled "militarized policing." This stemmed from the "war on terror." Tactically oriented police officers with weaponry fighting this "war" were my premise. Over the years, with liberal, conservative, then progressive administrations; the movement of "militarized policing" ebbed and flowed.

Current societal circumstances require that we "revisit" this approach. Through the pressures leading to increased violence and ambush attacks, police are increasingly being targeted. If this continues, police will protect themselves. Due to the current circumstances, this element is entitled *Protective Methods*, both for the public and for the police. Let's reassert why this approach is needed.

Ideologies that seek and foster the destruction of the capitalistic system are entrenched in this society. This is causing crime and chaos—manifested as lawlessness. It is just a matter of time before some radicals go "underground." Terrorist cells and direct action are inevitable. This was expected in 2009.

Some well-publicized attacks did occur, such as the Boston bombings, San Bernardino, Pulse Night club, Las Vegas, to name a few. Yet, my point here is not to rehearse what already happened. Looking forward with clear eyes at what may lie ahead requires articulating a few basic premises.

Initially, expect the police to be targeted by terroristic and extremist violence. The reason is grounded in the "logic" of terrorism: *If we can kill police and military, we can kill civilians.* This conveys a profound meaning. If the police and military cannot protect themselves, how can average citizens do so? Without the weapons and the training, citizens have little hope of protecting themselves. With weapons in hand, citizens may change this "protective dynamic" in favor of the law abider. Yet, this also brings back images of the "Wild, Wild West." As this plays out, what is certain is both people and public safety personnel know they must do more to protect themselves. This entails better training, tactics, weapons, and other "self-defense" methods.

The second premise: Police and other public safety providers, like most people, will protect themselves when attacked. While we will flesh this out in more detail below, suffice it to say that people will innovate when targeted. Self-defense is a powerful human trait deeply embedded in human nature. As cold as this may sound, police will not simply wait to die. They will protect themselves—what the military calls "force protection." As the "job description" is to provide "security services," police will counter attacks with similar—or superior—weapons and tactics.

Finally, the impact of being targeted and countering attacks has profound psychological implications for public safety personnel. Since much, if not most, terroristic violence is unpredictable (in terms of time, place, and method), the impact of this violence is difficult to cope with. The underlying goal of terrorism, *kill one, frighten thousands*, is directed not only at "civilian" audiences. It is also aimed at public-safety providers, who see their comrades wounded and killed.

Since this is part of the job, police must be ready for potential violence. However, they are not immune from the ill effects of seemingly random—and deadly—violence. Military personnel returning from deployments experience many adverse psychological and physical effects from such violence. Its uncertainty and unpredictability are extraordinarily difficult to cope with.[61] This is most relevant in predicting how terroristic and extremist violence will "trigger" a reciprocal response from American police.

Increased use of force incidents is clearly problematic. Critics of militarized police typically argue that police will use force because their weaponry and tactics foster it. This is a legitimate concern. Logically, more aggressive police practices may result in a more aggressive attitudes of individual police officers. Aggressive practices and attitudes may also result in more use-of-force incidents. Expecting more use of force incidents by police—and more controversial police shootings is not what one ought to desire. Yet, balancing protection against aggression is the challenge.

There is no real "solution." No reasonable person would advocate increased violence. However, assume for the sake of argument that this premise is correct: *that there will be a generalized increase in terrorism and extremist violence.* If correct, then the correlating premise is also likely to be correct: *the use of force by police will increase in response to a general increase in violence.*

This thinking is particularly relevant when the *target* of terrorist and extremist violence is often directed toward *police* and *other public-safety providers*. One must be cognizant of the impact of violence generally. If criminals and terrorists use more deadly and sophisticated weaponry, then it stands to reason that the police will do the same.

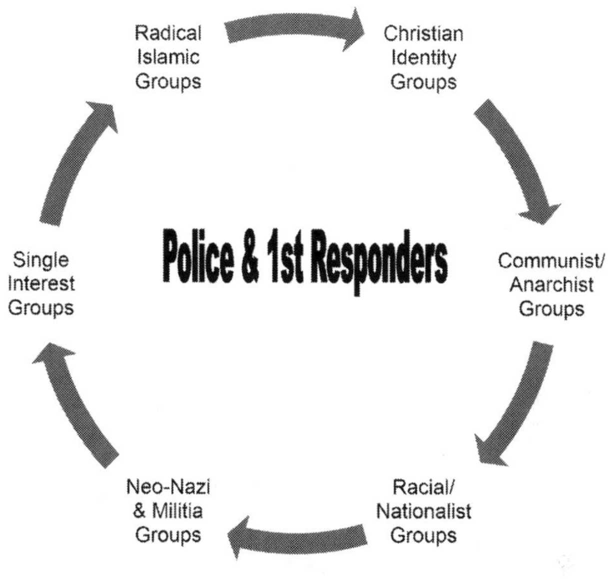

Copyright, James F. Pastor, 2009–2022

The above graphic illustrates this logic. While each of these ideologies has its own natural enemies as well as its potential allies, all see the police and first responders as a threat and a detriment. Detriment because they represent the system—as the most visible representatives of the government. Threat because they stand for stability and, hopefully, law and order. Police will arrest, prosecute, and sometimes even kill extremists. Consequently, the police must be defeated to achieve illicit power—either through revolution or otherwise.

No simple solutions are available. For example, gun-control laws, though appealing to many, are often presented in a simplistic, even naïve manner. These must be tied to this reality: *There are more guns in this country than people*. One may not like this, but it is a *hard fact* that cannot be ignored. Unless we are prepared to confiscate weapons, which amounts to "assisted-suicide" for those who are assigned to such tasks, then any notion of gun control has limited application. Yet can reasonable gun sale or transfer restrictions provide some remedy? If these are part of a larger multi-faceted program fashioned around legitimate 2nd Amendment protections, these may help. But the honest answer is blanket forms of gun control is *not* the solution. So what options are left?

Higher capacity and velocity weapons will be increasingly used by police. Expect the police to "arm up" to the level of weaponry used by criminals and terrorists. This may be perceived as "fighting violence with violence." This is acknowledged. When one thinks about any other alternatives, however, viable answers are absent. Many simply "hope" this will not happen, but *hope* is not a policy. Hope will not change the dynamics that have been taking root—for years. The seeds of this violence have been playing out for decades.

In short, the future portends increased violence and extremism. We cannot hope or wish this away. We will have to confront it on the streets and in public and private environments. While not wanting to discount any factor that will contribute to the "solution," we must realize that those who foster violence will have to be confronted.

Let's agree that the "solution" is not to ignore the obvious—that what was just summarized is coming—like it or not. If we believe as much, then we need to change the dynamics—and commence doing so before conditions further deteriorate. This means changing the selection, training, policies, and attitudes of police officers and public safety professionals. Changing cultural and organizational initiatives geared toward greater levels of discipline, fostered through revamping the way police agencies operate. As such, future policing agencies must find ways to both protect their officers—and limit the use of force to only those circumstances that require it. Correctly implementing this delicate balance—often in split-second decisions—is extraordinarily difficult.

As a result, look for more, not less, tactical units equipped with weapons that have been traditionally deemed military weapons. These tactical units, including SWAT teams, will play significant roles in combatting extremist and terroristic violence. Their mission must be to proactively find and arrest criminals and to engage those who carry or use weapons. They are to look for and arrest or engage those who seek to do harm.

The typical criticism of SWAT teams is that they have a "strong incentive" to expand their original "emergency" mission into more routine policing activities. Some think they do this to justify their existence.[62] While acknowledging the tendency to "use it because you have it," the real issue is more basic. Despite what some claim, raids or warrant service are *not* "routine." These are "routine" only when the subjects surrender peacefully. Heavily armed and trained SWAT units are excellent "motivators" for those to surrender without incident. Simply put, police weaponry and tactics may help level the playing field against individuals who have no rules or morals.

Conversely, not having heavy weapons or SWAT teams readily available can also contribute to *more* death. This played some role in the Uvalde school shooting. Should police have engaged the shooter sooner? Would this have been an appropriate tactical response? Was the failure to do so the result of lack of courage? Or would it have just been a reckless, useless act, resulting in police deaths? Notwithstanding the answers to these questions, the delay could, at least partly, be due to initially lacking the equipment and the firepower to effectively counter and neutralize the shooter. Though other mistakes were made, the dynamics of the incident—and its immediate and devastating results—with 19 dead children will be intensely analyzed. While the facts are still surfacing as this book is in its final edits, one can reasonably conclude that police tactics and weaponry will be hotly debated.

This debate will be emotional, yet impactive. Some contend that because of their close collaboration with the military, SWAT units bring the *warrior mentality* of military special forces. This includes being distinctly impersonal and elitist. Some contend that the *so-called* war on drugs and other *martial metaphors* are turning high-crime areas into "war zones," citizens into potential enemies, and police officers into soldiers. High-profile police killings over the past several years have validated this thinking—and have exasperated already volatile police-community relations.

Yet, the actual mindset lies somewhere between that of *warriors* and *peace officers*, represented by neither of these extremes. Although SWAT team officers consider themselves members of an elite unit with specialized skills, with more military ethos than typical police officers, this does not transform them into warriors. But it does come with caution as critics argue this "warrior mindset" is not appropriate for civilian police officers charged with enforcing the law.[63] With this thinking, the soldier confronts an enemy in a life-or-death situation. The soldier learns to use lethal force, follow orders instinctively, act in concert with his comrades, and initiate violence on command. This mentality, which new recruits are strenuously indoctrinated with in boot camp, can be a matter of survival for the soldier and the nation at war.

Despite this increase in police weaponry and tactics, and prior to any sustained terrorist campaign on American soil, we have seen "criminals" outgun the police. The Bank of America take-over robbery in the 1990s was a classic example. Years ago, this concern caused an International Association of Chiefs of Police (IACP) spokesman to say that police departments are "in an arms race" with criminals.[64] The consequence of this assertion has led a spokesman from the Brady Center to Prevent Gun Violence to assert that "police officers need to be able to defend themselves and the rest of us, and they need the weapons to do so." Since the Brady Center is devoted to gun-control laws, it is surprising to note that they advocated heavy weaponry for the police. This statement came years prior to heavily armed militias marching through urban areas, as seen with NFAC. So, too with gunmen entering grocery stores and schools.

Despite such pressures, civilian law enforcement officers must conduct themselves as being subject to the nation's laws and protected by the Bill of Rights. This is so basic to American policing that no additional comment is needed. Although police officers can legally use force in life-threatening situations, the Constitution and numerous Supreme Court rulings have circumscribed police use of force, as well as the power of search and seizure. To be clear, police must adhere to constitutional mandates. Overbearing tactics and violative behavior must be swiftly and consistently addressed. Balancing protective tactics with individual liberties, while sometimes exceedingly difficult, must be delicately and appropriately managed.

Yet, the inevitable question is: How will *Public Safety Policing* affect security and freedom? To most people, this issue is less about police weaponry and tactics and more about affecting the liberties and freedoms this country stands for. This is a fair and fundamental question. It's typically addressed by making hay when citizens are "terrorized" by heavily armed police. This makes the issue more about emotion than substance.

Yet, assessing the emotional impact—or better said, the perception—raised by highly armed police weaponry and tactics must be considered. Critics say that armored vehicles may only increase tensions by making residents feel as if they are under siege.[65] While this is a legitimate concern, it is also problematic. Should police die because they did not have the equipment and weaponry to counter an extremist, an armed gang member, or a terrorist?

With this mindset, looking at police tactics and weaponry is typically done without considering the perspective of the police. As is my approach, we miss much if we fail to see the viewpoint from the street and from police officers who know the streets.

Understanding the dynamics of ideology and terroristic violence brings us back to an era when the Los Angeles Police Department formed the first SWAT team and, it is said, originated the acronym SWAT to describe the elite force. The Los Angeles SWAT unit acquired national prestige when it was used successfully against the Black Panthers in 1969 and the Symbionese Liberation Army in 1973. What is the possibility that extremist groups like these will reappear in contemporary America? To reassert for emphasis, it is inevitable.

Please put yourself in the shoes of the typical police officer. A police officer, like most employees, wants to "do their job and go home." They desire job security. They pay bills, raise their children, juggle their debts, and spend time at home with their families. In short, they have human needs and dreams. Being police officers, however, they tend to be more cognizant of their safety than most other occupations.

When considering the protective methods of the police, one must understand what it's like to face weaponry you cannot counter. The implications of this point are made plain by Captain Phil Burton of the Marion County Indiana Sheriff's Department, who explained the reason why his department equipped its officers with assault weapons. He stated:

> "we felt the need . . . to equip ourselves, for lack of a better term, to meet force with force in order to provide safety to the public."[66]

This is the natural and pragmatic consequence of being targeted: police will respond with increased self-defense and self-protection techniques.

Being outgunned is a lonely—and helpless—feeling. It does not help the police or the community to be outgunned by criminals with ill intentions.

When faced with violent situations, it is extraordinarily difficult to remove emotion from the mix. Seeing violence from the perspective of those who must face it down, the legitimate human need for self-defense is obvious.

Being an enlightened, freedom-loving disciple, while never having to engage a heavily armed individual who would rather kill than go to jail separates concept from reality. Fortunately, this type of threat is not a daily occurrence. However, one such experience is sufficient to change one's perspective. Indeed, even the *possibility* of this occurring is enough to get your attention. "We live on being prepared for 'what if?'" said Pittsburgh Sgt. Barry Budd.[67] Many in this country have never had to even envision this possibility. To the average police officer, this is of little comfort.

This brings us back to my initial premise: the police officers see security and safety differently than most civilians. This is due to the nature of the job. However, the job is changing. As risky as it may have been in previous eras, these will pale by comparison to the years ahead. Police will be forced to protect themselves as they protect the community.[68]

Confronting threats that resemble *asymmetric warfare*, which is the military term for terrorism, will require great sacrifice—in blood and liberty—to overcome. *Asymmetric warfare* positions the weak against the strong. The "weak" (read the terrorists) declare "war" on the strong. The "strong" (read the police or more generally the US government) have superior weaponry, technology, resources, and personnel. These advantages are, nonetheless, constrained by several factors, including legal and moral considerations, public relations, operational capabilities, and the like.[69] The weak are not so constrained. When the "strong" are not able—or willing—to use their superior advantages, the battlefield in this "war" is leveled, sometimes even favoring the "weak."

As a consequence, those charged with protecting public safety will resemble the military, as asymmetric warfare has implications for both the military and the police. The "right" response requires some balance between the notion of war and crime. Police will need to "arm up," while simultaneously remaining cognizant of civil rights and principles. Is the prospect of heavily armed police officers on American streets problematic? My answer is yes—but it will be necessary!

It is fair to assert that heavily armed police may create an environment where individual rights may be violated. This could occur from the use of force inflicted by police against citizens. It could also occur from other constitutionally violative police practices stemming from an increase in the tactical orientation of policing. Each of these concerns is well-founded. Consider Balko's pointed assertion that:[70]

> "innocent American citizens had the sanctity of their homes invaded by agents of the government behaving more like soldiers at war than peace officers upholding and protecting our constitutional rights."

As this is a legitimate concern, many police administrators also worry about robberies in the subway. This type of crime, while problematic, pales in comparison to the suicide bomber on a train. Due to the changing nature of criminals, the destructive nature of their crimes, and the lethality of their weapons, police officers ought to have an array of high-tech military equipment previously reserved for use during wartime.[71] Consequently, *when* this "war" spills out into the US, police will face substantial increases in violence. When confronted with such lethal weaponry, police will respond with appropriate weapons and tactics.

This will require in a most delicate balance—protecting people and property in a manner consistent with legal and constitutional protections.[72] Achieving this balance when the "protectors" are in fear of their safety—from increasingly dedicated threats and increasingly lethal weaponry—will obviously complicate the dynamic.

As mentioned, this balance is extraordinarily difficult to obtain. According to Laqueur, "experience teaches that a little force is counter-productive . . . the use of massive, overwhelming force, on the other hand, is usually effective."[73] As such, Laqueur cautions against launching anti-terrorist campaigns unless the government is "able and willing to apply massive force."[74] While it is necessary and appropriate to examine police use of force incidents, the ability to do within a terrorist environment is extraordinarily difficult. Under these circumstances, being "willing and able" to launch such an anti-terror campaign is extremely questionable. Putting aside the political, legal, and public-relations arguments, one may question whether the police have the operational capability to perform massive anti-terror operations. Indeed, Poland agrees that massive force would be necessary, but he adds that:[75]

> "Unquestionably, a campaign of prolonged terrorism in the US would result in the federal government assuming direct police powers; and the temporary suspension of civil liberties would be deemed necessary to maintain order and locate offenders."

As would be expected, the notion that the police (plus security forces and/or the military) will respond to terrorist campaigns is disconcerting to many. Consider Balko's testimony before a congressional sub-committee, which argued that:[76]

> "the military has a very different and distinct role than our domestic peace officers. The military's job is to annihilate a foreign enemy. The police are supposed to protect us while upholding our constitutional rights. It's dangerous to conflate the two . . . It's time we stopped the war talk, the military tactics, and the military gear. America's domestic police departments should be populated by peace officers, not the troops of an occupying military force."

It is hard to imagine two completely different views of the world. Poland argues for massive force. Balko is averse to any force, as he desires "peace" officers. In the end, people will offer solutions based on how they see the problem. Some see the problem of police having too much force, too much weaponry, and too much authority. Others see the extremists and the terrorists as being too frightening, too well-armed, and too great a threat to combat with traditional policing modalities.

Either way, the debate will be heated and controversial. We have barely scratched the surface of the intensity of the coming controversy. To some, police will be seen as "shock troops,"[77] while others will desire the perceived *protection* from heavily armed police. The "right" approach will be much debated and fluid. The challenge will be to balance the security and safety principles desired by the police and the public, with the often-competing principles of rights and freedom. Depending upon the level of violence, this *balance* will weigh in favor of security and safety when violence (or the threat) is high. Conversely, it will weigh in favor of rights and freedom when violence is diminished.

Achieving an "optimal balance" will always be subject to disagreement. This is because a consensus will never be achieved on either the threat posed or the solutions to the threats. People "filter" their decisions according to disparate experiences, perceptions, and beliefs. These shape and define people's worldviews and determine the "right" approach. Debating how to address what lies ahead while faced with high levels of violence will be extraordinarily difficult. Our minds are unable to cope with both reasoned analysis and high levels of emotion at the same time. Hopefully, this book will spur such debate. In the meantime, please consider how worldview shapes our sense relating to the tactics and weaponry of the police.

In summary, this section articulates the *protective* methods in this element of *Public Safety Policing.* These include various policing strategies, supplemental non-policing approaches, and police tactics and weaponry. Articulating this vision is not pleasant, and it may not be pleasant to read. Yet, it was important to express, given the gravity of the predicted revolutionary climate. I said a lot of things I hope are wrong. Although, moving through the logic of the book, this chapter may be the "toggle" that moves this country closer to or farther away from revolution. If people see this chapter as it is written, my hope is that good people will stand up and support the police. If you are inclined to, do so sooner than later.

To close this chapter, consider again the formula and its vital importance . . .

Order + Surveillance + Protection = Control

CHAPTER VI

THINGS THAT MATTER . . .

We live in a fractured society seemingly going in opposite directions. On one hand, as we have chronicled throughout this text, lawlessness exists in urban areas. Mobs walking into stores, taking what they want. Pedestrians on the streets being brutally and randomly attacked. Shootouts and car jackings in broad daylight.

Yet, at the same time, businesses implement extraordinary precision along with legal and security instruments, policies, and protocols designed to protect business assets, customers, and employees. Having worked in various corporate counsel positions over the years, I am struck by the level of sophistication used to secure assets and people. Companies regularly use Non-Disclosure Agreements (NDA), Data Privacy Agreements, Service Level Agreements (SLA), and a host of other requirements within business contracts. These drive precision and protection. Yet, the society around them seems to be going in the opposite direction. Can we reconcile these . . .?

Coming off the *Public Safety Policing* chapter, we see the need for order, surveillance, and protection all come together to foster control in environments that are otherwise chaotic. But the environment is still in flux. Many things still need to happen to regain control.

Even as the elements of *Public Safety Policing* are articulated and developed, these come with certain complicating factors, such as reinstituting order and implementing protective methods. There will be pushback before control can be achieved. Those who benefit from disorder will not lie down just because they are told to. Those who desire to bring down "the system," will not simply give up because protective means are being utilized. Hence, a shifting but delicate balance still needs to occur. Yet, one cannot reconcile how corporations are dotting every "i" and crossing every "t" while cities try to cope with crime and chaos. These distinctions cannot be sustained. Something has to give. In a telling example, in March 2022, Amazon told hundreds of its employees to work at an alternative location after an uptick of violent crime rocked the area around its downtown Seattle office.[1] This will not be the last company to "adjust" its employment practices due to crime, disorder, and chaos.

An interesting historical parallel occurred in the late 1850s, going into 1860, just before the civil war. Coming off the partisan instability in the 1850s, young Northerners sought to regain control of an increasingly fractured society. The movement, known as the "Wide Awakes" campaigned for three important values: *free speech, free soil, and free men.* Wikipedia describes the Wide Awakes as "a youth organization and later a paramilitary organization cultivated by the Republican Party during the 1860 presidential election in the United States."

The social and political dynamic was dramatic. Here is how it was described:[2]

> "The Wide Awakes never marched anywhere in the South in 1860, but they represented the South's greatest fear, an oppressive force bent on marching down to their lands, liberating the slaves, and pushing aside their way of life . . .
>
> To the South, the Wide Awakes were only a taste of what was to come if Lincoln were to be elected. The North would not compromise and could force themselves upon the great

> South . . . That mindset was not appeased by the wide acceptance of the Wide Awakes in the North.
>
> On October 25, 1858, Senator Seward of New York stated to an excited crowd that '*a revolution has begun*' and alluded to Wide Awakes as 'forces with which to recover back again all the fields . . . and to confound and overthrow, by one decisive blow, the betrayers of the constitution and freedom forever.' To the South, the Wide Awakes and the North would be content only when the South was fully dominated (emphasis added)."

In a society dominated by woke culture, can one doubt that a countermovement will result? Just as corporations seek to control every element of their business model, people will not allow their cities to be mired in chaos. Indeed, how long will corporations operate in urban areas unless control is achieved? Somehow, forces to reassert control over chaos must result. For example, the "Wide Awakes" in the pre-Civil War era were described as "well-drilled" and "served as *political police* in escorting party speakers and in *preserving order at public meetings* (emphasis added)." Yet, just as in its earlier iteration, the woke will not stand by idly. Seeing the Wide Awakes coming to the fore, the south created its own force known as the "Minutemen." The rest, as they say, is history. A brutal and divisive civil war resulted.

Though the Wide-Awake name has been coopted by the woke,[3] there is no doubt some opposing mindset—or ideology—will try to regain control. That is, if the government, police, and public safety providers fail to do so. This is partially why progressives were so animated about the Kyle Rittenhouse incident. Having an armed "vigilante" attempt to regain control in a volatile environment was *beyond the pale*. But few progressives (if any) complained about the "mostly peaceful protests." Recall that the violence at these protests was never even mentioned during the Democratic Convention. Less than a week after the convention, Rittenhouse shot three men.

With this as set-up, this chapter will analyze *Things That Matter*. Taking a step back from the volatility, let's look at what really matters. These points can help us reorient and ground ourselves. Before getting started, let me present what I saw about a decade and a half ago. At that time, my sense of the biggest challenge was the delicate balance between security and rights. Passionately trying to articulate what was at stake, here is what I said then:[4]

> "I will close this book with what I consider the most important principles facing this country—and any individual. Since the reader made it this far through the book, I presume that you have determined that my tendency is to err on the side of security as opposed to rights. While I readily admit to this tendency, I do not discount the incredibly important notion of rights— or more broadly—freedom or liberty. In my mind, freedom is one of the most important human ideals. It is what has driven people for generations. Millions of people have died for this ideal. It is, in short, what drives the human soul to live a better life for themselves or for their children.
>
> The significance of this ideal may be best epitomized by the movie *Braveheart*. The Scottish leader, William Wallace, fought against England, seeking freedom for his country. He was captured and asked to renounce this movement. He refused...and cried out 'FREEEEE-DOMMMMMM' as his last words! . . ."

Let us continue from this perspective. Freedom is an extraordinarily powerful motivator. It's the only way to prevail over fanaticism. Referring to the War on Terror, in the end, my assertion was that it would be won when more people were willing to die for freedom compared to those willing to die for a fanatical worldview. These provocative questions were raised:

In the end, it is all about the reason you are living... Does your life have meaning larger than you? Are you willing to die for something? At the end of your life, do you "win" if you have the most toys or a lasting and meaningful legacy?

Freedom as the ultimate "solution" is partly tempered by socio-political realities. While freedom can prevail over fanaticism, the reality is that most people will not be willing (or able) to see it that way. Only some will understand the nature of the conflict!

Since most Americans do not recognize or intend to be part of the War on Terror—or the coming revolution—the only way to hold off defeat is to secure ourselves from those who seek to do harm. Hence, advocating for security over freedom may be pragmatic because most Americans do not understand the nature of the conflict—and are not ready for it. Until this occurs, if it occurs, emphasizing security to maintain something close to the American ideal may be necessary. This statement may sound ambiguous—even contradictory. In some ways it is.

The American ideal has always been more than a concept than a reality. We have many sins—many flaws. Our noblest ideals and principles, however, are real. Many have died for them. Those on the political Left, who tend to be the most critical of this country, are the very people who most ardently contend we must live up to the ideals of this country. In doing so, they strongly advocate for their rights, the rights of suspects, and the esteem of the world community. When they are not trumpeting these ideals, however, they are quick to criticize this country as racist, sexist, imperialistic, selfish, and on and on. My point is this: Are those who ardently advocate for their rights willing to die for them?

Consider again the motto of the original Wide-Awakes: *free speech, free soil, and free men*. These are the things that truly matter. These principles were so powerful, they inspired many to fight to keep the union together and that *all* should enjoy the principles inherent in our Constitution. As flawed as we were, the ideals of E pluribus Unum—Latin for "Out of many, One"—was so strong, many went to war to achieve it. As chronicled here, a new "war" is forthcoming. While still relatively calm, we need to know deep in our heart of hearts, that it is real.

There are hundreds of great quotes about freedom or liberty, but the one that may be most appropriate in our current circumstance is attributed to Ronald Reagan, who stated,[5]

> "Freedom is a fragile thing and is never more than one generation away from extinction. It is not ours by inheritance; it must be fought for and defended constantly by each generation, for it comes only

> once to a people. Those who have known freedom and then lost it have never known it again."

Are we at risk of losing freedom? Most would disagree. Few see that this is even possible. But is it possible people have not connected the dots? Consider, most progressives think that capitalism has failed, yet they cannot point to any country where socialism has succeeded. Absent a skewed perception of Cuba, the rhetoric from progressives is one of *hope* of equity and some ill-conceived notion of a classless, green society. They don't realize they are advocating their own constraints. It is not liberty or equity they will get. Yet, they mouth the mantras as if they matter. What *actually* matters is what this chapter attempts to convey.

Elements will be presented and analyzed, using certain issues—or triggers to illustrate the tension between the parings. Triggers act as catalysts, tensions, or even divisions. What may seem to be "solutions," may be part of the problem. This may seem illogical now but keep reading. In any case, these are the parings:

- *Rights & Freedom*
- *Security & Authoritarianism*
- *Truth & Love*

Consider again the quotes above. Security and rights were crucial elements at stake—and key principles to balance. Now, these seem too *simple.* Times have changed. Balancing security and rights are no longer optimal. Now, while similar, our alternatives are more *complicated.*

Security and rights are two associated but often distinctive principles. When security increases, rights decrease. When rights increase, security decreases. While not necessarily one for one, the ratio is like a pendulum, changing with the threat levels and with the circumstances. As threats, crimes, and fears increase, so typically do the provision of security methods. Controlling variables that cause disorder or lead to an attack is the goal of security. Countering, diminishing, or defeating these variables is the purpose of security methodologies.

What has changed, though, is that security and rights have given way to a more nuanced distinction. Though nuanced, it is extraordinarily important.

At first blush, rights and freedom seem complementary. Unlike security and rights, where the dynamic tends to give a little, take a little, both freedom and rights go to the same goal—liberty. Yet, they can also be mutually averse to each other.

RIGHTS & FREEDOM → SECURITY & AUTHORITARIANISM

Freedom—by its very nature—allows the free flow of people within society. Yet, "pure" freedom brings chaos, anarchy, and moral decay. Indeed, it's impossible to achieve "pure" freedom in a civilized society. Some restrictions or constraints on freedom—or on rights—are unavoidable. This is what some call "ordered liberty," which entails "understanding that laws exist to prevent individuals from infringing on the inalienable rights of others."[6]

Yet, ordered liberty is breaking down. What is supposed to happen is this: *Through the application of constitutional protections and through the application of law and order, citizens interact, reside, conduct business, and traverse in a relatively unencumbered manner.* The ability to do so is dependent on traversing without being subject to threats, violence, or chaos. Conversely, allowing some people "the right" to create disorder while interacting with law-abiding people creates perverse counter-incentives—hurting people and damaging property by those who are inclined to do so.

This dynamic encompasses both "normal" crimes, such as disorderly conduct, drinking and using drugs on the public way, robbery, and extremist/terroristic violence. For normal crimes, "giving people space" to create disorder and chaos, which was done in Baltimore in 2015 and more generally in 2020, is clearly beyond the norm of "ordered liberty."

Think about how ordered liberty relates to two significant threats: lawlessness and terrorism. These threats are fostered by disorder and result in chaos. Lawlessness is typically manifested in "normal" crime—open and notorious drug and alcohol usage, gang fights, smash-and-grab shoplifting, violent and brazen carjackings, and other violent acts. Terrorism is typically manifested in shootings, bombings, and assassinations. Though the motivations of these are different, the result is the same—a breakdown of the social fabric, chaos in public environments, and the deterioration of the legal and political systems. These are fostered when law and order is ignored, when ordered liberty breaks down. Picture this "dual dilemma" as you read on. Consider the implications as we go forward.

What is happening in 2022 across the country is some form of lawlessness. Letting some people behave in disorderly and illegal ways diminishes—even negates—the freedom of others to travel without being subject to abuse or worse. Civilized societies stop those who engage in disorderly behaviors and protect those who are law abiders.

Consider the application of order maintenance—and by extension ordered liberty. Not engaging people who create disorder and commit crimes affects the freedom of those who live, work, and shop in these areas. The freedom of many is directly hampered by the "rights" of some.

Do the "rights" of a few outweigh the freedom of all? Should the tyranny of the minority (or some small subset of the minority) dictate and hurt the well-being of the majority? Do some have a "right" to be on the public way, even though their presence diminishes the freedom of others in that environment? It's particularly ludicrous when the presence of certain people results in their "right" to commit crimes. In this way, many not only lose some freedoms but are also victimized by criminals. All to the detriment of many, for the benefit of few. Why?

The reason this is allowed to occur is that enforcing the law and maintaining order is construed by some as racist and based on white supremacy. We used to think that "lady liberty" was blindfolded. That the *law was the law*. Laws are to be enforced consistently and honestly, without regard for men (or their skin color). While not always living up to constitutional ideals and principles, this adage holds true: *Two wrongs don't make a right*. Claims of racism and the fear of adverse-impact lawsuits should not prevail over keeping people safe and secure. The primary duty of public officials is to keep people safe. *We used to think those who were to be kept safe were the law abiders*, not the *law violators*!

Adding one cautionary note, we ought to understand that allowing the rights of some to prevail over the freedom of others will not end well. Sooner or later, one or both will occur. Either people will decide to push back, like Rittenhouse and the "Wide-Awakes," or dramatic terroristic incidents will occur. These will result in greater levels of police and governmental intervention. Draconian controls and restrictions within the environment will result. Freedoms will be further diminished. Consequently, this is the operative question: Will freedom for all be the price we pay for the rights of some?

In a terroristic climate, the difficult balance described above is even more significant. Stuart Taylor, a widely respected constitutional attorney, concisely stated, "when dangers increase, liberties shrink." According to Taylor, it is preferable to adjust the rules and prevent violence than to adhere to rigid laws and suffer the consequences. He made this larger point: "Preventing mass murder is the best way of avoiding a panicky stampede into truly oppressive 'police statism,' in which measures now unthinkable could suddenly become unstoppable."[7]

As such, it is seen as better to avoid tragic and dramatic terrorist attacks *because* these attacks will lead to more draconian police and security practices. This "solution" is somewhat counterintuitive. *It is necessary to proportionately reduce rights to prevent terrorist attacks.* Stopping or at least minimizing terrorist attacks will result in the protection of rights and freedoms. Accordingly, one can make the argument that those who attempt to hold fast to each "small" right (see examples below) will bring about the loss of significant freedoms.

Former Judge on the US Court of Appeals and law professor Richard Posner notes that "the safer the nation feels, the more weight judges will be willing to give to the liberty interest."[8] If society feels safe, judges will further liberty interests. If society is fearful, judges will reduce rights in favor of security. A pointed analogy may help illustrate this dynamic: "a rattlesnake loose in the living room tends to end any discussion of animal rights."[9]

How should we respond to terrorism and lawlessness? The new model of policing described in the previous chapter is directly related to the level of lawlessness—and the threat of extremism and terrorism. Both order maintenance and surveillance are crucial to help deter crime and foster free movement in society. Protecting people, however, usually requires control and surveillance, both of which are likely to affect the liberty and constitutional rights of the controlled or the surveilled. This is not new. It has been happening for years.

Consider this quote from a civil rights observer regarding cameras and other surveillance devices. "If this technology ends up being deployed widely, it seems to be another step toward a society where you need to accept surveillance in every part of your life."[10] Similarly, UK sociologist Clive Norris concluded that cameras are becoming so "omnipresent that all Britons should assume their behavior outside the home is monitored."[11]

Now take this a step further. Consider how security can tend toward authoritarianism. Fostering a secure environment is a necessary and appropriate goal. Yet, there are many ways to achieve security. For example, locking down the population, declaring martial law, and stationing police and soldiers on the streets would likely provide a secure environment. But at what cost? Losing freedom while obtaining security would not be an ideal tradeoff. A quote from Benjamin Franklin is operative: "Those who would give up essential Liberty, to purchase a little temporary Safety, deserve neither Liberty nor Safety." Franklin's point leads to this: a society that abandons liberty because it desires *temporary* safety will not long have either. The result will likely be an authoritarian consequence.

How does an authoritarian society function? The late Hannah Arendt, a holocaust survivor and highly regarded scholar, stated such a society "is one which an ideology seeks to displace all prior traditions and institutions, with the goal of bringing all aspects of society under control of that ideology." This type of state "aspires to nothing less than defining and controlling reality. Truth is whatever the rulers decide it is."[12]

As we have chronicled, this observation of how an authoritarian system operates can be seen all around us. Think about the "traditions" of this country being redefined by the 1619 Project and by declaring the country as "systemically racist." Think about statues that were standing for multiple generations being either torn down by mobs or removed by legislative or executive action. Think about how leaders of institutions throughout this country have proclaimed the vacant mantras of "defunding" and "reimagining" almost without question. Think about BLM being grounded in Marxist thinking yet deemed by the "intellectuals" and "leaders" that all must believe one skin color is oppressive while another is oppressed.

There are many other examples to follow below, but a quote from Rod Dreher puts this directly in context with what we have articulated in this book. Here is his quote:[13]

> "One of contemporary progressivism's commonly used phases—*the personal is political*—captures the totalitarian spirit, which seeks to infuse all aspects of life with political consciousness. Indeed, the Left pushes its ideology ever deeper into the personal realm, leaving fewer and fewer areas of daily life uncontested. This, warned Arendt, is a sign that a society is ripening for totalitarianism, because that is what totalitarianism essentially is: *the politization of everything* (emphasis added)."

This quote aptly explains why *race, religion, and politics* have been the centerpiece of this book. These are all lumped into one bucket—all work together for one goal. In short, this thinking can lead one to conclude that this country is heading toward an authoritarian society. Much more evidence of this will be presented below.

Surveillance

Now, turn rights and liberty upside down. Instead of the rights of a few affecting the liberty of all, this is the opposite. The rights of many were *freely* given away to the detriment of everyone's freedom.

In this application, surveillance goes to "big tech" and the willingness to give away our rights. Here is the thinking. Giving away privacy rights in exchange for using *Facebook*, *Google*, and other social networks ultimately reduced everyone's freedom. Its consequence: *By giving away our rights, the result is unprecedented levels of surveillance of the general population.*

Consider the extraordinary analysis by Shoshana Zuboff, professor emeritus at Harvard Business School and the author of *The Age of Surveillance Capitalism.* In her view, companies like Google, Facebook, Amazon, Microsoft, and Apple have become "private surveillance empires," representing the largest publicly traded companies by market capitalization in the world. Describing *surveillance capitalism* as a "hidden revolution in how information is produced, circulated and acted upon," this economic system was built on the secret extraction and manipulation of human data.

The process of obtaining this information is both fascinating and frightening. It starts with massive data flows of personal information by those who create accounts and use social media. The data is then assessed through computational analyses to *predict* precise locations of advertising. These are designed for maximum "click-through." Such predictions were enabled by analyzing "data trails" that users unknowingly left behind as they searched and browsed *Google's* pages. *All* this data was collected on *everyone* who used the Internet—precisely but chillingly characterized as "better data" and "real data," as a front-row seat to "your whole life."

Following "data trails," *Google* is able to extract predictive metadata, also called "data exhaust." These were used to predict likely patterns of future behavior.

Dr. Zuboff said this process led to "lucrative predictions" from the flows of human data on an "unimaginable scale." Data came from unsuspecting users, who did not know it was being secretly hunted and captured. This occurred in *every corner of the Internet*, extending to apps, smartphones, devices, cameras, and sensors. The underlying aim was to maintain what Zuboff refers to as "user ignorance." Ignorance was fostered by new products. When introduced as part of the marketing strategy, new products enhanced "engagement," which Zuboff pointedly said was a "euphemism used to conceal illicit extraction operations."

The extraction of data then became *Google's* second imperative. "Massive-scale extraction operations were crucial. This created a new economic edifice and superseded other considerations, beginning with the quality of information."[14] This massive extraction "assumes the destruction of privacy as a nonnegotiable condition of its business operations." She continued with this damming assertion: ". . . with privacy out of the way, ill-gotten human data are concentrated within private corporations, where they are claimed as corporate assets to be deployed at will."[15]

With massive amounts of data came massive amounts of revenue. Revenue became the quest. Data integrity was the victim. According to Zuboff, in the "logic of surveillance capitalism, information integrity is not correlated with revenue." She points to a quote from Eric Schmidt, the executive chairman of *Google's* parent company, who acknowledged the role of *Google's* algorithmic ranking operations in spreading corrupt information. "There is a line that we can't really get across," he said. "It is *very difficult for us to understand truth* (emphasis added)." Consider the implications involved.

On one hand, the company boasts that ". . . we have better information than anyone else. We know gender, age, location, and it's real data as opposed to the stuff other people infer." Yet, with this data and its mission to organize and make accessible all the world's information using the most sophisticated computer systems, the company admits that it cannot discern corrupt information—it cannot understand truth! The result, according to Zuboff, is that this "leaves a trail of social wreckage in its wake: the wholesale destruction of privacy, the intensification of social inequality, the poisoning of social discourse with 'defactualized' information, the demolition of social norms, and the weakening of democratic institutions."[16]

When revenue is valued more than truth, obvious consequences result. Targeting mechanisms change real life, sometimes with grave consequences. These consequences can be manipulated based on the biases and ideology of those who are charged with monitoring content. Content monitors could *delete* or *allow* millions of comments made on social media sites. These are typically assessed based on "community standards." Defining standards is next to impossible. At best, assessments are subjective. At worse, they are outright biased. With these assessments, Zuboff correctly notes that depending upon the worldview of the monitor (or of the algorithms designed into the system), the result is this:[17]

> "Anger is rewarded or ignored. News stories become more trustworthy or unhinged. Publishers prosper or wither. Political discourse turns uglier or more moderate. People live or die."

Despite these negative consequences, surveillance capitalism is the dominant economic institution of our time. Its "business model" has been adopted by myriad industries, from insurance, retail, banking, and finance to agriculture, automobiles, education, healthcare, and more. "All apps and software, no matter how benign they appear, are designed to maximize data collection."

This desire to maximize data results in what Zuboff terms the "colossal asymmetry" between companies and users. They know much, much more about us than we know about them. The sheer size of this *knowledge gap* ingests "trillions of behavioral data points every day and producing six million behavioral predictions each second."[18]

All this information leaves one reeling. Think about the surveillance implications of our private lives held by companies who admittedly cannot discern truth from fiction. Frightening consequences come to mind. This "meta-crisis" leaves the ideal of human self-governance in a very tenuous condition. Zuboff concludes with these chilling words, "to survive the digital century, then all solutions point to one solution: a *democratic counterrevolution* (emphasis added)." Any notion of "regulating big tech should focus on the bedrock of surveillance economics: the secret extraction of human data from realms of life once called 'private.' "[19]

This conclusion is the result of multiple millions of individuals voluntarily giving away their privacy rights. This can upset the foundations of democracies in ways we cannot fully see nor understand. One thing seems clear: how we think of *freedom* will change. Indeed, can we even be "free" if we have no private information or private spaces? If we have no way to live without being surveilled? The implications are beyond what I can grasp. Yet, this is where we are.

Coming off the elements of *Public Safety Policing*, I trust you can see why this was called "pragmatic." It is not a solution. Though the model may reduce crime and diminish the probability and the consequences of extremist and terroristic violence, it also builds on and utilizes the extensive surveillance-based systems already in place. To get a window into where this is going, let's look at the most sophisticated surveillance system in the world: China.

This takes us past "rights and liberty" to "security and authoritarianism." As you read on, think about how this can be seen as a continuum, or a spectrum, starting with giving away one's rights to an authoritarian entity.

China created what it called the "Golden Shield Project." This incorporated surveillance networks implemented decades ago into what is euphemistically called *community-grid management.* The surveillance network is vast. Its "infrastructure" consisted of video systems, drone surveillance, networks of automated sensory systems which include CCTV cameras with facial recognition, automated license-plate recognition, infrared capabilities, along with "Wi-Fi sniffers" that collect identifying addresses of networked devices, and Internet/social-media monitoring and tracking. Such surveillance capacity is furthered through mobile apps, smartphones, biometric data collection, artificial intelligence, and more. Collection and surveillance are enhanced by embedding malicious software in apps and software, which can "remotely turn on a phone's microphone, record calls, or export photos, phone locations, and conversations on chat apps."[20]

By incorporating tactics of *intelligence-led policing* (ILP), which was presented as part of the "protective methods" element of *Public Safety Policing*, Chinese policing agencies collect and assess multitudes of data to address crime. Also, ironically, consider China is building so-called *safe cities* (which is the name used by US federal grants to fund policing and homeland security). China's safe cities program takes surveillance steps beyond the models used in the US. It integrates data from intrusive surveillance systems to predict and prevent everything from fires to natural disasters—and political dissent."[21]

A crucial element of these initiatives is "social scores," used to assess an individual in all facets of life. Individuals are scored on such things as lease and credit-card balances and payment timeliness, comments made on social media, music and movie selection, and websites and places visited. A host of other factors are also at play, including the central bank data, which is also adopting digital currency.

This will foster even greater levels of surveillance—and control—of financial transactions, which are critical to life. Think about the "Build Back Better" plan advocated by the Biden Administration which sought to hire 80,000 IRS analysts and obtain the authority to review *every* bank transaction over $500. One is hard-pressed to deny that China and the US are using each other as "models" to gain more and more control of their respective populations.

According to Sheena Chestnut Greitens, associate professor at the University of Texas at Austin, "China has figured out how to entwine surveillance with digital governance, not only to calibrate coercion and repression but also to provide public services and to co-opt citizens. Surveillance is an overall project to make citizens highly legible to the party-state." This was echoed by Human Rights Watch, which stated in a 2020 report that "Governments' impulse for surveillance is hardly new, but the Chinese government is presenting a new model of social control that, if we do not act now, may become the future for much of humanity."[22]

Still another surveillance apparatus voluntarily engaged by Americans comes from China. *TikTok* is described by *Google* as being "held by WangTouZhongWen (Beijing) Technology, which is owned by three Chinese state entities including a fund backed by the country's main internet watchdog, the Cyberspace Administration of China (CAC) . . ."[23] Many say the Chinese have a "backdoor" in this technology that allows user data to be surveilled. Given the analysis above, this seems a "safe bet."

Let's take this idea of social control and apply it to the pandemic. The connection is obvious if one has the "eyes to see."

Covid

Consider the implications of using an app with facial recognition software and geolocation to prove adherence to a fourteen-day quarantine. This policy was instituted in the fall of 2021 by the state of South Australia. To abide by this policy, two other Australian states, allow residents to spend post-travel quarantine at home, rather than in a hotel. But they must download and use the "Orwellian" app, developed by the South Australian government. Users may be randomly contacted, asking them to provide proof of their location within fifteen minutes. If the individual fails to verify their location or identity when requested, the South Australia Health Department will notify the police, who may conduct an in-person check on the person in quarantine.[24]

While registration to use the app for home quarantine is voluntary, the alternative is fourteen-day confinement in a hotel, payable by the traveler. So, the options are limited. Don't travel. If you do travel, be subject to hotel quarantine or voluntarily download the app and stay home. Each alternative has obvious controls built into the policy.

"I think it is accurate to describe it as Orwellian, but one has to understand the context," says Robert Carling, an economics senior fellow at The Centre for Independent Studies. "It is home quarantine Australian style, and the alternative is hotel quarantine Australian style, under police guard, which people hate." Carling went on to explain that "since March 2020, Australians have been banned even from leaving the country unless they can get a special permit to do so." He called this exit ban a "totalitarian, North Korea-style measure . . ."[25]

Carling noted that the "Orwellian" South Australia quarantine app trial—horrifying though it is—represents a step toward an "elusive normalcy." Or, as the "new normal."

In Canada, the federal government admitted to secretly surveilling its population's movements during the COVID-19 lockdown by tracking 33 million phones. The Public Health Agency of Canada (PHAC) clandestinely tracked phones to assess "the public's responsiveness during lockdown measures."[26] The PHAC bought location and movement data from Canadian telecom giant Telus to "understand possible links between the movement of populations within Canada."

Consider that its entire population totals 38 million, which means that almost the entire population was surveilled. Excluding children, the infirmed, and some percentage of people who do not have phones, this surveillance was extraordinarily exhaustive. This example is consistent with controls and surveillance instituted by many countries during the pandemic. David Lyon, author of *Pandemic Surveillance* pointedly said, "evidence is coming in from many sources, from countries around the world, that what was seen as a huge surveillance surge—post 9/11, is now completely upstaged by pandemic surveillance."

Surveillance modes will not end with the pandemic. According to PHAC, it plans to continue tracking population movement for *at least the next five years* to control "other infectious diseases, chronic disease prevention, and mental health (emphasis added)."[27]

With vast numbers of people working from home during the pandemic, companies using surveillance measures jumped 54 percent, according to research by online privacy site *Top10VPN*. Companies are enforcing *task tracking* via new technologies, such as Amazon's truck monitoring technology or Microsoft's productivity scoring software. Employers have also implemented virtual monitoring with programs like Time Doctor or StaffCop, which log keystrokes, watch screens, take over a computer remotely, track employees' locations, record audio, and more—all designed to prevent employees from committing "time theft" while working remotely.

This goes beyond technology. Employers also want to "inspect" the home office. Blaming insurance requirements, companies make "periodic unplanned visits" to homes.[28]

Colleges are also using surveillance means. For example, New York University uses "ProctorU," an online proctoring service that utilizes students' webcams and screen-sharing technology to ensure ethical remote test-taking. To accomplish this, students must download a location-tracking COVID-19 app (as above in Australia). Also, eye-tracking technology can be used to ensure students don't look away from their screens continuously (checking notes). The implications of widespread surveillance in educational setting were pointedly summarized as:[29]

> "The more common surveillance software is in education settings, the more desensitized young people will be to surveillance when they grow up and enter the workforce. It's all part of the plan: Tech companies want to make intrusive surveillance of every move part of our daily lives, like brushing our teeth or putting on shoes."

Making surveillance fit into daily lives may also require compulsion. Students who do not cooperate are often sanctioned. Consider a Rutgers University student barred from taking classes because he has not been vaccinated—even though he was taking classes virtually from home, about 70 miles from the campus. After being locked out of his school email account, the student was told vaccination was required. The student's response was telling, "I don't care if I have access to campus. I don't need to be there. They could ban me. I just want to be left alone."[30]

As the pandemic grinds on, the idea of going back to "normal" has divided people, often around ideological worldviews. In October 2021, comedian and traditional liberal Bill Maher told his audience, "Just resume living!" He added, "I know some people seem to not want to give up on the wonderful pandemic, but you know what? It's over. There's always going to be a variant. You shouldn't have to wear masks . . . I travel in every state now, back on the road, and the red states are a joy, and the blue states are a pain in the a--. For no reason," Maher said.

He described masks as an amulet. "A charm people wear around the neck that wards away evil spirits. It means nothing," Maher said. "I mean, can't we get people to understand the facts more?" He went on to slam Democrats over a poll that showed "41 percent" of them believed unvaccinated people have "over 50 percent" risk of hospitalization when it's actually "0.89 percent," adding that it's "0.1 percent" for vaccinated people. "So, in both cases, the correct answer is less than 1 percent. They thought it was over 50 percent. How do people, especially of one party, get such a bad idea? Where did that come from?" Maher asked.[31]

Covid mask mandates have resulted in disturbances and fights in restaurants and other public establishments. In one example, the mandates were exacerbated by racial overtones.[32] Others see masks as having implications on the psyche of people and on human dignity.

The class-based nature of masking was eviscerated by David Marcus. He wrote, "Americans are not by nature a jealous people. We do not begrudge the rich their luxuries. After all, those of more modest means have our own pleasures . . . But what we cannot abide is a legal or social system that gives the elites a different set of rights, a different set of freedoms."

He then cited New York City's mandate that all entertainment venue patrons must show a vaccine card, though it exempts "celebrity entertainers and their entourages," who don't need to show proof of vaccination. "Rather the rest of us, those of us who don't really matter, must produce our vaccine cards to ensure the health and welfare of our betters." He noted masking was supposed to be about protecting others around us, but on "what possible basis should they [celebrities] be exempt from masking rules?"

His answer: It is a new Covid *caste system* that has "nothing to do with politics. It is about fairness and human dignity" and that "it is immoral, it is ugly, and it is deeply un-American."[33]

Others see the distinctions created by Covid as being a struggle for power. Seeing the mandates imposed on the military, Tucker Carlson asserts the underlying reason is controlling those who "hold the guns," enabling the use of force "as an apparatus of a specific political party."

In Australia, politicians called in the military to enforce their totalitarian Covid restrictions, using violence, if necessary. Sydney imposed martial law. Instead, of acknowledging that marital law may involve draconian measures for corrupt reasons, many think the problem is "white supremacy." Canadian Prime Minister Justin Trudeau made similar allegations against truckers who were protesting Covid mandates in Ontario, criticizing them for "hate, abuse, and racism" and later invoked the Emergencies Act.[34]

Carlson asks, "sound familiar"? It goes without saying that none of this has anything to do with Covid or racism, obviously. It's about power."

Defense Secretary Lloyd Austin explained "that his very first and most pressing job was rooting out what he referred to as "extremism" in the US military." Carlson asked where this extremism might be. Where are the extremists in the military? How many were found? We were never told nor has any evidence come out since Austin's declaration. Nonetheless, "because we're keeping score, to this day, we're not aware of a single white supremacist on active duty who's been discovered by the Pentagon and fired." The only firing noted was a senior commander in the Space Force, Lt. Col. Matthew Lohmeier, who lost his job—for criticizing Marxism.

Those in the armed services who won't submit to the COVID-19 vaccination will be fired. It doesn't matter if they had natural immunity, as so many in the military do. "Their personal moral or religious objections were totally irrelevant," Carlson stated. "The point of mandatory vaccination is to identify the sincere Christians in the ranks, the freethinkers, the men with high testosterone levels, and anyone else who doesn't love Joe Biden and make them leave immediately. It's a takeover of the US military."[35]

Those who tie Covid mandates to religious beliefs have some powerful arguments. Elliot Resnick writing in *American Greatness*, laid out his reasons for refusing Covid vaccinations. The "Judeo-Christian tradition calls on man to use the unique divine gift with which he's been blessed—his mind—to conduct his life. If I shut off my brain, if I ignore clear scientific data that the COVID-19 vaccine is unnecessary for me, I would be rejecting God's gift." Consider this impassioned and logical case made by Resnick:[36]

> Thus, if I ignore scientific data—if I irrationally receive the COVID-19 vaccine despite having recovered from the disease—I would effectively be adopting the pre-biblical view of the ancient pagans who engaged in superstitious practices to ward off danger. I would be committing a form of idolatry.
>
> Finally, I would note that according to our founding fathers, 'rebellion to tyrants is obedience to God.' This country isn't yet run by tyrants, but the current vaccination campaign bears unmistakable totalitarian undertones. 'Get the vaccine or lose your job.' That's the message of the government. You can be a healthy 30-year-old who already had COVID, but the government doesn't care. It wants everyone vaccinated—facts be damned.
>
> I believe resisting such authoritarian orders is a religious imperative. As a Bible adherent, I worship one God and one God only. Only He can demand absolute obedience from me. Only He can ask me to walk with Him blindly, against all reason. No one else can. And if someone tries to, he is usurping God's role and asking me to worship someone other than Him . . . To take the

> vaccine would require me to act contrary to both reason and piety, reject modern science, and irrationally submit to a mortal power. All three are religious crimes.

As government demands more and more controls on American citizens, it simultaneously allows hundreds of thousands of migrants into this country with little or no viable controls relating to Covid. Why? This is illogical at every level. It is so indefensible that it must be ignored! With little media attention, few will even ask the questions that are so obvious as to be impossible to miss. Here is the obvious question: *Is this intended?*

The government needs legitimacy. If it loses legitimacy, it loses allegiance. When political leaders are seen ignoring Covid laws or mask regulations, it diminishes their credibility. When the government "allows" hundreds of thousands of migrants into the country without anything close to systematic Covid testing and compliance protocols, why should Americans comply? It reduces the willingness to follow the law.

In a country that once prided itself on being guided by "the rule of law," adherence to the law is crucial. With thousands of laws and regulations, the government cannot possibly enforce these without almost universal *voluntary* compliance. Yet, citizens are much more apt to comply when the government is seen as legitimate. Fostering the duty to respect the rule of law is what government should seek. Enacting laws and regulations that are ignored by those in power (or for special classes of people) will inevitably result in the perception of illegitimate use of power. When this occurs, the collective sense of duty and obligation ends.

If this occurs, mandates, surveillance, and draconian controls are the only option to sustain the government. We have seen in this section; that some extraordinary technologies foster this possibility. We have also seen here and throughout this book, some laws are being ignored, unenforced, inconsistently applied, and even downright draconian.

Vaccination mandates constitute the latter. This is a classic example of the tension between rights and freedom. This goes to the individual's right to decide what to put in their body. Yet, the government says the rights of the collective override the rights of the individual. Public safety is more important than individual rights. Yet, on the streets, this equation is reversed. Afraid to enforce quality-of-life policing and other order-maintenance techniques because these may result in disparate treatment and discrimination allegations, the Left has ensured that, there, individual rights trump public safety. Progressives get it wrong in both applications.

Here is the larger point. On Covid mandates, progressives favor public safety, siding with the collective over the individual. On law and order in the streets, progressives favor individual rights, siding with the individual over the collective. These go in different directions. This is intellectually dishonest at best. What's more, these mutually inconsistent positions are illustrative of an agenda—not even close to a principled position. As we have chronicled, this is yet another vacant, deceptive mantra. On second thought, maybe there *is* consistency: *progressives are about mantras and mandates!*

Yet another classic example of draconian and illogical thinking was illustrated for the world to see during the 2022 Super Bowl. In a stadium filled with tens of thousands of mask*less* fans, pre-game singers Erica and Tina Campbell performed "Lift Every Voice and Sing" (known as the "Black National Anthem") *outside* while the Youth Orchestra of Los Angeles accompanied them, playing musical instruments *while masked*! Essentially the entire audience, including the singers, did not wear masks, but the band did! The same children in attendance would then be required to attend school the next day *wearing a mask*—yet do people see the irony? Saying this is "science" is so far from reality as to take one's breath away—which is what happens when wearing the mandated masks!

One can laugh at such thinking, but when individuals lose the freedom to decide whether to be vaccinated, what option does the government have? Order mandates or back down. Mandates are often illogical (as with the youth orchestra) and often without exception. It's *authoritarian*. It's raw power. As Carlson noted earlier, if the government's option is reduced to raw power, then it behooves them to rid the military—and the police of those who are not inclined to obey.

Protests/ Riots

While protests are inherent to and even desirable within our system, as the First Amendment gives us freedom of association and assembly, the line between protests and riots has become blurred. Indeed, one can argue that the line no longer exists at all. News accounts from 2020 showing fires and chaos in the background while some "reporter" parrots the "mostly peaceful mantra" were widely panned. It would be funny if it weren't so serious. Contrast these incidents with the "insurrection" mantra describing the capital riot. These illustrate that some don't know the difference between protests, riots, and an insurrection. Understating riots as "protests" and overstating riots as an 'insurrection" is wrong—both go in favor of progressive interests and ideology.

Much has already been said of the silence and the failure to clearly condemn the riots in a timely manner. Without "re-litigating" the issue again, it is sufficient to say that the "peaceful protest template" will be hard to revise. Just like all the other progressive-inspired changes, almost $2 billion in damages from riots in more than 140 US cities will have a lasting impact. Damages will be difficult to repair, rebuilding will be costly, and the psychological impact will be lasting. For example, in Minneapolis, during a legislative hearing in February of 2021, nine months after the destruction of their livelihoods, business owners finally got the chance *to beg the state* for monetary relief. Rob Yang, the owner of two apparel stores in Minneapolis and St. Paul described his nightmare. "I was no more than fifteen feet away from the entrance where I would normally greet customers while complete strangers took their turns looting my American dream and fifteen years of hard work," he testified to lawmakers.

An Ethiopian immigrant made a similar plea, describing the destruction of his American dream, a furniture store in Minneapolis. "It was very emotional, and I still feel like the city is burning down. Let's rebuild this town. I don't want to see boarded businesses any longer. That's what this civil unrest created because the police protests got hijacked. We all know that."[37]

These are but a sliver of the horror stories emanating from the riots of

2020. As bad as these were, another even more lasting impact goes to this question: *Why do we think we can stop these from happening again?* This may sound cold, but when President Biden says that the protests "unified people of every race and generation in peace and with purpose to say enough, enough, enough of these senseless killings,"[38] why would the next "senseless killing(s)" not justify more rioting? When this happens, and it will, how do we walk back these words? How do we enforce law and order in response to *any* alleged senseless killing(s)?

In an interview with former Minnesota Governor Arne Carlson, he spoke frankly about what happened during the Minneapolis rioting and *why*.

First, he made clear that protocols exist to handle disorder. He recalled other riots while he was governor, noting that established protocols are clear: bring the team together and determine which person is most capable of handling the situation, typically the director of public safety. "Then, you empower that person and say okay, You're in charge. You work with the mayor, the county, and you bring all of the law enforcement together and you have a unified position, and partisan politics instantly disappears."

Speaking directly about Minneapolis, the former governor did not pull any punches. He referred to the "mayor who literally had no experience. He needed help. Instead, the governor was cowardly and refused to provide any assistance." And it just "spun out of control instantly... Yes, there's room for protest, no, there's no room for destruction. The National Guard should have been there instantly, and I mean instantly and it wasn't." He then closed the loop with this pointed and common-sense assertion:[39]

> "These things are not hard. Minneapolis has a lot of experience with riots and they're very predictable. On an episode of this nature, you can bet within a matter of hours every thief, every burglar, every bad actor's going to be out on the street looking for ways to hustle some bucks. That's when you draw the line on property and human destruction and they [the Walz administration] didn't do it. Once they didn't do it, they lost control because now it's very hard to get control."

This is from a man who once governed the state for eight years. That was "back in the day" in the 1990s, when leaders adhered to their constitutional duty to protect the people.

Yet, some rational thinking still exists today. Riots have motivated leaders to enact laws to crack down on chaos. A classic example surrounds Governor DeSantis in Florida, who in April 2021 signed an "anti-riot" bill, which increased penalties for crimes committed during riots. To "combat public disorder," DeSantis described the legislation: "If you look at the breadth of this particular piece of legislation, it is the strongest anti-rioting, pro-law enforcement piece of legislation in the country. There's just nothing even close."[40] Elements of the law are indeed significant. Many elements go directly to what we have advocated in this book: [41]

- Grants civil legal immunity to people who drive through protesters blocking a road
- Allows authorities to hold arrested demonstrators from posting bail until after their first court date
- Increases the charge for battery on a police officer during a riot
- Limits local governments' discretion to "justify a reduction in law enforcement budgets"
- Allows people to sue local governments over personal or property damages if they were determined to have interfered with law enforcement response during civil unrest
- Increases penalties for protesters who block roadways or deface public monuments
- Creates a new crime: "mob intimidation"

This law may help reverse the "template" created in 2020. Yet, this is a red state. What about people in blue states, such as the two store owners in Minneapolis quoted above? Consider this question rhetorical.

Recall the famous words of President Kennedy as he passionately plead this nation "would bear any burden, meet any hardship . . . in order to assure the survival and success of liberty." [42] How do his famous words resonate in

2022? What does the survival and success of liberty mean to us now? Kennedy most certainly did not think of liberty as the freedom to riot. He did not equate it with a draconian authoritarian system. He wanted to maintain this nation's liberty. This section described a system under great distress and disruption. Remember this principle: *when dangers increase, liberties decrease.*

Freedom of Speech

As a corollary to freedom of association and assembly, the protections surrounding freedom of speech are significant and well beyond the scope of this book. Instead, let me highlight two issues that are relevant to this book.

First, "controlling the narrative" and re-defining words have been methods used to control populations. It may be helpful to demonstrate its application coming from what were once the bastions of free speech and inquiry. Rikki Schlott passionately describes her experience as a student at NYU in the *New York Post*. She explains as soon as she entered the campus she was "taught that there is right-think and wrong-think. Everywhere I look, professors, administrators, and peers all fervently parrot the same beliefs." Even orientation involved "highly politicized" events that assumed "community values of radical progressivism." She goes on to describe how "speech codes, safe spaces, trigger warnings, and the conflation of speech with violence have all had a discernibly chilling effect on campus discourse. NYU identification cards even prominently display a bias report hotline to report any instances of offense." Here are some excerpts from the letter:[43]

> "Today's students recoil at the first hint of contention and demand insulation from controversial ideas. But, in the process of bubble-wrapping themselves, they undermine the very purpose of their education: the exploration of self that is paramount to intellectual maturity.
>
> Nonetheless, the movement to squash dissent is gaining steam. A 2021 survey found that 76 percent of liberal students believe peers who say something they deem offensive should be reported to the

university. Eighty-five percent insist professors who offend should be disciplined, too.

Most of these conversations are prefaced with, 'I'm scared to admit it, But . . .' and end with something along the lines of '. . .please don't tell anybody.' Saddest of all: 'I want to speak out like you, but I have a parent who works in academia. I'm afraid it could jeopardize their career.'

All around me, students and even faculty are going along to get along, ducking controversy and toeing the political line. After all, their social lives, grades, letters of recommendation and even careers all hang in the balance.

This frightening climate has led to a crisis of self-censorship. This isn't just my anecdotal hunch. Statistics reveal that there really is a silenced plurality, if not majority, across campuses nationwide. In fact, a 2020 survey revealed that nearly two-thirds of students feel the academic climate prevents them from expressing their beliefs.

The purpose of the university is to serve as a congregation point for the brightest minds, where diverse perspectives meet in colorful debate. Central to that dynamic is ideological difference.

Instead, self-identified liberal students paradoxically uphold illiberalism on campus by shutting down alternative ideas in pursuit of ideological safety. These 'conformists' are going unchallenged, while 'nonconformists' are intimidated into compliance.

Silent acquiescence is no longer tenable. When two-thirds of America's college students are afraid to speak their minds, they are truly facing a tyranny of the minority. We cannot continue to bow down to ideological authoritarians. The integrity of free minds hangs in the balance.

We must stand up now in defense of intellectual honesty, and, ultimately, personal integrity."

Trigger warnings, safe spaces, speech codes, warnings and the conflation of speech with violence have all had a discernibly chilling effect on campus discourse. These alleged attempts to keep people safe inevitably result in chilling speech. In his bestseller, *The Madness of Crowds*, Douglas Murray described the dynamic within schools of "higher education." [44]

> "The catastrophizing, the claims made which bore no resemblance to provable facts, the unleashing of entitlement in the guise of creating a level playing field, the turning of words into violence and violence into words."

An ironic element of Schlott's letter is our second highlight. That is, the quest to "protect" students by using trigger warnings. Recently, this thinking was subject to independent review. A body of peer-reviewed research shows these have little value—*or even may cause more harm than good.* According to a review by James Freeman, which involved seventeen studies using a range of media, the conclusion was: *Trigger warnings do not alleviate emotional distress*. And they do not significantly reduce negative effects or minimize intrusive thoughts.[45]

These two key indicators of post-traumatic stress disorder (PTSD) are not resolved by *illiberal* "protective" devices. Freeman elaborates, "we are not aware of a single experimental study that has found significant benefits of using trigger warnings . . . What's more, they found that trigger warnings actually increased the anxiety of individuals with the most severe PTSD, prompting them to "view trauma as more central to their life narrative." "Trigger warnings," they concluded, "may be most harmful to the very individuals they were designed to protect."[46]

There is no point in arguing as *definitive proof* that triggers warnings have no value. Yet, for millennia, people survived without them. Why are they needed now? Indeed, why were they rushed into schools without first studying the merits of such a dramatic change?

Just like "defunding" and "reimagining," these were implemented without any understanding of their implications. In keeping with progressive thinking, here is the provocative question: *Instead of "protecting" students, could the goal have been to foster an environment of fear?* Could this be to have a chilling effect on free speech? Schlott's letter says speech is now *chilled.* Based on what you read about the merits of progressive initiatives, you be the judge of their intent.

The better answer is what we used to believe for generations. That is, *more speech, not less.* This is what Murray recommended as the remedy for speech codes: "Disagreement is not oppression. Argument is not assault. Words—even provocative or repugnant ones—are not violence. The answer to speech we do not like is more speech."[47]

Social media makes the implications of speech even more insidious—and harmful. We are living at a time when legislators think it is "courageous" to flee the state when they know that they don't have the votes to assert their policy preferences. When the "world's most deliberate legislative body" seeks to *change the very rule that made it deliberate—the filibuster.* This rule fostered compromise, debate, and persuasion. Yet, when the votes are not sufficient to enact a law, then change the rule.

Writing an editorial for the *Wall Street Journal*, Salvatore Cordileone and Jim Daly call out the fundamentalists who unilaterally "seek to impose their own rigid certitude." This, they contend, results in not a more compassionate and liberal society but a more punitive one. "In the new public square of the Internet, power displaces liberty and conscience. In the past, religious-liberty issues could be resolved, or at least fruitfully argued, by appeals to the founding fathers. Their moral vision was shaped by a mix of biblical faith and Enlightenment thought: reason and faith working together."[48] This once widely shared basis for freedom is no longer viable.

Noting that the language of "rights" and social justice resonating in social unrest sound familiar, "but some of the key ideas that govern our current culture wars are found nowhere in the Constitution, or, for that matter, in reality." They cite Herbert Marcuse and his 1965 essay "Repressive Tolerance." Citing the "cultural turmoil" of the 1960s, Marcuse advocated "liberating tolerance" which may require "new and rigid restrictions on teachings and practices." Using "new and rigid" teaching practices for the purpose of "killing freedom in the name of freedom is the Orwellian proposition at work."

The remedy for "liberating tolerance is:[49]

> "This is why religious liberty should be important to everyone. It checks government's tendency to overreach, and it helps form citizens in the virtues necessary for democracy to work. There is a reason the Pledge of Allegiance places our national loyalty "under God." Without that protection, the ambitions of power tend to corrupt conscience and deform human rights.
>
> The American experiment was founded on, and has always thrived on, the freedom of religious believers to speak, teach, preach, practice, serve and work in peace—not only in private, but in the public square—for the truth about God and humanity that ennobles their lives and all lives.
>
> The more we diminish that freedom, the more crippled we become as a people. The more we feed it, the deeper and more robust the roots of our nation and its freedoms grow."

They conclude with this statement: "Those are the two paths before us. Here's the good news: We get to choose." The choices before us are clear.

Let's end this section with two perspectives that have driven people for thousands of years: *the belief in a greater being and the need to be free*. As noted above, these go hand in hand. Since this book was written to describe a *revolution that is in process*, it may be helpful to read what the Founding Fathers wrote in the Declaration of Independence:

> We hold these truths to be self-evident, that all men are created equal, that they are **endowed by their Creator** with certain unalienable Rights, that among these are Life, Liberty, and the pursuit of Happiness.
>
> That to secure these rights, Governments are instituted among Men, **deriving their just powers from the consent of the governed**,
>
> That whenever any Form of Government becomes destructive of these ends, it is the Right of the People to alter or to abolish it, and to institute new Government, laying its foundation on such

> principles and organizing its powers in such form, as to them shall seem most likely to effect their Safety and Happiness.
>
> Prudence, indeed, will dictate that Governments long established should not be changed for light and transient causes; and accordingly all experience hath shewn, that mankind are more disposed to suffer, while evils are sufferable, than to right themselves by abolishing the forms to which they are accustomed. But when a long train of abuses and usurpations, pursuing invariably the same Object evinces a design to reduce them under absolute Despotism, it is their right, it is their duty, to throw off such Government, and to provide new Guards for their future security . . .

A couple of crucial points demand review. Firstly, according to the Declaration of Independence, our rights *come from God.* When initially written, this was a revolutionary statement. No founding document had previously made such a claim. Its obvious intent was "we," meaning the founding fathers were *not* granting rights. God was. Think about this in terms of governing. Since God granted our rights, then subsequent leaders cannot take rights away. Since God granted our rights, only God could take them away.

The second point is less well known. The declaration *actually contains* language that could be construed as advocating *revolution.* By stating that the "Right of the People to alter or to abolish it [government]," the declaration accomplished two completely opposite premises. First, to declare freedom. Second, to declare the right to change the government, if the form of government "becomes destructive of these ends." What ends? To deny "certain unalienable Rights, that among these are Life, Liberty and the pursuit of Happiness." And to "secure these rights," the Governments [note plural] are instituted among Men, deriving their just powers from the consent of the governed.

Government must secure that *life, liberty, and the pursuit of happiness*—and citizens consent to be governed by that government. This book's title was written to convey that many *want* revolution. This connection to the Declaration of Independence is obvious but not intended. Yet, it is folly to think that a revolution ought to occur in a world ready to "bounce" on a battered America. Revolution is folly because it would destroy both the government *and* the revolution. America cannot withstand a revolutionary climate while maintaining its standing in the world order. It is impossible to sustain attacks from within and without. Lincoln knew that the house divided would fall. And that any such fall would come from within. For posterity, this is what he said:[50]

> "From whence shall we expect the approach of danger? Shall some trans-Atlantic military giant step the earth and crush us at a blow? Never. All the armies of Europe and Asia . . . could not by force take a drink from the Ohio River or make a track on the Blue Ridge in the trial of a thousand years. No, if destruction be our lot we must ourselves be its author and finisher. As a nation of free men we will live forever or die by suicide."

Establishing facts and logic to demonstrate that the forces of our destruction are at play has no doubt been hard to read—and to write. This is both a message of hope and a warning. We are at a crossroads—but we have a choice. Choose to follow two aspects of the Creator God that we are told to model—*truth and love.*

As we build to this, the *Wall Street Journal* annually re-prints an editorial written in 1949 by the late Vermont Royster. It's entitled "In Hoc Anno Domini," meaning: *The year of our Lord.* This fits perfectly in our current circumstances. We have a choice. Bondage or freedom. Royster provides insight into the 1st century when Saul's (who later was renamed Paul) world lay in bondage, as only Rome ruled the world with one master for all, Tiberius Caesar. "Everywhere there was civil order, for the arm of the Roman law was long. Everywhere, there was stability, in government and in society, for the centurions saw that it was so." Yet, there was oppression—for those who were *not* the friends of Tiberius Caesar.

"What was a man for but to serve Caesar?" Yet those who resisted Caesar were persecuted, as were "men who dared think differently, who heard strange voices or read strange manuscripts. And most of all, there was everywhere a contempt for human life. What, to the strong, was one man more or less in a crowded world?"

While recommending that you read the piece in its entirety, these are relevant—and powerful—conclusions:[51]

> "Then, of a sudden, there was a light in the world, and a man from Galilee saying, Render unto Caesar the things which are Caesar's and unto God the things that are God's. And the voice from Galilee, which would defy Caesar, offered a new Kingdom in which each man could walk upright and bow to none but his God. Inasmuch as ye have done it unto one of the least of these my brethren, ye have done it unto me. And he sent this gospel of the Kingdom of Man into the uttermost ends of the earth.
>
> So the light came into the world and the men who lived in darkness were afraid, and they tried to lower a curtain so that man would still believe salvation lay with the leaders.
>
> But it came to pass for a while in divers places that the truth did set man free, although the men of darkness were offended and they tried to put out the light. The voice said, Haste ye. Walk while you have the light, lest darkness come upon you, for he that walketh in darkness knoweth not whither he goeth . . .
>
> Then might it come to pass that darkness would settle again over the lands and there would be a burning of books and men would think only of what they should eat and what they should wear, and would give heed only to new Caesars and to false prophets. Then might it come to pass that men would not look upward to see even a winter's star in the East, and once more, there would be no light at all in the darkness . . .
>
> Stand fast therefore in the liberty wherewith Christ has made us free and be not entangled again with the yoke of bondage.

Even to those who don't believe in God, these words convey the notion of freedom that have moved people for eons. Desire for freedom is deep and powerful. As progressives are quick to assert, slavery cost millions of blacks their freedom. The brutality and inhuman nature of slavery are inexcusable. Yet, it has been a consistent feature of human nature. Every country, every culture, and every race used this brutal practice. America was no different. Yet, it was different. Unlike any other country, it waged a bloody civil war leading to the end of slavery. In the run-up to the civil war, Frederick Douglass, a brilliant and free black man stated these famous words:[52]

> "Liberty is meaningless where the right to utter one's thoughts and opinions has ceased to exist. That, of all rights, is the dread of tyrants. It is the right which they first of all strike down. They know its power. Thrones, dominions, principalities, and powers, founded in injustice and wrong, are sure to tremble, if men are allowed to reason of righteousness, temperance, and of a judgment to come in their presence. Slavery cannot tolerate free speech . . ."

Before we delve into the two great options, let's conceive of the two roads. Think again of the crossroad that is before us.

FEAR + CONTROL = POWER

Fear can be derived from chaos, crime, and extremist violence. Fear also comes from being careful to watch every word uttered from one's mouth or from one's keyboard. Fear comes from being afraid to lose employment, status, or acclaim because of what one said or didn't say. Fear is the undue threat of being exposed to Covid by others. Fear is being subject to mandates based supposedly on science. Fear is creating resentment toward those who don't look like you, pray like you, or vote like you.

These fears usually lead to draconian controls designed to "protect" you from threats. No amount of balance will suffice. *No risk* is the mantra and the only "solution." The goal of this equation is power! Power is the motivator and the driver. By fostering and creating chaos and its attendant fears, and by failing to seek balance or ordered liberty, the inevitable disruptions that result justify extensive controls. Because the *means* to the end are chaos and fear. Which bring the desired *end*: Power!

ORDER + SURVEILLANCE + PROTECTION = CONTROL

Fear is also relevant here. But here, fear is seen as an indicator that something is wrong and needs to change. Reasonable people—and prudent policymakers—will intercede in situations that cause fear. This includes establishing order on the streets. Addressing Covid with more than vaccinations, masks, and shutdowns. Remedies would be reasonable, balanced, and based on data and medical science. But medical science is not the *only* factor. Balancing *risks and threats* against *rights and freedom* would be crucial. These factors come in many forms, including medical, psychological, social, economic, spiritual, educational, and other considerations.

Threats are subjective, as are fears. What may terrify some may empower others. This is not in dispute. Yet, the key is to address fear and what causes fear. Sound public policy requires a balanced approach. *Balance is the crucial factor—but it is the hardest factor.*

Achieving balance does not occur with mandates. Mandates are the opposite of balance! As is defunding the police. Extreme positions are, on their face, unbalanced. This is what we should look for—evidence of balance or lack thereof. Articulating where the imbalance lies has been an underlying theme of this book.

Consequently, one can discern the *actual* policy goals or the *motivation* of the policymakers based on the presence or lack of balance.

This distinction can be seen from the equation. Order must first be maintained—but done in a balanced manner. These principles are at play: Too much freedom results in chaos. Too much control results in authoritarianism. Balancing these extremes is the challenge.

Surveillance, though not optimal, is necessary. The real question is *why* surveillance is used. Is it to protect against attacks by those who are inclined to attack? Or is it designed to watch everyone simply because technology and power enables and fosters this? Is it to control the "bad guys" from hurting others? Or to control everyone because those who control the technology have the power to do so?

Draconian methods like Communist China are obviously disfavored. But what about the examples from Canada and Australia? What about America? If the goal is protection, then it must be *balanced protection*. Blanket, across-the-board methods are too restrictive. Absolute and overbroad methods are obvious indicators of an authoritarian mindset.

Hence, the goal must be to control risks and threats—but not to foster power. Controls should always consider *who* needs to be controlled. Criminals and those who create danger or disorder ought to be the subject of legal and security remedies. Control the people and places that need control. Don't control for the sake of power. This is a crucial distinction. Think about the "who and the why," not just the means. Any attempt to exert overbroad and overreaching controls demonstrates the goal of the policy. *Overbroad* is the quest for power. *Balance* is the quest for appropriate levels of control. Get this distinction!

Finally, a famous quote from Thomas Jefferson aptly fits here: "When government fears the people, there is liberty. When the people fear the government, there is tyranny."[53]

TRUTH & LOVE

Finding the truth often takes work. It requires more than a soundbite. One must be prepared to *work* to find the truth. One of my favorite expressions is "the truth always comes out." But it takes time. It takes digging. Consider the adage about how quickly lies circulate, with truth so slow. This adage has many variations. The one that makes the most sense to me is from a collection of sermons by Thomas Francklin published in 1787. Here is his version:[54]

> "Falsehood will fly, as it were, on the wings of the wind, and carry its tales to every corner of the earth; whilst truth lags behind; her steps, though sure, are slow and solemn, and she has neither vigour nor activity enough to pursue and overtake her enemy . . .

Let's start with this premise. In a world flooded with information, the truth is hard to find and discern. Proving any specific "truth" is often a folly not worth the exercise. A "fool's errand" comes to mind. Throughout this book, the goal was to be fair, show facts, use logic, and make carefully worded assertions. Avoiding the *I know* "the truth" avoids getting into the weeds trying to "prove" facts. Digging out every relevant fact to "prove" anything is often folly.

Being in the "persuasion business" for decades—policing, lawyering, teaching, and working as an expert witness—this conclusion has ultimately resonated: *most people won't consider opinions they don't like.* Though this is not universal; some can and do get it. Minds open to new facts, logic, and ideas do occur but not very often. But when it does, it is refreshing and often inspiring. This often occurs in court settings, maybe because people appreciate the gravity of their decision. There, they are more apt to pursue the truth with an open mind.

Consequently, our focus here is not on definitive truth but instead on *how to find* the truth. We will explain the means and help explain why *the truth* is so rare these days.

Rational Thinking

Rational thinking is easier to get your mind around than discerning the truth. Plus, rational thinking will get us closer to the truth. So, let's look at rational thinking.

WR Wordsworth powerfully summarizes America's transition from the classical liberal tradition of America's founding, which was inspired *by* and stemmed *from* the Enlightenment tradition. Enlightenment rose in principled opposition to religious conflict in Reformation Europe. This thinking disavowed the religious orthodoxy of its time and abandoned theocracy as a governing ideal. These lasted centuries. Wordsworth contends that "these are now buckling under the relentless attacks of a morally bigoted, hateful, authoritarian Left."

Noting that a fundamental truth of the human experience is exercising political power, which motivates "vulgar climbers" into "paragons of virtue," Wordsworth emphasized that the "empowerment of virtue (however defined) is perhaps the most common founding myth of tyranny." Citing Enlightenment thinking, the fight *against* political fanaticism was best advocated through political liberty. The power of the state was limited; it could only exercise its authority over violent actions but not over controversial thoughts. Wordsworth points out that "*No political authority has a right to dictate to its subjects how they should think.*" Though authoritarian governments often seek to do so. For example, Benito Mussolini was quoted as saying "Everything within the state, nothing outside the state, nothing against the state."[55]

Wordsworth observed that the quest for free-thinking has deep historical roots. "The demand for liberty of conscience seems obvious to us only because it represents a deep assumption of our shared culture—a culture gradually wrested from the grip of fanatics by the teachings of the Enlightenment." This is the political culture we inherited, codified in our founding documents. Wordsworth cites fashionable mantras criticized in this book. Calling the current circumstances as an "attack by a contemporary form of political fanaticism that portrays classical liberalism itself *as a racist con* so as to justify its repudiation and nullification from a putatively higher moral ground (emphasis added)." His cutting analysis deserves our attention:[56]

> "Today's moral fanatics appear not as Biblical guardians, but as self- appointed racial vigilantes. The ugly rhetoric of this vigilantism has been eagerly embraced by the Democratic Party as a source of political advantage, but the promotion of contrived ancestral grievances for cheap political gains comes at the cost of lasting social damage, and one cannot help but wonder when and how the final bill will come due.
>
> And we must recognize: for some of the most dedicated activists on the Left, the social damage is the aim. The contemporary enemies of the Enlightenment seek to inflame tribal hatreds to mobilize their partisans just as the theocrats of old sought to inflame confessional hatreds to mobilize theirs. The classical liberal tradition, with its insistence on moderation, tolerance, and compromise, stands in the way of their ascendancy, so it must be discredited. The social justice fascist impugns the classical liberal heritage as a fraud and proclaims it no more worthy of respect than some crumbling statue in a public park—just another moldering monument to 'white

supremacy' to be contemptuously thrust aside in the name of 'social justice . . .'

The fabrication of racial insult would seem to have become politically obligatory as the nation's political leadership leaps past one other in their eagerness to reach a microphone through which they can denounce the nation they lead as systemically racist. Meanwhile, the old norms . . . are driven to the margins and left there to die of neglect. But one might ask, are these norms then wholly without defenders? Of course not! But the defenders themselves need defenders.

Those defaming the classical liberal tradition pose as sophisticates. Dismissing all traditionalist loyalties as embarrassing sub-intellectual anachronisms bolsters their own insatiable need for comparative self-aggrandizement. The American conservative is caricatured as a boorish nativist whose political attitudes amount to little more than a fetish for powdered wigs and yellowed parchment. But what these bile-spewing mediocrities fail to consider is that the American Experiment is worth defending not because it evokes some gauzy nostalgia, but because the gains of the Enlightenment informing it are worth preserving. It is these gains that are in jeopardy. The Enlightenment's insistence on the essential limits of political power has kept all manner of hellish brutality at bay by denying political fanatics an opportunity to instigate it. These limits—to the extent they are respected—invariably disappoint and frustrate tyrants . . .

If the liberal democratic state does not serve to protect individual rights and guarantee civil peace—if it does not zealously withhold its power from hyperventilating fanatics on behalf of their intended victims—then how does it differ from that which it rose to replace [i.e. the theocracy]? . . .

In rejecting the divisive, malignant slanders of the activist Left we reaffirm our dedication to a political culture that—at its

> best—devoted itself to the principled defense of political sanity. Our immediate reward for this is predictable: in the current environment, the defender of classical liberalism can expect to be dismissed as an accessory to racism. It is high time we recover the true value of limited government and stand against the vigilantes who shamelessly behave as though their superior virtue entitles them to wield the state as a weapon of group revenge."

Read this quote again. Let these words resonate in your heart and mind. Let rational thoughts dominate your mind. Do not doubt yourself when repeated mantras of vacant things meaning *nothing* bombard your mind. Even if these mantras are spoken confidently by people who are in positions that typically elicit respect, do not be fooled by irrational thinking regardless of where it comes from. Consider a powerful principle articulated by Barbara Tuchman: "the rejection of reason is the prime characteristic of folly."[57] This is what mantras do—they ask people to reject reason. They effectively require one to put aside common sense. Quoting Hannah Arendt, Mark Levin shows that common sense loses its impact when people don't have it, writing that "totalitarian propaganda can outrageously insult common sense only where common sense has lost its validity."[58] Propaganda has an impact only when common sense doesn't exist.

Another biting analysis of contemporary thinking comes from one of my favorite writers, Daniel Henninger, who says we are "living in a Peter Pan world: You just think lovely, wonderful thoughts and they lift you up in the air. The credibility cost is zero."[59]

Euphemisms are an important tool for asserting alternative realities. Two of the most important are "reframe" and "reimagine." Citing the "1619 Project" with its purpose to "reframe the country's history," the term came to mean *whatever one wants it to mean*. Henninger defines reframing as "displacing a proven reality with mere assertion, something previously difficult but now normalized." Wokeness says it is about "reimagining" the status quo. "It has reimagined sex by asserting new pronouns; reimagined race as a national "DNA" problem ("1619" again); reimagined merit in college admissions; and reimagined crime control from Seattle to New York."[60]

"All those people who today say they just don't get it may—in reality—be a majority. And they do get it." So, should you. As should all rational thinking people. Douglas Murray dealt directly with expecting people to accept with they don't believe. Murray goes to the heart by saying, "as anyone who has lived under totalitarianism can attest, there is something demeaning and eventually soul-destroying about being expected to go along with claims you do not believe to be true and hold to be true."[61]

Contrast this with the "woke." "The more radical their agenda becomes, the more stridently they demand obedience to it. Republicans, meanwhile, cower at charges of extremism, mostly because they lack a moral and intellectual framework on par with wokeism," says Glenn Elmers.[62] He believes a more effective way to counter the charges of extremism is to aim higher, reviving their belief in what Lincoln called "reason and justice," rooted in the proposition that all men are created equal. Citing Henry Jaffa, he saw Lincoln's sense of the founding as the only possible source of national renewal. "Today we are faced with an unprecedented threat to the survival of biblical religion, of autonomous human reason, and to the form and substance of political freedom," Jaffa wrote in 1990. "It is important to understand why the threat to one of these is also the threat to all. It is above all important to understand why this threat is . . . an internal one, mining and sapping our ancient faith, both in God and in ourselves."

These sentiments will be expanded in the next chapter. But for now, think about how "reason and justice" have been lost in the fog of political correctness—and Wokism. We will never get to the truth if we cannot think lucid thoughts. We will never obtain true justice if the system is inherently racist. We are in a bind so knotted that "connecting the dots" first requires that we untie the illogical, irrational, and destructive thinking that predominates this society. This reality was powerfully described by Rod Dreher in this insightful yet chilling book *Live Not By Lies*: "The foundation of totalitarianism is an ideology made of lies. The system depends for its existence on a people's fear of challenging the lies."[63] Much of the blame for this rests with the "fourth estate," the "arbiters" of truth, and the "referees" of fairness.

Media

For years, many argued that the media is biased. Though the bias is obvious, this is not *news*. What is new is the media has now made their biases known, and they are increasingly abandoning the notion of objectivity. Some quotes and comments go to these points.

In mid-2021, *NPR* announced that reporters should participate in activities that advocate the "freedom and dignity of human beings" on social media and in real life. What this means is far from clear. It is just another undefined mantra. How does one define what freedom and dignity means? As we developed here, freedom is crucial. But it is often used without any idea of how it is achieved and maintained. Dignity is similar. Both are obviously worthy goals. Yet, we ought to be suspicious. We have seen the agenda behind the mantras. This comes from those who are supposed to be the arbiters of truth.

"Stop calling it journalism," said Ayaan Hirsi Ali of the *NPR* report. "If you want to engage in activism, go ahead. But to call it journalism—it's a joke. It's not journalism. It's not reporting, it's not analyzing, it's not investigative reporting because, for all of those activities, you require an open mind, you require a kind of philosophy that you follow the facts to where they lead and then you have to have that disposition of honest, impartial reporting." She adds that media corporations decided "what sells is divisiveness, and hatred and sensationalism, and that's how they make their money, and I think that the general public is seeing that." Ali said. "And that why poll after poll after poll shows there is very, very low trust in media, because it's not media anymore, really."[64]

"The woke young journalists have completely taken over the field and are destroying what little remains of major media credibility," said Dan Gainor of the Media Research Center. "The New York Times, Washington Post, NPR, CNN, are all like watching one of those clown cars in the circus. Every single journalist that climbs out of the car is in makeup and clown shoes. This is what journalism has become and it's why media trust is in the toilet."[65]

But *why* does the public have such a negative impression of the media? As a summary statement from David Rutz. He notes that a "growing number of prominent journalists have declared once-bedrock press principles like fairness and objectivity to be outdated and unnecessary since the Donald Trump era rocked American politics, and while some observers appreciate the honesty, others feel blending opinion and reporting makes for a 'dangerous time' in America."[66]

I trust the reader sees this quote as consistent with the premise of this book. We will make some points on this, but it may be helpful to first get a sense of the journalists who are leaving behind the image (or the fiction) of the disinterested, impartial correspondent.

NBC News anchor Lester Holt won plaudits from mainstream colleagues after declaring "fairness is overrated." In his acceptance speech for a journalism award, he added it's not necessary to "always give two sides equal weight and merit." *CNN's* John Harwood publicly thanked Holt. *CNN's* "Reliable Sources" newsletter called it a "sharp critique of bothsiderism."

The rejection of "bothsiderism" was echoed by *Los Angeles Times* columnist Jackie Calmes, who published an opinion piece titled "Why journalists are failing the public with 'both-siderism' in political coverage." Calmes called out "journalistic pressure" to produce seemingly balanced stories that prevent journalists from reporting what she referred to as "the *new* truth" (emphasis added). She targeted journalists who "focus critically on President Biden and Democrats" as opposed to "Republicans' obstructions." Repeatedly criticizing Republicans, she warned that "democracy is literally at stake." "This is a Republican Party that is not serious about governing or addressing the nation's actual problems, as opposed to faux ones like critical race theory," Calmes wrote. She concluded her op-ed by writing, "Democrats can't be expected to deal with these guys like they're on the level. Nor should journalists cover them as if they are."[67]

Just as with Holt, acclaim followed Calmes' piece. *New Yorker* staff writer Jane Mayer tweeted, "Good point from longtime reporter @JackieCalmes: Missing from much political coverage is that only one party is even trying to govern." *New York Times Magazine* writer Nikole Hannah-Jones added, "Every political journalist should read this and the book *How Democracies Die*." Former VP at *NPR* Bill Buzenberg tweeted, "Great Op Ed—important message for every journalist. Please don't 'balance' the truth with an outright, calculated lie, and call it objective reporting or interviewing."[68]

This rejection of "bothsiderism" implies that the media (or individual reporters) *can discern when one side is wrong*. It also does not merit "the wrong" position being communicated to the public. That they can discern truth from lies is implicit in this thinking. They cannot be "objective" because one side is correct, and the other side is wrong. Let's flesh this out.

First, the obvious. Under what circumstances ought the media determine that one side's position has no merit? What standards or criteria can be used to make this determination? Note, as with the mantras, there is never any substantive explanation as to who, what, where, when, why, and how. These are supposed to be the essence of journalism. But they are all missing. Instead, the public is given a mantra. It does not even come with one concrete example.

Second, why should the public give any weight to these "editorial" decisions anyway? Deciding what to cover, how to cover it, who to talk to, and the like are all editorial decisions. This is part of the news-gathering process that takes place prior to publishing any piece. What is written or shown is only a small part of the overall "story." Any number of facts, angles, perspectives, and opinions are honed or eliminated through the editorial process. What appears is what the media sources wanted to convey. It is not the "whole story." Often what is *not* reported is just as important or relevant as what *is* reported. Hence, the notion of "media silence" has informed my thinking for decades. The silence is often the *real story*.

This fits what progressive *New York Times Magazine* writer Nikole Hannah-Jones declared when she said, "all journalism is activism." *PBS* reporter Yamiche Alcindor said that she considers it *her duty* to use journalism to bend the "moral arc toward justice (emphasis added)."[69] These comments should not surprise us. But they raise many questions covered in this book, such as: Activism for who? For what "causes"? Justice for whom? Who determines what "justice" is? Truth . . . who decides and based on what facts?

These and many others go to the heart of where we are as a society. Trust you know what "side" of the ledger these determinations will reside on. Yet, the *guise* of "objectivity" is at least being peeled away.

"On one hand, journalists abandoning objectivity, or as Lester Holt said even more insidiously, 'fairness,' just further cements the media's abandonment of principles it once maintained," said *Fourth Watch* editor Steve Krakauer. "Everyone in America with two eyes and a brain knows most of the establishment, legacy media isn't objective and hasn't been for a very long time. It's good they are finally admitting the obvious—to the public and to themselves."

Conservative writer Drew Holden added these thoughts. "Objectivity as a standard at least requires that outlets try to see and reconcile their own biases. Without it, we risk sinking even deeper into an environment where advocacy and partisanship get laundered as straight news to everyday Americans who see the media as honest brokers. . . . There's a whole group of people out there who want reporters to be partisans and are very critical whenever people who do what I do try to basically do our jobs . . . to be fair and balanced," Holden said.[70]

DePauw University professor and media critic Jeffrey McCall feels "there has always been a prominent role for opinion in journalism, and the First Amendment surely allows for the media to engage in activism. However, professional ethics in American journalism is to keep opinion and advocacy in a separate lane from the straightforward presentation of facts. We live in a *dangerous time today*, however, when professional journalists want to blend opinion and reporting into the same place (emphasis added)," said McCall. "This presents several problems, not the least of which is that the public can no longer trust many traditional news outlets to present news fairly and fully. This had led to broad declines in media credibility," McCall added.

University of North Carolina Professor Lois A. Boynton pointed out that colonial and early American newspapers and pamphlets were "openly partisan and did not employ objectivity," but there were so many competing publications that readers were able to gather multiple perspectives and draw their own conclusions. Roughly 100 years ago, legendary journalist Walter Lippmann "saw the value of reporters using what scientists employed—objectivity—a process to check, recheck and verify findings," Boynton said.

Objectivity requires journalists to develop a consistent method of testing information. This creates a transparent approach to evidence. Transparency reduces the personal and cultural biases that could undermine the accuracy of their work. "In other words, people are not objective, but with rigor, they can do objectivity," she added.

Let me end this section with a personal observation. As a police officer, I was present at many crime scenes that were covered by local news outlets in Chicago. Watching the news coverage of the incident was often like watching an alternative reality. I was almost always amazed that what I saw and heard at the crime scene was not what was covered by the news outlet. There were times I literally stared at the TV wondering what scene they had covered? This was sometimes deeply upsetting.

Over the years, I spoke with many reporters and generally received fair coverage. In several instances, though, I did lengthy interviews with reporters and was never mentioned in their reporting. Much of what I said appeared as "background" in the piece, but I was not cited or named. It took me a while to figure out that I did not "say the right thing." I did not say what they wanted to hear—or wanted to print.

One ought not care about media acclaim nor do I write for acclaim or to "please" the media. Conveying this message goes well beyond these "things," which are ultimately petty and unimportant anyway. The focus must be *the message*—this is what matters . . .

Race Relations

Since race relations play such an "outsized" role and since this book has focused some time and attention on race, it may be helpful to see "race relations" from a different perspective.

In the past few years, the American public has been exposed to these versions of race relations: 1619 Project, Black Lives Matter (BLM), Critical Race Theory (CRT), "systemic racism." "white fragility," "white supremacy," and a host of "racist" allegations and attacks. All these go one way. All these present America—and the American people—as either being outright racist or complicit by way of silence or simply by the color of their skin. All of these are overbroad, discriminatory, and intimidating. Indeed, these are so wrong they must be refuted. Since the media arbiters are either absent or downright complicit, let's at least attempt to level the playing field with some discussion on race relations.

Robert Woodson has a lot of relevant, profound things to say about race. As a man who worked with Dr. King and devoted his life to the principles derived from the 1960s civil rights movement, he has credibility, conviction, and context. Unfortunately, his message is not what most of the media want to hear. He counters the race mantras of progressives—and does so using the credibility and conviction of his long-standing service to civil rights.

Mr. Woodson makes the basic point that belies the notion of "systemic racism." He says that an "insistence on 'systemic' racism tells minority communities they have no power over their own lives." He condemns the notion that blacks must rely on white people to solve all their problems "by somehow ending systemic and institutional racism." Calling this "both nonsensical and self-defeating," he believes blacks are more than capable of helping themselves. Indeed, he rebuffs the help that progressives provide to black communities, which is *hurting* black communities.

He explains that by focusing on the past and present sins of white America as the source of all one's problems, blacks "ignore the enemy within, and that which is in our power to change." "We turn a blind eye to the destruction within our communities that is consuming more of our lives than the Klan ever did, even at the height of its power." As an aside, consider that about 10,000 blacks were killed in 2021. Since the vast number of blacks are killed by blacks, this has little or no consequence for the media and the racial provocateurs.

He then raises this provocative question: "Are only white people capable of hate crimes? If you get all your news from mainstream media sources, that's what you'd think." He noted that throughout 2020 there was a rise in violence against Asian-Americans, but "the race of the perpetrators was typically mentioned only when they were white."[71]

He goes on to describe the emphasis on so-called white supremacists. "Media and other elites obsessively push the narrative that the greatest threat in this country is coming from 'white supremacists.' This oversimplification has dire consequences for the most vulnerable in our society—those living in the poorest neighborhoods—and for the nation as a whole." He criticizes the "media environment in which the only acceptable villains are white." This he says, "creates a more dangerous world for all of us." Pointing to the segregated pre-Civil Rights South, he parallels the current media and political climate to the "rush to judgment based on skin color." Here is his perspective, comparing the "Old South" with what we may call "the *new* truth,"[72]

> "In those days, some in law enforcement couldn't care less about crimes committed by blacks against other blacks, but there were severe penalties for offenses against whites. We marched and demanded fair and equal treatment under the law. As far as the application of criminal law, much of what is happening today is a retreat to the pre-Civil Rights South.
>
> Every tragic police killing of a black person is amplified by radical progressives to accuse police of white supremacy and to push for defunding and anarchy . . . Meanwhile, the cries of the 81 percent of blacks who oppose defunding the police are chronically ignored.
>
> Thanks to so-called racial progressives . . . low-income black neighborhoods are experiencing some of what it was like to live in the pre-Civil Rights South."

Mr. Woodson injects some sanity and reason into discussions on race relations. He agrees that "race remains a salient issue in America, but not only because of whites victimizing minorities. Yet the US is the world's most prosperous and harmonious multiracial society. We have some serious problems we must address, but we can't solve them unless we're willing to speak about them honestly."[73]

Yet another source of honesty comes from commentator Bill Maher. As most other prominent liberals have "graduated" to progressive socialists, Maher is a force of reason, often by biting humor. The *Real Time* host blasted progressives who refuse to acknowledge the progress on racial and social issues that's been made in America.

Maher began by diagnosing the Left with "progressophobia," a term he defined as "a brain disorder that strikes liberals and makes them incapable of recognizing progress." "If you think America is more racist now than ever, more sexist than before women could vote, and more homophobic than when b---j--s were a felony, you have 'progressophobia' and should adjust your mask because it's covering your eyes," Maher told his viewers. He pointed out how only "4 percent" of Americans approved of interracial marriage in 1958. Gallup measured this question until 2013, stopping when "87 percent" of the population supported it. Maher noted this was a "sea change" from his childhood.[74]

"And yet there's a recurrent theme on the far-left that things have never been worse! This is one of the big problems with wokeness," he continued, "that what you say doesn't have to make sense or jive with the facts or even be challenged lest the challenge be conflated with racism."[75] As an aside, where are the rest of the liberals? Maher is not the only one seeing this.

Finally, there is Mayor Lightfoot. The Chicago mayor not only cannot see the progress America has made in race relations; she cannot see anything *but* race. Being gay, female, and black; rising to the height of power in the Windy City, one would think she would recognize how fortunate she was to be born in America. Educated as a lawyer, previously serving as an Assistant United States Attorney, she had many bountiful blessings and wonderful opportunities. And as the mayor of a city filled with violence and corruption, with assorted fiscal and housing challenges, she decided to focus on the race of reporters that she would talk to.

Mayor Lightfoot said in a two-page written statement that "I will be exclusively providing one-on-one interviews with journalists of color." She justified her decision as a response to "the overwhelming whiteness and maleness of Chicago media outlets, editorial boards, the political press corps, and yes, the City Hall press corps specifically."

She suggested the negative coverage she receives stems from racial bias. "For the past two years, more often than not, we have debated internally, then chosen to say nothing, to let it go, lest we be accused of whining about negative coverage or of 'playing the race card,'" Ms. Lightfoot wrote. "And the truth is, it is too heavy a burden to bear, on top of all the other massive challenges our city faces in this moment, to also have to take on the labor of educating white, mostly male members of the news media about the perils and complexities of implicit bias."[76]

As the *Wall Street Journal* notes, "like the racists of the Jim Crow South, the mayor will now judge journalists solely by the color of their skin." Though the mayor defended her decision for months after the letter was written, the "exclusivity" afforded to "journalists of color" allegedly was designed for her two-year anniversary as mayor. The fact that this controversy followed for months after the anniversary speaks to the volatile nature of race. The *Journal* calls it a "sign of the times. . . . America is again dividing itself by race. It is hard to imagine a more dangerous trend for social comity and democratic consent, and if Ms. Lightfoot's racist media policy is a guide, it promises to get worse."[77]

Things *are* getting worse, so bad that revolution may be seen as an option for some. The operative question may be "What can we do?" Can we step back from the abyss?

Two solutions are offered. Both are easy to say but difficult to define. Both are widely regarded, but not practiced enough. Both are eternal and universal but conceptual and subjective. These are *truth and love.*

Let's start with truth. In one of the most famous accounts in history. This question was posed: *What is truth?* The premise of this question—and the answer is as old as humankind. People have struggled to find the truth in many ways, in many places, and all times. The setting for this universal question was the trial of Jesus Christ. Here is the account from John:[78]

> "So Pilate entered his headquarters again and called Jesus and said to him, 'Are you the King of the Jews?'
>
> Jesus answered, 'Do you say this of your own accord, or did others say it to you about me?' Pilate answered, 'Am I a Jew? Your own nation and the chief priests have delivered you over to me. What have you done?'

> Jesus answered, 'My kingdom is not of this world. If my kingdom were of this world, my servants would have been fighting, that I might not be delivered over to the Jews. But my kingdom is not from the world.'
>
> Then Pilate said to him, 'So you are a king?' Jesus answered, 'You say that I am a king. For this purpose I was born and for this purpose I have come into the world—to bear witness to the truth. Everyone who is of the truth listens to my voice.'
>
> Pilate said to him, '*What is truth*?' After he had said this, he went back outside to the Jews and told them, 'I find no guilt in him (emphasis added).'

Christ previously answered this question in a conversation with His disciples, saying, "if you abide in my word, you are truly my disciples, and you will know the truth, and the truth will set you free."[79]

This answer is twofold. First, as Christ said, to know the truth, one must be "truly my disciple." This means that people must be a student (disciple) of Christ. Know Christ as the Word and the Savior. Model life based on what Christ said and how He lived. Thus, truth is dependent on the connection to Christ—His ways and His purpose. Yet, all have sinned and fallen short of the glory of God.

This goes to the second part: *the truth will set you free.* Knowing this way of life, we are free to live life to the fullest. A full and purposeful life worthy of one's calling. Living the truth sets one free to live this way. Yes, we will fall. But the important part is getting up and moving toward what really matters—a legacy in this life, God's kingdom, and eternal life.

I trust that some percentage of the readers will not think this way, though many will relate and want more. Both positions are understandable. People need something tangible to hang on to. People need to have hope for a better tomorrow.

Yet, seeking the truth can be analogized as an eternal quest. As with every generation of humans, we seek truth. Though, we have different ways of thinking. Different ways to filter facts and perceptions. Distinctions are partially based on our cultural, educational, social, and racial circumstances. Our history, our parents, and our upbringing, all come together to establish our unique and yet distinctly human worldview.

Human distinctions used to be celebrated. I grew up with the idea that America was a "melting pot." That people from all races, creeds, and ethnic backgrounds came together in the American experiment, enabling people from different perspectives to blend into "Americans."

Later, the idea of "diversity" took hold—and took over. Here the focus was on our differences. You heard the adage, "our strength is our diversity." This worked for a time to bring Americans together while acknowledging that some want to retain part of "who they are." This means retaining elements of one's culture, with values and life experiences being tied to one's race, religion, ethnic, and cultural background.

While the focus on diversity is not wrong, per se, it "opened the door" to a more insidious element that exists today. That is, one's race, religion, gender, self-identity, ethnic, and cultural conditions being prominent. This thinking propelled the idea of "my truth," which is intimately and naturally tied to that person's lived experiences. How can one understand a black woman, unless one is a black woman? This was essentially what Lori Lightfoot said. So, the "answer" is to surround oneself with black women, or least, "women of color." This thinking was even advocated by US Supreme Court Justice Sonia Sotomayor who stated, "I would hope that a wise Latina woman, with the richness of her experiences, would more often than not reach a better conclusion than a white male who hasn't lived that life."[80]

This is not to say that different experiences are not helpful. Indeed, they are. It is part of the "logic" of *strength through diversity*. But has the bright line been crossed, where "my truth" is so personal, so racial, so cultural, as to make the notion of "universal truth" a simple relic of the past? This question is *way more* than conceptual. As we have seen throughout this book, the "racially based" agenda does not even bother to contend that whites and blacks can be on the same page. That is, unless whites first bow at the altar of "white guilt" and admit to their racist sins derived from the color of their skin. This is not a formula for truth, or for racial relations. Instead, it is a blatant and obvious attempt to turn what may have been white supremacy into modern-day black supremacy.

How about abandoning the need to assert supremacy over others? How about agreeing with this standard: *that the best facts, the most merit, the hardest working, the smartest, and the most effective people are those who strive for and achieve success.* What if we ran society professional sport? Merit wins the day—merit wins the job and the game. Sports bring races together because players think as a team. No race is superior because that is not the goal. The goal is a better team—or a better country.

Reason and rational thinking *could* overcome bitter, hateful, and divisive thinking. Honestly addressing things this country did wrong, particularly relating to race, is why advocates of CRT say their "theory" is necessary.

In 2018, Jill Lepore, wrote a piercing examination of American history entitled *These Truths*.[81] Lepore's version of US history was both hard to read and enlightening. Hard because example after example of harm, hatred, and prejudice made my heart sick. Chronicling *These Truths* struck me as a thorough work with excellent scholarship. Designed to focus on the plight of blacks, rather than hard and difficult times others also struggled through, yet it served to highlight wrongs for which no living person is culpable.

Surely, history is filled with struggles; humanity is riddled with hate and hardship. Not to minimize historical faults and failures, but contemporary societal relations are also at stake. We cannot ignore history. But one wonders how a well-intended and well-researched book can also be used to foster division. Getting an accurate account of history ought not serve to motivate contemporary resentment. Using the previously described "Holy Trinity" as an example, *These Truths* do not validate modern theories designed to foster a progressive agenda. The operative question is thus: *Can we learn from history without seeking retribution or revenge today?*

Despite chronicling many decisions that resulted in many wrongs, Lepore acknowledges that this country still made revolutionary progress. Never in history of the world was such a bold and noble experiment undertaken. A classic example came from the Declaration of Independence, where Lepore makes this point about the hallowed document:[82]

> "The Declaration that Congress did adopt was a stunning rhetorical feat, an act of revolutionary political courage. It also marked a colossal failure of political will, in holding back in the tide of opposition to slavery by ignoring it, for the sake of a union that, in the end, could not and would not last."

Lepore is correct. The words of the hallowed document were better than its execution. A bloody civil war was needed because ignoring opposition to slavery was wrong. The Declaration declared that "all men are created equal." But this basic—yet unprecedented—principle was not fully abided. The founders carried out "an act of revolutionary political courage," (using Lepore's words), which was unprecedented in history. But in making this historical declaration about the nature of mankind, they violated their own declaration. Clearly, this was done for both political—and pragmatic purposes. The founders knew that a compromise or accommodation was needed to obtain the commitment of southern states. There was not going to be an agreement, and the American Revolution was not going forward without this compromise.

Looking back at this decision with modern eyes, this was obviously wrong. It's one of *These Truths* that cannot be justified. This "original sin" has been painful and attempts at redemption have been difficult and bloody.

The truth is that sin cannot be undone—only forgiven. The truth is that history cannot be undone. The truth is that we are all flawed, as is every human endeavor and every country. All we can do is do better. Accordingly, CRT, 1619 project, "systemic racism," and other "race-based revelations" are not solutions—these are *not* representative of doing better. These things are the opposite of doing better. These are harsh and divisive. No less so than the wrong decisions made at the foundation of this country. Most assuredly, we will not *right* wrongs with other wrongs. This is a *hard* truth.

The hard reality is that truth is a process. As Sohrab Ahmari aptly says, "truth thus becomes an ongoing project . . ."[83] It often takes hard work to discern and to resolve. These seldom come in the form of a "mantra." Elements of truth are often embedded with elements of falsehoods or perceptions.

Though truth is dependent on many factors and variables, it still matters, and it always finds its way to the light. Truth "always comes out." Aleksandr Solzhenitsyn, the great Russian novelist and philosopher said, "one word of truth outweighs the whole world."[84] Dreher adds this powerful belief: "It is up to us today to take up this challenge, to *live not by lies* and to speak the truth that defeats evil."[85]

Being closer to the truth requires a life of character. Living with integrity, abiding by what we understand to be true, being grounded in principles derived from universal or eternal values. Going forward, times *will* get hard. Character is shaped and wizened by adversity.

Let's close with this philosophical or spiritual approach. *Combat with Truth. Strengthen with Love.* Work to find and convey truth. Often, all relevant facts aren't discernable. Indeed, characterizations or conclusions are often mistaken for "facts." Discerning and assembling as many facts as possible is the challenge. John Adams famously stated, "facts are stubborn things; and whatever may be our wishes, our inclinations, or the dictates of our passion, they cannot alter the state of facts and evidence." [86] No amount of passion can change stubborn facts. Facts are what they are. Yet, finding facts can be a difficult task.

Search for facts with trusted sources, including balancing mainstream sites with other views to get a different, wider perspective. Indeed, mainstream media institutions are suspect—even dead, as former *Chicago Tribune* columnist John Kass described—from *root rot.* Years of "playing the game" have now digressed to the point that "journalists" have rejected objectivity.

Consequently, where we seek "truth" will give us a better chance of finding it. As Christ stated, *where one seeks matters*. But once truth is found, strengthen it with love. Care about the truth. Care how people are impacted by it. Use love as a guide. Love strengthens the quest for truth and strengthens our resolve. Live it. But use truth with discretion, as it is powerful. Temper its use as a weapon. If a weapon is needed, let it be more often a shield, not a sword. Going forward armed with truth, we will close the loop in the next chapter.

CHAPTER VII

CLOSING THE LOOP . . .

Telling the story of a pending revolution has been challenging and disconcerting. Yet, this is a story that needs to be told. Think of this analogy. In police parlance, the term "in progress" is used to describe a crime that is current—it is *happening now*. Having responded to thousands of "in-progress" calls, I know that many crimes have been interrupted prior to completion. In the same way, responding in a timely manner can intercede and stop the momentum toward revolution. At least, this is my hope.

Seeing the revolution as "in progress" gives us the opportunity to do something to intercede. Telling the story involves explaining what is happening and why. It is difficult to lay out yet crucial to understand.

This book commenced by projecting how certain crimes can be seen as representing a larger trend. Seeing the macro from the micro enables one to see what most miss. Understanding that these are reflective of something larger changes one's perspective. Seeing the *why* and the *how* is crucial.

The reason—the motives—why people commit crimes is what we ought to look for. Knowing what some *do* reflects what others are *thinking* can give insight into the future. Hence, showing that certain incidents may reflect larger trends gives us a window into the worldview of what others may do in the future. Similarly, showing that allowing crimes and disorder to go unabated may devolve into chaos is another window into the future. This was done by showing how policies directly impact results. It is cause and effect—seeing the future by understanding the dynamics of policy decisions. This also implies adjusting policies can achieve different results.

In short, this book took on progressive policies for what they really are—for what they are designed to do. We are getting what was intended.

This included looking closely at what most ignore—or are afraid to directly address: *race, religion, and politics*. Not only were these *not* ignored but were focused on with facts and logic, not emotion—nor groundless accusations. Ironically, because discussing these can be combustible, most do not honestly address what is most likely to divide us. Think of the *definitive speech on race* given by Barack Obama. Apparently, it was not *definitive*. If it was, why is it no longer relevant?

Addressing these factors separates this book from most. Using facts and logic instead of emotion and allegation is the only way to deal with controversial matters. Yet, this also takes courage and conviction. Taking on what has been likened to the "third rail" requires being prepared for the sword and shield of racism. I expect to be attacked as a racist—the "sword" is inevitable.

Using the "shield" of facts and logic, though insufficient, must still be applied. Believing that the truth is always slower than allegations, it is necessary to "step out in faith," while most "run for cover." Yet, many are standing up for truth, albeit a smaller number than the "crowd." Yet, history tells us that people who stand up are necessary. Do we have what it takes to stand up when others cower? If so, being armed with facts and logic is necessary.

Neo-racists do not operate at this level. All they have is emotion and allegation. Getting facts and logic into the mix is the only honest way to prevail. But expect to be attacked. Not buckling to emotion and groundless allegations are required. Do this through courage and conviction.

Another way to see the horizon is to understand ideologies. Ideologies fuel the fire. While race, religion, and politics often separate us; ideologies are what drive those who *want* to separate. While humans have more in common than not, ideology drives separation. Presenting those of the parties involved will provide a vital window into extremist worldviews. Unless one understands this thinking, making sense of contemporary America is akin to wandering through a maze.

Big things are happening. But these look disconnected, even illogical—unless one has the path through the maze. To use another analogy, ideology is the picture depicting what the completed puzzle will look like. Ideologies illustrate what is occurring beyond what most can see. They enable us to understand this revolutionary climate and *why* it has come to be.

Taking this to the natural conclusion, we delved deeply into policies that were clearly generated by a specific ideology—socialists imagining themselves as progressives. We can see "defunding" and "reimagining" emanating from Marxist thinking, while others simply wonder what were they thinking? Why is this happening? We saw the underlying motivations of criminal justice "reform" designed to divert offenders from the system. And of police policies designed to reduce, even preclude, *proactive* police enforcement. Detailing these changes and the resultant state of lawlessness takes the veil off their agenda. Crime data and the effects on policing, including the notion of a "thin blue line," were also presented and analyzed.

Lawlessness is not just an unfortunate result of misguided thinking. It could also be seen as a strategy designed to "collapse" the system. Understanding the ideologies underlying this thinking, one can conclude that the real purpose of *reforms* and *policies* was to create pressure on the system designed to *destroy* it. This is my conclusion. In *American Marxism*, Mark Levin pointed to what he termed a "Cloward and Piven-type approach"[1] and said something similar: "overwhelming the system, crashing the system, then blaming the system, and taking control of the system . . ."[2] One can think otherwise, but those who advocate such ideological thinking fail to explain—or do so in only mantras and simplistic terms—*why* CRT, 1619, and "systemic racism" are beneficial or necessary.

Due to advocates using mantras, such as "mass incarceration," "white supremacy," "systemic racism," and the like; the underlying goals of this thinking are not quantifiable—nor substantive. How does one even define such nebulous terms? How does one "fix" a society that is systemically racist?

Even if white supremacy *does* dominate this country (which we have disputed), can this be eliminated by interjecting racially-based thinking? These questions are left unanswered because advocates of such mantras have no answers. These were *not intended to be answered.* Instead, what is intended is the destruction of capitalism. The real "answer" is socialism.

Based on this premise, one can conclude that a revolutionary climate is at hand. If this is true, there will be push-back. It could come in many forms. From competing ideologies? From those who seek to maintain the capitalistic system? From those who want to live in freedom?

Fostering the latter can be achieved through the application of *Public Safety Policing*. Providing the theoretical and historical basis of this policing model was done to demonstrate its proven effectiveness. Unlike vague undefinable mantras, our approach was to let research, facts, and logic lead the way. Yet, the honest answer offered goes to a pragmatic response—the policing model is not a definitive answer to vexing societal circumstances. But reasserting order is crucial to regaining control of an increasingly disorderly and chaotic society. Hence, the remedy is to address disorder with order and to address chaos with control. These approaches will create tension and prove challenging. This will not be without controversy or without drama.

Indeed, the application of this policing model will be messy. Mistakes will be made. Allegations of "racism" will surely follow. Police officers will be killed. Police use of force incidents will increase in relation to the number of police killings, and from the increase in violent crime. These dilemmas and challenges lie ahead. Yet, it will be worse if needed changes are not made. Continuing the climate of lawlessness is worse—and fosters an inevitable increase in extremist and terroristic violence. Unfortunately, such violence will occur with or without implementing remedies designed to regain order and control.

Consequently, there is no "perfect" answer. There are too many challenges. Too many fights. Too much division. Societal dynamics will not allow for "solutions" with either consensus or without pain. Unfortunately, there is no easy answer forthcoming. In short, the gravity and complexity of our problems does not lend easy answers. If easy answers were out there, they would have already been applied. *This is why we are where we are*. Hostilities will mount as we go forward because any "solutions" will be resisted and challenged by those with different "answers."

We then presented *things that matter*—freedom, security, love, and truth. The tension with these and the means to achieve these were presented and analyzed. As these are so important—this analysis was crucial. The consequences of not getting this right ought to create profound thought and reflection. What was presented goes to the level of analysis befitting such crucial factors. Yet, this was just a primer. The scope here fit with the overall theme—a pending revolution.

The formulas presented can be used to assess the road ahead. Are we headed toward an authoritarian society? Or will we maintain necessary freedoms despite ideological actors seeking to collapse society? Understanding the distinction between control designed to sustain freedom and control designed to foster power is critical to our ability to think through the way forward.

BACK TO THE BEGINNING

With these as summaries of what has been said, let's now close the loop. Let's go back to the beginning. *You say you want a revolution?* was used to introduce this story. The answer about fifty years ago was: *But if you want money for people with minds that hate, all I can tell you is brother you have to wait.* The answer implied the motivation—minds that hate. This can be discerned by *how and what* is sought.

As asserted throughout this book, goals based on mere mantras are deceptive. They are largely mindless soundbites with no means to define or access. Revolutionary movements throughout history have used similar rhetoric. Even when they "succeed," they fail to achieve an equitable, classless, and "better" society. In previous quests for revolutionary changes, literally millions have died. Therefore, *vetting the motivations* of those who want to effect basic changes to society ought to be done diligently—and in the light of day! This was done in this book.

My conclusion: those seeking to "change" this society are doing so because they *hate* the status quo. They *hate* the capitalistic system. They accuse others of hate, yet they foster hate and destruction. With little detail, yet considerable flowery mantras, they do not and cannot articulate what the new society will consist of. Anyone who delves into the "empty" mantras is typically met with allegations of racism, sexism, and other "isms." If these cannot be substantively communicated now, why should we believe what they are offering? Levin says it this way: ". . . it is they [Marxists] who are using and promoting racism, sexism, ageism, etc., as weapons of disunity and rebellion while claiming to want to end them. Even worse, they are using America's freedom to destroy freedom and the Constitution to destroy the Constitution."[3]

One critical indicator of motivation is the ability to craft a detailed view of their worldview. Do your own research. See what you find. If you find what I contend, then the *absence of substance* goes to the *motivation of the heart and the mind*. Be well advised to use great caution in buying into something so profound yet so undefined. Those who "sell" as much either have corrupt motives or fail to understand the danger of their product.

Those who caution us about the motives of the progressives were thus cited, quoted, and explained in this text. Some extraordinary people of all races have been presented. Their words are precise, articulate, and powerful. Yet, these are largely voices in the wilderness. Most do not have the power to combat the deep-seated institutional forces that are aligned against them. Plainly, progressives hold much of the power in American institutions—or those who run these institutions are afraid to speak up. Academia, media, big tech, entertainment along with those in the political arena at all levels; their reach and influence are daunting to overcome. Still, at least for now, Americans still have the freedom to question these institutions—and those who run them. Signs of pushback are showing. As the song asserts, "but if you go carrying pictures of Chairman Mao, you ain't going to make it with anyone anyhow." This will be interesting to watch . . .

Many years ago, I learned of an interesting parallel to describe the dynamics of policing streets and of interactions within society. Coming from former Army Lieutenant Colonial David Grossman, who used an analogy of sheep, sheepdogs, and wolves to describe the state of society. In describing these in human terms, Grossman characterizes most people as "sheep." They are nonviolent with little, if any, desire to hurt others. Grossman cites statistics to show that the murder rate of only six per 100,000 to demonstrate that few people are violent—and very few commit murder. He explains that "I mean nothing negative by calling them sheep. . . . Someday the civilization of sheep they protect will grow into something wonderful. For now, though, the sheep need warriors to protect them from the predators."[4] In short, the sheep need protection from the hard-edged sheepdogs.

As in the *animal and human* world, the sheepdogs protect the sheep from the wolves. This is how these were described:[5]

> "Then there are the wolves, and the wolves feed on the sheep without mercy. Do you believe there are wolves out there who will feed on the flock without mercy? You better believe it. There are evil men in this world, and they are capable of evil deeds. The moment you forget that or pretend it is not so, you become a sheep. There is no safety in denial."
>
> Then there are sheepdogs . . . [who] live to protect the flock and confront the wolf. Or, as a sign in one California law enforcement agency put it, 'We intimidate those who intimidate others.' "

This gets us closer to understanding the dilemma in contemporary America. Many have confused sheepdogs with wolves—and vice versa. This is more understandable than one may consider. First, the body structure of these animals resembles the other. Both have strong teeth and necks—they are built to fight and run hard. Plus, they are carnivores. Conversely, sheep are herbivores and eat mainly plant material. Their teeth and bodies are not nearly as strong and robust as are the sheepdogs and wolves.

Second, because of the similarities in their body types, sheepdogs sometimes act like wolves. They can be aggressive. They sometimes even kill wolves who confront their sheep. You see the point. Sheepdogs sometimes act too much like wolves, so much so that the sheep can be fearful of them. Sheepdogs regularly herd the sheep, sometimes collide, and even bite them to get their attention.

It can be hard to distinguish the *why* between a bite of the sheepdog versus the bite of a wolf. They both hurt. But the difference lies in the motivation. Sheepdogs do what they do to protect the sheep. Wolves do what they do to destroy—and eat the sheep.

Just like sheep, modern America is now hard-pressed to tell the difference between sheepdogs and wolves. Sheepdogs have been demonized for tactics that often are fully *within the law* (note the section on the *Use-of-Force Model*). When a police officer *violates* the law, as in the George Floyd case, the template is the same: racist police officer who victimizes black citizen. What is usually lacking is any real analysis of what the "victim" did to precipitate the encounter. They are usually treated as "sheep," but, their arrest history, conduct, and resistive attitude are more closely akin to a wolf. In almost all such cases, these factors are glossed over in a manner that is designed to foster the "innocent" citizen (read sheep) being accosted by the bad cop (read sheepdog).

Significantly, when police violate the law, they are subject to the law. But this is not good enough. Broadly condemning police officers is the preferred approach. Cops are racist. The system is racist.

Given this dynamic—and this perception—it's understandable that the distinction between sheepdogs and wolves has been blurred. It may even be juxtaposed—with the sheepdogs viewed as bad while the wolves are seen as good, or at least innocent. Speaking generally, nothing could be further from the truth. Yet, this is what we have been "sold." This is partly what motivated *defunding* and *reimagining.*

Extricating society from this conceptual confusion will not be easy. This is in part because the wolves will continue intimidating and destroying the sheep. Wolves will also keep resisting and confronting—and even attacking sheepdogs. Faced with these realities, police officers will be forced to act like *wolves*—and confront and bite them. These encounters will often be videotaped. Trying to gain control of resisters or aggressors can be hard. It looks "messy" because it *is*. Handcuffing someone who does not want to be handcuffed is difficult. This is well known in police circles, but for obvious reasons not often communicated.

Simply stated, there are no easy ways to subdue someone who does not intend to surrender. Tasers and other technologies help. But just like the animal world with *real* sheep, sheepdogs, and wolves, sometimes violence is the only recourse. Just like the animal world made popular in nature shows, such as *Animal World* and *National Geographic*, cameras are often there to "document" the encounter for the world to see.

Drawing parallels to the animal world is helpful to demonstrate the nature of the conflict. This parallel is not meant to imply that "criminals are animals," as many used to criticize former President Trump when he compared MS-13 to "animals." Yet, the parallel and the dynamics between sheepdogs and wolves are illustrative because it "depersonalizes" the nature of the conflict. And there is no getting around the fact that these conflicts occur—and will continue to occur. Partially because the template is used so often and is so well-developed, one can expect more conflict, more resistance, and more aggression—between sheepdogs and wolves.

Ultimately, wolves understand one thing: *force or strength* (depending upon how it is characterized). Just as predators in the human realm, force/strength is the common denominator. Of all other "remedies," this is what they most respect. Indeed, in many cases, force/strength is the *only* thing they respect. This is something liberals generally do not understand or acknowledge. Progressives may "get this" but for the wrong reasons. Based on the summer of love riots, surely, they saw that those who create chaos had value. If chaos is desired, those so inclined can oblige.

What is lost in this analysis, and in the societal dynamic is the "why." It is the motivation that separates sheepdogs from wolves. Sheepdogs seek to protect. Wolves seek to destroy. When considered at the societal level, consider these questions. Should those who want to change the system be considered wolves? Surely, they are not sheep. Many who go along believing the mantras, though, likely *are* sheep. Those who blindly and naively abide the false hope of soundbites and mantras fit nicely into the definition of "sheep." Again, this is not to demean. But they blindly or gullibly go along with what will ultimately hurt them. They don't know they need to be protected from the wolves. Believing to one's detriment is not ideal—yet it happens all the time, and no one is immune.

A brief story may illustrate this dilemma. As a tactical police officer in the gang crime unit, my partner and I had engaged a high-level gang member of one of the "Disciple" gang factions. As we worked the case toward the execution of a search warrant, one of the older officers in the unit looked me in the eye and said, "Be careful. These people are different; they will kill you without blinking an eye." This stunned me. It was not just the words that impacted me. It was the way he said it. With a level of conviction that was unusual. He was generally a good-natured guy, often joking and laughing. Here his admonition seemed out of character. Yet, he drove home the point. I got it.

Yet, this was not "news" that I did not previously understand. I was street smart from a teenager and had been in the gang unit for some years—and dealt with many "bad guys." Yet, what he conveyed was a distinction that I didn't yet fully understand. That is, some people can be considered "evil." Not just lawbreakers, not just bad, but *evil.* This is the connection to those who seek to destroy the system. To those who are willing to kill and destroy. It is these people who can be considered "wolves." They are predators. They must be confronted. They will not back down without force—and this must be greater than the force that they are prepared to assert. This question naturally results: *Who will be those who confront them?* It will not be sheep.

Yet here we are in a society that has discredited and demonized sheepdogs. So much so that many cannot discern the difference between them and wolves. The good news is the wolves will distinguish themselves by their sheer hatred and brutality. Sooner than later, people will discern—and be repulsed by—the violence and chaos emanating from them. This is happening to some extent already, with those who *discovered* that defunding the police was not a good idea. The bad news is people will die until the wolves are confronted or deterred. Indeed, some of the sheepdogs who confront the wolves will also die.

In the meantime, what will the sheep do? Will they stand up and support the "thin blue line"? Will we stand up for truth and love? Will we have the courage and conviction to stand up for what this country once represented? Or will they "buy" the mindless, hateful mantras? Consider again Lennon's admonition regarding hate. Put another way, we ought to shun those that hate, and seek to support those who confront them. Even when doing so can sometimes get messy!

Lt. Col. Grossman cites William J. Bennett spoke at a lecture to the United States Naval Academy in 1997. His words are relevant yet unsettling. Here is what Bennett said,[6]

> "Honor never grows old, and honor rejoices the heart of age. It does so because honor is, finally, about defending those noble and worthy things that deserve defending, even if it comes at a high cost. In our time, that may mean social disapproval, public scorn, hardship, persecution, or as always, even death itself.
>
> The question remains: What is worth defending? What is worth dying for? What is worth living for?"

As we approach the end of this book, let this quote stand for the three most important aspects of life: God, Country & Family. It is with respect to these aspects of life that we will be judged, and we ought to focus our energies accordingly. We will articulate these one by one and though this discussion is not definitive, let it be a means to think deeper about these profound matters.

GOD

The belief in a great being—a creator, a savior—is as old as humankind. The belief in God was common to the founding fathers. It inspired their declaration that our rights were bestowed by God. 190 years later, in 1966, *Time Magazine* asked the provocative question: Is God dead?

As this society gradually loses its belief in a biblical or Judeo- Christian God, people gravitate to other gods. Let's be clear: Everyone has a god. Whether people see this or not is irrelevant. The definition of "god" is subjective. It could be some spiritual notion. It could be nature, Mother Earth, gold, money, sex, power, and the deities of all major and minor religions. In short, our DNA is programmed to "worship" something larger than ourselves. Yet, by losing belief in the biblical God, our culture and country lose their roots and its most distinctive galvanizing influence. Without the God of the bible, we are rudderless. As we lose understanding of God, we also lose our sense of a spiritual dimension. To quote Sohrab Ahmari, "faith in God assures us that there is ultimate meaning in creation, even if we can't always discern it."[7]

Contrast God with the notion of evil. Many years ago, while researching a book on the subject, Lance Morrow, who is a thoughtful observer of Americana, asked a variety of people whether they had ever known someone they considered evil. The response *overwhelmingly* was: "No—no one I would call truly evil. There was Hitler, of course. But I didn't know him."

Morrow noted that back then word *evil* still carried the weight of its old significance. Describing evil as inspiring "respect and humility, fear and awe. There is, after all, no appeal from evil. It is uncompromising, unforgivable." Over the years, people "settled into a routine of mass shootings: evil, of course, but soon enough demystified as a string of psychotic episodes." As a result, evil, "once an august item in the range of human possibilities, has been reduced to a cliché of political abuse."[8]

Recently revisiting this "evil question," Morrow asked progressives whether they ever knew anyone who was evil. Donald Trump was the most common answer. Other common answers were such "lesser devils" as Derek Chauvin, Dylann Roof (Charleston church shooter), Josh Hawley (US senator), Tucker Carlson (Fox News commentator). Morrow's conclusion, "there is no distinction in their minds between the mass murderer in the church in Charleston and someone with whose opinions they disagree." This thinking was not just displayed by people on the street. He cites Tony Norman, a *Pittsburgh Post-Gazette* columnist who referred to Trump as "the twice-impeached abomination of desolation," "Satan," and "the Antichrist," along with calling Trump's political base as a "death cult," and subscribers to his "End Times fever dream." These words are meaningless. Confusing evil with political personas and constituencies is frightening.

Morrow's conclusion is enlightening—and chilling. He notes that the "reckless use of *absolute language* freighted with old religious toxins causes political disagreements between fellow citizens to become invested with ultimate meanings (emphasis added)." Thinking about who or what to classify as evil and losing our "appetite for objective proof" (such as masses of people killed or some other quantitative assessment), has grave consequences. "If our *feelings are enough* to determine who or what is evil, then *evil by declaration* is the only thing that matters. If you feel that something or someone is evil, *then it is so"* (emphasis added). In short, our feelings "acquire the status of reality." This also goes to relative truth—also known as "my truth." Morrow warns that the Salem witch trials proceeded with the same premise.[9]

This conclusion was echoed by Hoover Institution fellow Niall Ferguson, a Scottish author and historian, who asserted that political figures and ideologies are increasingly viewed from a religious context. Ferguson sees this as constituting a "dire warning for all." He elaborated, "we are dealing not just with the decay of traditional religion but, far worse, the rise of new fake religions—*political* religions." As an aside, think about *Black Theology and Black Power* and *The White Man's Bible.* Both are racial religions—with a political spin. Ferguson cites evidence from the not-so-distant past: "when people take their religious feelings and they apply them to political ideologies, terrible things can happen." What made communism so deadly was the fact that "it's ultimately a religion: Karl Marx is ultimately a prophet and Marxism is a kind of religion."[10]

Though Adolf Hitler is now commonly viewed as "evil," in Nazi Germany he was viewed in a religious light. "The most ardent Nazis thought of Hitler and explicitly called him a *redeemer* of the German nation (emphasis added). His message: *Be very careful of political religions.* "Politics is not something that you should approach with a religious impulse."

Take this a step further with parallels from religion to science. Our political preoccupation with "science" can drive thinking to deity levels. "There is no such thing as 'the science.' Of course, there are scientists. And they'll tell you there are sciences, plural, and it's a constantly shifting dynamic system in which ideas are tested and frequently found to be false." Ferguson noted the view of "science" as some sort of "magical thinking" where there is an established "stated view [and] consensus." Instead, science is *ever-changing,* ever subject to new and better evidence. Yet, Ferguson said those who don't subscribe to science (and its consensus), are labeled heretics. "Well, that's "magical thinking," he said.[11]

Consider also that Marx despised religion, and instead sought to create a political economy with parallels to Christianity—particularly apocalyptic doctrine. Marx believed that a revolution would wrest control from the rich (capitalists) in the name of the workers (proletariats) to establish an all-powerful government that would redistribute resources. This would be done in a bloody revolution between Good (workers) and Evil (capitalists). In essence, Marx "prophesized" that an earthly paradise with justice for workers would prevail. Just as Christians hope for the second coming of Christ, which would come when the earth was about to destroy itself—and result in the kingdom of God—Marx hoped that a bloody revolution would result in an earthly paradise.[12]

Even more directly, modern Western thinking has been shaped by Enlightenment thinking that grew out of—and was opposed to—what then was faith in religious dogma rather than man. Enlightenment flipped this thinking to faith in man—particularly faith in science and technology. We are seeing another change in how we think about God—or more accurately what we worship.

Politicians used the pandemic to close thousands of churches, and some were jailed for practicing their faith. Tucker Carlson echoes my earlier, point: "All of us are born with the need to worship. The question is what?" Carlson's conclusion: "America has not lost its religion; it just replaced its religion." Christianity is dying, and in its place comes a "new creed, and like all religions, it has its own sacraments, its own sacred texts. It's the cult of coronavirus."

Calling the New York governor, Kathy Hochul, one of the "high priestesses of this new faith," with a *vaccination necklace* worn around her neck. "That necklace signified to the faithful gathered that Hochul is ascended to the select priesthood of those who have taken full intravenous communion."[13] The sterling silver necklace that the governor often wore is available for purchase. It spells out in cursive *vaccinated.* Also, available are Tony Fauci pins,

Tony Fauci mugs, and Tony Fauci Christmas ornaments. Carlson calls these *ornaments* of the new Covid cult.

Has science and politics crossed the line toward religion? Happening at a time when Victor Davis Hanson notes that "Americans of all classes and races are starting to fear a *self-created apocalypse* that threatens their families' safety and the American way of life," he describes this self-created apocalypse in much the same manner as we chronicled in this book.[14]

What does this all mean? Traditional religion is losing influence and converts. Politics and science are growing in influence, using the rhetoric and symbols of religion. As these occur, the society around us is experiencing increasing crime and chaos, which can be described through the religious term of *apocalypse*. So, as society redefines its notion of religion, those who understand biblical precepts, such as the apocalypse, cry out in despair and fear.

To close this section, dig deep to wrestle with your own proclivities and your sense of the challenges we face ahead. It is my sense that our "Westernized" and "civilized" minds are deeply ambivalent about the notion of God and of evil. As a believer in God, I trust in His word and His protection. God ought to be our primary emphasis—our primary purpose. Believers in God will see the chaos (and even an apocalypse) from a biblical perspective.

Yet, to many, the notion of a creator God is simplistic. It is not my desire to convince any reader of any religious conclusion. What is obvious, though, is that many are replacing God with other "deities." Indeed, many have also declared *evil* undefined concepts or feelings. Whether Hitler or Trump is "evil" has now simply become a matter of perspective. God and evil, like many of the mindless mantras analyzed in this book, have no connection to traditional thinking.

Ironically, this "sophisticated" thinking is naïve. Even if you dismiss the underlying truth of God and of evil, one is hard-pressed to deny that political opponents will use the declaration of evil to attack their enemies. Just as God was used to attack opponents for eons, some will do the same in this era. Yet, using God to physically attack is contrary to what Christ taught. But those who follow a different god are not subject to such constraints. Regardless of how evil is *defined,* this is clear: *anyone or anything deemed "evil" deserves to be attacked and/or destroyed.*

I trust the reader can see the danger of using deities, either good or evil, to further personal, ideological, political, or even scientific ends. This has application in foreign policy. Years ago, the Left complained that US foreign policy caused many of our enemies to hate us. Yet, if one actually paid attention to what our enemies said, they strongly criticized many aspects of American society—including our perceived moral and spiritual decadence. Simply stated, many international extremists see us as "evil." Radical Islamists see the US as the "Great Satan" and Israel as the "Little Satan." Communist countries have made similar allegations but without this direct religious component. If the US somehow "cured" its past faults, would our enemies ignore the "sins" of our culture and our lifestyle?

Of course, this also relates to the allegations made in domestic politics. Seeing this country as "systemically racist" allows no redemption or forgiveness for our "sins." Many of our most "enlightened" leaders have declared the society and system racist. Being deemed a "racist," of course, can be equated with evil. Is there a peaceful resolution to these declarations?

I think the answer is clear. In a worldview that seeks to separate "believers" from infidels, radical Islamists have a strong incentive to fight to the death. In a worldview that declares this society systemically racist, the incentive to destroy the system is obvious. The impact of this reality is clear—at least to those who understand the stakes. The implication of such was pointedly made by Laura Ingraham, who stated:[15]

> "It is not enough for us to defend American soil or to maintain a thriving economy. It will all be in vain if we fail to nurture and refresh America's soul. And that is only possible through individual belief demonstrated through action . . .
>
> If we lose faith in God, it will be very difficult to keep faith with our duty to defend America—from without or within...If we find unity in faith, there is no challenge—internal or external—that can overwhelm us."

Another way to think of this is what Christ said, "For whoever wants to save his life will lose it, but whoever loses his life for me will find it."[16]

To illustrate just one example of people doing amazing things to make a difference, Pastor Corey Brooks commenced a 100-day vigil on a rooftop on a cold November night in 2021 to take a stand against violence and poverty on the south side of Chicago. He "camped" on the roof during a Chicago winter to make a point—and to raise money to build a leadership and economic opportunity center for his community. His solitary and his faithful act forced many to look within themselves, whether consciously or unconsciously. Noting the divisions in this country, Brooks said: "we're Black and White and Christians and non-Christians and Republicans and Democrats, but there comes a time when there have to be some causes where we have to be unified, and that's the reason why I think violence is something that we could all come to the rescue for."[17] As this book nears publication, Brooks is still on the roof, long after the 100 day goal failed to bring in the necessary funds to build the community center. Ironically, BLM failed to give him any money—and even failed to respond to his many requests.[18]

In yet another irony, Pastor Brooks is encamped on 66th and Martin Luther King Drive. His message is consistent with Dr. King, which can be summarized as "the body of Christ overrides tribalism." We have seen that tribalism, whether racial, religious, or political, ultimately dehumanizes people. These are both wrong and divisive. Getting past tribalism toward God was echoed by Ahmari, who said that "without an absolute standard that reflects the will of the supreme being, men and women could countenance and rationalize any evil in their dealings with one another, everything could be relativized."[19] We have seen the dramatic implications of what may lie ahead, and this should give us pause.

Yet, individuals stepping forward together *into the unknown* based on their faith in God can make a difference! Creating bridges—and good faith—is needed to solve the most enduring problems can be accomplished. Belief in God can be *the* bridge over tribal tendencies in contemporary America. People of God, of *good faith*, and of *goodwill* could prevail in this divisive climate. Even more directly and poignantly, can this help to create individual or collective redemption—or even a religious revival?

Ultimately, the answer to the questions posed above is in each of our hearts and minds. This turns on how much faith we have in God, and how much conviction we *really* have. These questions deserve deep contemplation. Citing a Christian pastor, Rod Dreher offers that there are two kinds of Christians, "those who sincerely believe in God and those who, just as sincerely, believe that they believe. You can tell them apart by their actions in decisive moments."[20]

Let's end this section by reminding ourselves of what a great leader sought in times of great struggle. Consider that on March 30, 1863, President Lincoln signed a Proclamation Appointing a National Fast Day. In this powerful text, Lincoln sought we *recognize our God* and *pray for His help* to resolve a bloody and divisive war that was pulling the country apart. I recommend reading this entire proclamation (see link in citation), but in pertinent part:[21]

> "And whereas it is the duty of nations as well as of men, to own their dependence upon the overruling power of God, to confess their sins and transgressions, in humble sorrow, yet with assured hope that genuine repentance will lead to mercy and pardon; and to recognize the sublime truth, announced in the Holy Scriptures and proven by all history, that those nations only are blessed whose God is the Lord.
>
> And, insomuch as we know that, by His divine law, nations like individuals are subjected to punishments and chastisements in this world, may we not justly fear that the awful calamity of civil war, which now desolates the land, may be but a punishment, inflicted upon us, for our presumptuous sins, to the needful end of our national reformation as a whole People?
>
> We have been the recipients of the choicest bounties of Heaven. We have been preserved, these many years, in peace and prosperity. We have grown in numbers, wealth and power, as no other nation has ever grown. *But we have forgotten God.*

> We have forgotten the gracious hand which preserved us in peace, and multiplied and enriched and strengthened us; and we have vainly imagined, in the deceitfulness of our hearts, that all these blessings were produced by some superior wisdom and virtue of our own. Intoxicated with unbroken success, we have become too self-sufficient to feel the necessity of redeeming and preserving grace, *too proud to pray to the God that made us!* . . . (emphasis added)

COUNTRY

The founding of this country was an extraordinary development in human history. James Freeman tells the story of Independence Hall, where America's founding documents were created, both the US Constitution and the Declaration of Independence. In 1926, President Calvin Coolidge came to Philadelphia to celebrate the 150th anniversary of the Declaration of Independence, saying:[22]

> "If no one is to be accounted as born into a superior station, if there is to be no ruling class, and if all possess rights which can neither be bartered away nor taken from them by any earthly power, it follows as a matter of course that the practical authority of the Government has to rest on the consent of the governed."

Freeman called the Declaration of Independence the most important civil document in the world, containing immortal truths. Harvard history professor David Armitage wrote that "the Declaration's influence wasn't limited to the American colonies of the late 18th century. No American document has had a greater impact on the wider world." Professor Armitage added:[23]

> "As the first successful declaration of independence in history, it helped to inspire countless movements for independence, self-determination and revolution after 1776 and to this very day. As the 19th-century Hungarian nationalist, Lajos Kossuth, put it, the US Declaration of Independence was nothing less than 'the noblest, happiest page in mankind's history.' "

If the implications of a *pending revolution in contemporary America* are seen, the words of Abraham Lincoln should resonate in our hearts and minds. In February of 1861, just prior to the civil war, Lincoln visited Independence Hall on his way to begin his presidency and said—please read these inspiring words, as they reflect much about the current state of America:[24]

> "I am filled with deep emotion at finding myself standing here, in this place, where were collected together the wisdom, the patriotism, the devotion to principle, from which sprang the institutions under which we live. You have kindly suggested to me that in my hands is the task of restoring peace to the present distracted condition of the country . . . from the sentiments which originated and were given to the world from this hall.
>
> I have never had a feeling politically that did not spring from the sentiments embodied in the Declaration of Independence. I have often pondered over the dangers which were incurred by the men who assembled here, and framed and adopted that Declaration of Independence. I have pondered over the toils that were endured by the officers and soldiers of the army who achieved that Independence. I have often inquired of myself what great principle or idea it was that kept this Confederacy so long together. It was not the mere matter of the separation of the Colonies from the motherland; but that sentiment in the Declaration of Independence which gave liberty, not alone to the people of this country, but, I hope, to the world, for all future time.
>
> It was that which gave promise that in due time the weight would be lifted from the shoulders of all men. This is the sentiment embodied in that Declaration of Independence. Now, my friends, can this country be saved upon that basis? If it can, I will consider myself one of the happiest men in the world if I can help to save it. If it can't be saved upon that principle, it will be truly awful.
>
> But, if this country cannot be saved without giving up that principle—I was about to say I would rather be assassinated on

> this spot than to surrender it. Now, in my view of the present aspect of affairs, there is no need of bloodshed and war. There is no necessity for it. I am not in favor of such a course, and I may say in advance, there will be no blood shed unless it be forced upon the Government. The Government will not use force unless force is used against it.
>
> My friends, this is a wholly unprepared speech . . . but I have said nothing but what I am willing to live by, and, in the pleasure of Almighty God, die by."

Compare Lincoln's speech to that of our current president, Joe Biden's inaugural speech in 2021. Our new president left little doubt about his focus. His presidency, he pledged *repeatedly*, would be devoted to *healing* a fractured nation. Speaking just two weeks after the Jan. 6 Capitol riot, President Biden used variations of the words "unity" and "together" more than a dozen times, as when he declared: "Today, on this January day, my whole soul is in this: Bringing America together. Uniting our people. And uniting our nation." After citing earlier national crises, from the Civil War to 9/11, Biden described leading the nation to a better place. This is what he said:[25]

> "History, faith, and reason show the way of unity," he said. "We can see each other not as adversaries but as neighbors. We can treat each other with dignity and respect. We can join forces, stop the shouting, and lower the temperature. For without unity, there is no peace, only bitterness and fury."

Michael Goodwin noted these as "excellent ideas. Too bad he hasn't practiced what he preached. Or even tried." Of course, words need action. Words also must be equated with reality—and with unifying policies. Here is how Goodwin viewed his words as compared to his actions:[26]

> "Biden has pursued radical policies and a race-driven agenda that are by definition divisive, leading to doubts about whether there was an ounce of sincerity in his January 20th address . . .

> Far from it. In a party bursting with flamethrowers, the president stands out for the harshness of his rhetoric. He brazenly and repeatedly lies about the efforts in numerous states to reform voting laws. His claim that the demand for voter ID in Georgia and other states is the new Jim Crow is preposterous and proves he prefers fearmongering to facts.
>
> He did it again in his July 13 speech in Philadelphia, where he foolishly insisted the new voting laws are "the most significant test of our democracy since the Civil War."
>
> At this point, it is impossible to see such language as anything other than an intentional attempt to further divide the nation. It exposes the president as a hypocrite and reveals the desperation of his party.
>
> All these events and others make it feel as if the inaugural address was given by another president in another era."

From my perspective, President Biden's words have obviously not reconciled with his actions and policies. Ironically, in his inaugural speech, he *appeared to understand* what was at stake. "We must end this uncivil war that pits red against blue, rural versus urban, conservative versus liberal. We can do this if we open our souls instead of hardening our hearts, if we show a little tolerance and humility." Goodwin correctly asks this question: Where is *that* guy?[27]

Much more could be said—and many other examples provided as to how the Biden Administration is either intellectually sympatico with the progressive wing of the Democratic party or has succumbed to its dominance. Progressives yield significant power. As of January 2022, they have ninety-six members in the progressive caucus.[28]

Citing Mark Levin, David Limbaugh describes the current political climate as a "counterrevolution to the American revolution." What he calls an *insurrection* is "no longer a fringe movement but is in the mainstream of our culture and institutions." Echoing many of the points made in this book, consider this quote:[29]

> "What makes the counterrevolutionaries particularly dangerous is their sophisticated techniques of distorting language, disguising their true intent with deceitful euphemisms to disarm patriots and facilitate their scheme to fundamentally transform this nation into something unrecognizable to its founders and wholly unacceptable to all who cherish and revere the glorious American experiment in self-governance.

"Levin soberly observes that to defeat the threat we face, 'a unified, patriotic front of previously docile . . . factions and forces' that believes America is worthy of defending must emerge. People of good will must wake up to the gravity of the threats we face and recognize 'the urgency of the moment' and rise up to take back this nation."[30]

Ways to bridge the ideological divide are available if we embrace a nonviolent approach like what Dr. King advocated in the 1960s. What better person to emulate than Robert Woodson? As mentioned previously, Mr. Woodson started his quest for civil rights with Dr. King. His roots were long and hard. His father was veteran of World War I's legendary Harlem Hellfighters, but he died when Robert was just a kid.

His work in the Woodson Center demonstrates resolve and toughness to pursue true virtues and principles. The center's approach is to develop people whom others "turn to in times of crisis" and "try to resource them so that they can scale up," thereby strengthening "informal networks" responding to problems of crime, addiction, and family breakdown.[31]

Even more significantly, the Woodson Center's latest project, *1776 Unites*, is an answer to the "1619 Project," Critical Race Theory, and other progressive indoctrination attempts. Through this project, the center seeks and collects essays that celebrate "the resilience and perseverance of blacks in the past under some of the worst conditions." Mr. Woodson says that "America's history of racial oppression should be studied not just in a spirit of moral accusation, but to understand black Americans' resistance to it, their resilience."

This combination of resistance and resilience is crucial, particularly *without* the racist allegations commonly thrust into people's faces. Allegations in contemporary America are landing on people who had little or nothing to do with historical discrimination. Blaming people today for slavery that ended over 150 years ago is not fruitful or even accurate. Accusing people today of discrimination during reconstruction or during the Jim Crow era has the same negative impact. Yet, showing blacks what their forefathers encountered and overcame conveys a positive message: *If they overcame these struggles, then I can do so too!* Thus, Woodson "flips the script." He emphasizes positive examples from history, instead of accusing people today, who had no part in the decisions or the behaviors of our country's past.

Another goal is to influence those who are instrumental in today's messaging. For example, addressing the National School Boards Association, the center said it was standing "in unqualified opposition to any curricula that depict America as irredeemably racist; teach that the legacies of slavery, racial segregation, and other appalling crimes are insurmountable; or fail to provide examples from history of black achievement against the odds."[32]

Mr. Woodson explains this thinking: "those who focus on systemic racism know their history, but they aren't accurately judging the present. 'Name one job in America that a black person cannot occupy,' he says. 'Name one place in America where a black cannot purchase a home.'" These questions go to the heart of how America has progressed from its "original sin," and how we *could* heal going forward.

As a Christian, Mr. Woodson, is hopeful of redemption, even though "continued emphasis on race is taking us toward chaos." "America is thirsty to reward grace and virtue," Mr. Woodson says. "I believe that there's going to be a revival coming soon, and that revival is going to come from low-income black neighborhoods, because those neighborhoods are untouched by wokeness." No one there, he says pointedly, claims that "fathers are not relevant."

As demonstrated earlier, Mr. Woodson doesn't see the problems of black America through a racial prism. The institutions and traits that make healthy communities are the same for all human beings. "Tell me how ending institutional racism is going to prevent a kid in Silicon Valley from taking his life, or a kid in Appalachia taking drugs, or a kid from shooting somebody in the head," he says. Mr. Woodson wants to "deracialize race"—to make it an incidental category in social-improvement projects rather than the salient one. His hope for the future is to "*get race off the table, so we can deal with the moral and spiritual free fall that is consuming all races of people* (emphasis added)." He says, "the emphasis on race now is acting as a primary barrier for us to address the deeper malaise facing this country."[33]

There are so many positive things one can say about Mr. Woodson's work and beliefs. Yet, let his words speak to you. This is the guidepost to America's solutions—including its revival. If a revival comes, it will be from those who think and work like Mr. Woodson.

There are other positive signs amongst the discord and disorder in this country. For example, in the summer of 2021, after the tragic killing of Chicago Police Officer Ella French, Mayor Lori Lightfoot said some things that both surprised me and gave me hope. The surprise comes because the mayor had been previously very critical of the Chicago Police Department—which was unfair and even smacked of racism.

Yet, the hopeful part is what the mayor said after the officer's tragic death. She stated in pertinent part, "there are some who say that we do not do enough for the police and that we are handcuffing them for doing their jobs. There are others who say we do too much for the police and that we never hold them accountable for what they do particularly in Black and Brown neighborhoods. But to all of this, I say, 'stop, just stop.' This constant strife is not what we need in this moment." It gets better. She then said, "of course we need to continue the journey to achieve constitutional and accountable policing," Lightfoot continued with words that people need to hear—and take to heart:[34]

> "That cannot be a debate at this point. But let me also reiterate what I've said before and what I know to be true. The *police are not our enemies. They're human, just as we are. Flawed, just as we are. But also risking their lives every day for our safety and security"* (emphasis added).

Chicago Police Superintendent David Brown added these helpful words: "our officers need this city to pray for their strength, to pray for peace that they are comforted that their families are comforted. I'm asking Chicago to wrap our arms around our police officers today."[35]

While such words come only *after* a tragedy; they give hope. If this helps focus on the safety of police, then better late than never. Police need the support of good people—and from policymakers. Though, with great reservations, it is refreshing to see that *some* positive words are conveyed about the police. Yet, these are just words. As with President Biden's words revolving around unity and tolerance, actions and policies are even more important.

While America faces bitter and difficult domestic conflicts, the world is watching. A reminder of what awaits us in the larger geopolitical arena—comes from former National Security Advisor H.R. McMaster. Following the disastrous exit from Afghanistan, McMaster poignantly stated that,[36]

> "the long war against jihadist terrorist organizations isn't over; it is entering a new, more dangerous phase. America's rivals—including China, Russia, North Korea and Iran—are emboldened. They are watching a Defense Department that seems to focus more on climate change than being prepared to fight, one that promotes postmodernist theories that undermine the warrior ethos and valorize victimhood. Our leaders have an obligation to protect the warrior ethos and build America's military capabilities, rather than promote destructive philosophies and attempt to solve problems better handled by other departments.

The disastrous exit from Afghanistan coincides with the equally disastrous "entry" from our southern border. These twin slow-moving disasters portend significant problems on the horizon. One being geopolitical, the other domestic.

Throughout 2021 and into 2022, the southern border was a sieve. An estimated 1.5 to 2 million people flowed through the border in the calendar year. One article puts the estimate at 1.8 million, which would set a dubious record. The tragedy is far and wide—a national security and humanitarian nightmare. As of September 2021, eighteen bodies were discovered in Arizona's Yuma Sector's desert.[37] This is just one district along a 2000-mile border.

"The cartel owns every bit of property along the international boundary," says the sheriff in the Yuma sector. "They coordinate everything, even controlling where people from certain countries cross." Likened by some as an "invasion," border-crossers come from around the world, ninety-three countries so far this year, and "arrests so far this year include seventeen people from special interest countries with ties to terrorism, a particular issue now with the world's bad actors energized by the Afghanistan bugout." [38]

Then there are the "got-a-ways" . . . who are these people? "No one knows their names, home countries, what they're carrying, or whether they wish Americans well or ill. They are given no background check and certainly no Covid test. But they are with us now. Agents are alternately demoralized and defiant. Many are angry at being treated like babysitters with badges. Some borderland residents feel betrayed by an administration that seems to care more for those crossing the border illegally than the safety of US citizens." As one southern Arizona rancher said, "I feel hopeless. Great nations don't behave this way."[39]

Except one great country does. Though something has to give. We either must change our ways. Or we will regret it . . .

So, what can go wrong? Allowing the Taliban to act as gatekeepers in Afghanistan where we rushed about 120,000 people out of the country. Considering the frenzied pace and chaotic manner this was done, one does not need to be an expert on terrorism to conclude that some percentage of the people who were airlifted did not have good intentions. The same goes for the southern border. With the cartels acting as gatekeepers, the likelihood that "bad actors" have crossed the border is near certainty.

While this country has survived much adversity over its history, current circumstances give great pause—and great concern. As we have connected dots around the ideologies targeting the capitalistic system, one can connect similar threats in the geopolitical arena. Unfortunately, we have "invited" threats upon us. Some are operating internationally; others are certain to have crossed the borders. Yet, few talk about these. Though beyond the scope of this book, I would be remiss if these threats were not at least mentioned.

With all of this percolating, consider that every year around Thanksgiving, the *Wall Street Journal* publishes a reminder of what this country has done and overcome. The piece cited still uses these words, "air of unease that hangs everywhere." It takes readers through the myriad of wars and troubles that have been overcome yet serves as a reminder of the abundant blessings still enjoyed. For this reason, the entire piece is worth reading to help put our times in perspective, offering pertinent sentiments of both visitors and citizens who consider all that we have overcome yet still face:[40]

> ". . . they see young arrayed against old, black against white, neighbor against neighbor, so that they stand in peril of social discord. Or not despair when they see that the cities and countryside are in need of repair, yet find themselves threatened by scarcities of the resources that sustain their way of life. Or when, in the face of these challenges, they turn for leadership to men in high places—only to find those men as frail as any others.
>
> How can they pass on to their children a nation as strong and free as the one they inherited from their forefathers? How is their country to endure these cruel storms that beset it from without and from within? . . .
>
> We can remind ourselves that for all our social discord we yet remain the longest enduring society of free men governing themselves without benefit of kings or dictators. Being so, we are the marvel and the mystery of the world, for that enduring liberty is no less a blessing than the abundance of the earth . . .

FAMILY

As we close this book, let's do so with an appeal to family. Realizing that some are not inspired by an appeal to God. Others may not be motivated by an appeal to country. Yet, those who find nothing of value in these may still see the need to sacrifice for their family. In a country as racially, ethnically, socially, and religiously diverse as America, there may be yet one common thread that can bring us together. That is family.

Much good can be said about families. Fond and loving memories abound.

Reaching for something to believe in may be easily found in the family unit. It is the building block of society. Every healthy society is made up of healthy and viable families. Yet, the American family is under great stress. Even prior to the pandemic, families were fragile.

Healing this society must include the family unit. While it is beyond our scope to delve into this, what is clear is that dysfunctional and fractured families have played an outsized role in the deterioration of this society. It is another equation. Families and societies are tied together. Think of the family as the part of the foundation, with the superstructure being society. Crumbling families will collapse the structure.

While we will conclude this book with some words of encouragement—and hopefully inspiration—one cannot ignore the reality of our crucial superstructures. For decades, the family structure has been deteriorating—even in crisis. Recall that data on out-of-wedlock children in black families reveal that almost 75 percent of children are born to a single-parent family. The impact of the "great society" upon the black family has been devastating. Remember that in 1963, 72 percent of non-white families were married and together. By 2017, this data was essentially reversed, with only 27 percent of black households being married.[41]

Citing these statistics, Kendall Qualls provocatively writing for *Fox News* stated that if, "the American Black family was a spotted owl or a gray wolf, it would be on the endangered species list." Comparing the focus on maintaining animal species while people are ignored is a compelling way to bring attention to the dire circumstances we face. Qualls continues by condemning those who *blame racial disparities on white privilege and systemic racism*, yet they fail to focus on the cultural roots of faith, family, and education that sustained the Black family. "We know the damaging effects fatherless homes [have on] children after seeing the steep decline of two-parents in the Black community for five decades: 85 percent of children with behavioral disorders; 90 percent of homeless and runaways; young boys and girls suffer higher rates of physical and sexual abuse, and the list continues."[42]

As a man writing from experience, he has devoted his adult life to mentoring, coaching, and encouraging young people that their past doesn't have to define their future. "There are some who do make it out and achieve success in life. However, the numbers reveal that they are the exception, not the rule." His criticism of the great society reflects my earlier assertions. "What happened to the American Black family is not the dream King had in mind and is nothing short of a cultural genocide. It has been a nightmare for children born during this period. The Black community has been a political pawn for fifty years, and I plan to lead a crusade to change that forever."[43]

Qualls saved his strongest criticism for the Congressional Black Caucus (CBC), which in 2021 celebrated fifty years as a political caucus. On its website, while first acknowledging "we [blacks] have come a long way," it then condemned the usual litany of social wrongs from: "racist and discriminatory policies and institutions that result in disparities across almost every facet of life, from access to quality affordable health care and education to police brutality and voter suppression." Qualls counters that the "disparities the CBC references are not a result of racism." Instead, Qualls contends that "90 percent of the problems in the Black community can be attributed to the fatherless home crisis." Continuing his critique, he stated that, "nowhere does the CBC reference the decline of two-parent families and its impact on women, children, health, or education. The reason they hide this is sorrowful and treasonous to their communities and the country."[44]

Those who call this society systemically racist would be much more credible if it addressed the underlying impact of just this one factor. Yet, the silence is deafening. Indeed, BLM advocated on its website to essentially eliminate the family—or at least diminish the family in favor of the "care" provided by the state, cradle-to-grave support being the goal of the socialist state. But this is another empty promise. Not only does the state not do a good job of raising its children but believing that we have the money to do so is an illusion. As Margaret Thatcher famously said, "the problem with socialism is that you eventually run out of other people's money."[45]

So, we need healthy, viable families. Much work needs to be done. I am not optimistic. The forces aligned against the family are one problem. But so is the *protection* given to dysfunctional families. An example may be illustrative. A headline of a *Chicago Tribune* column by Dahleen Glanton in May

2021 proclaimed: "You can't be a gang-banger and a good parent, no matter how much you love your kids."

The story revolved around the killing of a seven-year-old child who was shot dead because the shooter missed his target—the child's father. While this was tragic enough, it gets worse. After the shooting, McDonald's CEO Chris Kempczinski text-messaged Mayor Lori Lightfoot about the "tragic shootings." In his text, the McDonald's CEO said, ". . . the parents failed those kids, which I know is something you can't say. Even harder to fix." When the text became public, calls for Mr. Kempczinski's resignation followed.

Jason Riley rejected the call for his resignation. Writing in the *Wall Street Journal*, Riley said:[46]

> "Mr. Kempczinski was stating a plain truth, making an observation surely shared by an overwhelming majority of rational adults. The problem, as he also noted in his text, is that stating plain truths has become verboten— especially in regard to the behavior of racial and ethnic minorities like the victims in Chicago. We are supposed to pretend that the high rates of violent crime and other social pathologies among low-income blacks and Hispanics can be blamed entirely on systemic racism and that the individuals themselves are blameless."

Riley concludes that "it's hard to see how we can address these and other social disparities if we can't have honest conversations about what's driving them. And the political Left's attempts to silence truth-tellers will only delay those conversations." With the family and society at stake, one would think that honest and prudent people could find reasonable means to address the dysfunction and violence that it brings. *Yet, we cannot even talk about it!*

Writing on the same matter, Matt Rosenberg, called the black crime data "inconvenient facts." He then made this assertion: "Black-on-Black violence cannot possibly be called out. Excuses must be made. It is a way of saying, as Progressives now implicitly so often do, that Blacks are not capable of adhering to broadly held community standards." He then quoted two black mothers who had these piercing words:[47]

- "If the parents are not responsible, then who is? Society is responsible for these children's behavior? The greatest youth program is the family . . .Nobody wants the police defunded. Because our greatest enemy is ourselves . . .My Black sons have more chance to be killed by somebody that looks like them, than a cop."
- "Parents need to parent…Nothing in the entire world can replace parents teaching the basics of humanity and responsibility to their children."

So, what happens when progressives seek to parent and teach today's children? One example lies in a remarkable yet twisted program coming out of the City of Portland, which hosted a summer camp called *Budding Roses.* The camp was founded by an "Anarchist Federation" called Black Rose/Rosa Negra Anarchist Foundation. The group's website proclaims its efforts are meant to turn children into the next generation of protesters in Portland:[48]

- "We believe that empowering youth to become critically engaged with social justice issues lays the groundwork for transformational social change tomorrow and today."
- "We see returning campers taking on leadership roles at camp, getting involved in their communities, holding banners at marches, and initiating discussion about social issues with their parents."
- Campers have access to the "Budding Roses Protest and Chant Book, "which includes Antifa classics like 'no borders, no nation, stop deportations' and 'cops and borders, we don't need them, what we want is total freedom.' "

As twisted as training young children to chant such things is, it gets worse. Though the camp uses the typical soundbite mantras, the mission statement of Black Rose Anarchist Federation is more direct. It states the organization is of "revolutionaries who share common visions of a new world" where they hope "people collectively control their own workplaces" and "society is organized for peoples' aspirations, passions, and needs rather than profit." Of course, the desired "Marxist society can only be accomplished by overthrowing the state and capitalism." Specifically, the website lays it out plainly:[49]

> "We believe that this vision can only be brought about through the revolutionary power of the working class organized in the workplaces, community, schools, and streets to overthrow the state and capitalism and build a new world from the bottom up."

Given their stated ideology, one would not be surprised to know that it promotes Antifa in their blogs, including the 2017 book by Mark Bray, *Antifa: The Anti-Fascist Handbook*. Even more direct, Mark Bray is a member of Black Rose Anarchist Federation.[50]

The federation also published a "handy guide," which reads in pertinent part, "abolishing police means looking at how we can care for each other instead of punishing people and communities for being poor. We would all be a lot safer if everyone had access to the things they needed. That could mean a lot of different things!" The instructional guide contains a download for these young campers to learn about "the effects of tear gas, and also provides illustrated pictures on how to contain tear gas that police use when people are rioting."

And of course, the guide wouldn't be complete without its section "Reflections of Privilege and White Supremacy." This provides an activity portion specifically "for white youth" that tasks kids with asking themselves "What parts of white supremacy do you see in yourself or in your family."[51]

One cannot make this up. Yet, here it is in plain sight in contemporary America. Who cares that this is happening? Surely, the media—and the leaders of the City of Portland ought to care. Certainly, they know. One can only assume it's okay with them. Is it okay with you?

Finally, one last bit of "good news." This comes from a hidden video released by James O'Keefe's *Project Veritas* (note *Veritas* is Latin for "Truth"). The twelve-minute video purports to show a high-school teacher (whose name I will not mention, but he is named in the article) talking about his involvement with the Antifa Sacramento chapter and how he gives students extra credit for attending protests. "I have 180 days to turn them into revolutionaries . . . scare the f--k out of them," the man said in the video. Photos taken by undercover journalists purported to show an "Antifascist Action" flag and a

Mao Zedong poster prominently displayed in the classroom.[52]

The teacher also said he tracks his students' political leanings throughout the course of the year and that "every year, they get further and further left. I've met so many people in my life who, when they met me, thought I was off the wall, and now they're all Marxists," he said in the video.

Let's end this section with a couple of quotes from the "teacher," who was quoted saying:[53]

> ". . . Like, why aren't people just taking up arms? Like why can't we, you know, take up arms against the state? We have historical examples of that happening, and them getting crushed and being martyrs for a cause and it's like, OK, well, it's slow going because it takes massive amounts of organization."
>
> "We need to create parallel structures of power because we cannot rely on the state. So we need to distribute food, necessities, we need to create those mutual aid programs that we can look back at groups like the [Black] Panthers and learn from their successes as well as their mistakes, as well as consistently focusing on education and a change of cultural propaganda. We have to hit both fronts. We have to convince people that this is what we actually need."

AS WE GO FORWARD . . .

We will end this book with three quotes from three very different people. Each discusses war and revolution. The first is from Sun Tzu, who authored one of history's most famous books on military tactics. The second is from Vicente Fox, the former president of Mexico, who wrote a powerful book entitled *The Revolution of Hope.* The third is from William A. Galston, who wrote a compelling piece about revolution from the perspective of the ancient Israelites. Each of these address the theme of this book but does so from different directions or perspectives.

The first quote is attributed to Sun Tzu. His work *The Art of War* has been a manual for commanders and military strategists for hundreds of years. His approach to war is simple yet profound. These principles have sustained the test of time. They speak to the basic tenets of human existence and human nature. As you read these words, please juxtapose them with the quote from Vincente Fox. They go to the same place. Each relate to why we live—and what we live for. The message from Tzu is as follows:[54]

> "If you know the enemy and know yourself, you need not fear the results of a hundred battles. If you know yourself and not the enemy, for every victory gained, you will also suffer a defeat. If you know neither yourself or the enemy, you will succumb in every battle"

A couple of points from Tzu's quote. There are two things we need to know: *Ourselves* and the *enemy*. As to the enemy, Barbara Tuchman in her classic book *The March of Folly* said that the "most frequent and fatal of self-delusions" is the "underestimation of the opponent."[55] So, who is our opponent? Who is our enemy? Most "leaders" now would say "white supremacy" or "systemic racism." Are these *actually* our enemies? Is this an accurate assessment of our opponent? My conclusion: this is dishonest and divisive.

Instead, these constitute what Tuchman calls "folly." Tuchman views as "folly" when a "perverse persistence in a policy demonstrably unworkable or counter-productive."[56] As you know, the "defunding" mantra has been proven unworkable and counter-productive. Yet, even when funding decisions are reversed, the implications of "defunding" have not been solved. Many other "theories," such as CRT, 1619 project, systemic racism, and others live on as being the height of folly. Counter-productive is an understatement.

What should we think of these "theories"? Are they being forwarded to help or to hurt? Are they designed to improve society or destroy it? Murray weighs in with this poignant assertion:[57]

> "Few people think that a country cannot be improved on, but to present it as riddled with bigotry, hatred and oppression is at best, a partial and at worst a nakedly hostile prism through which to view society. It is an analysis expressed not in the manner of a critic hoping to improve, but as an enemy eager to destroy."

This brings us to the other thing we need to know—*ourselves*. Take this to mean both individually and collectively. *Collectively* relates to who we are as a country. In a population so divided, in a society so "race-conscious," in a political spectrum that is increasingly hardened, who we are collectively is hard to know.

Weakened geo-politically, struggling to find our "center," we say we are a "great nation," yet we do not act like one. So, who are we? Are we great? Do we want to be *great again*, or are we happy to be just another state in the world order? Even worse, after reading this book, is it not fair to conclude that some desire to destroy, or at least diminish, this nation?

These questions can be answered with question: Do we want to foster *globalism* or *nationalism*? If our goal is the former, policies like the Afghanistan exit, the open southern border, CRT, 1619 project, and systemic racism fit this goal. Further, we saw that every extremist ideology targets the capitalistic system—and by extension nationalistic thinking. These also support the globalist agenda.

Meanwhile, nationalism requires the emphasis on God, Country, and Family. You know my sentiments.

What about you? Who are you? Do you *really* know yourself? Do you know what you want collectively? How do you see your country? How do you see your individual destiny, whether as an American or as an individual living in this country? The collective answer to these questions may determine our destiny.

The next quote is from Vicente Fox, the former president of Mexico. In this book: *The Revolution of Hope,* he powerfully asserted that:[58]

> "Only when we are fully immersed in challenge can we forget our weakness and our fears and summon the courage, stamina, and strength to overcome all obstacles . . .
>
> In order to move mountains, first we must move souls. This is our challenge. This is how we become men and women for others. This is our revolution of hope."

Are we fully immersed in the challenges that lie ahead? If we are, we will have the courage, the stamina, and the strength to forge on—to overcome all obstacles. To do this, we must move souls. Our souls go to our destiny. Which goes to who we are at our core, and what we live for. These are very personal and subjective perspectives, which require decisions.

Finally, we have the words of William A. Galston, who wrote a long editorial entitled *Lessons for Politicians at Passover*, which addresses a long view of humanity. Galston introduces it with "there are lessons for today's political revolutionaries . . ." He then eloquently describes the illusion of revolution. Again, I recommend reading the piece in its entirety, but for now, in pertinent part:[59]

> ". . . Liberation is a precondition of freedom, but no guarantee of it. Revolutions can go awry, and usually do. Throwing off the shackles of tyranny often ends in new forms of bondage.
>
> The shared experience of oppression holds the oppressed together, but once the tyranny ends, so does the unity. Revolutionary leaders can claim only tenuous authority, at least at first, unless they are buttressed by character and accomplishment.
>
> The newly liberated Israelites weren't ready for freedom. Confronted with the rigors of life in the desert, they yearned for the guaranteed sustenance of oppression, and they blamed Moses for failing to meet their unrealistic expectations. The Exodus generation, which hadn't been responsible for its own liberation, lacked the courage to fight for freedom. It took a new generation, hardened by deprivation and conflict, to develop the character needed to enter the Promised Land.
>
> During the modern era, the Exodus became an inspirational template for Secular revolutions, and so it is important to understand the full and rich message of the departure from Egypt.
>
> Most revolutions fail, at least initially. Undertaken in the name of republican principles, the French Revolution soon yielded to the

Terror, imperial rule and a restored monarchy. It took more than 100 years to establish self-government in France. Those who wage wars against colonialism often become authoritarian kleptocrats. Leaders of the struggle against communist domination in Eastern and Central Europe split into warring factions after the collapse of the Soviet Union. Many have sought to entrench their power by curtailing democratic liberties such as freedom of the press and an independent judiciary.

The same may be said of the Arab Spring that engulfed much of the Middle East and North Africa two centuries later. Demonstrations erupted everywhere from Algeria to Iraq, and revolutions came in Libya and Syria. Who can forget the events in Cairo's Tahrir Square, where students armed with cellphones brought down an autocracy? It was dubbed the "Facebook Revolution" and heralded as the dawn of a new political era. We know what happened next.

Millennia ago, the Israelites were given the Law at Sinai . . . Secular revolutions are not so fortunate; they must give the law to themselves, which means that they must reach a consensus. When a new constitution is one-sided, as so many are, the excluded parties are bound to resist.

Wise revolutionaries will do their best to include the forces they have defeated, as Nelson Mandela understood. But this requires a rare degree of magnanimity. Too often, revolutions are occasions for settling old scores and creating new hierarchies of oppressors and oppressed.

In his commentary on the Haggada, the liturgy of Passover, the late Rabbi Jonathan Sacks notes that Hebrew has two words for freedom— hofesh and herut. The former means "freedom from," the latter, "freedom to." Hofesh is liberation from oppression; herut is a system in which each individual respects the freedom of others.

Liberation is exhilarating. A system of liberty is slower and harder; it requires restraint and forbearance. In a stable free society, leaders

> understand that victories are temporary and that the rights of minorities are protections that they may need when their fortunes shift. The imperative of forbearance is a lesson that politicians everywhere . . ."

This quote requires additional commentary. The premise is that people are often not ready for revolutions and the *freedom* that may follow. The "success" of a revolution depends both on the character of the leaders and of the led. How people deal with their newfound freedom is tenuous. Often, factions develop. Often, violence results. Often, *freedom* becomes bondage. Creating a new society requires the institution of laws, which itself creates conflict and struggles for power.

The Hebrew words are instructive. *Hofesh* means "freedom from." This could entail freedom from the bondage they once lived through. It brings liberation from oppression. *Herut* means "freedom to." Here, people have the freedom *to seek* revolution or dramatic societal change. Yet, those who seek revolution must respect the freedom of others.

In short, liberation can be exhilarating, but short-lived. Many transitionary elements must occur *after* the initial birth of liberation. These can be good or bad. And even worse than *before* the revolution. Ancient Israelites wanted to go *back* to Egypt. They missed the life they had before they left. They left slavery yet wanted to go back to it. Freedom in the desert was too hard. Given the false premises that the progressives use to drum up resentment, this should be a cautionary tale with an ironic twist imparted to those who willingly accept their own figurative or literal chains.

History demonstrates that liberty comes slower than liberation. Indeed, it comes well after liberation—if it comes at all. Liberty *requires* restraint and forbearance. Yet, once liberation occurs, there is no guarantee that restraint and forbearance will result. History also demonstrates that most revolutions do not accomplish what was desired. Factions and power struggles *after* liberation are common. So is bondage and authoritarian rule. In her study of history, Tuchman offers this cautionary tale: "the process of gaining power employs means that degrade or brutalize the seeker, who wakes to find that power has been possessed at the price of virtue—or moral purpose—lost."[60]

Consequently, the operative question: *You say you want a revolution?* The first chapter provides the quick response: *Be careful what you ask for!* Throughout this book, we sought to connect reality's dots, demonstrating that a revolutionary climate is upon us. But we still have time to make crucial adjustments. We still have time to expose and engage those who have heretofore been able to conceal their *real* goals. We still have time to support the police, public safety providers, and those who will help keep this country safe. We still have time to make necessary public policy changes to secure environments and to maintain freedom to live, work, study, play, and pray in.

Added to this dynamic is the "great reset" from the pandemic, whereby so many elements of life will never be the same. The *new normal* from this great reset will manifest itself in the months and years to come. Meanwhile, the "great resignation" where millions of people decided to quit their jobs is bound to forever change the workforce and the employment market. How these "twin greats" play out going forward is beyond the scope of this book. Yet, these will surely impact a society already in a tenuous and fragile state.

The road ahead is still obscured by clouds, but a storm is no doubt coming. Times will get harder and more hazardous before they get better—*if* they get better. People will cope in different ways. Some will divert their eyes, putting their heads in the sand. Others will deny reality with flowery "it's-going-to-get-better" mantras. Others will actively seek to bring the revolution to fruition. Others will actively resist and seek to maintain the system. Still others will seek their God, pray for their country, and try to protect their family.

Regardless of our individual options or coping mechanisms, it's as former Defense Secretary Gates stated: "we may not be interested in the long war, but the long war is interested in us."[61] Ironically, this quote was paraphrased from Leon Trotsky, who being a "founder" of Communism stated, "You may not be interested in war, but war is interested in you."[62] This is applicable to the times ahead. Something big is coming. Is it a civil war? Or an ideological war? Or a redemption? Or a revival? A political earthquake? A revolution?

Each of us has a choice. Our character counts. The content of our character, not the color of our skin is the better standard—and the healthier approach.

Our collective choice . . . revolution or redemption? Are there other options? If there are, they are limited, at best. How about individually? Are you part of the solution or the problem . . .?

Most pointedly, whether we *choose* to hate is probably our most important and lasting decision. There are a million "reasons" to hate, yet the simple answer is that *it's wrong*. More emphatically, Ahmari goes further by quoting Howard Thurman, a black American minister born in 1899 and who lived through the Jim Crow south:

> "Jesus rejected hatred. It was not because he lacked the vitality or the strength. It was not because he lacked the incentive. Jesus rejected hatred because he saw that hatred meant death to the mind, death to the spirit, death to communion with his Father. He affirmed life; and hatred was the *great denial* (emphasis added)."

We can never justify what is wrong . . . Hate is wrong! As developed throughout this book, hate cannot be justified—regardless of Race, Religion, or Politics. Yet, people often do what can't be justified. This is at the core of our divide. Hatred fuels divisions. Hatred drives extremist ideologies. Hatred causes people to do violent—and evil acts. Hatred destroys the hater—and seeks to destroy the target. The direct target is "the other side." The ultimate target is the system, capitalism and democracy. We've been warned. There is no good end. Nothing good will result from hatred.

All of us have a choice. Let's end the story the way it started: *You say you want a revolution?*

ENDNOTES

CHAPTER I

1 Louis Casiano, France rejects American "woke" culture that is "racializing" country; *Fox News*, 10-2-21 @ https://www.foxnews.com/world/france-american-woke-racializing

2 See Jacobin Magazine @ https://jacobinmag.com/issue/lower-the-crime-rate viewed on 11-16-2021.

3 King James Bible, Luke 11:17.

4 *The Wall Street Journal* on Aug. 30, 2021 @

https://www.wsj.com/articles/jim-webb-afghanistan-withdrawal-debacle-american-founding-constitution-accountability-11630357157

5 James Freeman, *The Wall Street Journal*, July 2, 2021 @

https://www.wsj.com/articles/the-noblest-happiest-page-in-mankinds-history-11625222292

6 Louis Casiano, Police chief association releases number of officers injured during violent riots, *Fox News*, December 1, 2020 @ https://www.foxnews.com/us/police-chief-officers-injured-riots

7 Noah Manskar, Riots following George Floyd's death may cost insurance companies up to $2B, *The New York Post*, September 16, 2020 @ https://nypost.com/2020/09/16/riots-following-george-floyds-death-could-cost-up-to-2b/

8 Louis Casiano (2021) op. cit.

9 Police Union says 140 officers were injured in Capitol Riot; *The Washington Post*, January 27, 2021 @ https://www.washingtonpost.com/local/public-safety/police-union-says-140-officers-injured-in-capitol-riot/2021/01/27/60743642-60e2-11eb-9430-e7c77b5b0297_story.html

10 Spencer S. Hsu, Jan. 6 riot caused $1.5 million in damage to Capitol—and U.S. prosecutors want defendants to pay; *The Washington Post*, June 3, 2021 @ https://www.washingtonpost.com/local/legal-issues/capitol-riot-defendants-pay-damages-restitution/2021/06/03/74691812-c3ec-11eb-93f5-ee9558eecf4b_story.html

11 Madison Hall, Skye Gould, Rebecca Harrington, Jacob Shamsian, Azmi Haroun, Taylor Ardrey, and Erin Snodgrass, 753 people have been charged in the Capitol insurrection so far. This searchable table shows them all, https://www.insider.com/all-the-us-capitol-pro-trump-riot-arrests-charges-names-2021-1 retrieved on 11-23-21.

12 Spencer S. Hsu, Tom Jackman, Ellie Silverman and Rachel Weiner, Court hearings, guilty pleas belie right-wing recasting of Jan. 6 defendants as persecuted patriots, *The Washington Post*, September 17, 2021 @ https://www.washingtonpost.com/local/legal-issues/j6-rally-capitol-riot-defendants/2021/09/17/b433ecb6-1657-11ec-a5e5-ceecb895922f_story.html.

13 https://en.wikipedia.org/wiki/Weather_Underground retrieved on 11-23-21.

14 Jeremy Herb, Evan Perez, Donie O'Sullivan and Mark Morales, *CNN*, May 31 2020 @ https://www.cnn.com/2020/05/31/politics/outside-influence-extremists-riots-us/index.html

15 Ron Grossman, Martin Luther King Jr. brought the fight to Chicago; *Chicago Tribune*, Apr 07, 2013 @ https://www.chicagotribune.com/news/ct-per-flash-mlk-0407-20130407-story.html

16 Kyle Smith, Why must everything—from 'Real Housewives' to the NFL to yoga—be about race, *NY Post*, on July 16, 2021 @ https://nypost.com/2021/07/16/why-must-everything-from-real-housewives-to-the-nfl-to-yoga-be-about-race-it-is-toxic-for-america/?utm_source=gmail&utm_campaign=android_nyp

17 BabylonBee.com, July 16th, 2021 @ https://babylonbee.com/news/scientists-warn-that-in-the-next-decade-well-run-out-of-things-to-call-racist

18 James Freeman, Leading Like a Marine in Virginia, Immigrant Winsome Sears lives her American dream; *The Wall Street Journal* on Nov. 4, 2021 @ https://www.wsj.com/articles/leading-like-a-marine-in-virginia-11635962909

19 Eberhart, Christopher; Race relations in the US between black and white adults are at the lowest point in more than two decades, *Dailymail.com,* 7-21-21 @ https://www.dailymail.co.uk/news/article-9812245/Black-white-race-relations-lowest-20-years-poll-finds.html

20 Charles Murray, Identity crisis: how the politics of race will wreck America; *The Spectator*, June 16, 2021 @ https://spectatorworld.com/topic/identity-crisis-politics-race-wreck-america-charles-murray/

21 Charles Murray (2021) op. cit.

22 James F. Pastor (2010). *Terrorism and Public Safety Policing: Implications for the Obama Presidency*, CRS Press-Taylor & Francis Group, 2010.

23 Mark Levin (2021). *American Marxism*, Threshold Editions, New York at 246.

24 adl.com; Black Nationalist Arrested Following Shooting of Florida Officer, June 28, 2021 retrieved 11-18-21 @

https://www.adl.org/blog/black-nationalist-arrested-following-shooting-of-florida-officer

25 Officer.com compiled from The Daytona Beach News-Journal, 9-2-21 retrieved 11-18-21 @

https://www.officer.com/features/honoring-the-fallen/news/21236789/man-faces-firstdegree-murder-charge-in-shooting-of-florida-police-officer

26 Dom Calicchio, Arvada police also released a video that shows the suspect chasing down and shooting 19-year veteran Officer Gordon Beesley; *Fox News*, June 26, 2021 @ https://www.foxnews.com/us/colorado-cop-killers-chilling-words-revealed-my-goal-today-is-to-kill-arvada-pd-officers

27 Bill Hutchinson and Jeffrey Cook; Denver police feared mass shooting near MLB All-Star Game, documents show; *ABC News*, July 12, 2021 @

https://abcnews.go.com/US/denver-police-feared-mass-shooting-mlb-star-game/story?id=78797363

28 FOX 11 Digital Team; Man wearing body armor with cache of weapons stopped outside Roybal Federal Building in DTLA, July 15, 2021 @

https://www-foxla-com.cdn.ampproject.org/c/s/www.foxla.com/news/cache-of-weapons-discovered-in-vehicle-stopped-outside-roybal-federal-building-in-dtla.amp

29 Ryan Lucas, Two California Men Have Been Charged with Plotting to Bomb a Democratic Party Building; *NPR*; July 16, 2021 @ https://www.npr.org/2021/07/16/1016844817/2-california-men-have-been-charged-with-plotting-to-bomb-a-democratic-building

30 Smokinggun.com; Nazi Enthusiast Blames Antifa for Shooting, July 26 @

http://www.thesmokinggun.com/documents/crime/antifa-made-me-do-it-726508

31 Louis Casiano, Capitol bomb threat suspect appears in court, charged with threatening use of weapon of mass destruction; *Fox News*, August 21, 2021 @ https://www.foxnews.com/us/capitol-bomb-suspect-court-charged-destruction

32 Andrew Court, *Dailymail.com*, 3 July 2021 @

https://www.dailymail.co.uk/news/article-9752493/Massachusetts-cops-issue-urgent-shelter-place-warning-eight-heavily-armed-men-run.html

33 Alexander Mallin, Newly released FBI tapes show white supremacist members of 'The Base' plotting terror attacks; *ABC News*, November 4, 2021 @ https://abcnews.go.com/Politics/newly-released-fbi-tapes-show-white-supremacist-members/story?id=80975917

34 Samuel Chamberlain, NYC shrink tells Yale audience she fantasizes about shooting white people in head, *NY Post*, June 4, 2021 @ https://nypost.com/2021/06/04/nyc-pyscho-fantasizes-about-shooting-white-people-in-yale-talk?utm_source=gmail&utm_campaign=android_nyp

35 Tony Messenger, Messenger: Ending the 'lullaby of gunshots' is goal of St. Louis violence interrupters, *St. Louis Post-Dispatch*, November 7, 2021 @ https://www.stltoday.com/news/subscriber/messenger-ending-the-lullaby-of-gunshots-is-goal-of-st-louis-violence-interrupters/article_43730892-440d-5e64-926a-47cce94e6284.html

CHAPTER II

1 James F. Pastor (2010). *Terrorism and Public Safety Policing: Implications for the Obama Presidency*, CRS Press-Taylor & Francis Group.

2 Barack Obama speech at 2004 Democratic Convention @ https://www.pbs.org/newshour/show/barack-obamas-keynote-address-at-the-2004-democratic-national-convention retrieved on 11-25-21.

3 Joseph C. Phillips, Commentary: Barack Obama Can't Win as Long as He Continues to Play That Tired, Dog-Eared Race Card, www.blackamericanweb.com on August 19, 2008 @ https://web.archive.org/web/20080819212134/http://www.blackamericaweb.com/site.aspx/sayitloud/phillips819 retrieved on 11-24-21. Note the original post was removed from blackamericaweb.com, so this was retrieved from way back on 11-24-21 @ https://archive.org/web/.

4 Joseph C. Phillips (2008) op. cit.

5 Elisha Fieldstadt, James Alex Fields, Driver in deadly car attack at Charlottesville rally, sentenced to life in prison; *NBC News*, June 28, 2019 @ https://www.nbcnews.com/news/us-news/james-alex-fields-driver-deadly-car-attack-charlottesville-rally-sentenced-n1024436

6 Carly Sitrin, Read: President Trump's remarks condemning violence "on many sides" in Charlottesville; *Vox*, Aug 12, 2017 @ https://www.vox.com/2017/8/12/16138906/president-trump-remarks-condemning-violence-on-many-sides-charlottesville-rally

7 Full text: Trump's comments on white supremacists, 'alt-left' in Charlottesville, *Politico*, August 15, 2017 @ https://www.politico.com/story/2017/08/15/full-text-trump-comments-white-supremacists-alt-left-transcript-241662

8 Matt Pearce, Q&A: What is President Trump's relationship with far-right and white supremacist groups? *Los Angeles Times*, September 30, 2020 @ https://www.latimes.com/politics/story/2020-09-30/la-na-pol-2020-trump-white-supremacy

9 Matt Pearce (2020) op. cit.

10 Karen Ruiz, Jennifer Smith, *Daily Mail, November 24, 2021 @ https://www.dailymail.co.uk/news/article-10235869/Waukesha-suspect-shared-social-media-posts-promoting-violence-white-people.html*

11 Affidavit of FBI Special Agent Scott J. Bierwirth filed on October 20, 2018 in case #18MJ02791 retrieved from https://www.courthousenews.com/wp-content/uploads/2018/10/RAM-rioting-Rundo-et-al-COMPLAINT133873.pdf on 3-11-22.

12 Bierwirth Affidavit (2018) op. cit. at page 8.

13 Stanford University, Center for International Security and Cooperation, Rise Above Movement, Last modified September 2020, retrieved from @ https://cisac.fsi.stanford.edu/mappingmilitants/profiles/rise-above-movement on 3-11-22.

14 Huang Lanlan and Cui Fandi, GT investigates: Evidence suggests US may have supported neo-Nazi Azov Battalion, *Global Times*, March 7, 2022 @ https://www.globaltimes.cn/page/202203/1254217.shtml

15 Huang Lanlan and Cui Fandi (2022) op. cit.

16 Jill Schrider, Ukrainian Neo-Nazi Group—Documents Show Ties Between Azov Battalion, US Rioters, *Daily Veracity*, March 10, 2022 @ https://www.dailyveracity.com/2022/03/10/breaking-fbi-documents-reveal-ties-between-ukraine-neo-nazi-group-azov-battalion-charlottsville-rioters-u-s-funding-helped-train-cville-rioters/

17 James F. Pastor, A Critical Analysis of Terrorism; Master's Thesis submitted in March 1988 at the University of Illinois at Chicago.

18 Pastor, James (1988) op. cit. at page 8.

19 Pastor, James (1988) op. cit. at page 55.

20 Google search of "What is Critical Race Theory" retrieved 321,000,000 results on November 26, 2021.

21 What is Critical Race Theory @ https://www.fairfightinitiative.org/critical-race-theory/ retrieved in 11-26-21.

22 Definition of Critical Race Theory @ https://www.britannica.com/topic/critical-race-theory retrieved on 11-26-21.

23 Candance Owens, Blackout, Threshold Editions, 2020 at page 51.

24 What is Critical Race Theory @ https://www.fairfightinitiative.org/critical-race-theory/ retrieved in 11-26-21.

25 Gene Demby, Two Justices Debate The Doctrine Of Colorblindness, *NPR*, April 23, 2014 @ https://www.npr.org/sections/codeswitch/2014/04/23/306173835/two-justices-debate-the-doctrine-of-colorblindness

26 Caroline Downey, MSNBC Guest on Winsome Sears: 'There Is a Black Mouth Moving but a White Idea Running on the Runway of the Tongue', *National Review*, November 5, 2021 @ https://www.nationalreview.com/news/msnbc-guest-on-winsome-sears-there-is-a-black-mouth-moving-but-a-white-idea-running-on-the-runway-of-the-tongue/

27 Sen. Tim Scott predicts 'coming backlash to this liberal oppression' on *Hannity*, *FOX News*, April 29, 2021 @

https://www.foxnews.com/politics/sen-tim-scott-predicts-backlash-liberal-oppression

28 What is Critical Race Theory? @ https://www.fairfightinitiative.org/critical-race-theory/ retrieved in 11-26-21.

29 Isabel Vincent, Activist Shaun King lives lavishly in lakefront New Jersey home, *The New York Post*, July 31, 2021 @ https://nypost.com/2021/07/31/activist-shaun-king-lives-lavishly-in-lakefront-nj-home/?utm_source=gmail&utm_campaign=android_nyp

30 Isabel Vincent (2021) op. cit.

31 Isabel Vincent (2021) op. cit

32 Charles Love, Who is leading BLM and where are their millions going? No one can say, *The New York Post*, February 12, 2022 @ https://nypost.com/2022/02/12/who-is-blms-leader-and-where-are-donations-going-no-one-can-say/?utm_source=gmail&utm_campaign=android_nyp

33 Charles Love (2022) op. cit.

34 Christopher F. Rufo, Battle Over Critical Race Theory: Advocates and media circle the wagons and try to conceal the truth about a pernicious ideology, *The Wall Street Journal*, June 27, 2021 @ https://www.wsj.com/articles/battle-over-critical-race-theory-11624810791

35 Christopher F. Rufo (2021) op. cit.

36 Christopher F. Rufo (2021) op. cit.

37 Charles Murray, Identity crisis: how the politics of race will wreck America; *The Spectator*, June 16, 2021 @ https://spectatorworld.com/topic/identity-crisis-politics-race-wreck-america-charles-murray/

38 Charles Murray (2021) op. cit.

39 Paul Mirengoff, The Washington Post's Attack on Tucker Carlson Misses the Mark; July 15, 2021 @ https://www.powerlineblog.com/archives/2021/07/the-washington-posts-attack-on-tucker-carlson-misses-the-mark.php

40 Victor Davis Hanson, An American apocalypse—why people of all classes, races are filled with fear; *Tribune Media Services,* August 14, 2021 @ https://www.foxnews.com/opinion/american-armageddon-woke-victor-davis-hanson,

41 Andrew Gutmann and Paul Rossi, Inside the Woke Indoctrination Machine, *The Wall Street Journal,* February 11, 2022 @ https://www.wsj.com/articles/inside-the-woke-indoctrination-machine-diversity-equity-inclusion-bipoc-schools-conference-11644613908

42 Charles Murray (2021) op. cit.

43 William McGurn, Gavin Newsom's White Privilege; *The Wall Street Journal* on 9-13-21 @ https://www.wsj.com/articles/gavin-newsom-white-privilege-larry-elder-racism-inequality-california-recall-election-11631566580

44 Liz Peek, Biden flip-flops on US racism—here's what prompted the new White House message How can country be racist if its people are not? *Fox News*, May 3, 2021 @ https://www.foxnews.com/opinion/biden-flip-flops-racism-prompted-new-message-liz-peek

45 Liz Peek, (2021) op. cit.

46 Victor Davis Hanson, The secret that Biden, Obama, Hillary won't say aloud about today's Democratic Party, *Tribune Media Services*, July 17, 2021 @ https://www.foxnews.com/opinion/biden-obama-hillary-democratic-party-victor-davis-hanson

47 Victor Davis Hanson (2021) op. cit.

48 Victor Davis Hanson (2021) op. cit.

49 Definition of "Woke" @ https://www.merriam-webster.com/dictionary/woke retrieved on 11-29-21.

50 Definition of "Culture War" @ https://en.wikipedia.org/wiki/Culture_war retrieved on 11-29-21.

51 Peggy Noonan, The Culture War Is a Leftist Offensive; *The Wall Street Journal*, July 8, 2021 @ https://www.wsj.com/articles/the-culture-war-is-a-leftist-offensive-11625784024

52 Peggy Noonan (2021) op. cit.

53 Peggy Noonan (2021) op. cit.

54 Peggy Noonan (2021) op. cit.

55 William McGurn, Virginia's 'Phony' Culture War: It's getting ridiculous when Winsome Sears is called a face of white supremacy; *The Wall Street Journal,* Nov. 8, 2021 @ https://www.wsj.com/articles/virginia-phony-culture-war-youngkin-governor-critical-race-mcauliffe-reid-obama-lincoln-project-11636409757

56 William McGurn (2021) op. cit.

57 William McGurn (2021) op. cit.

58 Joseph Epstein, The Culture War Must Go On; *The Wall Street Journal,* July 6, 2021 @ https://www.wsj.com/articles/the-culture-war-must-go-on-11625608694

59 Joseph Epstein (2021) op. cit.

60 Louis Casiano, France rejects American 'woke' culture that is 'racializing' country; *Fox News*, 10-2-21 @ https://www.foxnews.com/world/france-american-woke-racializing |

61 Victor Davis Hanson (2021) op. cit.

62 Joseph A. Wulfsohn, Bill Maher schools Whoopi Goldberg on Black national anthem: 'Separate but equal' is out of step!; *Fox News*, September 25 @ https://www.foxnews.com/entertainment/bill-maher-whoopi-goldberg-black-national-anthem-debate

63 Joseph A. Wulfsohn (2021), op. cit.

64 Joseph A. Wulfsohn (2021), op. cit.

65 Lee Brown, BLM chapter calls American flag 'symbol of hatred' only used by racists, *The New York Post*, July 8, 2021 @ https://nypost.com/2021/07/08/blm-chapter-calls-american-flag-symbol-of-hatred/?utm_source=gmail&utm_campaign=android_nyp

66 Emily Crane, North Korean defector says she was robbed by 3 black women, accused of being racist; New York Post, August 5, 2021 @ https://nypost.com/2021/08/05/n-korean-defector-

says-she-was-robbed-by-black-women-accused-of-being-racist/?utm_source=gmail&utm_campaign=android_nyp

67 http://www.tucc.org/store/index.cfm?action=catbrowse&catid=69 retrieved on April 25, 2008.

68 www.adl.org and State and Local Anti-Terrorist Training (SLATT) at page 21.

69 Jonathan R. White (2008). "A Theology of Anti-government Extremism," *Terrorism in Perspective* (2nd). Ed. Mahan, Sue and Pamela L. Griset. Thousand Oaks, CA: Sage Publications at page 193.

70 http://www.adl.org/Learn/ext_us/WCOTC.asp?xpicked=3&item=17 retrieved on May 5, 2008

71 http://www.adl.org/Learn/ext_us/WCOTC.asp?xpicked=3&item=17 retrieved on May 5, 2008

72 Becky Shay (2009). "Billings group wants to change image of white supremacists," *Billings Gazette (Montana)* @ http://www.missoulian.com/articles/2009/01/08/bnews/br60.txt retrieved on January 8, 2009.

73 Douglas Murray (2019). *The Madness of Crowds: Gender, Race and Identity*, Bloomsbury Continuum, at 254.

CHAPTER III

1 Definition of "Ideology" taken from Dictionary.com @ https://www.dictionary.com/browse/ideology retrieved on 12-2-21.

2 Definition of "Domestic Terrorism" taken from the Federal Bureau of Investigation @ https://www.fbi.gov/investigate/terrorism retrieved 12-2-21.

3 https://en.wikipedia.org/wiki/Almighty_Black_P._Stone_Nation retrieved on 11-23-21.

4 Kerby Anderson, *Arguments Against Abortion* @ http://www.leaderu.com/orgs/probe/docs/arg-abor.html retrieved on 12-2-21.

5 Psalms 139: 13–16; Holy Bible – English Standard Version

6 Kerby Anderson, op. cit. @ http://www.leaderu.com/orgs/probe/docs/arg-abor.html retrieved on 12-2-21.

7 Kerby Anderson, op. cit. @ http://www.leaderu.com/orgs/probe/docs/arg-abor.html retrieved on 12-2-21..

8 Kerby Anderson, op. cit. @ http://www.leaderu.com/orgs/probe/docs/arg-abor.html retrieved on 12-2-21.

9 Taken from Army of God website @ https://www.armyofgod.com/ which referenced Hill's homepage @ https://www.armyofgod.com/Paulhillindex.html retrieved on 12-2-21.

10 Taken from Army of God website @ https://www.armyofgod.com/EricRudolphHomepage.html retrieved on 12-2-21.

11 Jonathon Turley, Dems threaten Supreme Court over abortion – their 'revolution' will destroy fair, impartial judicial system; *FOX News*, December 1, 2021 @ https://www.foxnews.com/opinion/democrats-supreme-court-abortion-revolution-judicial-system.

12 State & Local Anti-terrorist training (SLATT) manual, Domestic Terrorist Groups, @ :\content\section3domestic\pdfs\narrative.pdf on p. 13.

13 Nathan I. Yungher, (2008). *Terrorism: The Bottom Line.* Upper Saddle River, NJ: Pearson-Prentice Hall at p. 129.

14 Steven Best and Anthony J. Nocella. "Defining Terrorism" retrieved on May 2, 2008 @ http://www.criticalanimalstudies.org/JCAS/Journal_Articles_download/Issue_2/DefiningTerrorism.doc

15 SLATT, Domestic Terrorist Groups, Narrative, op. cit. at p. 14.

16 http://www.fbi.gov/congress/congress02/jarboe021202.htm retrieved on May 2, 2008

17 http://www.earthliberationfront.com/main.shtml retrieved on May 2, 2008

18 Ibid @ http://www.earthliberationfront.com/main.shtml

19 http://www.salvationinc.org/archives/2004_08.html on May 2, 2008

20 SLATT, Domestic Terrorist Groups, Narrative, op. cit. at p. 2.

21 Sue Mahan and Pamela L. Griset (2008). *Terrorism in Perspective* (2nd). Thousand Oaks, CA: Sage Publications at pps. 7-8.

22 SLATT, Domestic Terrorist Groups, Narrative, op. cit. at p. 3.

23 SLATT, Domestic Terrorist Groups, Narrative, op. cit. at p. 4.

24 http://www.knowgangs.com/gang_resources/profiles/ms13/ retrieved on June 12, 2007

25 Matthew Quirk, (2008). "How to Grow a Gang," *The Atlantic.* May at p. 24.

26 John Robb (2007). "The Coming Urban Terror: Systems disruption, networked gangs, and bioweapons," *City Journal*, Summer @ http://www.city-journal.org/html/17_3_urban_terrorism.html retrieved on May 16, 2008.

27 http://www.knowgangs.com/gang_resources/profiles/ms13/ retrieved on June 12, 2007

28 Sue Mahan and Pamela L. Griset (2008) op. cit. at p. 6.

29 SLATT, Domestic Terrorist Groups, Narrative, op. cit. at p. 4-5.

30 Jessica Stern (2008). The Ultimate Organization: Networks, Franchises and Freelancers. *Terrorism in Perspective* (2nd). Ed. Mahan, Sue and Pamela L. Griset. Thousand Oaks, CA: Sage Publications at p. 173.

31 Jessica Stern (2008) op. cit. at p. 175.

32 Definition of "Antifa" taken from Wikipedia @ https://en.wikipedia.org/wiki/Antifa_(United_States) retrieved on 12-2-21.

33 Jessica Chasmer, Rep. Nadler says Antifa violence in Portland is a "myth," *The Washington Times*, July 27, 2020 @ https://www.congress.gov/116/meeting/house/110938/documents/HHRG-116-JU00-20200728-SD037.pdf

34 Chris Tomlinson, Slovenian Prime Minister: Antifa Is 'International Terrorist Organization'; *Breitbart.com*, November 1, 2021 @ https://www.breitbart.com/europe/2021/11/01/slovenian-prime-minister-antifa-is-international-terrorist-organisation/

35 Chris Tomlinson (2021) op. cit.

36 Boogaloo Ideology taken from https://en.wikipedia.org/wiki/Boogaloo_movement retrieved on 1-5-22.

37 Michael J. Mooney, "The Boogaloo Bois prepare for civil war," *The Atlantic*, January 15, 2021 @ https://www.theatlantic.com/politics/archive/2021/01/boogaloo-prepare-civil-war/617683/

38 Nathan I. Yungher (2008) op. cit. at p. 126.

39 SLATT, Domestic Terrorist Groups, Narrative, op. cit. at page 6; and Yungher, Nathan I. (2008) op. cit. at p. 126.

40 SLATT, Domestic Terrorist Groups, Narrative, op. cit. at p. 6.

41 SLATT, Domestic Terrorist Groups, Narrative, op. cit. at p. 7-8.

42 Freddy Cruz, In Plain Sight: Uncovering Border Patrol's Relationship with Far-Right Militias at the Southern Border, Southern Poverty Law Center, July 29, 2021 @ https://www.splcenter.org/hatewatch/2021/07/29/plain-sight-uncovering-border-patrols-relationship-far-right-militias-southern-border

43 SLATT, Domestic Terrorist Groups, Narrative, op. cit. at p. 10-11.

44 www.kkk.com/intro.htm retrieved on August 17, 2007.

45 SLATT, Domestic Terrorist Groups, Narrative, op. cit. at p. 11.

46 www.adl.org retrieved on August 17, 2007.

47 SLATT, Domestic Terrorist Groups, Narrative, op. cit. at p. 12.

48 http://www.newblackpanther.com retrieved on May 5, 2008.

49 Hisham Aidi (2005). "Jihadi's in the Hood: Race, Urban Islam & the War on Terror," *Violence & Terrorism*. Ed. Thomas J. Badey: McGraw-Hill/Dushkin, at p. 129.

50 Hisham Aidi (2005) op. cit. at p. 129.

51 Hisham Aidi (2005) op. cit. at p. 134.

52 ADL website @ https://www.adl.org/ retrieved on 12-2-21.

53 ADL website (2021) op. cit.

54 ADL website (2021) op. cit.

55 Frank Fernandez and Mark Harper; What we know about NFAC, the extremist group linked to accused cop-shooter Othal Wallace?, June 26, 2021 @ https://www.news-journalonline.com/story/news/local/volusia/2021/06/26/nfac-a-danger-democracy-volusia-sheriff-mike-chitwood-says/5356781001/

56 Frank Fernandez and Mark Harper (2021) op. cit.

57 Graeme A. Wood, Black Army Rises to Fight the Racist Right; *The Atlantic*, April 2, 2021 @ https://www.theatlantic.com/politics/archive/2021/04/the-many-lives-of-grandmaster-jay/618408/

58 Graeme Wood (2021) op. cit.

59 Graeme Wood (2021) op. cit.

60 Graeme Wood (2021) op. cit.

61 Graeme Wood (2021) op. cit.

62 Paul Crespo, Largest Armed Extremist 'Insurrectionist' Militia in US Isn't White – It's Black; *American Defense News*, October 8, 2021 @ https://americandefensenews.com/2021/10/08/largest-armed-extremist-insurrectionist-militia-in-us-isnt-white-its-black/

63 Taken from Black Lives Matter website @ https://blacklivesmatter.com/herstory/?__cf_chl_jschl_tk__=KSfd0jBmLAKwmNWG8Ge72jicNxTNGhd3301hccV3a58-1638671827-0-gaNycGzNCKU on 12-5-21.

64 Mike Gonzalez and Andrew Olivastro; The Agenda of Black Lives Matter Is Far Different From the Slogan; Heritage.com, on July 3, 2020 @ https://www.heritage.org/progressivism/commentary/the-agenda-black-lives-matter-far-different-the-slogan.

65 Mike Gonzalez and Andrew Olivastro (2021) op. cit.

66 Mike Gonzalez and Andrew Olivastro (2021) op. cit.

67 Patrick J. Buchanan, Who Is Killing 10,000 Black Americans Every Year? *CNS News*, October 1, 2021 @ https://cnsnews.com/commentary/ patrick-j-buchanan/who-killing-10000-black-americans-every-year

68 Mike Gonzalez and Andrew Olivastro (2021) op. cit.

69 Bob Price, BLM Activist Asks When People 'Ready to Get Blood on Their Hands?; *Breitbart*; April 16, 2021 @ https://www.breitbart.com/law-and-order/2021/04/16/watch-blm-activist-asks-when-people-ready-to-get-blood-on-their-hands/

70 Joseph Epstein, Black Lives Matter Poisons a Young Athlete's Mind, *The Wall Street Journal*, Aug. 16, 2021 @ https://www.wsj.com/articles/black-lives-matter-noah-lyles-sprinter-bronze-holt-black-power-systemic-racism-11629141520

71 http://www.knowgangs.com/gang_resources/profiles/ms13/ retrieved on June 12, 2007

72 Laurie Wood, (2007). *Intelligence Report*, p. 56-57, Fall.

73 http://www.dc.state.fl.us/pub/gangs/prison.html retrieved on May 5, 2008

74 http://www.splcenter.org/intel/intelreport/article.jsp?aid=569 retrieved on May 5, 2008

75 www.adl.org retrieved on August 17, 2007

76 http://www.splcenter.org/intel/intelreport/article.jsp?aid=569 retrieved on May 5, 2008

77 SLATT, Domestic Terrorist Groups, Narrative, op. cit. at p. 8.

78 Nathan I. Yungher (2008) op. cit. at p. 125.

79 Proud Boys ideology taken from https://en.wikipedia.org/wiki/Proud_Boys retrieved on 1-5-22.

80 Joseph A. Wulfsohn, NYT reporter suggests declaring Trump supporters 'enemies of the state' to combat 'national security threats;' *Fox News,* July 27, 2021 @ https://www.foxnews.com/media/new-york-times-katie-benner-trump-supporters-enemies-of-the-state

81 Brooke Singman, Biden WH strategy for battling domestic terror labels White supremacy, militia 'extremists' as biggest threats, *Fox News,* June 15, 2021 @ https://www.foxnews.com/politics/biden-strategy-domestic-terrorism-white-supremacy-militia-extremists-threats

82 Brooke Singman (2021) op. cit.

83 Thomas H. Johnson and M. Chris Mason (2008). "All Counterinsurgency is Local," *The Atlantic,* October at p. 38.

84 When considering the sources of terrorism, the "link between terrorism and nationalist, ethnic, religious and tribal conflict is far more tangible [than other so-called sources of such violence]," as asserted by: Laqueur, Walter (2004). The Terrorism to Come, *Policy Review*, No. 126 @ www.policyreview.org/aug04/laqueur_print.html retrieved on November 1, 2004.

CHAPTER IV

1 Allan Smith, Progressive DAs are shaking up the criminal justice system. Pro-police groups aren't happy, *NBC News*, Aug. 19, 2019 @ https://www.nbcnews.com/politics/justice-department/these-reform-prosecutors-are-shaking-system-pro-police-groups-aren-n1033286

2 Allan Smith (2019) op. cit.

3 Sam Dorman, BLM attacks Booker for defund the police vote, says 'NO ONE' in Senate had their back, *Fox News*, August 21, 2021 @ https://www.foxnews.com/politics/black-lives-matter-booker-defund-police-senate

4 *Chicago Sun Times* wire, December 7, 2021 @ https://chicago.suntimes.com/crime/2021/12/6/22821727/12-year-old-girl-wounded-in-downtown-shooting

5 Noah Manskar, Riots following George Floyd's death may cost insurance companies up to $2B, *The New York Post*, September 16, 2020 @ https://nypost.com/2020/09/16/riots-following-george-floyds-death-could-cost-up-to-2b/

6 Google search for "Define reimagine policing" done on 12-8-21 with 873,000 hits. The number one listing was https://www.obama.org› policing-pledge, which is the Obama Foundation @ https://www.obama.org/policing-pledge/

7 Obama Foundation website @ https://www.obama.org/policing-pledge/ retrieved on 12-8-21.

8 Gerrard Kaonga, Lori Lightfoot Says Chicago Retailers Aren't Doing Enough to Defend Against Theft, *Newsweek*, December 8, 2021 @ https://www.newsweek.com/chicago-mayor-lori-lightfoot-theft-store-smash-grab-1657330

9 Edmund DeMarche, New York BLM leader warns Eric Adams of 'bloodshed,' 'riots' if city brings back tougher policing, *Fox News*, November 11, 2021 @

https://www.foxnews.com/politics/blm-leader-in-new-york-warns-mayor-elect-against-returning-to-the-old-ways-of-policing

10 Lizzy Murica, San Francisco to shift $120 million from law enforcement budget to 'reparations' to the black community, *Law Enforcement Today*, February 28, 2021 @ https://www.lawenforcementtoday.com/walgreens-closes-17-stores-in-san-fran-due-to-out-of-control-shoplifting/

11 Lizzy Murica (2021) op. cit.

12 Lizzy Murica (2021) op. cit.

13 Zusha Elinson, Dan Frosch and Joshua Jamerson; Cities Reverse Defunding the Police Amid Rising Crime, *The Wall Street Journal*, May 26, 2021 @ https://www.wsj.com/articles/cities-reverse-defunding-the-police-amid-rising-crime-11622066307

14 Editorial Board; The Assault on Seattle's Police, *The Wall Street Journal*, Aug. 29, 2021 @ https://www.wsj.com/articles/seattle-police-city-council-federal-monitor-violent-crime-shooting-homicide-blm-defund-11630253834

15 Mike Carter, *Seattle Times, November 4 2021 @ https://www.seattletimes.com/seattle-news/seattle-leaders-failed-lorenzo-father-of-chop-victim-files-new-lawsuit-naming-durkan-sawant/*

16 Gregory J. Wallance, *The Hill, June 30, 2020 @ https://thehill.com/opinion/criminal-justice/505157-the-occupation-of-seattles-capitol-hill-district-is-a-cautionary*

17 Tim Gordon, *KGW.com*, March 1, 2021 @ *https://www.kgw.com/article/news/crime/portland-protests-vandalism-pearl-district/283-9b5cac12-5d1c-437a-8001-4c669033f673*

18 *Personal interview with Stan Penkin, November 4, 2021 Transcription on file*

19 Robert Mackey, August 23, 2021, *The Intercept, https://theintercept.com/2021/08/23/portland-police-proud-boys-protest/*

20 *https://www.wsj.com/articles/anarchy-in-portland-oregon-ted-wheeler-chuck-lovell-11630014195*

21 *https://policetribune.com/portland-police-give-up-let-proud-boys-antifa-brawl-through-portland/*

22 *Personal interview with Stan Penkin, November 4, 2021 Transcription on file*

23 Zusha Elinson, Dan Frosch and Joshua Jamerson (2021) op. cit.

24 Crimethinc twitter post on September 3, 2021 @ https://twitter.com/crimethinc/status/1433910534575955971 retrieved on 12-9-21.

25 Joe Schoffstall, Soros bankrolls group pushing to 'dismantle,' replace Minneapolis Police Department, *Fox News*, August 5, 2021 @ https://www.foxnews.com/politics/george-soros-dismantle-replace-minneapolis-police

26 Journal Editorial Board (2021) op. cit.

27 Zusha Elinson, Dan Frosch and Joshua Jamerson (2021) op. cit.

28 James Freeman, Seattle Residents: Fund the Police, *The Wall Street Journal*, April 27, 2021 @ https://www.wsj.com/articles/seattle-residents-fund-the-police-11619561775

29 Journal Editorial Board, Austin's Defund the Police Lesson, *The Wall Street Journal,* Oct. 10, 2021 @ https://www.wsj.com/articles/austin-texas-defund-the-police-murder-burglary-response-budget-cut-staffing-shortage-11633881864

30 Journal Editorial Board (2021) op. cit.

31 Audrey Conklin, AOC, 'Squad' members promote 'Defund the Police' but spend thousands on private security, *Fox News*, April 20, 2021 @ https://www.foxnews.com/politics/aoc-defund-police-squad-private-security

32 Dorothy Moses Schulz, 'Defund police' Squad members are biggest spenders on private security, *New York Post*, September 13, 2021 @ https://nypost.com/2021/09/13/defund-police-squad-members-spend-on-private-security/?utm_source=gmail&utm_campaign=android_nyp

33 Dorothy Moses Schulz (2021) op. cit.

34 Dorothy Moses Schulz (2021) op. cit.

35 Dorothy Moses Schulz (2021) op. cit.

36 Allan Smith (2019) op. cit.

37 Abha Bhattarai and Gerrit De Vynck - 'Flash mob' robberies roiling U.S. retailers, traumatizing workers, *The Washington Post*, December 3, 2021 @ https://www.msn.com/en-us/news/us/e2-80-98flash-mob-e2-80-99-robberies-roiling-us-retailers-traumatizing-workers/ar-AARqtwi

38 Journal Editorial Board; San Francisco's Drug Store Anarchy, *The Wall Street Journal*, Oct. 14, 2021 @ https://www.wsj.com/articles/san-franciscos-drug-store-anarchy-walgreens-closes-theft-11634245898 and Jason L. Riley, San Francisco Has Become a Shoplifter's Paradise, *The Wall Street Journal*, Oct. 19, 2021 @ https://www.wsj.com/articles/san-francisco-shoplifters-theft-walgreens-decriminalized-11634678239

39 Editorial Board and Jason Riley (2021) op. cit.

40 Journal Editorial Board (2021) op. cit.

41 Allan Smith, Parents guilty of murder and raised by radicals, Chesa Boudin is San Francisco's next district attorney, *NBC News*, December 16, 2019 @ https://www.nbcnews.com/politics/elections/parents-guilty-murder-raised-radicals-chesa-boudin-san-francisco-s-n1101071

42 Andrew Mark Miller, San Francisco prosecutors quit progressive DA Chesa Boudin's office, join recall effort, *Fox News*, October 25, 2021 @ https://www.foxnews.com/politics/san-francisco-prosecutors-quit-chesa-boudin-office-recall-joined

43 Andrew Mark Miller (2021) op. cit.

44 Andrew Mark Miller (2021) op. cit.

45 Journal Editorial Board (2021) op. cit.

46 Jason L. Riley (2021) op. cit.

47 Andrew Mark Miller (2021) op. cit.

48 Jason L. Riley, Shrinking Blue States Have 'Defund the Police' to Blame, *Fox News*, May 18, 2021 @ https://www.wsj.com/articles/shrinking-blue-states-have-defund-the-police-to-blame-11621375938

49 Brittany De Lea, Derek Chauvin trial judge slams Maxine Waters' inflammatory comments, *Fox News*, April 19, 2021 @ https://www.foxnews.com/politics/derek-chauvin-defense-maxine-waters-comments-trial

50 News Staff, Report finds racial disparities in stops, arrests, use-of-force by Seattle Police officers, *KOMO*, July 15th 2021 @ https://katu-com.cdn.ampproject.org/c/s/katu.com/amp/news/local/report-finds-racial-disparities-in-stops-arrests-use-of-force-by-seattle-police-officers

51 James F. Pastor, *Terrorism and Public Safety Policing: Implications for the Obama Presidency*, CRS Press-Taylor & Francis Group, 2010.

52 Ben Singleton, Drawing comparisons on race and crime, *Seattle Times*, August 5, 2016 @ https://www.seattletimes.com/opinion/drawing-comparisons-on-race-and-crime/

53 KOMO Staff Report (2021) op. cit.

54 Danielle Wallace, Portland police's newly resurrected gun violence team can't find officers to fill unit: Gun Violence Reduction Team disbanded last summer amid Black Lives Matter protests, *Fox News*, August 2, 2021 @ https://www.foxnews.com/us/portland-police-gun-violence-unit-struggles-find-officers-homicide-rate

55 Danielle Wallace (2021) op. cit.

56 Heather Mac Donald, Police Vindicate the 'Thin Blue Line' Patch Every Day, *The Wall Street Journal*, August 23, 2021 @ https://www.wsj.com/articles/police-thin-blue-line-shootings-black-homicide-crime-proactive-policing-blm-defund-11629750911

57 Danielle Wallace (2021) op. cit.

58 Sohrab Ahmari, A world of crack, urine and catatonia: Welcome to Washington Square Park, *New York Post*, July 8, 2021 @ https://nypost.com/2021/07/08/a-world-of-crack-urine-and-catatonia-welcome-to-washington-square-park/?utm_source=gmail&utm_campaign=android_nyp

59 Sohrab Ahmari (2021) op. cit.

60 Journal Editorial Board, Breaking Bill de Blasio's Windows, *The Wall Street Journal*, July 28, 2021 @ https://www.wsj.com/articles/bill-de-blasio-new-york-city-crime-broken-windows-washington-square-park-11627509372

61 Audrey Conklin, 'Quality-of-life crimes' in Philadelphia, including public urination and prostitution, to get new treatment, *Fox News*, July 29, 2021 @ https://www.foxnews.com/us/philadelphia-quality-of-life-crimes-changes

62 Heather Mac Donald, Anticop Movement Wants Road Anarchy Too, *The Wall Street Journal*, April 22, 2021 @ https://www.wsj.com/articles/anticop-movement-wants-road-anarchy-too-11619132197

63 Heather Mac Donald, (2021) op. cit.

64 Heather Mac Donald, (2021) op. cit.

65 Heather Mac Donald, (2021) op. cit.

66 Warren Kozak, Social Breakdown Starts with Skipping a Stop Sign, *The Wall Street Journal*, July 25, 2021 @ https://www.wsj.com/articles/traffic-fatalities-society-danger-11627238246

67 Warren Kozak (2021) op. cit.

68 David Aaro, Portland police hands-off strategy during violent political clashes criticized by some, praised by mayor, *Fox News*, August 24, 2021 @ https://mail.google.com/mail/u/0/?tab=km&pli=1#inbox/QgrcJHsbhNPjRZpgmPLHGJmPChwTbrcSSrq

69 Journal Editorial Board, Anarchy in Portland, *The Wall Street Journal*, August 26, 2021 @ https://www.wsj.com/articles/anarchy-in-portland-oregon-ted-wheeler-chuck-lovell-11630014195

70 Sara Cline, 'Lawless city?' Worry after Portland police don't stop chaos, *ABC News*, October 16, 2021 @ https://abcnews.go.com/US/wireStory/lawless-city-worry-portland-police-stop-chaos-80613763

71 Holman W. Jenkins, How to Have More Police Shootings, *The Wall Street Journal*, April 23, 2021 @ https://www.wsj.com/articles/how-to-have-more-police-shootings-11619213893

72 Jason L. Riley, Race Relations in America Are Better Than Ever, *The Wall Street Journal*, April 27, 2021 @ https://www.wsj.com/articles/race-relations-in-america-are-better-than-ever-11619561751

73 Heather Mac Donald, (2021) op. cit.

74 Marisa Schultz, Number of police officers shot this year reaches 128, union says 'defund' movement a factor, *Fox News*, June 2, 2021 @ https://www.foxnews.com/us/police-officers-shot-128-union-dehumanization-law-enforcement

75 Stephanie Pagones, Over 60K police, law enforcement officers assaulted in 2020, up by 4,000+ from year before, FBI says, Fox News, October 19, 2021 @ https://www.foxnews.com/us/police-law-enforcement-officers-assaulted-fbi

76 National Law Enforcement Officers Memorial Fund, 2021 END-OF-YEAR PRELIMINARY LAW ENFORCEMENT OFFICERS FATALITIES REPORT @ https://nleomf.org/wp-content/uploads/2022/01/2021-EOY-Fatality-Report-Final-web.pdf

77 National Law Enforcement Officers Memorial Fund (2021) op. cit.

78 Stephanie Pagones (2021) op. cit.

79 Danielle Wallace, Chicago police identifies 'hero' officer killed during traffic stop: 'We will #NeverForget', *Fox News*, August 9, 2021 @ https://www.foxnews.com/us/chicago-officer-killed-traffic-stop-increased-shootings-targeting-police

80 Danielle Wallace (2021) op. cit.

81 Stephanie Pagones, Seattle Police Department losing officers at 'record pace' amid budget uncertainty, lack of support: officials, *Fox News*, May 5, 2021 @ https://www.foxnews.com/us/seattle-police-department-exodus-record-pace-political-support

82 Talia Kaplan, Officers resign from team that polices protests: 'Tired of being managed by politics', *Fox News*, April 19, 2021 @ https://www.foxnews.com/us/albuquerque-officers-resign-protest-squad-lack-support

83 Stephanie Pagones (2021) op. cit.

84 Associated Press, Police departments struggle to recruit since killing of George Floyd, *Fox News*, June 11 @ https://www.foxnews.com/us/law-enforcement-police-recruiting-george-floyd

85 Miranda Devine, Why would anyone want to be a cop with the way they're being treated, *New York Post*, April 14, 2021 @ https://nypost.com/2021/04/14/the-truth-about-racism-cops-devine?utm_source=gmail&utm_campaign=android_nyp

86 Miranda Devine (2021) op. cit.

87 Miranda Devine (2021) op. cit.

88 Miranda Devine (2021) op. cit.

89 Peter Aitken, Atlanta mayor suggests officer fired to prevent riots, defends decision as he is reinstated, *Fox News*, May 6, 2021 @ https://www.foxnews.com/us/atlanta-mayor-officer-fired-prevent-riots-reinstated

90 Gerard Baker, The Chauvin Trial and the Chelsea Handler Standard of Justice, *The Wall Street Journal*, April 19, 2021 @ https://www.wsj.com/articles/americas-new-chelsea-handler-standard-of-justice-11618847816

91 Heather Mac Donald, A Year After George Floyd's Murder, It's 'Open Season' in Minneapolis, *The Wall Street Journal*, May 24, 2021 @ https://www.wsj.com/articles/a-year-after-george-floyds-murder-its-open-season-in-minneapolis-11621893383

92 Heather Mac Donald (2021) op. cit.

93 Heather Mac Donald (2021) op. cit.

94 Stephanie Pagones, Residents of ritzy Atlanta suburb push for separate police force as crime rages in 'war zone': neighbor, *Fox News*, June 9,2021 @ https://www.foxnews.com/us/buckhead-ritzy-atlanta-suburb-separate-police-force-crime-rages

95 Stephanie Pagones (2021) op. cit.

96 Bill Hutchinson, 'It's just crazy': 12 major cities hit all-time homicide records, *ABC News*, December 8, 2021 @ https://abcnews.go.com/US/12-major-us-cities-top-annual-homicide-records/story?id=81466453

97 Priya Krishnakumar and Peter Nickeas, 10 of the country's most populous cities set homicide records last year, CNN, January 4, 2022 @ https://www.cnn.com/2022/01/03/us/homicide-rate-us-statistics/index.html

98 Bill Hutchinson (2021) op. cit.

99 Bill Hutchinson (2021) op. cit.

CHAPTER V

1 German Lopez, Murders are spiking, Police should be part of the solution, *VOX*, September 27, 2021 @ https://www-vox-com.cdn.ampproject.org/c/s/www.vox.com/platform/amp/22580710/defund-the-police-reform-murder-spike-research-evidence

2 German Lopez (2021) op. cit.

3 German Lopez (2021) op. cit.

4 James F. Pastor (2003). *The Privatization of Police in America: An Analysis & Case Study,* McFarland, Jefferson, N.C.

5 Jeanette Covington and Ralph B. Taylor (1991). "Fear of Crime in Urban Residential Neighborhoods: Implications of Between and Within Neighborhood Sources for Current Models," *The Sociological Quarterly* 32 (2): pps. 231–249; Dan A. Lewis and Michael G. Maxfield (1980). "Fear in the Neighborhoods: An Investigation of the Impact of Crime," *Journal of Research in Crime & Delinquency*, July, Pp. 160–189; and George Kelling (1995). "Reduce Serious Crime by Restoring Order," *The American Enterprise*, May/June.

6 James Pastor (2003) op. cit.

7 Barbara N. McLennan, ed. (1970). *Crime in Urban Society*. London: Cambridge University Press.

8 Lawrence E. Cohen, and Marcus Felson (1979). "Social Change and Crime Rate Trends," *American Sociological Review* 44: pps. 588–607.

9 Jack P., Gibbs and Maynart L. Erickson (1976). "Crime Rates of American Cities in an Ecological Context," *American Journal of Sociology* 82: pps. 605–620. Also see Reppetto who concluded that social cohesion and informal surveillance declines when a large number of people live in a given area in: Jackson, Pamela Irving (1984). "Opportunity and Crime: A Function of City Size," *Sociology & Social Research* 68 (2): pps. 173–193.

10 Dan A. Lewis and Michael G. Maxfield (1980). "Fear in the Neighborhoods: An Investigation of the Impact of Crime," *Journal of Research in Crime & Delinquency*, July, pps. 160–189.

11 George Kelling (1995) op. cit.

12 These "theoretical" concepts have been widely recognized in police operations. For example, numerous physical and social factors contributing to crime reduction and problem solving are enumerated in policies and procedures by municipal police departments, such as "Community and City Services Problem Strategies," *Chicago Alternative Policing Strategy* (CAPS), Chicago Police Department, pps. 1–14, December 12, 2000.

13 Bonnie Fisher and Jack L. Nasar (1995). "Fear Spots in Relation to Microlevel Physical Cues: Exploring the Overlooked," *Journal of Research in Crime & Delinquency* 32 (2): pps. 214–239.

14 James Pastor (2003) op. cit.

15 James Pastor (2003) op. cit

16 Robert Kaplan (1994). "The Coming Anarchy," *The Atlantic Monthly*, February.

17 Marcus Felson (2002). *Crime & Everyday Life*. Sage Publications, Thousand Oaks, CA.; and Atlas, Randy I. (2008). "Fear of Parking," *Security Management*, p. 54, February

18 See example: Mark H. Moore and Robert C. Trojanowicz (1988). "Perspectives on Policing: Corporate Strategies for Policing," *National Institute of Justice*. Office of Justice Programs, U.S. Department of Justice, No. 6, November; Paul Palango (1998). "On the Mean Streets: As the Police Cut Back, Private Cops are Moving In," *MacLeans*, 111 (2), January 12; Thomas M. Seamon (1995). "Private Forces for Public Good," *Security Management*, September; Thomas A. Kolpacki (1994). "Neighborhood Watch: Public/Private Liaison," *Security Management*, November; Steven M. Cox (1990). "Policing into the 21st Century," *Police Studies* 13 (4), Pp. 168–177; Les Johnston (1992). *The Rebirth of Private Policing*. London: Routledge; George L. Kelling and Catherine M. Coles (1996). *Fixing Broken Windows: Restoring Order & Reducing Crime in Our* Communities, Simon & Schuster, New York; and Karin Schmerler, Matt Perkins, Scott Phillips, Tammy Rinehart, and Meg Townsend (2002). "Problem Solving Tips: A Guide to Reducing Crime & Disorder through Problem-Solving Partnerships," *Office of Community Oriented Policing Services,* U.S. Department of Justice, June.

19 David B. Muhlhausen (2001). "Do Community Oriented Policing Services Grants Affect Violent Crime Rates," *The Heritage Foundation*, May 25 at p. 4.

20 See for example: Marcia Chanken and Jan Chaiken (1987). "Public Policing-Privately Provided," *National Institute of Justice*. Office of Justice Programs, U.S. Department of Justice, June; Clifford D. Shearing and Philip C. Stenning (1983). "Private Security: Implications for Control," *Social Problems* 30 (5): Pp. 493–506; and William C. Cunningham, John J. Strauchs and Cliffiord W. Van Meter (1991). "Private Security: Patterns and Trends," *National Institute of Justice*. Office of Justice Programs, U.S. Department of Justice, August.

21 James Pastor (2003) op. cit.

22 James F. Pastor, (2006). *Security Law & Methods,* Butterworth-Heinemann, Burlington, MA.

23 James Pastor (2006) op. cit.

24 See for example: Bruce L. Benson (1990). *The Enterprise of Law: Justice Without State*. Pacific Research Institute for Public Policy, San Francisco, California; Ross McLeod (2002). *Para-Police*. Toronto: Boheme Press; Marcia Chanken and Jan Chaiken (1987) op cit.; and Paul Palango (1998) op. cit.

25 James F. Pastor, Doctoral Dissertation entitled: Assessing the Constitutional & Functional Implications of Private Security Patrols on Public Streets. Defended on September 10, 2001 @ The University of Illinois at Chicago.

26 James Pastor (2003) op. cit., James Pastor (2006) op. cit.

27 This division of labor approach was characterized as "blended policing" by Ross McLeod (2002) op. cit. at 129.

28 Robert C. Davis and Sarah Dadush (2000). "The Public Accountability of Private Police: Lessons from New York, Johannesburg, and Mexico City," *Vera Institute of Justice*, August.

29 Morgan O. Reynolds (1994). "Using the Private Sector to Deter Crime," *National Center for Policy Analysis*, March; and James Pastor (2003) op. cit.

30 A pointed example of this dilemma was discussed by Kelling and Coles where they cite data from Boston. From 1975 to 1991, the total number of 911 calls rose about 33 percent. In 1975, the "non-index" calls were 350,000. By 1991 they rose to 600,000. See George L. Kelling and Catherine M. Coles (1996) op. cit. at p. 91; David Hyde (2001) op. cit. at p. 14; and James Pastor (2005) op. cit.

31 Josiah Bates, Criminal Justice Researchers Studied Over 4 Million 911 Calls. Here's How Their Findings Could Influence Calls for Police Reform, *Time*, August 18, 2021 @

https://time-com.cdn.ampproject.org/c/s/time.com/6090633/911-calls-criminal-justice-study-defund-police/?amp=true

32 Josiah Bates (2021) op. cit.

33 Michael S. Scott and Herman Goldstein (2005). "Shifting and Sharing Responsibilities for Public Safety Problems: Problem Oriented Guides for Police Response," Guide Series No. 3, *Office of Community Oriented Policing Services,* U.S. Department of Justice, pps. 1-53, August.

34 "Call stacking" is a process that the computer system performs where non-emergency, lower priority calls are ranked and held ("stacked") so that higher priorities are continually dispatched first. For most busy departments, call stacking and delayed response have become the norm. For analysis of this process, see: Tom McEwen, Deborah Spence, Russell Wolff, Julie Wartell, and Barbara Webster (2003). "Call Management & Community Policing: A Guidebook for Law Enforcement," *Institute for Law & Justice,* U.S. Department of Justice, February.

35 Mary Litsikas (1994) op. cit.

36 Marty L. West (1993). "Get a Piece of the Privatization Pie," *Security Management*, March; Alan Farnham (1992) op. cit.; Adam Walinsky (1993) op. cit.; and Mary Litsikas (1994) op. cit.

37 Kasey Chronis, Bucktown group hiring private security to address crime, *FOX 32 Chicago*, December 14, 2021 @ https://www-fox32chicago-com.cdn.ampproject.org/c/s/www.fox32chicago.com/news/private-security-firm-hired-to-patrol-chicagos-bucktown-neighborhood.amp

38 Robert C. Wadman and William Thomas Allison (2004). *To Protect & To Serve: A History of Police in America.* Upper Saddle River, NJ, Pearson, Prentice Hall.

39 Tau Byron, The Business of Homeland Security Thrives in the Two Decades Since 9/11, The Wall Street Journal, Sept. 6, 2021 @ https://mail.google.com/mail/u/0/#inbox/QgrcJHrttkPPszBlXwBSLMsWvvMtmXrNxbq

40 "National Strategy for Homeland Security" (2007). *Homeland Security Council,* Office of the President of the United States, October.

41 *Law Enforcement Prevention and Deterrence of Terrorist Acts*, Department of Homeland Security, Version 1.0, p. 2/9.

42 Practical Guide to Intelligence-Led Policing, New Jersey State Police, 2006.

43 SLATT, p. 25.

44 http://www.manhattan-institute.org/html/cb_43.htm retrieved on October 16, 2007.

45 Video Surveillance: Information on Law Enforcement's Use of Closed Circuit Television to Monitor Selected Federal Property in Washington D.C. *Government Accounting Office,* GAO-03-748, June 2003 at p. 6–7.

46 G.A.O. op. cit. at pps. 5-6.

47 SecurityInfoWatch.com "Eye on Video: Adding Audio Intelligence" retrieved on July 22, 2008.

48 "Video Cameras on the Look-out for Terrorists" found on www.cnn.com retrieved on September 1, 2006 @ http://edition.cnn.com/2006/tech/08/07/terrorism.technology.ap.

49 Frank Thomas (2007). "TSA to Test New Thermal Cameras in Rail Stations," *USA Today,* October 4, 2007.

50 Pam Frost Gorder (2009). "Smart Cameras Are Watching You," *The Lantern* (Ohio State University) @ https://www.thelantern.com/2009/01/smart-cameras-are-watching-you/ on January 09, 2009.

51 Project Hostile Intent description taken from Department of Homeland Security website @ https://www.dhs.gov/publication/dhsstpia-005-project-hostile-intent-technology retrieved on 12-16-21.

52 Definition of Malintent from Department of Homeland Security website @ https://www.dhs.gov/sites/default/files/publications/Future percent20Attribute percent20Screening percent20Technology-FAST-508_0.pdf retrieved on December 16, 2021.

53 Allison Barrie (2008). "Homeland Security Detects Terrorist Threats by Reading Your Mind," *Fox News* @ http://www.foxnews.com/story/0,2933,426485,00.html on September 23, 2008.

54 Allison Barrie (2008) op. cit.

55 David Uberti, After backlash, predictive policing adapts to a changed world, *The Wall Street Journal*, July 8, 2021 @ https://www.wsj.com/articles/after-backlash-predictive-policing-adapts-to-a-changed-world-11625752931

56 David Uberti (2021) op. cit.

57 U.S. Department of Justice, Bureau of Justice Assistance, Understanding Community Policing A Framework for Action, August 1994 @ https://www.ojp.gov/pdffiles/commp.pdf

58 German Lopez (2021) op. cit.

59 German Lopez (2021) op. cit.

60 German Lopez (2021) op. cit.

61 For an excellent analysis of the psychological effects of violence, see David Grossman, who has published various research projects and developed books and presentations, including *On Killing* and *The Bullet Proof Mind*, which can be found at http://www.killology.com/index.htm.

62 Diane Cecilia Weber (2008) op. cit.

63 Radley Balko (2008) op. cit.

64 Matt Sedensky (2008). op cit.

65 Ramit Plushnick-Masti (2008). "U.S. Police Departments deploying Heavy Armor," posted on May 13, 2007 @ http://www.policeone.com/police-products/vehicles/specialty/articles/1244834-U-S-police-departments-deploying-heavy-armor retrieved on May 6, 2008.

66 Tom Spalding (2008) op. cit.

67 Plushnick-Masti, Ramit (2008) op. cit.

68 James F. Pastor, (2005). "Public Safety Policing," *Law Enforcement Executive Forum,* Vol. 5, No. 6, November at p. 14.

69 Walter Laqueur (2004). "The Terrorism to Come," *Policy Review*, No. 126 @ www.policyreview.org/aug04/laqueur_print.html retrieved on November 1, 2004 at p. 8.

70 Radley Balko (2008) op. cit.

71 U.S. Department of Justice and U.S. Department of Defense, Department of Justice and Department of Defense Joint Technology Program: Second Anniversary Report (Washington: U.S. Department of Justice, February 1997), pps. 8–18.

72 Robert C. Wadman and William Thomas Allison (2004). *To Protect & To Serve: A History of Police in America.* Upper Saddle River, NJ, Pearson, Prentice Hall at p. 159.

73 Walter Laqueur (2004) op. cit. at p. 9.

74 Walter Laqueur (2004) op. cit. at p. 9.

75 James M. Poland (2005). *Understanding Terrorism: Groups, Strategies & Responses*. Upper Saddle River, NJ: Pearson/Prentice Hall at p. 286.

76 Radley Balko (2008) op. cit.

77 Joel Miller (2008) op. cit.

CHAPTER VI

1 Patrick Reilly, Amazon relocating employees from Seattle office after violent crime surge, *New York Post*, March 14, 2022 @ https://nypost.com/2022/03/14/amazon-relocating-employees-from-seattle-office-after-crime-surge/

2 Description of the Wide Awakes taken from https://en.wikipedia.org/wiki/Wide_Awakes retrieved on 12-23-21.

3 Wide Awake website @ https://wideawakes.com/ reviewed on 12-23-21.

4 James F. Pastor (2010). *Terrorism and Public Safety Policing: Implications for the Obama Presidency*, CRS Press-Taylor & Francis Group.

5 Ronald Reagan's first inaugural address @ https://www.google.com/search?q=those+who+have+known+freedom+and+lost+it+will+never+know+freedom+again percentE2 percent80 percentA6&oq=those+who+have+known+freedom+and+lost+it+will+never+know+freedom+again percentE2 percent80 percentA6&aqs=chrome..69i57.1924j0j15&sourceid=chrome&ie=UTF-8 retrieved on 12-23-21.

6 Dan Crenshw (2020). Fortitude: American Resilience in the Era of Outrage, Twelve, Hachette Book Group, NY.

7 Nathan I. Yungher (2008). *Terrorism: The Bottom Line.* Upper Saddle River, NJ: Pearson-Prentice Hall at pps. 265-266.

8 Nathan I. Yungher (2008) op. cit. at p. 266.

9 Nathan I. Yungher (2008) op. cit. at p. 270.

10 http://www.usatoday.com/news/nation/2008-09-17-car-scanner_N.htm?csp=34 retrieved on September 19, 2008.

11 G.A.O. op. cit. at p. 16.

12 Rod Dreher (2020). Live Not By Lies, Sentinel at 8.

13 Rod Dreher (2020) op. cit. at 39.

14 Shoshana Zuboff, You Are the Object of a Secret Extraction Operation, *The New York Times*, Nov. 12, 2021 @ https://www-nytimes-com.cdn.ampproject.org/c/s/www.nytimes.com/2021/11/12/opinion/facebook-privacy.amp.html

15 Shoshana Zuboff (2021) op. cit.

16 Shoshana Zuboff (2021) op. cit.

17 Shoshana Zuboff (2021) op. cit.

18 Shoshana Zuboff (2021) op. cit.

19 Shoshana Zuboff (2021) op. cit.

20 Megan Gates, The Rise of the Surveillance State, *Security Technology*, June 1, 2021 @ https://www.asisonline.org/security-management-magazine/monthly-issues/security-technology/archive/2021/june/The-Rise-of-The-Surveillance-State/

21 Megan Gates (2021) op. cit.

22 Megan Gates (2021) op. cit.

23 *TikTok* description taken from https://tinyurl.com/49bn7d6a retrieved on 12-31-21.

24 Tyler O'Neil, Australia debuts 'Orwellian' new app using facial recognition, geolocation to enforce quarantine, *Fox News*, 9-3-21 @ https://www.foxnews.com/world/australia-debuts-new-orwellian-app-using-facial-recognition-geolocation-to-enforce-quarantine

25 Tyler O'Neil (2021) op. cit.

26 Conor Skelding, Canada secretly tracked 33 million phones during COVID-19 lockdown: report, *The New York Post*, December 25, 2021 @ https://nypost.com/2021/12/25/canada-secretly-tracked-33-million-phones-during-lockdown/?utm_source=gmail&utm_campaign=android_nyp

27 Conor Skelding (2021) op. cit.

28 Brooke Kato, All the ways you're being surveilled due to COVID-19, *The New York Post*, November 13, 2021 @ https://nypost.com/2021/11/13/all-the-ways-youre-being-surveilled-due-to-covid-19/?utm_source=gmail&utm_campaign=android_nyp

29 Brooke Kato (2021) op. cit.

30 Lee Brown, Rutgers bars unvaccinated student from attending virtual classes, *The New York Post*, September 7, 2021 @ https://mail.google.com/mail/u/0/#inbox/QgrcJHrjCsNGRMPBkmQDmDNxmXZLJHvJHtV

31 Joseph A. Wulfsohn, Bill Maher rails against COVID restrictions: It's time to admit pandemic is 'over,' *Fox News*, October 30, 2021 @ https://www.foxnews.com/entertainment/bill-maher-covid-restrictions-coronavirus-pandemic-over

32 Jessica Chasmar, Black Lives Matter chapter to protest in support of Texas tourists accused of assaulting NYC hostess, *Fox News*, September 20, 2021 @ https://www.foxnews.com/politics/black-lives-matter-protest-texas-tourists-assaulting-nyc-hostess

33 David Marcus, The Emmys prove it's time to destroy the COVID caste system, *Fox News*, September 20, 2021 @ https://www.foxnews.com/opinion/emmys-covid-caste-system-david-marcus

34 Andrew Naughtie, Trudeau accuses Canada truckers of 'hate, abuse and racism' as he tests positive for Covid after evacuation, *Independent*, January 31, 2022 @ https://www.independent.co.uk/news/world/americas/justin-trudeau-covid-canada-convoy-b2004245.html

35 Tucker Carlson, The military's COVID vaccine mandate amounts to a power grab, *Fox News*, September 21, 2021 @ https://www.foxnews.com/opinion/tucker-carlson-military-covid-vaccine-mandate

36 Elliot Resnick, A Religious Exemption Request for Those Who Have Already Had Covid, *American Greatness*, October 22, 2021 @ https://amgreatness.com/2021/10/22/a-religious-exemption-request-for-those-who-have-already-had-covid/

37 Brian Bakst, Owners of burned, looted businesses plead for state help, *NPR*, February 16, 2021 @ *https://www.mprnews.org/story/2021/02/16/owners-of-burned-looted-businesses-plead-for-state-help*

38 Michael Ruiz, PROTESTS . . . Where do we draw the line . . . how do we "define" the line, *Fox News* April 20, 2021 @ https://www.foxnews.com/politics/biden-rioting-george-floyd-derek-chauvin-conviction

39 *Personal interview with Gov. Arne Carlson, November 22, 2021. Transcription on file.*

40 Michael Ruiz, (2021) op. cit.

41 Michael Ruiz, (2021) op. cit.

42 http://nothingbuttruth.com/maximum-crane/2008/03/let-every-nation-know/ retrieved on February 20, 2009.

43 Rikki Schlott, Freedom of speech is endangered on college campuses — and I'm fighting back, *The New York Post*, July 31, 2021 @https://nypost.com/2021/07/31/freedom-of-speech-is-endangered-at-colleges-so-im-fighting-back/?utm_source=gmail&utm_campaign=android_nyp

44 Douglas Murray (2019). *The Madness of Crowds: Gender, Race and Identity*, Bloomsbury Continuum, at 132.

45 James Freeman, College Students Don't Need Protection from the Truth, *The Wall Street Journal*, September 16, 2021 @ https://www.wsj.com/articles/college-students-dont-need-protection-from-the-truth-11631825498

46 Freeman, James (2021) op. cit.

47 Douglas Murray (2019) op. cit. at 134.

48 Salvatore J. Cordileone and Jim Daly, Social Media's Threat to Religious Freedom, *The Wall Street Journal*, August 12, 2021 @ https://www.wsj.com/articles/social-media-religious-freedom-youtube-first-amendment-section-230-carl-trueman-sacramento-gospel-conference-11628802706

49 Salvatore J. Cordileone and Jim Daly (2021) op. cit.

50 Abraham Lincoln quote taken from https://www.goodreads.com/quotes/135212-from-whence-shall-we-expect-the-approach-of-danger-shall retrieved on 12-27-21.

51 Journal Editorial Board, In Hoc Anno Domini, The Wall Street Journal, December 23, 2021 @ https://www.wsj.com/articles/in-hoc-anno-domini-vermont-royster-editorial-11640296509

52 Frederick Douglass quote taken from https://lawliberty.org/frederick-douglass-plea-for-freedom-of-speech-in-boston/ retrieved on 12-26-21.

53 Quote for The Jefferson Monticello website @ https://www.monticello.org/site/research-and-collections/when-government-fears-people-there-liberty-spurious-quotation retrieved on 12-28-21.

54 https://quoteinvestigator.com/2014/07/13/truth/ retrieved on 11-24-21

55 Rod Dreher (2020) op. cit. at 30.

56 W.R. Wordsworth, The Fragility of Political Sanity, *American Thinker*, October 2, 2021 @ https://www.americanthinker.com/articles/2021/10/9_30_2021_23_54.html

57 Barbara W. Tuchman (1984). The March of Folly: From Troy to Vietnam, Random House, New York at 403.

58 Mark Levin (2021). *American Marxism*, Threshold Editions, New York at 200.

59 Daniel Henninger, Biden and Nothingness, *The Wall Street Journal*, October 13, 2021 @ https://www.wsj.com/articles/joe-biden-alternative-realities-reconciliation-spending-cost-nothing-border-closed-psaki-11634158213

60 Daniel Henninger (2021) op. cit.

61 Douglas Murray (2019) op. cit. at 9.

62 Glenn Ellmers, Harry Jaffa's Lesson for the GOP, *The Wall Street Journal*, September 16, 2021 @ https://www.wsj.com/articles/harry-jaffa-republican-gop-political-philosophy-natural-law-liberty-rightwing-extremist-11631805675

63 Rod Dreher (2020) op. cit. at xiv.

64 Cortney O'Brien, Ayaan Hirsi Ali rips NPR for new policy allowing reporters to protest: 'Stop calling it journalism', *Fox News*, July 30, 2021 @ https://www.foxnews.com/media/ayaan-hirsi-ali-npr-new-policy-reporters-protest-journalism

65 Cortney O'Brien (2021) op. cit.

66 David Rutz, More journalists admit and embrace bias, dismissing 'fairness' in new era of media, *Fox News*, July 24, 2021 @ https://www.foxnews.com/media/journalists-bias-dismissing-fairness-era

67 Lindsay Kornick, Liberal journalists promote column condemning 'both-siderism': 'Every political journalist should read this', *Fox News*, October 18, 2021 @ https://www.foxnews.com/media/liberal-reporters-promote-article-condemning-both-siderism

68 Lindsay Kornick (2021) op. cit.

69 David Rutz (2021) op. cit.

70 David Rutz (2021) op. cit.

71 Robert L. Woodson, Media's Racial Narrative Targets Whites, Harms Blacks, *The Wall Street Journal*, April 16, 2021 @ https://www.wsj.com/articles/medias-racial-narrative-targets-whites-harms-blacks-11618597161

72 Robert L. Woodson (2021) op. cit.

73 Robert L. Woodson (2021) op. cit.

74 Joseph A. Wulfsohn, Bill Maher scolds left's refusal to admit racial, social progress in America: 'We've come a long way, baby'y, *Fox News*, June 12, 2021 @ https://www.foxnews.com/entertainment/bill-maher-racial-social-progress

75 Joseph A. Wulfsohn (2021) op. cit.

76 The Editorial Board, Racism at Chicago's City Hall, The Wall Street Journal, May 20, 2021 @ https://www.wsj.com/articles/racism-at-chicagos-city-hall-11621550316

77 The Editorial Board (2021) op. cit.

78 John 18:33–38 from the English Standard Version of the Holy Bible.

79 John 8: 31–32 from the English Standard Version of the Holy Bible.

80 Justice Sonia Sotomayor quote taken from https://www.cnn.com/2009/POLITICS/05/28/sotomayor.latina.remark.reax/ retrieved on 12-28-21.

81 Jill Lepore (2018). *These Truths: A History of the United States*, W.W. Norton & Company, New York.

82 Jill Lepore (2018) op. cit. at 99.

83 Sohrab Ahmari (2021). *The Unbroken Thread: Discovering the Wisdom of Traditional in an Age of Chaos*, Convergent Books, New York at 19.

84 Rod Dreher (2020) op. cit. at 100.

85 Rod Dreher (2020) op. cit. at 100.

86 John Adams quote taken from https://www.goodreads.com/quotes/32621-facts-are-stubborn-things-and-whatever-may-be-our-wishes retrieved on 2-17-22.

CHAPTER VII

1 For an explanation of the Cloward and Piven approach see Wikipedia @ https://en.wikipedia.org/wiki/Cloward percentE2 percent80 percent93Piven_strategy retrieved on 2-17-22.

2 Mark Levin (2021). *American Marxism*, Threshold Editions, New York at 253.

3 Mark Levin (2021). op. cit. at 240-241.

4 Sheep, Sheep Dogs & Wolves taken from David Grossman's website at https://www.killology.com/sheep-wolves-and-sheepdogs retrieved on 1-3-22.

5 Grossman website op. cit.

6 Grossman website op. cit.

7 Sohrab Ahmari (2021). *The Unbroken Thread: Discovering the Wisdom of Traditional in an Age of Chaos*, Convergent Books at 47.

8 Lance Morrow, Not That Long Ago, 'Evil' Really Meant Something, *The Wall Street Journal*, September 26, 2021 @ https://www.wsj.com/articles/evil-meaning-trump-hitler-pol-pot-exaggeration-politics-political-polarization-11632676439

9 Lance Morrow (2021) op. cit.

10 Charles Creitz, Organized religion 'decays' as political ideologies increasingly viewed in 'religious light': Niall Ferguson, *Fox News*, June 15, 2021 @ https://www.foxnews.com/media/organized-religion-decays-political-ideologies-niall-ferguson

11 Charles Creitz (2021) op. cit.

12 For an interesting discussion on this parallel, see Rod Dreher (2020). Live Not By Lies, Sentinel at 24–27.

13 Tucker Carlson, Christianity is dying and being replaced by cult of coronavirus, *Fox News*, September 29, 2021 @ https://www.foxnews.com/opinion/tucker-carlson-christianity-dying-replaced-cult-coronavirus

14 Victor Davis Hanson, An American apocalypse – why people of all classes, races are filled with fear, *Fox News*, August 14, 2021 @ https://www.foxnews.com/opinion/american-armageddon-woke-victor-davis-hanson

15 Laura Ingraham (2007). *Power to the People*. Washington DC: Regnery Publishing at pps. 316-317.

16 Holy Bible, Matthew 16:25.

17 Eli Steele, Rooftop Revelations: The message of 'the body of Christ' overrides tribalism, *Fox News*, January 14, 2022 @ https://www.foxnews.com/opinion/rooftop-revelations-chicago-message-body-of-christ-tribalism

18 Corey B. Brooks, "Chicago pastor: 'I live on a roof to raise cash for black youths—but BLM won't help,'" *The New York Post*, May 28, 2022 @ https://nypost.com/2022/05/28/chicago-pastor-lives-on-roof-raises-cash-for-black-youthbut-blm-wont-help/

19 Sohrab Ahmari (2021) op. cit. at 74.

20 Rod Dreher (2020). *Live Not By Lies*, Sentinel at 204.

21 Proclamation Appointing a National Fast Day @ http://www.abrahamlincolnonline.org/lincoln/speeches/fast.htm#:~:text=We percent20have percent20been percent20the percent20recipients,But percent20we percent20have percent20forgotten percent20God. retrieved on 2-5-22.

22 James Freeman, The Noblest, Happiest Page in Mankind's History', *The Wall Street Journal*, July 2, 2021 @ https://www.wsj.com/articles/the-noblest-happiest-page-in-mankinds-history-11625222292

23 James Freeman (2021) op. cit.

24 James Freeman (2021) op. cit.

25 Michael Goodwin, Joe Biden's unity vow 'left' behind, *The New York Post*, July 24, 2021 @ https://nypost.com/2021/07/24/joe-bidens-unity-vow-left-behind-goodwin/?utm_source=gmail&utm_campaign=android_nyp

26 Michael Goodwin (2021) op. cit.

27 Michael Goodwin (2021) op. cit.

28 Progressive Caucus membership taken from https://progressives.house.gov/caucus-members retrieved on 1-3-22.

29 David Limbaugh, American Marxism, *The Liberty Loft*, July 17, 2021 @ https://thelibertyloft.com/american-marxism/

30 David Limbaugh (2021) op. cit.

31 Jason Willick, An Urban Organizer Wants 'Race off the Table', *The Wall Street Journal*, October 15, 2021 @
https://www.wsj.com/articles/urban-organizer-robert-woodson-center-mentorship-race-poverty-crime-11634328348

32 Jason Willick (2021) op. cit.

33 Jason Willick (2021) op. cit.

34 Danielle Wallace, Chicago police identifies 'hero' officer killed during traffic stop: 'We will #NeverForget', *Fox News*, August 9, 2021 @ https://www.foxnews.com/us/chicago-officer-killed-traffic-stop-increased-shootings-targeting-police

35 Danielle Wallace (2021) op. cit.

36 H.R. McMaster, H.R., If civilian leaders send troops into battle without a commitment to victory, who will sign up to serve?, *The Wall Street Journal*, November 10, 2021 @

https://www.wsj.com/articles/honor-vets-the-will-to-win-war-military-service-veterans-day-afghanistan-taliban-mcmaster-11636576955

37 Leo W. Banks, Arizona's Border Crisis Threatens Public Safety and Health, *The Wall Street Journal*, September 10, 2021 @ https://www.wsj.com/articles/arizona-border-crisis-public-safety-health-crossings-illegal-alien-immigrant-covid-terrorist-11631304060

38 Leo W. Banks (2021) op. cit.

39 Leo W. Banks (2021) op. cit.

40 And the Fair Land, *The Wall Street Journal*, Nov. 23, 2021 @ https://www.wsj.com/articles/and-the-fair-land-11637710823

41 Candance Owens, *Blackout*, Threshold Editions, 2020 at page 51.

42 Kendall Qualls, Martin Luther King's dream is alive but liberal policies are destroying Black communities, *Fox News*, January 15, 2022 @ https://www.foxnews.com/opinion/american-black-family-dream-martin-luther-king-kendall-qualls

43 Kendall Qualls (2022) op. cit.

44 Kendall Qualls (2022) op. cit.

45 Margaret Thatcher quote taken from https://www.goodreads.com/quotes/138248-the-problem-with-socialism-is-that-you-eventually-run-out retrieved on 1-4-22.

46 Jason L. Riley, McDonald's CEO Apologizes for Telling a Simple Truth, *The Wall Street Journal*, November 9, 2021 @ https://www.wsj.com/articles/mcdonalds-ceo-apologizes-race-crime-shooting-chicago-adam-toledo-jaslyn-adams-kempczinski-11636493025

47 Matt Rosenberg, McDonald's vs The Woke Mob: If Parents Are Not Responsible For Their Children, Then Who Is? @

https://johnkassnews.com/guest-column-matt-rosenberg-mcdonalds-vs-the-woke-mob-if-parents-are-not-responsible-for-their-children-then-who-is/?utm_source=rss&utm_medium=rss&utm_campaign=guest-column-matt-rosenberg-mcdonalds-vs-the-woke-mob-if-parents-are-not-responsible-for-their-children-then-who-is

48 Gregory Hoyt, Revealed: A disturbing look inside the pro-Antifa/Black Lives Matter summer camp for kids in Portland, *Law Enforcement Today*, August 9, 2021 @ https://www.lawenforcementtoday.com/revealed-a-disturbing-look-inside-the-pro-antifa-black-lives-matter-summer-camp-for-kids-in-portland/

49 Black Rose website taken from https://blackrosefed.org/mission-statement/ retrieved on 1-4-22.

50 Gregory Hoyt (2021) op. cit.

51 Gregory Hoyt (2021) op. cit.

52 Jessica Chasmar, Pro-Antifa teacher brags about turning students into 'revolutionaries,' undercover video shows, *Fox News*, September 1, 2021 @ https://www.foxnews.com/politics/video-antifa-teacher-bragging-students-revolutionaries

53 Jessica Chasmar (2021) op. cit.

54 Sun Tzu, *Art of War* as translated by Lionel Giles in http://www.chinapage.com/sunzi-e.html retrieved on February 20, 2009.

55 Barbara W. Tuchman (1984). *The March of Folly: From Troy to Vietnam,* Random House, New York at 27.

56 Barbara W. Tuchman (1984) op. cit. at 35.

57 Douglas Murray (2019). *The Madness of Crowds: Gender, Race and Identity*, Bloomsbury Continuum, at 245.

58 Vincente Fox and Rob Allyn (2007). *Revolution of Hope: The Life, Faith & Dreams of a Mexican President,* Viking Penguin Press, New York at pps. 132 and 355.

59 William A. Galston, Lessons for Politicians at Passover, *The Wall Street Journal,* March 30, 2021 @ https://www.wsj.com/articles/lessons-for-politicians-at-passover-11617136889

60 Barbara W. Tuchman (1984) op. cit. at 112.

61 Former Defense Secretary Robert Gates quote taken from https://www.stripes.com/news/text-of-secretary-of-defense-robert-gates-speech-at-west-point-1.77986 retrieved on 1-4-22.

62 Leon Trosky quote taken from https://www.goodreads.com/quotes/152853-you-may-not-be-interested-in-war-but-war-is retrieved on 1-4-22.

Made in the USA
Columbia, SC
02 September 2022